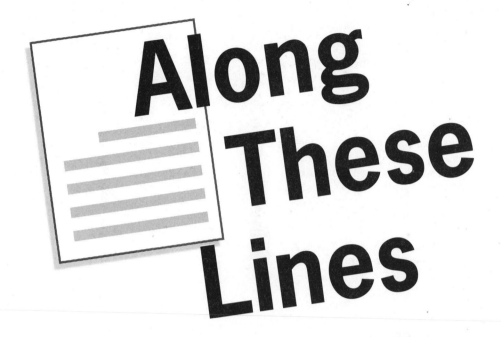

Along These Lines

Writing Sentences and Paragraphs

John Sheridan Biays
Broward Community College

Carol Wershoven
Palm Beach Community College

Prentice Hall

Upper Saddle River, New Jersey 07458

Library of Congress Cataloging-in-Publication Data

Biays, John Sheridan.

    Along these lines : writing sentences and paragraphs / John Sheridan Biays and Carol Wershoven.
        p.   cm.
    Includes index.
    ISBN 0-13-085070-5 (pbk.)
      1. English language—Sentences.   2. English language—Paragraphs.   3. English
    language—Rhetoric.   I. Wershoven, Carol.   II. Title.

    PE1441 .B53   2001
    808'.042—dc21
                                                         00-061977

Editor in Chief: Leah Jewell
Acquisitions Editor: Craig Campanella
Editorial Assistant: Joan Polk
Director of Production and Manufacturing: Barbara Kittle
Managing Editor: Mary Rottino
Production Editor: Joan E. Foley
Production Assistant: Elizabeth Best
Copyeditor: Virginia Rubens
Prepress and Manufacturing Manager: Nick Sklitsis
Prepress and Manufacturing Buyer: Ben Smith
Marketing Director: Beth Gillett Mejia
Marketing Manager: Rachel Falk
Text Permissions Specialist: The Publisher's Domain
Image Permissions Coordinator: Charles Morris
Creative Design Director: Leslie Osher
Interior and Cover Designer: Anne DeMarinis
Cover Art: Piet Mondrian (1872–1944). *Tableau II*. Dutch. Superstock, Inc.
Development Editor in Chief: Susanna Lesan
Development Editor: Elizabeth Morgan

This book was set in 11/13 ITC Century Book by TSI Graphics
and was printed and bound by Courier Companies, Inc.
Covers were printed by Phoenix Color Corp.

Prentice-Hall International (UK) Limited, *London*
Prentice-Hall of Australia Pty. Limited, *Sydney*
Prentice-Hall Canada Inc., *Toronto*
Prentice-Hall Hispanoamerica, S.A., *Mexico*
Prentice-Hall of India Private Limited, *New Delhi*
Prentice-Hall of Japan, Inc., *Tokyo*
Pearson Education Asia Pte. Ltd., *Singapore*
Editora Prentice-Hall do Brasil, Ltda., *Rio de Janeiro*

Contents

Nov. 27,28,29 out for thanksgiving
Dec 2 preregister
Dec 12 don't come
Dec. 20. report cards

iii

CHAPTER 17 Spelling   209

CHAPTER 18 Words That Sound Alike/Look Alike   220

CHAPTER 19 Using Prepositions Correctly   238

WRITING IN STEPS: The Process Approach   247

CHAPTER 20 Writing a Paragraph: Generating Ideas— Thought Lines   251

CHAPTER 21
Writing a Paragraph: Devising a Plan—Outlines   269

CHAPTER 22
Writing a Paragraph: Writing, Revising, and Editing the Drafts—Rough Lines   280

CHAPTER 23
Writing a Paragraph: Polishing, Proofreading, and Preparing the Final Copy—Final Lines   286

CHAPTER 24
Writing a Paragraph: Focus on Coherence and Unity   295

25 Writing a Paragraph: Focus on Support and Details   338

26 Writing From Reading   371

APPENDIX
ESL
Appendix: Grammar for ESL Students   401

Preface

TO INSTRUCTORS

Along These Lines: Writing Sentences and Paragraphs is a grammar and writing text (with selected readings) designed for beginning writers. As we planned the book, we recalled our struggles to learn the basics of using a computer. No *one* method seemed to work for us. Listening to an instructor didn't work; he or she went too fast. Watching other students in the class provided some help, but we soon got lost trying to follow their lead. Reading manuals alone in our offices was no solution, either. And simply turning on the computer, clicking and double-clicking, often left us floundering. While no *single* method taught us everything we needed to know, a combination of all these strategies did the trick.

We realized that the way we learned to be computer literate is the same way students learn to write—not by any one method, but by a variety of strategies. Merely listening to a teacher talk about writing or simply reading about how to write is not enough. Beginning writers, like computer novices, need to try all approaches: reading, listening, practicing, and experiencing the collegiality of working with their peers. Therefore, this book is filled with exercises and activities, both individual and collaborative, that involve students in the *process* of learning to write. We designed this book as a menu of instruction and activities, providing ample options to accommodate a diversity of teaching strategies and student populations.

Organizational Features

At the same time, this menu is structured around a simple, consistent pattern for writing. The word *Lines* in the title serves as a cue to the stages of the writing process:

- **Thought Lines:** the time spent generating ideas
- **Outlines:** the steps of planning and focusing
- **Rough Lines:** the steps of drafting and revising
- **Final Lines:** the last step, proofreading

The **writing chapters** of *Along These Lines: Writing Sentences and Paragraphs* are structured around these stages. A chapter on "Writing from Reading" also uses these steps in explaining how students can write summaries, reaction paragraphs, or essay tests from reading selections. An eclectic mix of activities is thus supported by a flexible framework for thinking, planning, drafting, and revising, providing students with the security of a clear and simple process as they develop their writing skills.

The **grammar chapters** also follow a consistent pattern, providing three kinds of exercises:

- **Practice:** exercises for simple reinforcement of the grammar principle being discussed
- **Collaborate:** more complex exercises to be done with a partner or group
- **Connect:** application of the grammar principle to paragraphs

Throughout the book, you will notice these features:

- No more than two pages of print are without an example, a chart, a checklist, a box, a list, or an exercise.
- The text has a lively, conversational tone, including question-and-answer formats and dialogues.

- The design features small, simple clusters of information surrounded by white space rather than intimidating expanses of small print.
- Exercises are integrated throughout each chapter, so each concept is reinforced as soon as it is introduced.

Distinctive Features

The **grammar chapters** include these distinctive features:

- Clear, simple steps, as in "Two Steps in Recognizing Sentence Fragments" or "Three Steps in Checking for Sentence Errors with Modifiers"
- Numerous collaborative activities, including exercises that ask students to devise their own examples to illustrate principles they've just learned
- Exercises based on the work of writers such as Edgar Allan Poe and Pulitzer Prize–winning author Edna Buchanan, along with historical figures such as Martin Luther King, Jr., and Winston Churchill

The **writing chapters** have these distinctive features:

- A clear and detailed example of one writing assignment, taken through all its stages
- Exercises placed immediately after explanatory material
- Collaborative exercises directing students to write with peers, interview classmates, react to others' suggestions, and build on others' ideas
- Numerous writing topics and activities, providing additional flexibility for the instructor
- Peer Review Forms, so students can benefit from classmates' reactions to their drafts

The **reading sections** include these distinctive features:

- A separate and detailed chapter on "Writing from Reading," explaining and illustrating the steps of prereading, reading and rereading, annotating, summarizing, reacting (in writing) to another's ideas, and writing for an essay test
- Vocabulary definitions for each reading selection
- Readings that appeal to working students, returning students, students recently out of high school, students who are parents, and students who are spouses. The selections focus on such diverse topics as working in a service industry, engaging in risky behavior, reinventing one's life, and losing a beloved pet.
- Readings by authors accessible to a student audience—from Judith Ortiz Cofer to Maya Angelou to John Grisham
- Topics for writing sparked by the content or strategies of the readings—designed to elicit thinking and develop specific writing skills, such as unity, coherence, or support

Along These Lines: Writing Sentences and Paragraphs combines the traditional and the innovative; while it provides a comprehensive study of conventional grammar, spelling, and word choice skills, it does so by using both individual and collaborative exercises. The division of the book into two parts, grammar and writing, enables instructors to start with either part, or to skip back and forth, and to cover as little or as much grammar or writing as they prefer. **Both traditionalists and innovators will find something useful in the many varied activities, assignments, and exercises designed to get students thinking, reacting, and connecting ideas.**

Instructors who select from the varied menu can connect and integrate the skills most valuable to their individual classes. They will find the text easy to use, for several reasons:

- Perforated tear-out exercises reinforce every instructional concept and eliminate the pressure instructors feel in preparing supplemental materials.
- Peer review forms, each clearly marked at the end of a chapter, provide easy access.
- Exercises serve as an instant lesson plan for any class period or as individualized work for students in a writing lab.

Years ago, when we first confronted the mysteries of the computer keyboard and gingerly tapped the mouse, we wanted the security of a manual close at hand and a teacher by our side. We wanted to write down the steps for using our email or saving a file, but we also wanted to practice on our own or ask a friend for help. Student writers are no different; they need to listen and read, and they need a plan. But they also need to work on their own and to learn with others. *Along These Lines: Writing Sentences and Paragraphs* addresses these needs. Through a structured yet stimulating approach, it is designed to involve students in their *own* learning without imposing instruction on a captive audience. As you and your students work through the writing process, we wish you much success along *all* lines.

ACKNOWLEDGMENTS

Veteran writing instructors are well aware that periodic group work and constructive peer interaction can help students thrive within an atmosphere of civility, trust, and active learning. As authors, we have enjoyed these same benefits thanks to the ongoing collegial and constructive feedback from many individuals. We are especially indebted to the following professionals for their insightful reviews and practical suggestions:

Donald Brotherton	DeVry Institute of Technology
Keith Coplin	Colby Community College
Janet M. Cutshall	Sussex County Community College
Kate Gleason	Interborough Institute
Patrick Haas	Glendale Community College
Jill A. Lahnstein	Cape Fear Community College
Maria Villar-Smith	Miami-Dade Community College

Many thanks to Joan Polk, editorial assistant, for coordinating these reviews and for providing updates during the drafting stages.

We are also grateful to the dedicated team of professionals in the Humanities and Social Science Division at Prentice Hall. Leah Jewell, editor in chief, and Craig Campanella, English editor, set the groundwork for expanding the *Along These Lines* philosophy into the current two-book series. Craig's enthusiasm and encouragement never waned as he oversaw every stage of development for the series. We are also extremely fortunate to have had Betty Morgan as our development editor again; she streamlined chapters, reshaped exercises, and maintained our original vision.

We also benefitted from the herculean efforts of our skillful copyeditor, Virginia Rubens. She tightened our prose, inserted the complex typesetting codes, kept our voice intact, and transformed a work-in-progress into production-ready copy. Thanks also to Mary Rottino, Ben Smith, and Susanna Lesan for keeping the project on schedule, and to The Publisher's Domain for securing the necessary permissions for our reading selections.

For their help in preparing supplemental material, we are very grateful to Evelyn Kelly and Jamie Barrett for writing the Instructor's Resource Manuals, and to Tom Hartman for developing the *Along These Lines Online Course.* Additionally, Rachel Falk, marketing manager, made us feel very comfortable as she introduced us to the remarkable possibilities of online instruction and cyberspace interaction. Thanks, Rachel, for your enthusiasm and creativity.

Once again, the design and production staffs at Prentice Hall excelled. The attractive cover and user-friendly design of this text reflects the collective talent of Anne DeMarinis, Nancy Wells, and Leslie Osher; the easily-referenced instructor annotations, chapter headings, and well-spaced exercises are the results of our superb production editor, Joan Foley. Joan methodically reviewed every page proof, kept in constant contact with us, and served as a liaison to every department involved in the final product. Thanks for keeping us in good spirits and on schedule, Joan. You've been the vital link in the entire process.

Finally, we want to thank our students and colleagues at Broward Community College and Palm Beach Community College. You are a constant source of information, insight, and inspiration. Thanks in particular to Dave Shaw, Margo Butler, and Joel Nydahl for your suggestions and encouragement, and to Susan Heslekrants and Flora Cohen for your wit and sanity along *all* lines.

John Sheridan Biays
Carol Wershoven

Supplements

Annotated Instructor's Edition. (0-13-086991-0) The *AIE* features the answers to all of the exercises and includes marginal annotations to enhance instruction. Written by John Biays and Carol Wershoven, these annotations are derived from their years of experience teaching developmental writing. "Teaching Tips" offer practical, proven ideas for getting the most out of each class session. They include specific activities to help students master the material. "Notes" provide chapter cross-references and suggestions for helping the class run more smoothly. "Discussion Questions" offer ideas on promoting class interaction. "Answers Will Vary" alert instructors to the questions that have a range of responses.

Instructor's Resource Manual. (0-13-091279-4) An additional free supplement for instructors, the *Instructor's Resource Manual* provides additional teaching strategies, additional collaborative exercises, sample syllabi, chapter summaries, and more.

Companion Website: www.prenhall.com/biays Free to students, the Companion Website is an interactive study resource for students. In includes Chapter Objectives, self-grading quizzes, essay-writing exercises, and web destinations for further study.

ALONG THESE LINES, The Online Course. Prentice Hall's new online developmental writing course offers you all the advantages of a custom-built program without the hassle of writing it from scratch. This course supports and augments the ALONG THESE LINES series by providing a complete array of writing concepts and exercises at your fingertips—to use just as it is presented *or* to be customized to fit your specific course syllabus.

Compatible with WebCT™, Blackboard, and eCollege platforms, ALONG THESE LINES Online includes the following features: Chapter Introductions, Lecture Notes, and Writing Workshops for each writing chapter; Quizzes that are auto-scored and recorded; Essay Questions; E-mail Accounts for each student and instructor; and Course Management.

> To view a demonstration, go to www.prenhall.com/cms

English on the Internet: A Critical Thinking Guide, 2001. This guide focuses on developing the critical thinking skills necessary to evaluate and use online sources effectively. The guide also provides a brief introduction to navigating the Internet, along with complete references related specifically to the English discipline and how to use the companion websites available for many Prentice Hall textbooks. This 96-page supplementary book is **free** to students when shrinkwrapped as a package *with any English title.*

To receive any of these supplements, contact your local Prentice Hall representative or call Faculty Services at 1-800-526-0485.

CHAPTER 1

The Simple Sentence

Identifying the crucial parts of a sentence is the first step in many writing decisions: how to punctuate, how to avoid sentence fragments, and how to be sure that subjects and verbs *agree* (match). Moving forward to these decisions requires us to take a few steps backward—to basics.

RECOGNIZING A SENTENCE

Let's start with a few definitions. A basic unit of language is a **word.**

> **examples:** cap, desk, tree

A group of related words can be a **phrase.**

> **examples:** battered baseball cap, on the desk, tall palm tree

When a group of words contains a subject and a verb, it is called a **clause.** When the word group has a subject and a verb and makes sense by itself, it is called a **sentence** or an independent clause.

If you want to check whether you have written a sentence and not just a group of related words, you first have to check for a subject and a verb. It is often easier to locate the verbs first.

RECOGNIZING VERBS

Verbs are words that express some kind of action or being. **Action verbs** tell what somebody or something does.

> **action verbs:**
>
> Computers *hold* an amazing amount of information.
> We *call* our parents once a month.
> The boxer *exercises* at my local gym.
> You *missed* the bus yesterday.
> David *dented* the back of my car.
> He *drives* like a maniac.
> They *study* together on weekends.
> I *believe* her story.

Sometimes a verb tells what something or somebody is. Such verbs are called **being verbs.** Words like *feels, looks, seems, smells, sounds,* and *tastes* are part of the group called being verbs. Look at some examples of being verbs and their functions in the following sentences:

being verbs:

Computers *are* a great invention.
The boxer *looks* tired today.
You *sound* happy.
David *is* a good candidate for traffic school.
He *seems* unaware of traffic lights.
They *are* the best students in my class.
I *feel* confident about her story.
Gossip *is* nasty and mean.

Exercise 1 Recognizing Action Verbs

Practice Underline the action verbs in the following sentences.

   1. The Doberman barked at the mail carrier.

   2. On Mondays, he brings coffee and doughnuts.

   3. The ice makes the road slick.

   4. My mother-in-law cooked Thanksgiving dinner.

   5. Christine talks like a lawyer.

   6. Some people hate surprise parties.

   7. Skydiving takes daring and a sense of adventure.

   8. An old sheet covered the sofa.

   9. Canned soup contains a great deal of salt.

   10. She takes the bus to work.

Exercise 2 Recognizing Being Verbs

Practice Underline the being verbs in the following sentences.

   1. That garlic bread smells wonderful.

   2. Eduardo was a good friend to me.

   3. That little boy looks confused.

   4. After the concert, the crowd seemed disappointed.

   5. Today's moviegoers are easily bored.

   6. Jason's mother and father were very strict parents.

7. My best friend Celine is a professional singer.

8. On the first day of summer vacation, I am carefree.

9. It seemed like a good idea.

10. A car is a necessity in this town.

Exercise 3 **Writing Sentences with Specific Verbs**

👥 Collaborate

With a partner or a group, write two sentences using each of the verbs listed below. Each sentence must have at least five words. When you have completed the exercise, share your answers with another group or with the class. The first one is done for you.

1. verb: removed

sentence 1: _The doctor removed the patient's appendix._

sentence 2: _Yesterday my brother removed that old carpet stain._

2. verb: smells

sentence 1: _____

sentence 2: _____

3. verb: delivers

sentence 1: _____

sentence 2: _____

4. verb: sounded

sentence 1: _____

sentence 2: _____

5. verb: concealed

sentence 1: _____

sentence 2: _____

6. verb: annoys

sentence 1: _____

sentence 2: _____

7. verb: are

sentence 1: _____

sentence 2: _____

8. verb: feel

sentence 1: _____

sentence 2: _____

9. verb: smashed

sentence 1: _____

sentence 2: _____

10. verb: broke

sentence 1: _____

sentence 2: _____

Helping Verbs

The verb in a sentence can be more than one word. There can be **helping verbs** in front of the main verb (the action verb or being verb). Here is a list of some frequently used helping verbs:

Infobox

Common Helping Verbs

am	do	might	were
are	had	must	will
can	have	shall	would
could	is	should	
did	may	was	

Here are some examples of sentences with main and helping verbs:

main and helping verbs:

You *should have answered* the question. (The helping verbs are *should* and *have*.)
Laurie *will notify* the lottery winner. (The helping verb is *will*.)
Babies *can recognize* their mothers' voices. (The helping verb is *can*.)
I *am thinking* about a career in medicine. (The helping verb is *am*.)

Exercise 4 **Recognizing the Complete Verb: Main and Helping Verbs**

Practice Underline the complete verb (both main and helping verbs) in each of the following sentences.

1. You <u>could have called</u> me about the party for Matthew.

2. Two of the birds <u>were picking</u> seeds out of the bird feeder.

3. My cousin <u>will be visiting</u> me next week.

4. The cabdriver <u>may have been robbed</u> before.

5. The sailors <u>were risking</u> their lives in the rescue mission.

6. Armand <u>can concentrate</u> under the most difficult conditions.

7. You <u>must clean</u> the windows with a solution of vinegar and water.

8. Last night I <u>was practicing</u> my speech for my public speaking class.

9. They <u>can say</u> anything about the incident.

10. Sylvester <u>might have known</u> the girl on the beach.

Exercise 5 **Writing Sentences with Helping Verbs**

👥 Collaborate

Complete this exercise with a partner or a group. First, ask one person to add at least one helping verb to the verb given. Then, work together to write two sentences using the main verb and the helping verb(s). Appoint a spokesperson for your group to read all of your sentences to the class. Notice how many combinations of main and helping verbs you hear. The first one is done for you.

1. **verb:** complained

   verb with helping verb(s): must have complained

   sentence 1: My supervisor must have complained about me.

   sentence 2: She must have complained twenty times yesterday.

2. **verb:** cheating

   verb with helping verb(s): _____

   sentence 1: _____

   sentence 2: _____

3. **verb:** improve

   verb with helping verb(s): _____

   sentence 1: _____

   sentence 2: _____

4. **verb:** demanded

   verb with helping verb(s): _____

   sentence 1: _____

   sentence 2: _____

5. verb: written

verb with helping verb(s): _____

sentence 1: _____

sentence 2: _____

6. verb: repeating

verb with helping verb(s): _____

sentence 1: _____

sentence 2: _____

7. verb: taken

verb with helping verb(s): _____

sentence 1: _____

sentence 2: _____

8. verb: control

verb with helping verb(s): _____

sentence 1: _____

sentence 2: _____

9. verb: speaking

verb with helping verb(s): _____

sentence 1: _____

sentence 2: _____

10. verb: defended

verb with helping verb(s): _____

sentence 1: _____

sentence 2: _____

More Than One Main Verb

Helping verbs can make the verb in a sentence more than one word long, but there can also be more than one main verb.

more than one main verb:

Antonio *begged* and *pleaded* for mercy.

I *ran* to the car, *tossed* my books on the back seat, and *jammed* the key in the ignition.

My dog *steals* my shoes and *chews* on them.

Exercise 6   **Recognizing Main Verbs**

Practice

Some of the sentences below have one main verb; some have more than one main verb. Underline all the main verbs in each sentence.

1. Mr. Pulaski and Mrs. Coelho <u>teach</u> tennis in the morning and <u>coach</u> the college teams in the afternoon.

2. Shopping <u>takes</u> too much time, <u>tests</u> my patience, and <u>leaves</u> me broke at the end of the day.

3. The mouse in our back yard <u>ate</u> all the seed in the bird feeder.

4. He <u>offered</u> me a discount but <u>refused</u> payment by credit card.

5. My mother's favorite vacation spot <u>is</u> a beach about fifty miles from here.

6. The volunteers <u>collected</u> and <u>sorted</u> all the recyclable items.

7. The puppy <u>grabbed</u> the baby's rattle, <u>raced</u> across the room, and <u>skidded</u> under the sofa with the toy.

8. Some people <u>find</u> friends in their workplace and also at neighborhood activities.

9. The casserole <u>looked</u> inviting, <u>smelled</u> enticing, and <u>tasted</u> delicious.

10. The best restaurant in town <u>served</u> its last meals yesterday.

Exercise 7   **Recognizing Verbs in a Selection from "The Tell-Tale Heart"**

Connect

This selection is from "The Tell-Tale Heart," a horror story by Edgar Allan Poe. In it, an insane murderer has killed an old man and buried him under the floor. When the police arrive, they find nothing, but the murderer is convinced that he—and the police—can hear the old man's heart beating under the floor. In this selection, the murderer describes what he feels as he hears the heart beat louder and louder.

Underline all the verbs in the selection. Notice how a careful choice of verbs can make writing exciting and suspenseful.

The officers were satisfied. My manner had <u>convinced</u> them. I was singularly at ease. They sat, and while I answered cheerfully, they chatted familiar things. But, ere* long, I felt myself getting pale and wished them gone. My head ached, and I fancied* a ringing in my ears: but still they sat and still chatted. The ringing became more distinct: —it continued and became more distinct: I talked more freely to get rid of the feeling: but it continued and gained definitiveness—until, at length,* I found that the noise was not within my ears.

No doubt I now grew very pale; —but I talked more fluently, and with a heightened voice. Yet the sound increased—and what could I do? . . . I gasped for breath—and yet the officers heard it not. I talked more quickly, more vehemently;* but the noise steadily increased. I arose and argued about trifles, in a high key and with violent gesticulations,* but the noise steadily increased. Why would they not be gone? I paced the floor to and fro with heavy strides, as if excited to fury by the observation of the men—but the noise steadily increased. Oh God! What could I do? I foamed—I raved—I swore! . . . It grew louder—louder—louder! And still the men chatted pleasantly, and smiled. Was it possible they heard not?

Almighty God!—no, no! They heard! —they suspected! —they knew!

* **ere** means before
* **fancied:** imagined
* **at length:** after a time
* **vehemently:** forcefully
* **gesticulations:** gestures

RECOGNIZING SUBJECTS

After you learn to recognize verbs, you can easily find the subjects of sentences because subjects and verbs are linked. If the verb is an action verb, for example, the **subject** will be the word or words that answer the question "Who or what is doing that action?" Follow these steps to identify the subject:

sentence with an action verb:

The cat slept on my bed.

Step 1: Identify the verb: *slept*

Step 2: Ask, "Who or what slept?"

Step 3: The answer is the subject: The *cat* slept on my bed. The *cat* is the subject.

If the verb is a being verb, the same steps apply to finding the subject:

sentence with a being verb:

Clarice is his girlfriend.

Step 1: Identify the verb: *is*

Step 2: Ask, "Who or what is his girlfriend?"

Step 3: The answer is the subject: *Clarice* is his girlfriend. *Clarice* is the subject.

Just as there can be more than one word making up a verb, there can be more than one subject.

examples: *Coffee* and a *doughnut* are a typical breakfast for me.
His *father* and *grandfather* own a landscaping service.

Exercise 8 **Recognizing Subjects in Sentences**

Practice   Underline the subjects in the following sentences.

1. Mr. Wong should have completed the work on time.

2. The police were investigating the crime yesterday.

3. Detergent and water will remove that greasy stain.

4. Something must have fallen in the night.

5. René and Robert designed a clear plan for the surprise party.

6. Nagging will not help the situation.

7. Recognition and respect were the things he wanted most.

8. Snakes can be ideal pets.

9. We supplied the food and cleaned the kitchen.

10. Soup tastes better on a cold day.

Exercise 9 **Adding Subjects to Sentences**

Collaborate   Working with a partner or a group, complete the paragraph below by adding subjects in the blanks. Before you fill in the blanks, discuss your answers and try to come to an agreement about the worst movie, the worst album, and so on. When you have completed the paragraph, share your answers with another group or with the class.

This year has seen many achievements in the arts and entertainment, but it has also seen many creative disasters. On movie screens, there have been some terrible movies. Without a doubt, _____ was the worst movie of the year. It should never have been made. On television, _____ was the worst and also the most irritating show. Every time I see it, I want to turn it off or kick in the television screen. _____ and _____ take the prize for the worst actor and actress of the year. They should consider other careers. In the field of music, _____ ranks as the least successful album of the year. _____ is the most annoying song because the radio played it far too often. Last, _____ is the most annoying singer.

MORE ABOUT RECOGNIZING SUBJECTS AND VERBS

Recognizing the Core Subject

When you look for the subject of a sentence, look for the core word or words; do not include descriptive words around the subject. Look for the subject, not for the words that describe it.

the core subject:

Light blue *paint* will brighten these walls.
Cracked *sidewalks* and rusty *railings* made the old school dangerous for children.

Prepositions and Prepositional Phrases

Prepositions are usually short words that often signal a kind of position or relationship, as shown in the following list:

Infobox

Some Common Prepositions

about	before	by	into	over	with
above	below	during	like	through	within
across	behind	except	near	to	without
after	beneath	for	of	toward	
among	beside	from	off	under	
around	between	in	on	up	
at	beyond	inside	onto	upon	

A **prepositional phrase** is made up of a preposition and its object. Here are some prepositional phrases. In each one, the first word is the preposition; the other words are the object of the preposition.

Prepositional Phrases

about the movie	of mice and men
around the corner	off the wall
between the lines	on the mark
during recess	up the chimney
near my house	with my sister and brother

An old memory trick can help you remember prepositions. Think of a chair. Now, think of a series of words you can put *in front of* the chair:

around the chair	*with* the chair
by the chair	*to* the chair
behind the chair	*near* the chair
between the chairs	*under* the chair
of the chair	*on* the chair
off the chair	*from* the chair

These words are prepositions.

You need to know about prepositions because they can help you identify the subject of a sentence. Here is an important grammar rule about prepositions:

Nothing in a prepositional phrase can ever be the subject of a sentence.

Prepositional phrases describe people, places, or things. They may also describe the subject of a sentence, but they never *include* the subject. Whenever you are looking for the subject of a sentence, begin by putting parentheses around all the prepositional phrases:

parentheses and prepositional phrases

The park (behind my apartment) has a playground (with swings and slides).

Nothing in the prepositional phrase can be the subject. Once you have eliminated these phrases, you can follow the steps to find the subject of the sentence:

Step 1: Identify the verb: *has*.

Step 2: Ask, "Who or what has?"

Step 3: The answer is the subject: The *park*. The *park* is the subject.

By marking off the prepositional phrases, you are left with the core of the sentence. There is less to look at.

(Across the street) a *child* (with a teddy bear) sat (among the flowers).
subject: *child*
The *student* (from Jamaica) won the contest (with ease).
subject: *student*.

Exercise 10 **Recognizing Prepositional Phrases, Subjects, and Verbs**

Practice Put parentheses around the prepositional phrases in the following sentences. Then underline the subjects and verbs and put an *S* above each subject and a *V* above each verb.

1. Several (of my friends) are members of the (Volunteer Crimestoppers' club.)

2. The restaurant was (off the highway) between (Riverdale and Parkland Heights.)

3. The car (in the garage) dripped oil (onto the cement floor.)

4. The best entry (in the cooking contest) was a seven-layer cake (with chocolate roses) (on a bed of mocha icing.)

5. He pulled a handkerchief (from his pocket) and began to wipe the tears (from the child's face.)

6. The boy (with my sister) is a visitor (from a rural area) (of Nicaragua.)

7. The prize (inside the Cracker Jack box) was a secret decoder ring (with a magic seal) (on the front.)

8. (With a smile,) she slipped the love letter (between the pages) (of her book.)

9. He drove around the neighborhood but got lost near the entrance to the freeway.

10. One of the easiest things in the world is making excuses for your bad habits.

Exercise 11 **Writing Sentences with Prepositional Phrases**

👥 Collaborate

Do this exercise with a partner. First, add one prepositional phrase to the core sentence. Then, ask your partner to add a second prepositional phrase to the same sentence. For the next sentence, switch places: let your partner add the first phrase, and you add the second. Keep switching places throughout the exercise. When you have completed the exercise, share your sentences (the ones with two prepositional phrases) with the class. The first one is done for you.

1. **core sentence:** Employees are concerned.

   Add one prepositional phrase: Employees are concerned about their
   paychecks.

   Add another prepositional phrase: Employees at the central plant are
   concerned about their paychecks.

2. **core sentence:** Children visited the zoo.

   Add one prepositional phrase: _____

   _____

   Add another prepositional phrase: _____

   _____

3. **core sentence:** The ball fell.

   Add one prepositional phrase: _____

   _____

   Add another prepositional phrase: _____

   _____

4. **core sentence:** The plane was delayed.

   Add one prepositional phrase: _____

   _____

   Add another prepositional phrase: _____

   _____

5. core sentence: Some families should be more concerned.

Add one prepositional phrase: _____

_____

Add another prepositional phrase: _____

_____

6. core sentence: The detective ran.

Add one prepositional phrase: _____

_____

Add another prepositional phrase: _____

_____

Word Order

When we speak, we often use a very simple word order: first, the subject; then, the verb. For example, someone might say, "He lost the key." *He* is the subject that begins the sentence; *lost* is the verb that comes after the subject.

However, not all sentences use such a simple word order. Prepositional phrases, for example, can change the word order. To identify the subject and verb, follow these steps:

prepositional phrase and changed subject-verb order:
Behind the cabinet was a box of coins.

Step 1: Mark off the prepositional phrases with parentheses: (Behind the cabinet) was a box (of coins). Remember that nothing in a prepositional phrase can be the subject of a sentence.

Step 2: Find the verb: *was*

Step 3: Who or what was? A box was. The subject of the sentence is *box*.

After you change the word order of this sentence, you can see the subject *(S)* and the verb *(V)* more easily:

   S   **V**
A *box* of coins *was* behind the cabinet.

(Even though *coins* is a plural word, you must use the singular verb *was* because *box* is the singular subject.)

Exercise 12 **Finding Prepositional Phrases, Subjects, and Verbs in Complicated**
Practice **Word Order**

Put parentheses around the prepositional phrases in the following sentences. Then underline the subjects and verbs, putting an *S* above each subject and a *V* above each verb.

1. From the top of the hill came a piercing scream.

2. At the back of the room sat a small boy with an enormous book bag.

3. In the depths of the basement are a box of old clothes and a trunk with old photographs in it.

4. With the rescue team came a trained nurse.

5. Beside the sleeping bulldog sat a fluffy gray kitten.

6. In the neighborhood near the train station were several old hotels and restaurants.

7. Down the road loped a large dog with a spotted black and white coat.

8. Beneath his friendly manner is an angry and troubled man.

9. Toward me came a stylish young man in an expensive suit.

10. Across the street from his store is an old market.

More on Word Order

The expected word order of a subject followed by a verb will change when a sentence starts with *There is/are*, *There was/were*, *Here is/are*, or *Here was/were*. In such cases, look for the subject after the verb:

S-V order with *There is/are, Here is/are*:

      V   S   S

There *are a supermarket* and a *laundromat* near my apartment.

       V   S

Here *is* my best *friend.*

If it helps you understand this pattern, you can change the word order:

      S   S   V

A *supermarket* and a *laundromat are* there, near my apartment.

         S   V

My best *friend is* here.

You should also note that even when the subject comes after the verb, the verb has to *match* the subject. For instance, if the subject refers to more than one thing, the verb must refer to more than one thing:

There *are a supermarket* and a *laundromat* near my apartment. (Two things, a supermarket and a laundromat, *are* near my apartment.)

Word Order in Questions

Questions may have a different word order. The main verb and the helping verb may not be next to each other.

word order in questions:

question: Did you study for the test?
subject: *you*
verbs: *did, study*

If it helps you to understand this concept, think about answering the question. If someone accused you of not studying for the test, you might say, "I *did study* for it." You'd use two words as verbs.

question: Will she call her mother?
subject: *she*
verbs: *will, call*

question: Is Charles making the coffee?
subject: *Charles*
verbs: *is, making*

Exercise 13 **Recognizing Subjects and Verbs in Questions and in *Here is/are, There***
Practice ***is/are* Word Order**

Underline the subjects and verbs in the following sentences, putting an *S* above each subject and a *V* above each verb.

1. Here are your sneakers and your tube socks.

2. Did Sharon borrow my notebook with the Introduction to Biology notes in it?

3. Can the plumber fix the sink today?

4. There is a great used car for sale in today's paper.

5. Behind the house there are an old apple tree and a cluster of pines.

6. Will you arrange for the furniture delivery?

7. Here are the best books on the subject of air pollution.

8. Do you want another helping of turkey?

9. Have they cleaned and sorted the clothes yet?

10. There is someone in the back of the car.

Words That Cannot Be Verbs

Sometimes there are words that look like verbs in a sentence but are not verbs. Such words include *adverbs* (words like *always, often, nearly, never, ever*) that are placed close to the verb but are not verbs. Another word that is sometimes placed between a helping verb and a main verb is the word *not. Not* is not a verb. When you are looking for verbs in a sentence, be careful to eliminate words like *often* and *not.*

They will not accept his apology. (The complete verb is *will accept.*)
Matthew can often repair his truck by himself. (The complete verb is *can repair.*)

Be careful with *contractions:*

> He hasn't called me in a long time. (The complete verb is *has called. Not*
> is not a part of the verb, even in contractions.)
> Don't you speak Spanish? (The complete verb is *do speak.*)
> Won't you come inside? (The complete verb is *will come. Won't* is a con-
> traction for *will not.*)

Recognizing Main Verbs

If you are checking to see if a word is a main verb, try the pronoun test. Combine your word with this simple list of pronouns: *I, you, he, she, it, we, they.* A main verb is a word such as *look* or *pulled* that can be combined with the words on this list. Now try the pronoun test.

> For the word *look:* I look, you look, he looks, she looks, it looks, we look, they look

> For the word *pulled:* I pulled, you pulled, he pulled, she pulled, it pulled, we pulled, they pulled

But the word *never* can't be used, alone, with the pronouns:

> ~~I never, you never, he never, she never, it never, we never, they never~~
> (Never did what?)

Never is not a verb. *Not* is not a verb, either, as the pronoun test indicates:

> ~~I not, you not, he not, she not, it not, we not, they not~~ (These combinations don't make sense because *not* is not a verb.)

Verb Forms That Cannot Be Main Verbs

There are forms of verbs that can't be main verbs by themselves, either. An *-ing* verb, by itself, cannot be the main verb, as the pronoun test shows:

> For the word *taking:* ~~I taking, you taking, he taking, she taking, it taking, we taking, they taking~~

If you see an *-ing* verb by itself, correct the sentence by adding a helping verb.

> He ~~taking~~ his time. (*Taking*, by itself, cannot be a main verb.)
> **correction:** He *is taking* his time.

Another verb form, called an *infinitive*, also cannot be a main verb. An **infinitive** is the form of the verb that has *to* placed in front of it.

Infobox

Some Common Infinitives

to call	to fall	to live	to talk
to care	to give	to run	to work
to drive			

Try the pronoun test and you'll see that infinitives can't be main verbs:

> For the infinitive *to live:* ~~I to live, you to live, he to live, she to live, it to live, we to live, they to live~~

So if you see an infinitive being used as a verb, correct the sentence by adding a main verb.

He ~~to live~~ in a better house.
correction: He *wants* to live in a better house.

The infinitives and the *-ing* verbs just don't work as main verbs. You must put a verb with them to make a correct sentence.

Exercise 14 **Correcting Problems with Infinitive or *-ing* Verb Forms**

Practice

Most—but not all—of the following sentences are faulty; an *-ing* verb or an infinitive may be taking the place of a main verb. Rewrite the sentences that have errors.

1. One of the best ideas for the party to send invitations to all my cousins.

2. School and work responsibilities leaving me with no chance to relax.

3. All the noise at the gymnasium was giving me a terrible headache.

4. In her soul, Cecilia facing the truth about her sister's frantic phone calls.

5. Several of the most successful broadcasters in television news to present a panel at our college tomorrow.

6. The chairman of the committee expressing his doubts about the proposal for a new budget.

7. The once-popular singer to sell his valuable art collection at an auction next week.

8. The driver in the next car needs to signal when he changes lanes.

9. Toys for my grandchildren, books for my nephews, and albums for my sister costing me several hundred dollars.

10. A tiny brown mouse suddenly sticking its head out of the cookie jar.

Exercise 15 **Finding Subjects and Verbs: A Comprehensive Exercise**

Practice

Underline the subjects and verbs in the following sentences, putting an *S* above each subject and a *V* above each verb.

1. Has she ever seen the inside of a log cabin with pioneer furnishings?

2. We weren't listening to the conversation at the other end of the dining room table.

3. Beneath her tears was the beginning of a smile.

4. Sylvia likes to cook spaghetti on Saturday nights.

5. Can't Miguel make his own bed?

6. Violent criminals are often the subject of television movies.

7. Procrastinating and forgetting will not erase their responsibilities.

8. Here are my best friend and my sister.

9. Wayne could have made that phone call before the trip.

10. At the top of the cupboard in the kitchen is an electric mixer.

11. Her mother mowed the lawn and trimmed the bushes around the fence.

12. A line of ants stretched from the refrigerator to the spilled Pepsi.

13. A firm mattress and fluffy pillows can make all the difference in the quality of your night's sleep.

14. Kathleen has never been to Disney World with me.

15. From the bottom of the hill you can't see the country roads and farms.

16. The insurance salesman has been calling the house all morning.

17. Jamal wrote to the doctor and asked for a copy of his records.

18. A singer from Haiti and a dancer from Peru won the international talent contest.

19. On weekends, Roberta ran two miles and exercised at the local gym.

20. Among the gifts was a sterling silver bowl with a gold rim.

Exercise 16 **Creating Your Own Text**

👥 Collaborate

Do this exercise with a partner or a group. Following is a list of the rules you have just studied. Write two examples for each rule. When your group has completed the examples for each rule, trade your group's completed exercise with another group's exercise and check their examples while they check yours. The first rule has been done for you.

Rule 1: The verb in a sentence can express some kind of action.

example 1: My cousin studies biology in college.

example 2: Yesterday the rain destroyed the rose bushes.

Rule 2: The verb in a sentence can express some state of being.

example 1: _____

example 2: _____

Rule 3: The verb in a sentence can consist of more than one word.

example 1: _____

example 2: _____

Rule 4: There can be more than one subject in a sentence.

example 1: _____

example 2: _____

Rule 5: If you take out the prepositional phrases, it is easier to identify the subject of a sentence because nothing in a prepositional phrase can be the subject of a sentence. (Write sentences containing at least one prepositional phrase. Put parentheses around the prepositional phrases.)

example 1: _____

example 2: _____

Rule 6: Not all sentences have the simple word order of subject first, then verb. (Give examples of sentences with more complicated word order.)

example 1: _____

example 2: _____

Rule 7: Words like *not, never, often, always, ever* are not verbs. (Write sentences using one of these words, but underline the correct verb.)

example 1: _____

example 2: _____

Rule 8: An *-ing* verb form by itself or an infinitive (*to* preceding the verb) cannot be a main verb. (Write sentences with *-ing* verb forms or infinitives, but underline the main verb.)

example 1: _____

example 2: _____

Exercise 17   **Recognizing Subjects and Verbs in a Paragraph**

Connect

Underline the subjects and verbs in the following paragraph, putting an *S* above each subject and a *V* above each verb.

    A letter can send a powerful message. For example, a love letter can bring joy (to a special person) and strengthen the bonds (between two peo-ple.) A note (of sympathy) (on the death) (of a family member) expresses a personal feeling. A store-bought sympathy card can't do the same thing. An individual's written words are a sign of caring. One of the greatest thrills for a child at camp is getting a long letter from home. A college student also loves to receive a letter from a good friend, boyfriend, girl-friend, sister, or brother. A phone call is great and can brighten a person's day. However, a call is over quickly and soon fades away. A letter can be saved and reread. An old letter is a treasure. In it are memories, emotions, and dreams.

CHAPTER 2

Beyond the Simple Sentence: Coordination

A group of words containing a subject and a verb is called a **clause.** When that group makes sense by itself, it is called a sentence or an independent clause. A sentence that has one independent clause is called a **simple sentence.** If you rely too heavily on a sentence pattern of simple sentences, you risk writing paragraphs like this:

> My father never got a chance to go to college. He had to struggle all of his life. He struggled to make a good living. He dreamed of sending his children to college. He saved his money for their education. Today, all three of his children are in college. Two of them are working toward degrees in business. My father is very proud of them. His third child has pleased my father the most. The third child, my brother, is majoring in education. My father will be proud of his son, the teacher. He thinks a teacher in the family is a great gift.

instead of

> My father never got a chance to go to college, and he had to struggle all of his life to make a good living. He dreamed of sending his children to college, so he saved his money for their education. Today, all three of his children are in college. Two of them are working toward degrees in business. My father is very proud of them, yet his third child has pleased my father the most. The third child, my brother, is majoring in education. My father will be proud of his son, the teacher, for he thinks a teacher in the family is a great gift.

If you read the two paragraphs aloud, you'll notice how choppy the first one sounds. The second one is smoother. The first one is made up of simple sentences, while the second one combines simple sentences for a more flowing style.

OPTIONS FOR COMBINING SIMPLE SENTENCES

Good writing involves sentence variety. This means mixing a simple sentence with a more complicated one and using both short and long sentences. Sentence variety is easier to achieve if you can combine related, short sentences into one.

Some students avoid such combining because they're not sure how to do it. They don't know how to punctuate the new combinations. It's true that punctuating involves memorizing a few rules, but once you know them, you'll be able to use them automatically and write with more confidence. Here are three options for combining simple sentences, followed by the punctuation rules you need to use in each case.

OPTION 1: USING A COMMA WITH A COORDINATING CONJUNCTION

You can combine two simple sentences with a comma and a coordinating conjunction. The coordinating conjunctions are *and, but, or, nor, for, yet, so.*

To **coordinate** means to *join equals.* When you join two simple sentences with a comma and a coordinating conjunction, each half of the combination remains an **independent clause,** with its own subject (S) and verb (V).

Here are two simple sentences:

> S   V   S   V
> *Joanne drove* the car. *Richard studied* the map.

Here are two simple sentences combined with a comma and the word *and,* a coordinating conjunction (CC):

> S   V   , CC S   V
> *Joanne drove* the car, *and Richard studied* the map.

The combined sentences keep the form they had as separate sentences; that is, they are both still independent clauses, with a subject and verb and with the ability to stand alone.

The word that joins them is the **coordinating conjunction.** It is used to join *equals.* Look at some more examples. These examples use a variety of coordinating conjunctions to join two simple sentences (also called independent clauses).

sentences combined with *but*:

> S   V   , CC S   V
> *She brought* a cake, *but she forgot* a cake slicer.

sentences combined with *or*:

> S   V   ,CC S   V
> *Mr. Chung can call* my office, *or he can write* me.

sentences combined with *nor*:

> S V   V   , CC V S   V
> *We couldn't see* the stage, *nor could we hear* the music. (Notice what happens to the word order when you use *nor.*)

sentences combined with *for*:

> S   V   , CC   S   V
> *My mother was* furious, *for the doctor was* two hours late. (Notice that *for* means *because.*)

sentences combined with *yet*:

S   V   , CC S   V
I loved botany, *yet I* never *got* a good grade in it. (Notice that *yet* means *but* or *nevertheless*.)

sentences combined with *so*:

    S   V   ,CC S   V
Marshall brought her flowers, *so she forgave* him for his rudeness. (Notice that *so* means *therefore* or *as a result*.)

Where Does the Comma Go?

The comma goes *before* the coordinating conjunction (*and, but, or, nor, for, yet, so*). It comes before the new idea—the second independent clause. It goes where the first independent clause ends. Try this punctuation check: After you've placed the comma, look at the combined sentences. For example:

John saved his money, and he bought a new car.

Now split it into two sentences at the comma:

John saved his money. And he bought a new car.

If you put the comma in the wrong place, after the coordinating conjunction, like this:

comma in wrong place:

~~John saved his money and, he bought a new car.~~

your split sentences would look like this:

John saved his money and. He bought a new car. (The split doesn't make sense.)

This test helps you see whether the comma has been placed correctly—where the first independent clause ends. (Notice that you can also begin a sentence with *and, but, or, nor, for, yet, so*—as long as you've written a complete sentence.)

Caution: Do *not* use a comma every time you use the words *and, but, or, nor, for, yet, so;* use one only when the coordinating conjunction joins independent clauses. Do not use a comma when the coordinating conjunction joins words:

tea or coffee
exhausted but relieved
love and happiness

Do not use a comma when the coordinating conjunction joins phrases:

on the patio or in the garden
in the glove compartment and under the seats
with harsh words but without anger

A comma is used when the coordinating conjunction joins two independent clauses. Another way to state the same rule is to say that a comma is used when the coordinating conjunction joins two simple sentences.

Placing the Comma by Using *S-V* Patterns

An independent clause, or simple sentence, follows this basic pattern:

S (subject)   V (verb)

Here is an example:

S V
He ran.

You can add to the basic pattern in several ways:

S S V
He and I ran.

S V V
He ran and swam.

S S V V
He and I ran and swam.

Study all the examples above, and you'll notice that you can draw a line separating the subjects on one side and the verbs on the other:

S	V
SS	V
S	VV
SS	VV

So whether the simple sentence has one subject or more than one, the pattern is subject(s) followed by verb(s).

Compound Sentences

When you combine two simple sentences, the pattern changes:

two simple sentences:

S V
He swam.

S V
I ran.

two simple sentences combined:

S V S V
He swam, but I ran.

In the new pattern, *SVSV*, you can't draw a line putting all the subjects on one side and all the verbs on the other. The new pattern is called a **compound sentence:** two simple sentences, or independent clauses, combined into one.

Learning the Coordinating Conjunctions

You've just studied one way to combine simple sentences. If you are going to take advantage of this method, you need to memorize the coordinating conjunctions—*and, but, or, nor, for, yet, so*—so that your use of them, with the correct punctuation, will become automatic.

Exercise 1 **Recognizing Compound Sentences and Adding Commas**

Practice Add commas only where they are needed in the following sentences.

1. Steve bought tickets for the game, but it was rained out.

2. A woman in the crowd waved a banner and stamped her feet against the bleachers. *No correction needed*

3. After my job interview I wrote a thank-you note to the interviewing committee, and I waited for the committee's decision. *no correction needed*

4. The dancers are working at a small club and are auditioning for a job on a television show. *no correction needed*

5. Snow was beginning to fall, so I put snow tires on the car.

6. Betty smiled a friendly smile, yet her words revealed a hidden anger.

7. I searched the phone book for a typewriter repair shop but couldn't find one anywhere. *no correction needed*

8. Harry dressed carefully, for he wanted to impress his date.

9. The police were not afraid of the gunman's threats nor were they intimidated by his weapons. *no correction needed*

10. Mark has to take good notes in class, or he forgets the main points of the lectures.

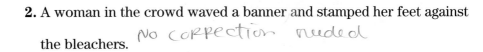

Exercise 2   **More on Recognizing Compound Sentences and Adding Commas**

Practice   Add commas only where they are needed in the following sentences.

1. My uncle was thinking about moving to California or opening a restaurant in Chicago. *no commas needed*

2. My boss at the Quick Mart gave me a stern yet sympathetic lecture about falling asleep on the job. *no commas needed.*

3. Idell and Conrad have been studying line dancing, so they are eager to show off their steps at the party.

4. There are three kinds of pasta in the refrigerator, for your brother has been cooking all afternoon.

5. I took the necklace out of its box, and I held the diamonds up to the light.

6. The doorbell rang, so Steve walked to the front door.

7. Lynn's cousins can go to the fashion show, or they can visit a museum.

8. Mr. Morales will fix the leaky faucet, but he can't fix the drain.

9. Criticism will help neither the team nor the coach.

no correction needed

10. Anthony and Sylvia gave me dinner and drove me home.

no correction needed

Exercise 3 **Writing and Punctuating Compound Sentences**

👥 Collaborate Working with a partner or a group, write the compound sentences described below. Be sure to punctuate them correctly. When you have completed the exercise, share your answers with another group or with the class.

1. Write a compound sentence using the coordinating conjunction *and*.

I went to the store, and I bought myself a pair of shoe.

2. Write a compound sentence using the coordinating conjunction *but*.

_____

3. Write a compound sentence using the coordinating conjunction *or*.

_____

4. Write a compound sentence using the coordinating conjunction *nor*.

_____

5. Write a compound sentence using the coordinating conjunction *for*.

_____

6. Write a compound sentence using the coordinating conjunction *yet*.

_____

7. Write a compound sentence using the coordinating conjunction *so*.

_____

OPTION 2: USING A SEMICOLON BETWEEN TWO SIMPLE SENTENCES

Sometimes you may want to combine two simple sentences (independent clauses) without using a coordinating conjunction. If you want to join two simple sentences that are related in their ideas and you do not want to use a coordinating conjunction, you can combine them with a semicolon.

two simple sentences:

S   V   S   V
I washed the floor. *He dusted* the furniture.

two simple sentences combined with a semicolon:

S   V   ; S   V
I washed the floor; *he dusted* the furniture.

Here are more examples of this option in use:

S   V ; S V
He swam; I ran.

S   V   V ; S V   V
Jacy couldn't sleep; she was thinking about her job.

S   V   ; S   V
Skindiving is expensive; you need money for equipment.

Notice that when you join two simple sentences with a semicolon, the second sentence begins with a lowercase letter, not a capital letter.

Exercise 4

Practice

Recognizing Compound Sentences and Adding Semicolons

Add semicolons only where they are needed in the following sentences.

1. She called me at home and asked for a copy of the letter from our lawyer.

2. I'll take the baby to the day-care center; you can take your sister to work.

3. Something is wrong at home; I can feel it in my bones.

4. His ambition cost him a family life and a good relationship with his eldest son.

5. Dr. Karram is a wonderful teacher; his lectures are easy to follow and full of interesting facts.

6. Computers were once a mystery to me; I was afraid of touching the wrong key and destroying the machine.

7. She wanted to do well in college but disliked reading and was easily distracted.

8. The sun baked the pavement; my bare feet hurt on the hot concrete.

9. Sam and Johnnie had a picnic in the park; the food was delicious.

10. Driving too fast can cost you a speeding ticket and higher insurance rates.

Exercise 5

Practice

More on Recognizing Compound Sentences and Adding Semicolons

Add semicolons only where they are needed in the following sentences.

1. My doctor gave me a prescription for an antibiotic and told me to take the medicine with food.

2. The movie was boring; it had too many car chases.

3. A fluffy white dog and a small child ran across the lawn and jumped into a small red wagon.

4. Complaining can become a bad habit;it can make a person frustrated and unhappy.

5. Michael was covered in mud;he had fallen into a ditch.

6. My truck hit a pothole in the road;the whole truck bounced and creaked.

7. Something is wrong with this can opener;it will not turn properly.

8. Ghost stories are a treat for children with active imaginations and brave spirits.

9. Harry usually offered sympathy;Richard gave practical advice.

10. Six letters came in the mail;they were all selling credit cards.

OPTION 3: USING A SEMICOLON AND A CONJUNCTIVE ADVERB

Sometimes you may want to join two simple sentences (independent clauses) with a connecting word called a **conjunctive adverb.** This word points out or clarifies a relationship between the sentences.

Infobox			
Some Common Conjunctive Adverbs			
also	furthermore	likewise	otherwise
anyway	however	meanwhile	similarly
as a result	in addition	moreover	still
besides	incidentally	nevertheless	then
certainly	indeed	next	therefore
consequently	in fact	now	thus
finally	instead	on the other hand	undoubtedly

You can put a conjunctive adverb (CA) between simple sentences, but when you do, you still need a semicolon in front of the adverb.

two simple sentences:

S V   S   V
I got a tutor for college algebra. *I improved* my grade.

two simple sentences joined by a conjunctive adverb and a semicolon:

S V   ; CA S   V
I got a tutor for college algebra; *then I improved* my grade.

S V   ;   CA   S   V
I got a tutor for college algebra; *consequently, I improved* my grade.

Punctuating After a Conjunctive Adverb

Notice the comma after the conjunctive adverb in the sentence *I got a tutor for college algebra; consequently, I improved my grade.* Here's the generally accepted rule:

> **Put a comma after the conjunctive adverb if the conjunctive adverb is more than one syllable long.**

For example, if the conjunctive adverb is a word like *consequently, furthermore,* or *moreover,* you use a comma. If the conjunctive adverb is one syllable, you do not have to add a comma after it. One-syllable conjunctive adverbs are words like *then* or *thus.*

> **punctuating with conjunctive adverbs:**
>
> Every month I paid my whole credit card debt; thus I avoided paying interest.
>
> Every month I paid my whole credit card debt; consequently, I avoided paying interest.

Exercise 6

Practice

Recognizing and Punctuating Compound Sentences with Conjunctive Adverbs

Add semicolons and commas only where they are needed in the following sentences.

1. My nephew begged and pleaded; finally, I gave him his surprise.

2. Jamal loves cold weather; in fact, he keeps his bedroom window open in the middle of winter.

3. My brother comes over every weekend but never offers to help with the chores around my house.

4. He will undoubtedly have a reason for coming to the meeting.

5. I know you didn't mean to be rude; however, you hurt my feelings with your sarcasm.

6. That actor used to be a big star; now you can't find him on television or in movies.

7. Several people have offered to buy my car; undoubtedly, I can sell it for a good price.

8. The phone was ringing in the kitchen; meanwhile, someone rang the door bell.

9. Freshly ground coffee is expensive but is worth every penny.

10. Freshly ground coffee is expensive; on the other hand, it is worth every penny.

Exercise 7
Practice **More on Recognizing and Punctuating Compound Sentences with Conjunctive Adverbs**

Add semicolons and commas only where they are needed in the following sentences.

1. The leader of the group sings beautifully; incidentally, she is my wife.

2. I run two miles every day; as a result, I am in good physical shape.

3. Christopher had always dreamed of owning a sports car; besides, he had been saving for one for years.

4. The rain began as a gentle drizzle; then it became a downpour.

5. His parents offered the little boy candy and toys; still the child screamed and stamped his feet.

6. My parents constantly talk about driving to New Orleans for a long weekend yet never take the trip.

7. Fresh strawberries taste great; besides, they are good for you.

8. My best friend will listen to my stories for hours and even pay attention to my late-night phone calls.

9. A college education can certainly help your chances of getting a challenging and rewarding job.

10. Jasmine should win the contest; certainly, she will be among the finalists.

Exercise 8
Collaborate **Writing Sentences with Conjunctive Adverbs**

Working with a partner or a group, write one sentence for each of the conjunctive adverbs below. When you have completed this exercise, share your answers with another group or with the class. The first one is done for you.

1. Write a compound sentence using *instead*.

   She couldn't find her notes for her speech to the jury; instead, she relied on her memory.

2. Write a compound sentence using *then*.

   _____

   _____

3. Write a compound sentence using *furthermore.*

_____

_____

4. Write a compound sentence using *meanwhile.*

_____

_____

5. Write a compound sentence using *consequently.*

_____

_____

6. Write a compound sentence using *therefore.*

_____

_____

Exercise 9 **Combining Simple Sentences Three Ways**

Practice

Add (1) a comma, (2) a semicolon, or (3) a semicolon and a comma to the following sentences. Do not add, change, or delete any words; just add the correct punctuation.

1. I gave you several chances to apologize; now I am out of patience and understanding.

2. Sport-utility vehicles are very popular, but they are terrible gas guzzlers.

3. Mrs. Lee was the best physics teacher in the school; moreover, she was a mentor to me.

4. I wrapped his gift carefully, for I wanted to impress him with my good taste.

5. Ann missed six classes in a row; consequently, she has no chance of passing the final exam.

6. The fair was a spectacular event; however, it was a big disappointment to the children.

7. My father was promoted at his job; he took the family out to celebrate.

8. Roberto had nothing to do with the surprise party; furthermore, he hates large parties full of strangers.

9. I had laryngitis all last week; I could barely talk on the phone.

10. Amelia designed the plans for the new house, and she interviewed the heads of several construction companies.

11. The puppy chewed his way out of the screened porch; then he dug an enormous hole in the flower bed.

12. Richard read the child a bedtime story; meanwhile, Cal did the dishes.

13. I wasn't prepared for my sister's news, for I hadn't seen her in two years.

14. The salesman walked us around the auto showroom; next he took us to his cubicle to make a deal.

15. Once I was a heavy smoker; now I lecture my friends about the dangers of smoking.

16. I bring a sandwich to work, or I pop a frozen pizza in the office microwave.

17. Sharing an apartment with Charlie can be irritating; still it is better than paying the rent by myself.

18. Danielle was late for work, so she took a shortcut through the mall.

19. That man is not a liar, nor is he a thief.

20. My brother never went to college; instead, he joined the navy after high school.

Exercise 10 **Combining Simple Sentences**

👥 Collaborate

Following are pairs of simple sentences. Working with a partner or a group, combine each pair into one sentence. Remember the three options for combining sentences: (1) a comma and a coordinating conjunction, (2) a semicolon, (3) a semicolon and a conjunctive adverb. When you have combined each pair into one sentence, exchange your exercise with another group. Write a new sentence below each sentence prepared by the other group. The first one is done for you.

1. Takeout pizza for a family of six is expensive.
   My children and I make our own pizza at home.

combination 1: Takeout pizza for a family of six is expensive, so my chil-dren and I make our own pizza at home.

combination 2: Takeout pizza for a family of six is expensive; instead, my children and I make our own pizza at home.

2. The concert was loud, crowded, and outrageously overpriced.
It was the most exciting night out of my life.

combination 1: The concert was loud, crowded, and outrageously overpriced, but it was the most exciting night out of my life

combination 2: The concert was loud, crowded, and outrageously overpriced; however, it was the most exciting night out of my life.

3. Damian's parents paid all his bills.
He remained totally dependent on his family.

combination 1: Damian's parents paid all his bills, so he remained totally dependent on his family

combination 2: Damians parents paid all his bills, still he remained totally dependent on his family.

4. Your plan for a new student center seems interesting.
I have some questions about your fund-raising strategies.

combination 1: Your plan for a new student center seems interesting, but I have some questions about your fund-raising strategies.

combination 2: Your plan for a new student center seems interesting, however, I have some questions about your fund-raising strategies.

5. Christine called me on her cell phone.
Jim tried to call me from a pay phone at the airport.

combination 1: Christine called me on her cell phone; Jim tried to call me from a pay phone at the airport.

combination 2: Christine called me on her cell phone; meanwhile Jim tried to called me from a pay phone at the airport.

Exercise 11 **Punctuating Compound Sentences in a Paragraph**

Connect Add commas and semicolons only where they are needed in the paragraph below.

Taking care of a cold means taking care of myself. At the first signs of a cold, I make sure to increase my consumption of vitamin C. I drink extra glasses of orange juice or I swallow a couple of vitamin C tablets with meals. I slow down at work I cut down on chores at home. I take life a little easier; consequently, I avoid the exhaustion of a bad cold. Sometimes I even pamper myself; I spend a whole day in bed and eat chicken soup. The hot liquid helps my sinuses; moreover, the bed rest gives me time to recover from my cold. I never fight a cold; instead, I give myself rest and comfort. I relax and nurse myself for a day or two, and I avoid a long, lingering illness.

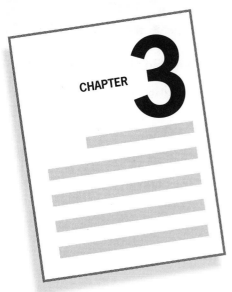

CHAPTER **3**

Avoiding Run-on Sentences and Comma Splices

RUN-ON SENTENCES

fused sentences - run on sentence.

If you run two independent clauses together without the necessary punctuation, you make an error called a **run-on sentence.** This error is also called a **fused sentence.**

run-on sentence error:

I worked hard in the class and I earned a good grade.

run-on sentence error corrected:

I worked hard in the class, and I earned a good grade. (To correct this error, you need a comma before the coordinating conjunction *and.*)

run-on sentence error:

I worked hard in the class I earned a good grade.

run-on sentence error corrected:

I worked hard in the class; I earned a good grade. (To correct this error, you need a semicolon between the two independent clauses.)

Steps for Correcting Run-on Sentences

When you edit your writing, you can correct run-on sentences by following these steps:

Step 1: Check for two independent clauses.

Step 2: Check that the clauses are separated by either a coordinating conjunction (*and, but, or, nor, for, yet, so*) and a comma or by a semicolon.

Follow the steps in checking this sentence:

Spaghetti is cheap so I buy it often.

Step 1: Check for two independent clauses. You can do this by checking for the subject-verb, subject-verb pattern that indicates two independent clauses:

S V   S V
Spaghetti is cheap so *I buy* it often.

The pattern indicates that you have two independent clauses.

> **Step 2:** Check that the clauses are separated by either a coordinating conjunction (*and, but, or, nor, for, yet, so*) and a comma, or by a semicolon.

There is no punctuation between the independent clauses, but there is a coordinating conjunction, *so*. Without the proper punctuation, the sentence is a run-on sentence. Correct it by adding a comma in front of the coordinating conjunction:

run-on sentence error corrected:

Spaghetti is cheap, so I buy it often.

Follow the steps once more, checking this sentence:

> I had a flat tire I couldn't get to school.

> **Step 1:** Check for two independent clauses. Do this by checking the subject-verb, subject-verb pattern:

S V   S V
I had a flat tire *I was* late for work.

> **Step 2:** Check that the clauses are separated by either a coordinating conjunction (*and, but, or, nor, for, yet, so*) and a comma, or by a semicolon.

There is no punctuation between the independent clauses. There is no coordinating conjunction, either. Without the proper punctuation, this is a run-on sentence. Correct it by putting a semicolon between the independent clauses:

run-on sentence error corrected:

I had a flat tire; I was late for work.

Using the steps to check for run-on sentences can also help you avoid unnecessary punctuation. Consider this sentence:

> Alan stuffed the papers into the trash and carried the trash bag to the curb.

> **Step 1:** Check for two independent clauses. Do this by checking the subject-verb, subject-verb pattern:

S V   V
Alan stuffed the papers into the trash and *carried* the trash bag to the curb.

The pattern is *SVV,* not *SV, SV.* You have one independent clause, not two. The sentence is not a run-on sentence.

Following the steps in correcting run-on sentences can help you avoid a major grammar error.

Exercise 1 **Correcting Run-on Sentences**

Practice

Some of the following sentences are correctly punctuated. Some are run-on sentences. If the sentence is correctly punctuated, write *OK* in the space provided. If it is a run-on sentence, put an *X* in the space provided and correct the sentence. To correct a sentence, you do not need to add any words; just add the necessary punctuation (a semicolon or a comma).

1. __X__ Abner took his sister to the mountains for her birthday, he wanted her to enjoy the fresh air.

2. __X__ We like that brand of applesauce, but we have decided to take a chance on a new brand.

3. __X__ Hidden inside the tissue paper was a lace shawl, it was a delicate shade of pink.

4. __OK__ Some of the most successful people in town give generously to the homeless shelter and volunteer at the food bank.

5. __X__ The movie was an enormous disappointment, it had no plot and far too much violence.

6. __OK__ Cars with their windows down and their stereos cranked up roam through my neighborhood every night and keep me awake.

7. __X__ Ron wanted to look stylish, for all his friends were dressed in the latest fashion.

8. __X__ Janet studied art throughout her high school years, yet she became an English major in college.

9. __OK__ I saved every penny from my summer salary, yet couldn't save enough for a new truck.

10. __OK__ My best friend looks snobbish, but is really shy and afraid of strangers.

Exercise 2 **More on Correcting Run-on Sentences**

Practice

Some of the following sentences are correctly punctuated. Some are run-on sentences. If the sentence is correctly punctuated, write *OK* in the space provided. If it is a run-on sentence, put an *X* in the space provided and correct the sentence. To correct a sentence, you do not need to add any words; just add the necessary punctuation (a semicolon or a comma).

1. __X__ I am outgoing and talkative on the outside, thus I appear calm and confident.

2. __X__ Your first impression of a person can be wrong, knowing a person takes time and effort.

3. __OK__ Pizza from the freezer section of the supermarket and pizza from a good Italian restaurant can't be compared.

4. __X__ The Super Bowl is my uncle's favorite sports event, he turns Super Bowl Sunday into a festival.

5. __X__ The summer storm arrived without a warning, then it hit with thunder and furious lightning.

6. __X__ Thunder rumbled in the sky, yet no rain fell in my neighborhood.

7. ___ Sam is grateful to Mrs. Singh for she gave him a good letter of recommendation.

8. ___ A highway patrol officer stopped Amy and asked for her license and registration.

9. ___ Ants covered the picnic table they were all over the sandwiches and cookies.

10. ___ Next week I can take a break from studying or I can get ahead in my math assignments.

COMMA SPLICES

A **comma splice** is an error that occurs when you punctuate with a comma but should use a semicolon instead. If you are joining two independent clauses without a coordinating conjunction, you *must use* a semicolon. A comma isn't enough.

comma splice error:

The rain fell steadily, the valley filled with water.

comma splice error corrected:

The rain fell steadily; the valley filled with water.

Note: If you had joined the independent clauses without any punctuation, you would have made an error called a *run-on sentence*.

Correcting Comma Splices

When you edit your writing, you can correct comma splices by following these steps:

Step 1: Check for two independent clauses.

Step 2: Check that the clauses are separated by a coordinating conjunction (*and, but, or, nor, for, yet, so*). If they are, then a comma in front of the coordinating conjunction is sufficient. If they are not separated by a coordinating conjunction, you have a comma splice. Correct it by changing the comma to a semicolon.

Follow the steps to check for a comma splice in this sentence:

The puppy jumped up, he licked my face.

Step 1: Check for two independent clauses. You can do this by checking for the subject-verb, subject-verb pattern that indicates two independent clauses.

       S   V   S   V
The *puppy jumped* up, *he licked* my face.

Step 2: Check that the clauses are separated by a coordinating conjunction.

There is no coordinating conjunction. To correct the comma splice error, you must use a semicolon instead of a comma:

comma splice error corrected:

The puppy jumped up; he licked my face.

Be careful not to mistake a short word like *then* or *thus* for a coordinating conjunction. Only the seven coordinating conjunctions (*and, but, or, nor, for, yet, so*), with a comma in front of them, can join independent clauses.

comma splice error:

Suzanne opened the letter, then she screamed with joy.

comma splice error corrected:

Suzanne opened the letter; then she screamed with joy.

Then is not a coordinating conjunction; it is a conjunctive adverb. When it joins two independent clauses, it needs a semicolon in front of it.

Also remember that conjunctive adverbs that are two or more syllables long (like *consequently, however, therefore*) need a comma after them *as well as* a semicolon in front of them when they join independent clauses:

Anthony passed the placement test; consequently, he can take Advanced Mathematics.

(For a list of some common conjunctive adverbs, see Chapter 2.)

Sometimes writers see commas before and after a conjunctive adverb and think the commas are sufficient. Check this sentence for a comma splice by following the steps:

The van held all my tools, however, it used too much gas.

Step 1: Check for two independent clauses by checking for the subject-verb, subject-verb pattern.

      S   V   S   V
The *van held* all my tools, however, *it used* too much gas.

Step 2: Check for a coordinating conjunction.

There is no coordinating conjunction. *However* is a conjunctive adverb, not a coordinating conjunction. Without a coordinating conjunction, a semicolon is needed between the two independent clauses.

comma splice error corrected:

The van held all my tools; however, it used too much gas.

Following the steps in correcting comma splices can help you avoid a major grammar error.

Exercise 3 Correcting Comma Splices

Practice
Some of the following sentences are correctly punctuated. Some contain comma splices. If the sentence is correctly punctuated, write *OK* in the space provided. If it contains a comma splice, put an *X* in the space provided and correct the sentence. To correct the sentence, you do not need to add words; just correct the punctuation.

1. ___X___ The marching band from Minneapolis was the best in the parade; the crowd loved the band's precision and style.

2. _____ Charlie gave me a lottery ticket, he said I needed some good luck.

3. ___X___ Some television shows start out funny; then they become stale and repetitive after a few weeks.

   4. __C__ The search team was combing the mountains for the lost boy, meanwhile, helicopters searched the valley.

   5. __C__ He worked full time at a hotel and attended college at night, thus he had no time for a social life.

   6. __C__ Leonard was eager to be my friend, but he had no social skills.

   7. __C__ I lost the address of the warehouse; nevertheless, I managed to find the place.

   8. __X__ Children need firm guidelines at home; otherwise, they feel lost and uncertain everywhere.

   9. __X__ A possible solution to your problem is to borrow the money from

   Dad; another solution is to go into partnership with me.

   10. __C__ You can't drink away your misery, nor can you drink your way to a better life.

Exercise 4 **More on Correcting Comma Splices**

Practice Some of the following sentences are correctly punctuated. Some contain comma splices. If the sentence is correctly punctuated, write *OK* in the space provided. If it contains a comma splice, put an *X* in the space provided and correct the sentence. To correct the sentence, you do not need to add words; just correct the punctuation.

   1. __OK__ I had never been to a ballet, yet I had always dreamed of seeing one.

   2. __OK__ Gina lied to get out of an embarrassing situation, then she got stuck in a tangle of lies.

   3. __OK__ My parents loved my brother, however, they wouldn't clean up his messes anymore.

   4. __X__ A truck jackknifed on the interstate highway; as a result, traffic was backed up for hours.

   5. __X__ Barnacle Ben's has great shrimp; I eat there every weekend.

   6. __OK__ I had to work on Friday night, so I missed a good party at my brother's house.

   7. __X__ Job interviews make me nervous; moreover, they do not show me at my best.

   8. __X__ My grandfather took a computer course; he is learning about e-mail and the Internet.

   9. __X__ Dr. Kosinski is a wonderful pediatrician; children love him.

   10. __X__ Our neighbors were robbed; now the whole neighborhood is frightened.

Exercise 5 Collaborate   **Completing Sentences**

With a partner or a group, write the first part of each of the following incomplete sentences. Make your addition an independent clause. Be sure to punctuate your completed sentences correctly. The first one is done for you.

1. <u>My candle suddenly blew out;</u>   then I saw the ghost.

2. <u>It was a great game,</u> however, the team lost the game.

3. <u>I waited all day,</u>   but no one called.

4. <u>We waited two hours and</u> finally, the concert began.

5. _____ now Christian wants a raise.

6. <u>I didn't have enough money for the car,</u> therefore, I bought a bicycle.

7. <u>Your account has to be balanced</u> or you will lose your deposit.

8. <u>We watched movies;</u>   meanwhile, the children cried.

9. <u>I turned on the lights, but</u> nothing worked.

10. <u>The car stopped in the middle of the road;</u> something was wrong with the car.

Exercise 6 Connect   **Editing a Paragraph for Run-on Sentences and Comma Splices**

Edit the following paragraph for run-on sentences and comma splices. There are six errors.

Looking at a photograph of myself can be a startling experience. I usually look at pictures with dread for I expect to see a terrible shot of myself. My typical reaction is horror; I always look fat and bloated in photos. Even worse is looking at old pictures of myself. I always forget about the old fashions of years ago; as a result, I am appalled at my outfits in old pictures. In some I look like a fool in huge, ugly shoes in others I look like a member of a very bad rock and roll group. Worst of all are the photos of ten years ago. In them I look so young consequently, I feel so old today. I have decided never to get in front of the camera again instead, I will get behind one. I will take the pictures and be spared those embarrassing photographs of myself.

CHAPTER **4**

Beyond the Simple Sentence: Subordination

MORE ON COMBINING SIMPLE SENTENCES

You may remember these principles of grammar:

- A clause has a subject and a verb.
- An independent clause is a simple sentence; it is a group of words, with a subject and a verb, that makes sense by itself.

Chapter 2 described three options for combining simple sentences (independent clauses). There is another kind of clause called a **dependent clause.** It has a subject and a verb, but it does not make sense by itself. It cannot stand alone because it is not complete by itself. That is, it *depends* on the rest of the sentence to give it meaning. You can use a dependent clause as another option in combining simple sentences.

OPTION 4: USING A DEPENDENT CLAUSE TO BEGIN A SENTENCE

Often, you can combine simple sentences by changing an independent clause into a dependent clause and placing it at the beginning of the new sentence:

two simple sentences:

If come at the beginning of sentence, it needs a comma

 S   V   S   V
I missed my bus. *I slept* through my alarm.

changing one simple sentence into a beginning dependent clause:

subordination

             S   V   S   V
Because *I slept* through my alarm, *I missed* my bus.

OPTION 5: USING A DEPENDENT CLAUSE TO END A SENTENCE

You can also combine simple sentences by changing an independent clause into a dependent clause and placing it at the end of the new sentence:

 S   V   S   V
I missed my bus because *I slept* through my alarm.

Notice how one simple sentence can be changed into a dependent clause in two ways:

two simple sentences:

S   V   S   V

Nicholas played his guitar. *Jared sang* an old song.

changing one simple sentence into a dependent clause:

S   V   S   V

Nicholas played his guitar while *Jared sang* an old song.

or

S   V   S   V

While *Jared sang* an old song, *Nicholas played* his guitar.

Using Subordinating Words: Subordinating Conjunctions and Relative Pronouns

Changing an independent clause to a dependent one is called **subordinating.** How do you do it? You add a subordinating word, called a **subordinating conjunction** or a **relative pronoun,** to an independent clause, which makes it dependent—less "important"—or subordinate, in the new sentence.

Keep in mind that the subordinate clause is still a clause; it has a subject and a verb, but it does not make sense by itself. For example, here is an independent clause:

S   V

David cooks.

Somebody (David) does something (cooks). The statement makes sense by itself. But if you add a subordinating word to the independent clause, the clause becomes dependent—incomplete, unfinished—like this:

When David cooks (When he cooks, what happens?)
Unless David cooks (Unless he cooks, what will happen?)
If David cooks (If he cooks, what will happen?)

Now, each dependent clause needs an independent clause to finish the idea:

dependent clause   **independent clause**
When David cooks, he makes wonderful meals.

dependent clause   **independent clause**
Unless David cooks, you will not get a decent dinner.

dependent clause   **independent clause**
If David cooks, dinner will be delicious.

There are many subordinating words. When you put any of these words in front of an independent clause, you make that clause dependent. Here is a list of some subordinating conjunctions and relative pronouns that are common subordinating words.

Infobox

Subordinating Words:
Subordinating Conjunctions and Relative Pronouns

after	how	until	whether
although	if	what	*which
as	in order that	whatever	whichever
because	since	when	while
before	*that	whenever	*who
even if	though	where	whoever
even though	unless	whereas	*whose

---

* The starred words are relative pronouns.

If you pick the right subordinating word, you can effectively combine simple sentences (independent clauses) into a more sophisticated sentence pattern. Such combining helps you add sentence variety to your writing and helps to explain relationships between ideas.

simple sentences:

  S V   V   S V
Emily had never *studied* art. *She was* a gifted painter.

new combination:

     dependent clause   independent clause
Although Emily had never studied art, she was a gifted painter.

simple sentences:

 S V   S   V
I bought a new leash last night. My *puppy chewed* up his old one.

new combination:

   independent clause   dependent clause
I bought a new leash last night because my puppy chewed up his old one.

Punctuating Complex Sentences

A sentence that has one independent clause and one or more dependent clauses is called a **complex sentence.** Complex sentences are very easy to punctuate. See if you can figure out the rule for punctuating by yourself. Look at the following examples. All are punctuated correctly.

   dependent clause   independent clause
Whenever I visit my mother, I bring flowers.

 independent clause   dependent clause
I bring flowers whenever I visit my mother.

   dependent clause   independent clause
While he was talking, I was daydreaming.

  independent clause   dependent clause
I was daydreaming while he was talking.

In the examples above, look at the sentences that have a comma. Now look at the ones that don't have a comma. Both kinds of sentences are punctuated correctly. Do you see the rule?

When a dependent clause comes at the beginning of the sentence, the clause is followed by a comma. When a dependent clause comes at the end of a sentence, the clause does not need a comma.

Here are some correctly punctuated complex sentences:

Although he studied hard, he failed the test.
He failed the test although he studied hard.

Until I started running, I was out of shape.
I was out of shape until I started running.

Exercise 1 **Punctuating Complex Sentences**

Practice

All of the following sentences are complex sentences—they have one independent clause and one or more dependent clauses. Add a comma to each sentence that needs one.

1. Unless you buy your tickets today, you won't be able to see that show.

2. Be sure to bring me a bagel with cream cheese when you go to the deli.

3. After Neil met Karen at work, he began coming to the office early every day.

4. When it starts to get dark early, I miss Daylight Saving Time.

5. My dog feels sleek and shiny after I brush her long red coat.

6. Whenever I see a frog in my yard, I remember Kermit the Frog on television.

7. Before the game started, the coach had an uneasy feeling about his star player.

8. The children sang a song about friendship as their teacher played a tinkly old piano.

9. As I have told you many times, I will not accept late papers.

10. The neighborhood looks cleaner since the old tavern was torn down.

Exercise 2 **More on Punctuating Complex Sentences**

Practice All of the following sentences are complex sentences—they have one independent clause and one or more dependent clauses. Add a comma to each sentence that needs one.

if comes at the end don't need comma

1. I stashed the birthday presents under my bed before my son came home from school.

2. Because my mother can't drive at night, I have to take her to her adult education class.

3. My girlfriend worries unless I call her every day.

4. Trinette broke up with Robert because she wanted more freedom.

5. Even if she apologizes to her brother, he will carry a grudge for a long time.

6. Since the weather is warm, we will eat outdoors.

7. My daughter was born after I was promoted at the training center.

8. Jack's parents had no idea where he had left his glasses.

9. Adrian can sleep while you drive the van.

10. Although Anatomy and Physiology is a difficult course, it is preparing me for nursing school.

Exercise 3 **Combining Sentences**

Practice

Combine each pair of sentences below into one smooth, clear sentence. The new combination should include one independent and one dependent clause and an appropriate subordinating word.

1. The turkey was dry. Mark had overcooked it.

combined: The turkey was dry because Mark had overcooked it.

2. Postcards make a good souvenir. They are no substitute for the genuine experience of traveling.

combined: Postcards make a good souvenir eventhough They are no substitute for the genuine experience of traveling.

3. Catherine watched a movie on television. Joanna washed the car.

combined: Catherine watched a movie on television whereas Joanna washed the car.

4. The mail carrier brings mail to my house. The dogs go wild.

combined: The mail carrier brings mail to my house before the dog go wild.

5. David prepares an impressive résumé. He will have a better chance of getting a job interview.

combined: Because David prepares an impressive resumé, he will have a better chance of get a job interview.

6. Denise apologizes to her sister. The two will never rebuild their relationship.

combined: Denise apologizes to her sister although the two will never rebuild their relationship.

7. Stephen spent fifty dollars on his haircut. It didn't look attractive.

combined: Stephen spent fifty dollars on his hair cut although it didn't look attractive.

8. The computer will not appeal to teens. It isn't fast enough.

combined: <u>the computer will not appeal to teens</u>
<u>because it isn't fast enough.</u>

9. Our team schedules a softball game. The weather turns nasty.

combined: <u>Our team schedules a softball game,</u>
<u>while the weather turns nasty.</u>

10. The first snow falls. We put an extra blanket on our beds.

combined: <u>Because of the first snow fall, we put an</u>
<u>extra blanket on our beds.</u>

Exercise 4 **Creating Complex Sentences**

👥 Collaborate

Do this exercise with a partner or a group. Each item below lists a dependent clause. Write two different sentences that include the dependent clause. One sentence should begin with the dependent clause; the other sentence should end with the dependent clause. The first one is done for you.

1. dependent clause: whenever I visit my grandmother

sentence 1: <u>Whenever I visit my grandmother, she tells me stories about</u>
<u>life in Havana.</u>

sentence 2: <u>I bring a box of chocolates whenever I visit my grandmother.</u>

2. dependent clause: although Maureen is an excellent swimmer

sentence 1: <u>Although Maureen is an excellent swimmer, she</u>
<u>doesn't like going to the beach.</u>

sentence 2: <u>Going to the beach is not fun, although Maureen</u>
<u>is an excellent swimmer.</u>

3. dependent clause: unless a dozen extra people show up for the party

sentence 1: <u>Unless a dozen extra people show up for the</u>
<u>party, we will not start.</u>

sentence 2: <u>We will not begin unless a dozen extra</u>
<u>people show up for the party.</u>

4. dependent clause: because you didn't follow the directions

sentence 1: You missed the question because you didn't follow the directions.

sentence 2: Because you didn't follow the directions, you don't know where to start.

5. dependent clause: while the car alarm was shrieking

sentence 1: While the car alarm was shrieking, I was inside the house.

sentence 2: I was away, while the car alarm was shrieking.

6. dependent clause: after he smashed the window

sentence 1: After he smashed the window, she had to clean it up.

sentence 2: His hand started bleeding after he smashed the window.

7. dependent clause: since he hates violent movies

sentence 1: Since he hates violent movies, he never buys them.

sentence 2: He doesn't have to come along with us since he hates violent movies.

8. dependent clause: before you lose your temper

sentence 1: Before you lose your temper, you should calm down.

sentence 2: You should stop shouting before you lose your temper.

9. dependent clause: as the German shepherd lunged for the fleeing robber

sentence 1: As the German shepherd lunged for the fleeing robber, the cops got them.

sentence 2: _the robbers tried to shoot, as the_
german shephard lunged for the fleeing
robber.

10. dependent clause: even if he apologizes

sentence 1: _I wont accept his apologease even_
if he apologizes

sentence 2: _Even if he apologizes, I wont_
accept it.

CHAPTER **5**

Combining Sentences: A Review of Your Options

Combining sentences helps you to avoid a choppy writing style in which all your sentences are short. The pattern of one short sentence after another makes writing repetitive and boring. When you mix the length of sentences, using some long ones and some short ones, you use a strategy called **sentence variety.**

You can develop a style that includes sentence variety by combining short, related sentences clearly and smoothly. There are several ways to combine sentences. The following chart helps you to see them all, at a glance. It also includes the punctuation necessary for each combination.

Infobox

Options for Combining Sentences

Coordination

Option 1
Independent clause
$\left\{\begin{array}{l}, \text{and} \\ , \text{but} \\ , \text{or} \\ , \text{nor} \\ , \text{for} \\ , \text{yet} \\ , \text{so}\end{array}\right\}$
independent clause.

Option 2
Independent clause
;
independent clause.

$\left\{\begin{array}{l}; \text{also,} \\ ; \text{anyway,} \\ ; \text{as a result,} \\ ; \text{besides,} \\ ; \text{certainly,} \\ ; \text{consequently,} \\ ; \text{finally,} \\ ; \text{furthermore,} \\ ; \text{however,} \\ ; \text{in addition,} \\ ; \text{incidentally,}\end{array}\right.$

A Review of Your Options

Option 3 Independent clause	; indeed, ; in fact, ; instead, ; likewise ; meanwhile, ; moreover, ; nevertheless, ; next ; now ; on the other hand, ; otherwise, ; similarly, ; still ; then ; therefore, ; thus ; undoubtedly,	independent clause.

Subordination

Option 4 Independent clause	after although as because before even if even though how if in order that since that though unless until what whatever when whenever where whereas whether which whichever while who whoever whose	dependent clause.
Option 5	After Although As Because Before Even if Even though	Dependent clause, independent clause. (When you begin with a dependent clause, put a comma at the end of the dependent clause.)

(continued)

	How		
Option 5 (continued)	If In order that Since That Though Unless Until What Whatever When Whenever Where Whereas Whether Which Whichever While Who Whoever Whose		Dependent clause, independent clause. (When you begin with a dependent clause, put a comma at the end of the dependent clause.)

Exercise 1 Combining Simple Sentences

Practice

Following are pairs of simple sentences. Combine each pair of sentences into one clear, smooth sentence. Create two new combinations for each pairing. The first one is done for you.

1. My car wouldn't start yesterday.
The car battery was dead.

combination 1: My car wouldn't start yesterday because the battery was dead.

combination 2: The car battery was dead; as a result, my car wouldn't start yesterday.

2. Stephen had a hard time with calculus.
Stephen managed to earn a C in the class.

combination 1: Stephen had a hard time with calculus but he managed to earn a c in the class.

combination 2: Even though Stephen had a hard time with calculus, he managed to earn a C in the class.

3. I balanced myself on the very top of the ladder.
I lost my footing and fell.

combination 1: _I balance myself on the very top of the ladder; however, I lost my footing and fell._

combination 2: _____

_____

4. Lenny never invited me to his house.
   I am not inviting Lenny to my party.

combination 1: _Since Lenny never invited me to his house, I am not inviting Lenny to my party._

combination 2: _____

_____

5. My little sister adores Uncle Frank.
   Uncle Frank lets her play with his electric train collection.

combination 1: _Because my little sister adores Uncle Frank, he lets her play his electric train collection_

combination 2: _____

_____

6. Every autumn I see lovely brown ducks on the lake.
   The ducks stop at the lake on their way south.

combination 1: _Every autumn I see lovely brown ducks on the lake because the ducks stop at the lake on their way south._

combination 2: _____

_____

7. The cousins get together for Thanksgiving.
   The cousins always talk about old times on the farm.

combination 1: _Whenever the cousins get together for Thanksgiving the cousins always talk about old times on the farm._

combination 2: _____

_____

8. I love almost anything chocolate.
   I am not fond of chocolate doughnuts.

combination 1: _____

_____

combination 2: _____

_____

9. Emily wears stylish clothes.
The clothes don't always look good on her.

combination 1: _Emily wears stylish clothes, but_
the clothes don't always look good on here.

combination 2: _____

_____

10. We couldn't get a baby sitter.
We couldn't go to the movies.

combination 1: _Since we couldn't get a baby sitter,_
we couldn't go to the movies.

combination 2: _____

_____

Exercise 2 **Creating Your Own Text**

Collaborate

Following is a list of rules for sentence combining through coordinating and subordinating. Working with a group, create two examples of each rule and write those sentences on the lines provided. After your group has completed this exercise, share your examples with another group.

Option 1: You can join two simple sentences (two independent clauses) into a compound sentence with a coordinating conjunction and a comma in front of it. (The coordinating conjunctions are *and, but, or, nor, for, yet, so.*)

example 1: _I'm going to the grocery store and_
I'll stop by McDonald to get something to eat.

example 2: _____

_____

Option 2: You can combine two simple sentences (two independent clauses) into a compound sentence with a semicolon between independent clauses.

example 1: _We were_ _____

_____

example 2: _____

_____

Option 3: You can combine two simple sentences (two independent clauses) into a compound sentence with a semicolon and a conjunctive adverb between independent clauses. (Some common conjunctive adverbs are *also, anyway, as a result, besides, certainly, consequently, finally, furthermore, however, in addition, incidentally, indeed, in fact, instead, likewise, meanwhile, moreover, nevertheless, next, now, on the other hand, otherwise, similarly, still, then, therefore, thus,* and *undoubtedly.*)

example 1: _We went to the store, moreover we had a picnic at the park_

example 2: _____

_____

Option 4: You can combine two simple sentences (two independent clauses) into a complex sentence by making one clause dependent. The dependent clause starts with a subordinating conjunction or relative pronoun. If the dependent clause begins the sentence, the clause ends with a comma. (Some common subordinating conjunctions and relative pronouns are *after, although, as, because, before, even if, even though, how, if, in order that, since, that, though, unless, until, what, whatever, when, whenever, where, whereas, whether, which, whichever, while, who, whoever,* and *whose.*)

example 1: _Kate attended the birthday party even though she wasn't invited._

example 2: _____

_____

Option 5: You can combine two simple sentences (two independent clauses) into a complex sentence by making one clause dependent. If the dependent clause comes after the independent clause, no comma is needed.

example 1: _I had to go to the store because I needed some papers._

example 2: _____

_____

Exercise 3 **Editing a Paragraph with Compound and Complex Sentences**

Connect

Edit the following paragraph, adding commas and semicolons where they are necessary and taking out unnecessary commas. There are twelve errors.

When I was a high school junior, I had to follow several family rules. My parents were strict with me; on the other hand they were fair. On school nights there were three rules. I was expected to call home, whenever I was going to be home later than dinner time. I had to be home by eleven; there were no exceptions to this curfew. And I could not have friends in the house after eleven. Weekend rules were less strict but still tough to follow. My curfew was midnight, and the only exceptions were for big events like prom night or a homecoming dance. Whenever I went out, my father or mother had to meet my companions. They were always very friendly to my buddies; nevertheless, they were keeping an eye on my friends. My parents were fair to me because I had very clear rules to follow. Although these rules made me furious at the time, today I understand them. Now, I am the parent of a teen myself; consequently, my views have changed. I want to know where my son is and I want to know his friends. I have become just like my parents, so I can now see their point of view.

Exercise 4 **Combining Sentences in a Paragraph**

Connect

In the following paragraph, combine each pair of underlined sentences into one clear, smooth sentence. Write your combination in the space above the old sentences.

One of the most important job skills is the ability to relate well to others. <u>Almost every employee has to deal with a manager and co-workers. Many workers have to deal with customers.</u> Learning how to behave around a boss, a peer, or customers can be a difficult process. <u>A worker is rude or sarcastic around a supervisor. The worker may be fired.</u> The employee does not want to learn this lesson the hard way. <u>A worker gossips about co-workers. Co-workers no longer trust the worker.</u> The talkative worker has lost valuable friends in the workplace. <u>A demanding or agitated</u>

customer can provoke a worker to anger. The same customer can complain to the worker's boss. Therefore, the skilled worker is patient, especially with customers. This worker wants to tell tales about another employee. He or she thinks twice and remains silent. This worker knows that gossip in the workplace can be deadly. Disrespect can also be dangerous. Good people skills include respect for those in charge. In fact, people skills are based on three kinds of respect: respect for managers' authority, for co-workers' privacy, and for customers' concerns.

CHAPTER 6

Avoiding Sentence Fragments

A **sentence fragment** is a group of words that looks like a sentence, is punctuated like a sentence, but is not a sentence. Writing a sentence fragment is a major error in grammar because it reveals that the writer is not sure what a sentence is. The following groups of words are all fragments:

fragments:

Because parents with small children want a car with room for car seats, stroller, diaper bags, and toys.
Her father being an open-minded individual.
For example, the controversy over the safety of air bags.

There are two simple steps that can help you check your writing for sentence fragments:

Infobox

Two Steps in Recognizing Sentence Fragments

Step 1: Check each group of words punctuated like a sentence; look for a subject and a verb.

Step 2: If you find a subject and a verb, check that the group of words makes a complete statement.

RECOGNIZING FRAGMENTS: STEP 1

Check for a subject and a verb. Some groups of words that look like sentences may have a subject but no verb, or they may have a verb but no subject, or they may have no subject *or* verb.

fragments:

The bowl with the bright gold rim. (*Bowl* could be the subject of the sentence, but there is no verb.)
Can't be a friend of mine from college. (There is a verb, *Can be,* but there is no subject.)

On the tip of my tongue. (There are two prepositional phrases, *On the tip* and *of my tongue*, but there is no subject or verb.)

Remember that an *-ing* verb by itself cannot be the main verb in a sentence. Therefore, groups of words like the following may look like sentences but are missing verbs and are really fragments.

fragments:

The man cooking the Texas chili for the barbecue contest.
A few brave souls taking the plunge into the icy lake in mid-March.
My friend Cynthia being loyal to her selfish and manipulative sister.

An infinitive (*to* plus a verb) cannot be a main verb in a sentence, either. The following groups of words, which contain infinitives, are also fragments.

fragments:

Next week a representative of the airlines to meet with travel agents from across the country.
My hope to help the children of the war-torn nation.
Something nutritious to eat for supper.

Groups of words beginning with words like *also, especially, except, for example, for instance, in addition,* and *such as* need subjects and verbs. Without subjects and verbs, these groups can be fragments, like the ones below:

fragments:

Also a dangerous neighborhood in the late hours of the evening.
Especially a house with a large basement.
For example, a box of high-priced chocolates.

Checking for subjects and verbs is the first step in recognizing the major sentence errors called fragments.

Exercise 1 **Checking Groups of Words for Subjects and Verbs**

Practice   Some of the following groups of words have subjects and verbs; these are sentences. Some groups are missing subjects, verbs, or both; these are fragments. Put an *S* next to each sentence; put an *F* next to each fragment.

1. ___F___ Definitely can't be the person at the movies with Wilson last night.

2. ___S___ For example, you can paint a room in white or yellow to brighten it up.

3. ___F___ For instance, a second helping of turkey and cranberry sauce.

4. ___F___ A crazed shopper racing through the store, frantically searching the sales racks for the biggest bargain in raincoats.

5. ___F___ Except for one driver obeying the speed limit.

6. ___S___ My purpose is to explain the steps for changing the oil in your car.

7. ___F___ At the end of the line with a dollar bill in his hand.

8. ___F___ Donald's intention being to clarify the issues before tomorrow's vote.

9. _S_ In addition, the view from the hotel room was spectacular.

10. _F_ Bob having absolutely no sense of responsibility for his errors.

Exercise 2 **More on Checking Groups of Words for Subjects and Verbs**

Practice Some of the following groups of words have subjects and verbs; these are sentences. Some groups are missing subjects, verbs, or both; these are fragments. Put an *S* next to each sentence; put an *F* next to each fragment.

1. _F_ An old friend from Honduras to visit me over the summer vacation.

2. _S_ Two of the Siamese kittens were chewing on the old, smelly sock.

3. _F_ A supervisor with a real understanding of his staff and their needs.

4. _F_ Should have called the house before coming over on a Saturday night.

5. _S_ Luke has to give half of the money to his brother.

6. _F_ Especially a student running out of money at the end of the semester.

7. _F_ The reason being a driver with a suspended license.

8. _F_ Has neglected to water the plants or mow the lawn.

9. _F_ Came from the center of the dark, dense woods.

10. _S_ Checking the battery is a good idea.

RECOGNIZING FRAGMENTS: STEP 2

If you are checking a group of words to see if it is a sentence, the first step is to look for a subject and verb. If you find a subject and a verb, step 2 is to check that the group of words makes a complete statement. Many groups of words have both a subject and a verb but don't make sense by themselves. They are **dependent clauses.**

How can you tell if a clause is dependent? After you've checked each group of words for a subject and verb, check to see whether it begins with one of the subordinating words, the subordinating conjunctions or relative pronouns that start dependent clauses.

Infobox			
Subordinating Words:			
Common Subordinating Conjunctions and Relative Pronouns			
after	how	until	whether
although	if	what	*which
as	in order that	whatever	whichever
because	since	when	while
before	*that	whenever	*who
even if	though	where	whoever
even though	unless	whereas	*whose

*The starred words are relative pronouns.

A clause that begins with a subordinating word is a dependent clause. When you punctuate a dependent clause as if it were a sentence, you have a kind of fragment called a **dependent-clause fragment.** These fragments do not make a complete statement.

dependent-clause fragments:

After she gave him a kiss. (What happened after she gave him a kiss?)

Because lemonade tastes better than limeade. (What will happen because lemonade tastes better than limeade?)

Unless you leave for the movie right now. (What will happen unless you leave for the movie right now?)

It is important to remember both steps in checking for fragments:

Step 1: Check for a subject and a verb.

Step 2: If you find a subject and verb, check that the group of words makes a complete statement.

Exercise 3 **Checking for Dependent-Clause Fragments**

Practice Some of the following groups of words are sentences. Some are dependent clauses punctuated like sentences; these are sentence fragments. Put an *S* next to each sentence and an *F* next to each fragment.

1. _F_ Whenever my girlfriend forgets my birthday or ignores our anniversary.

2. _F_ As the detectives investigated the crime scene for fingerprints and other evidence.

3. _S_ In the top drawer of my desk is a letter from Catherine.

4. _F_ Even though the holidays are supposed to be a time for celebration and cheerfulness.

5. _S_ At the end of the day my father is worn out.

6. _F_ If the shoes pinch or cut across the top of the foot and cause pain.

7. _S_ Hidden resentment can destroy any friendship.

8. _F_ Before I had even met our noisy neighbors.

9. _F_ Although saving money isn't easy in these times of unemployment and layoffs.

10. _F_ Because Rebecca and Ramon know exactly how to get to the stadium.

Exercise 4 **More on Checking for Dependent-Clause Fragments**

Practice Some of the following groups of words are sentences. Some are dependent clauses punctuated like sentences; these are sentence fragments. Put an *S* next to each sentence and an *F* next to each fragment.

1. _S_ Within seconds, the plumber had stopped the leak in the sink.

2. _F_ When the weather is warmer and more suitable for a picnic.

3. _F_ After the conference ended and most of the speakers had left for the night.

4. _F_ Since Dad gave me that lecture yesterday afternoon.

5. _S_ With him was his sister-in-law.

6. _F_ How the detective solved the mystery and found the famous jewel thief.

7. _F_ Even if the promotion at work pays more money.

8. _S_ From his father James inherited beautiful dark eyes.

9. _F_ Since the movie is too frightening for children to see.

10. _S_ Aggressive driving puts many lives at risk.

Exercise 5 **Using Two Steps to Recognize Sentence Fragments**

Practice Some of the following are complete sentences; some are sentence fragments. To recognize the fragments, check each group of words by using the two-step process:

Step 1: Check for a subject and a verb.

Step 2: If you find a subject and a verb, check that the group of words makes a complete statement.

Then put an *S* next to each sentence and an *F* next to each fragment.

1. _S_ _F_ Sylvia's biggest problem with her father being his refusal to accept her as an adult.

2. _S_ The teacup with the gold rim was smashed beyond repair.

3. _F_ When Bertrand had done his best to finish the assignment on time.

4. _S_ From the hallway to the dining room, gold ribbons decorated every available surface.

5. _F_ Without a trace of anger in her voice or sarcasm in her choice of words.

6. _S_ A central warehouse supplying the three supermarkets in our city.

7. _F_ For instance, a quick dive into icy cold water.

8. _F_ As if he had done this routine at least a hundred times.

9. _S_ _F_ An inspirational speech to be given at the graduation ceremonies tomorrow.

10. _S_ One of the kindergartners was being silly about washing his hands before lunch.

Exercise 6 **More on Using Two Steps to Recognize Sentence Fragments**

Practice Some of the following are complete sentences; some are sentence fragments. To recognize the fragments, check each group of words by using the two-step process:

Step 1: Check for a subject and a verb.

Step 2: If you find a subject and a verb, check that the group of words makes a complete statement.

Then put an *S* next to each sentence and an *F* next to each fragment.

1. _F_ Which gave me no choice about visiting my sister in Mexico City.

2. _F_ Has never been a real fan of that group's music.

3. _F_ Because he pretends to be your friend and flatters you with phony compliments.

4. _S_ In the middle of the lawn was a plastic flamingo.

5. _F_ When the days start to get shorter and the weather cooler.

6. _S_ Suddenly, a burst of loud and obnoxious music filled the arena.

7. _S_ Calling for help is the wisest move.

8. _F_ The real reason being Jamal's fear of looking like a fool in front of his friends.

9. _F_ To him fashionable clothes appearing to be the ticket to acceptance and respect.

10. _S_ Around the corner came a spotted, grinning dog.

CORRECTING FRAGMENTS

You can correct fragments easily if you follow the two steps for identifying them.

Step 1: Check for a subject and a verb. If a group of words is a fragment because it lacks a subject or a verb, or both, *add what is missing.*

fragment: Jonette giving ten percent of her salary. (This fragment lacks a main verb.)

corrected: Jonette gave ten percent of her salary. (The verb *gave* replaces *giving,* which is not a main verb.)

fragment: Can't study with the television on. (This fragment lacks a subject.)

corrected: Salvatore can't study with the television on. (A subject, *Salvatore,* is added.)

fragment: Especially at the end of the day. (This fragment has neither a subject nor a verb.)

corrected: I often feel stressed, especially at the end of the day. (A subject, *I,* and a verb, *feel,* are added.)

Step 2: If you find a subject and a verb, check that the group of words makes a complete statement. To correct the fragment, you can turn a dependent clause into an independent one by removing the subordinating conjunction, *or* you can add an independent clause to the dependent one, to create something that makes sense by itself.

fragment: When Mrs. Diaz offered him a job. (This statement does not make sense by itself. The subordinating conjunction *when* leads the reader to ask, "What happened when Mrs. Diaz offered him a job?" The subordinating conjunction makes this a dependent clause, not a sentence.)

corrected: Mrs. Diaz offered him a job. (Removing the subordinating conjunction makes this an independent clause—a sentence.)

corrected: When Mrs. Diaz offered him a job, he was very happy. (Adding an independent clause to the end of the sentence turns this into something that makes sense by itself.)

corrected: He was very happy when Mrs. Diaz offered him a job. (Adding an independent clause to the beginning of the sentence turns this into something that makes sense by itself.)

Note: Sometimes you can correct a fragment by adding it to the sentence before or after it.

fragment (in italics): *Even if he lowers the price.* I can't afford that car.
corrected: Even if he lowers the price, I can't afford that car.

fragment (in italics): Yvonne hates large parties. *Like the one at Matthew's house.*
corrected: Yvonne hates large parties like the one at Matthew's house.

You have several choices for correcting fragments: you can add words, phrases, or clauses; you can take words out or combine independent and dependent clauses. You can change fragments into simple sentences or create compound or complex sentences. If you create compound or complex sentences, be sure to use correct punctuation.

Exercise 7	**Correcting Fragments**

Practice   Correct each sentence fragment below in the most appropriate way.

1. Every winter he buys me a warm piece of clothing. Such as gloves or mittens.

corrected: _____

_____

2. If you do the laundry today. You'll have time to go shopping tomorrow.

corrected: _____

_____

3. Watching the last exciting moments of the game. We forgot about the turkey roasting in the oven.

corrected: _____

_____

4. After dinner, drowsiness fell on all of us. Especially Tom.

corrected: _____

_____

5. Because the movie was sold out. We had to see a less popular film.

corrected: _____

_____

6. Whoever ate the last piece of carrot cake.

corrected: _____

_____

7. The swimmer barely making it to shore before the storm hit.

corrected: _____

_____

8. Tiffany was anxious to see the new apartment. To plan how to place her furniture and to check the size of the closets.

corrected: _____

_____

9. Mark and Jared were still arguing about money. As I decided to get out of the house.

corrected: _____

_____

10. Most of his friends thinking Alan had nowhere to go for Thanksgiving dinner.

corrected: _____

_____

Exercise 8 **Correcting Fragments Two Ways**

👥 Collaborate

The following groups of words all contain fragments. Working with a partner or a group, construct two ways to eliminate the fragment. You can add words, phrases, or clauses, take out words, combine independent and dependent clauses, or attach a fragment to the sentence before or after it. When you have completed the exercise, be ready to share your answers with another group or with the class. The first one is done for you.

1. When she calls me and starts complaining.

corrected: <u>When she calls me and starts complaining, I try to be sympa-</u>

<u>thetic.</u>

corrected: <u>She calls me and starts complaining.</u>

_____

2. Even though Philip spent a fortune on the leather jacket.

corrected: _____

_____

corrected: _____

_____

3. As the band began to play a slow dance. The couple left the dance floor.

corrected: _____

_____

corrected: _____

_____

4. If the baby cries in the middle of the night again.

corrected: _____

_____

corrected: _____

_____

5. My sister having no interest in fashion and hating to waste time at the mall.

corrected: _____

_____

corrected: _____

_____

6. Whenever that song comes on the radio. I change the station immediately.

corrected: _____

_____

corrected: _____

_____

7. The thief stole the diamond ring. While his accomplice distracted the salesperson.

corrected: _____

_____

corrected: _____

_____

8. At the drive-through window, where she worked.

corrected: _____

_____

corrected: _____

_____

9. I can't go to Disney World this weekend. Unless I can get somebody to cover for me at work.

corrected: _____

_____

corrected: _____

_____

10. Who loves her husband and children very much and makes them the center of her life.

corrected: _____

_____

corrected: _____

_____

Editing Paragraphs for Fragments

Connect

Both of the paragraphs below contain sentence fragments. Edit the paragraphs, correcting the fragments by writing in the space above each fragment. There are two fragments in the first paragraph and six fragments in the second.

1.   Fridays are my hardest days at work because they are my busiest days. I work behind the counter at a dry cleaner's, and it seems like everybody comes to my store on Fridays. Maybe all the businessmen suddenly remember to drop off their dirty shirts at the end of the week. Or suddenly remember to pick up their clean shirts. In addition, many people who need sweaters, coats, or even draperies cleaned show up on Friday. Maybe they think they can get this errand done before the weekend and have more free time on Saturday or Sunday. Whatever the reasons, I am swamped with customers at the end of the week. Sometimes they are lined up ten deep. With their cleaning ticket or soiled clothing in their hand. They are crabby and tired, and so am I. After all, it's Friday, and we all want to take life easy until Saturday arrives. Unfortunately for me, there's nothing easy about my busy Fridays.

2.   David and I got into an argument last night. When he got lost on the turnpike. Before we left, I told David he should call our friend Nathan for directions to the restaurant where we were meeting. David didn't want to call and rushed me out the door and into the car. The reason for the hurry being that we were already late for dinner. David figured we'd waste time calling when we could be halfway to the restaurant instead. Well, of course we got lost and missed the exit for the restaurant. We spent the next half hour turning around, retracing our steps. After thirty minutes, I made a suggestion. All I suggested was that David do something sensible. Something like ask for directions at a gas station. David lost his temper, pulled the car over to the side of the road, and stopped. He told me to go ahead and drive. If I thought I could do a better job of finding the restaurant. David's temper tantrum showed me. How immature he is.

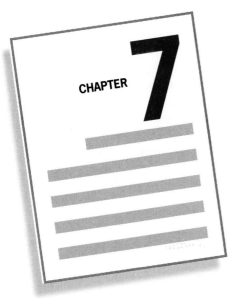

Using Parallelism in Sentences

Parallelism means balance in sentences. To create sentences with parallelism, remember this rule:

Similar points should get similar structures.

Often, you will include two or more points—related ideas, examples, or details—in one sentence. If you express these ideas in a parallel structure, they will be clearer, smoother, and more convincing.

Here are some pairs of sentences with and without parallelism:

not parallel: Of all the household chores, the ones I hate the most are cooking, to iron, and dusting.

parallel: Of all the household chores, the ones I hate the most are *cooking*, *ironing*, and *dusting*. (Three words are parallel.)

not parallel: When I need a pencil, I look in my purse, the table, and beside the telephone.

parallel: When I need a pencil, I look *in my purse*, *on the table*, and *beside the telephone*. (Three prepositional phrases are parallel.)

not parallel: Inez should get the promotion because she gets along with her co-workers, she works hard, and a knowledge of the business.

parallel: Inez should get the promotion because *she gets along with her co-workers*, *she works hard*, and *she knows the business*. (Three clauses are parallel.)

From these examples, you can see that parallelism involves matching the structures of parts of your sentence. There are two steps that can help you check your writing for parallelism:

Infobox

Two Steps in Checking a Sentence for Parallel Structure

Step 1: Look for the list in the sentence.

Step 2: Put the parts of the list into a similar structure.

You may have to change or add something to get a parallel structure.

ACHIEVING PARALLELISM

Let's correct the parallelism of the following sentence:

not parallel: If you want to pass the course, you have to study hard, taking good notes, and attendance at every class.

To correct this sentence, we'll follow the steps.

Step 1: Look for the list. If you want to pass the course, you have to do three things:
1. to study hard
2. taking good notes
3. attendance at every class

Step 2: Put the parts of the list into a similar structure.
1. *to study* hard
2. *to take* good notes
3. *to attend* every class

Now revise to get a parallel sentence.

parallel: If you want to pass the course, you have *to study* hard, *to take* good notes, and *to attend* every class.

If you follow steps 1 and 2, you can also write the sentence like this:

parallel: If you want to pass the course, you have to *study* hard, *take* good notes, and *attend* every class.

But you can't write the sentence like this:

not parallel: If you want to pass the course, you have to study hard, take good notes, and to attend every class.

Think of the list again. You can write

If you want to pass the course, you have
1. to study
2. to take   } parallel
3. to attend

Or you can write

If you want to pass the course, you have to
1. study
2. take   } parallel
3. attend

But you *cannot* write

If you want to pass the course, you have to
1. study
2. take   } not parallel
3. to attend

In other words, either use *to* once (if it fits every part of the list), or use it with *every* part of the list.

Sometimes making ideas parallel means adding something to the sentence because all the parts of the list cannot match exactly.

not parallel: After the toddler threw his bowl of cereal, oatmeal splattered down the walls, the floor, and the table.

Step 1: Look for the list: After the toddler threw his bowl of cereal, oatmeal splattered

1. down the walls
2. the floor
3. the table

As this sentence is written, *down* goes with *walls*, but it doesn't go with *floor* or *table.* Check the sense of this sentence by looking at each part of the list and how it is working in the sentence: "After the toddler threw his bowl of cereal, oatmeal splattered *down the walls*" is clear. But "oatmeal splattered *down the floor*"? Or "oatmeal splattered *down the table*"? These parts of the list are not right.

Step 2: The sentence needs some words added to make the structure parallel.

parallel: After the toddler threw his bowl of cereal, oatmeal splattered *down* the walls, *on* the floor, and *under* the table.

When you follow the two steps to check for parallelism, you can write clear sentences and improve your style.

Exercise 1 **Revising Sentences for Parallelism**

Practice

Some of the following sentences need to be revised so they have parallel structures. Revise the ones that have faulty parallelism.

1. The Festival of Flowers begins on June 5; ~~June 15 is when it ends.~~ *and ends on*

   revised: The festival flowers begins on June 5; and ends on June 15.

2. Rick is considerate, sympathetic, and ~~has tact.~~ *tactful*

   revised: Rick is considerate, sympathetic, and tactful.

3. My children have so many after-school activities that I have to take them for haircuts, *to* buying them new shoes, and share family dinners on the weekend.

   revised: _____

4. It's perfectly acceptable to come to the party in jeans or shorts.

   revised: correct

5. Rachel is a dancer with great style and who is talented.

revised: _____

_____

6. After the conference, the director and I met to assess the program, planning next month's session, and coordinate the schedule.

revised: _____

_____

7. The pager's color, its compact size, and what it cost made it attractive to Gary.

revised: _____

_____

8. I would rather go to a movie than spending forty dollars on a concert.

revised: _____

_____

9. Getting engaged is not the same as when you get married.

revised: _Getting engaged is not the same as_

getting Married.

10. If you want to be friends with him, you have to accept his shyness and excuse his awkwardness.

revised: _____

_____

Exercise 2 **Writing Sentences with Parallelism**

👥 Collaborate

With a partner or with a group, complete each sentence. Begin by brainstorming a draft list; then revise the list for parallelism. Finally, complete the sentence in a parallel structure. You may want to assign one task (brainstorming a draft list, revising it, etc.) to each group member, then switch tasks on the next sentence. Following is a sample of how to work through each question, from list to sentence.

sample incomplete sentence: The three parts of college I like best are

Draft List	Revised List
1. new friends	1. making new friends
2. doing well in English	2. doing well in English
3. Fridays off	3. having Fridays off

sentence: The three parts of college I like best are making new friends, doing well in English, and having Fridays off.

1. Three ways to meet new people are

Draft List   **Revised List**

1. _____   1. _____

2. _____   2. _____

3. _____   3. _____

sentence: _____

_____

2. Two suggestions for saving money are

Draft List   **Revised List**

1. _____   1. _____

2. _____   2. _____

sentence: _____

_____

3. Three annoying driving habits are

Draft List   **Revised List**

1. _____   1. _____

2. _____   2. _____

3. _____   3. _____

sentence: _____

_____

4. Children need firm guidelines at home because (give three reasons)

Draft List   **Revised List**

1. _____   1. _____

2. _____   2. _____

3. _____   3. _____

sentence: _____

_____

5. Four ways to contribute your time to the community are to

Draft List   **Revised List**

1. _____   1. _____

2. _____   2. _____

3. _____   3. _____

4. _____   4. _____

sentence: _____

_____

Exercise 3 **Recognizing Parallelism in Famous Speeches**

Collaborate

Some of the most famous speeches in history contain parallel structures. This parallelism adds emphasis and dignity to the points expressed. Working in a group, have one member read each segment of the following speeches aloud while the others listen carefully. Then underline all the words, phrases, clauses, or sentences that are in parallel form. When you have completed the exercise, share your answers with another group.

1. Inaugural Address
   John F. Kennedy

President John F. Kennedy delivered this speech when he was inaugurated on January 20, 1961. His theme was the renewal of American values and the changes and challenges we must face.

Let the word go forth from this time and place, to friend and foe alike,

that the torch has been passed to a new generation of Americans—born

in this century, tempered* by war, disciplined by a hard and bitter peace,

proud of our ancient heritage—and unwilling to witness or permit the

slow undoing of those human rights to which this nation has always been

committed, and to which we are committed today at home and around

the world.

* **tempered** means hardened, toughened

2. I Have a Dream
   Martin Luther King, Jr.

Martin Luther King, Jr., a Southern minister, was a leading advocate of civil rights in the 1960s. He delivered this speech to 200,000 people in Washington, D.C., where they had gathered to demonstrate peacefully for the cause of equality.

I have a dream that one day every valley shall be exalted, every hill

and mountain shall be made low, the rough places shall be made plain, and the crooked places shall be made straight, and the glory of the Lord will be revealed, and all flesh shall see it together.

This is our hope. This is the faith that I go back to the South with.

With this faith we will be able to hew* out of the mountain of despair a stone of hope. With this faith, we will be able to transform the jangling discords of our nation into a beautiful symphony of brotherhood.

With this faith we will be able to work together, to pray together, to go to jail together, to stand up for freedom together, knowing that we will be free one day.

* **hew** means to make or shape with cutting blows

Exercise 4

Connect **Combining Sentences and Creating a Parallel Structure**

In the paragraph below, some sentences need to be combined in a parallel structure. Combine each cluster of underlined sentences into one sentence with a parallel structure. Write your sentences in the space above the old ones.

Regular exercise and a healthy diet have many benefits. Many experts recommend that we get at least thirty minutes of moderate exercise at least three times a week. Such exercise can lower our stress levels. In addition, energy levels can be raised by exercise. Also, regular exercise burns calories. Exercise does not have to involve a workout at an expensive health club; it can be a vigorous walk around the neighborhood or a bike ride to town. Staying active is good for us, and so is eating right. Eating right means limiting the amount of fat in our diets. Cutting back on junk food also helps. Concentrating on fruits and vegetables is important, too. A healthy diet is low in fats and animal protein and high in whole grains, fruits, and vegetables. Eating healthfully can help us avoid heart disease, strokes, and other serious illnesses. Diet and exercise are not punishments; they are gifts we give ourselves. If we watch what we eat and get regular exercise, we improve the quality of our lives.

Revising a Paragraph for Parallelism

The following paragraph contains sentences with errors in parallelism. In the space above the lines, rewrite the sentences that contain errors in parallelism. There are four sentences with errors.

When I went to the mall, I had three objectives. I wanted to get in and out fast, to get a birthday present for my sister, and buy myself a new pair of sneakers. As soon as I got inside the mall, I knew I wouldn't get out fast. The place was mobbed with shoppers pushing, shoved, and shouting. The stores were having a Labor Day weekend sale, and everybody was there for the bargains. I roamed through four department stores but couldn't find a thing for my sister. Everything I liked was too big or in a size too small. As for finding a pair of sneakers, I couldn't get any I wanted. There were sneakers with jazzy colors, sneakers with expensive insignia, with thick soles, sneakers with corrugated soles. All I wanted was plain old sneakers, and no one had them. I left the mall without meeting any of my objectives.

CHAPTER 8

Using Adjectives and Adverbs

WHAT ARE ADJECTIVES?

Adjectives describe nouns (words that name persons, places, or things) or pronouns (words that substitute for a noun).

> **adjectives:**
>
> She stood in a *dark* corner. (*Dark* describes the noun *corner.*)
> I need a *little* help. (*Little* describes the noun *help.*)
> She looked *happy.* (*Happy* describes the pronoun *she.*)

An adjective usually comes before the word it describes:

> He gave me a *beautiful* ring. (*Beautiful* describes *ring.*)

Sometimes it comes after a *being* verb, a verb that tells what something is. Being verbs are words like *is, are, was, am, has been.* Words like *feels, looks, seems, smells, sounds,* and *tastes* are part of the group called being verbs.

> He seems *unhappy.* (*Unhappy* describes *he* and follows the being verb *seems.*)
> Alan was *confident.* (*Confident* describes *Alan* and follows the being verb *was.*)
> Your tires are *bald.* (*Bald* describes *tires* and follows the being verb *are.*)

Exercise 1 **Recognizing Adjectives**

Practice   Circle the adjective in each of the following sentences.

1. Jack jumped into the cold sea.

2. The chili tastes delicious.

3. Ramona was a thoughtful friend.

4. The house has a spacious kitchen.

5. They look upset.

6. An expensive car parked in the driveway.

7. The small boy began to howl.

8. The roses smell wonderful.

9. I needed a quiet room.

10. We are enthusiastic about the project.

Exercise 2 **More on Recognizing Adjectives**

Practice Circle the adjective in each of the following sentences.

1. An enthusiastic puppy jumped up.

2. The hall led to an elegant room.

3. His cry sounded desperate.

4. My hair feels greasy.

5. The pianist has thin fingers.

6. Mike was wearing a wrinkled shirt.

7. Selena offered me some shiny coins.

8. Dirty laundry filled the basket.

9. We went to a cheap restaurant.

10. Ungrateful friends irritate me.

ADJECTIVES: COMPARATIVE AND SUPERLATIVE FORMS

The **comparative** form of an adjective compares two persons or things. The **superlative** form compares three or more persons or things.

comparative: Your car is *cleaner* than mine.
superlative: Your car is the *cleanest* one in the parking lot.

comparative: Hamburger is *cheaper* than steak.
superlative: Hamburger is the *cheapest* meat on the menu.

comparative: Lisa is *friendlier* than her sister.
superlative: Lisa is the *friendliest* of the three sisters.

For most adjectives of one syllable, add *-er* to form the comparative, and add *-est* to form the superlative:

The weather is *colder* today than it was yesterday, but Friday was the *coldest* day of the year.

Orange juice is *sweeter* than grapefruit juice, but the *sweetest* juice is grape juice.

For longer adjectives, use *more* to form the comparative and *most* to form the superlative:

I thought College Algebra was *more difficult* than English; however, Beginning Physics was the *most difficult* course I ever took.

My brother is *more outgoing* than my sister, but my father is the *most outgoing* member of the family.

The three forms of adjectives usually look like this:

Adjective	Comparative (two)	Superlative (three or more)
sweet	sweeter	sweetest
fast	faster	fastest
short	shorter	shortest
quick	quicker	quickest
old	older	oldest

Or they may look like this:

Adjective	Comparative (two)	Superlative (three or more)
confused	more confused	most confused
specific	more specific	most specific
dangerous	more dangerous	most dangerous
confident	more confident	most confident
beautiful	more beautiful	most beautiful

However, there are some irregular forms of adjectives:

Adjective	Comparative (two)	Superlative (three or more)
good	better	best
bad	worse	worst
little	less	least
many, much	more	most

Exercise 3 **Selecting the Correct Adjective Forms**

Practice Write the correct form of the adjective in each of the following sentences.

1. Of the two sons of Senator Menendez, Dr. Sam Menendez is the

more intelligent _____ (intelligent).

2. Carissa is the ____ youngest ____ (young) of the four girls.

3. David thinks basketball is _ more exciting _ (exciting) than

baseball, but he is sure that hockey is the _ fastest _
(fast) game of all.

4. That movie was the ____ baddest ____ (bad) movie I have ever
seen.

5. Studying hard the night before a big test may be good for you, but

studying a little each day can be ____ better ____ (good) than
cramming.

6. Skiing is the _Most enjoyable_ (enjoyable) sport I've ever learned.

7. Simon is _More compassionate_ (compassionate) than his friend Lev.

8. Driving in sleet is _badder_ (bad) than driving in rain.

9. Which of these three cards is the _cheapest_ (cheap) one?

10. My three brothers gave me the _best_ (good) gift I've ever received.

Exercise 4 **Writing Sentences with Adjectives**

Collaborate

Working with a partner or a group, write a sentence that correctly uses each of the following adjectives. Be prepared to share your answers with another group or with the class.

1. more fortunate _She is more fortunate than her friend._

2. worst _That shirt is one of the worst one I've ever seen._

3. kinder _Ally is kinder than Joey_

4. most attractive _Which one of these two dress is the most attrative one._

5. cutest _Which of these two dogs is the cutest._

6. more nutritious _Which part of the food group is more nutritious._

7. bigger _Anggie is bigger than her older sister._

8. worse _____

9. better _Chocolate bars taste better than Lolipop._

10. more respected _____

WHAT ARE ADVERBS?

Adverbs describe verbs, adjectives, or other adverbs.

adverbs:

As she spoke, Steve listened *thoughtfully*. (*Thoughtfully* describes the verb *listened*.)

I said I was *really* sorry for my error. (*Really* describes the adjective *sorry*.)

The cook worked *very* quickly. (*Very* describes the adverb *quickly*.)

Adverbs answer questions like "How?" "How much?" "How often?" "When?" "Why?" and "Where?"

Exercise 5 **Recognizing Adverbs**

Practice Circle the adverbs in the following sentences.

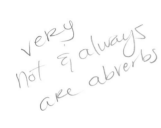

1. When I asked him a question, he responded graciously.

2. That statue is a truly beautiful work of art.

3. Suzanne stepped cautiously around the broken glass.

4. Nick examined the box carefully.

5. I am not really concerned about the flat tire.

6. The best actors perform intensely.

7. When he was criticized, my brother responded rudely.

8. He will speak tomorrow.

9. The mail disappeared very mysteriously.

10. *Titanic* is an extremely long movie.

Exercise 6 **More on Recognizing Adverbs**

Practice Circle the adverbs in the following sentences.

1. Customers frequently complain about the prices.

2. Be sure you speak clearly.

3. In a crisis, he will react quickly.

4. The child is not completely awake.

5. We need a highly skilled technician.

6. Traffic is moving slowly.

7. My dog is extremely intelligent.

8. My mother thought the movie was very amusing.

9. The tired boy answered angrily.

10. Michelle always drives safely.

Exercise 7 **Writing Sentences with Adverbs**

Collaborate

Working with a partner or a group, write a sentence that correctly uses each of the following adverbs. Be prepared to share your answers with another group or with the class.

1. suspiciously _____

_____

2. really _____

_____

3. often _____

_____

4. usually _____

_____

5. nearly _____

_____

6. regularly _____

_____

7. simply _____

_____

8. recently _____

_____

9. sometimes _____

_____

10. carefully _____

_____

HINTS ABOUT ADJECTIVES AND ADVERBS

Do not use an adjective when you need an adverb. Some writers make the mistake of using an adjective when they need an adverb:

not this: Talk to me ~~honest~~.
but this: Talk to me honestly.

not this: You can say it ~~simple~~.
but this: You can say it simply.

not this: He was breathing ~~deep~~.
but this: He was breathing deeply.

Exercise 8 **Changing Adjectives to Adverbs**

Practice

In each pair of sentences, change the underlined adjective in the first sentence to an adverb in the second sentence. The first one is done for you.

1. a. That light is <u>bright</u>.

   b. That light gleams _____brightly_____.

2. a. Nancy is an <u>intelligent</u> writer.

   b. Nancy writes _intelligently_.

3. a. David has a <u>mysterious</u> smile.

   b. David smiles _mysteriously_.

4. a. Carmen seems <u>shy</u>.

   b. Carmen speaks _shyly_.

5. a. The paramedics made a <u>quick</u> response.

   b. The paramedics responded _quickly_.

6. a. The detectives conducted a <u>careful</u> search.

   b. The detectives searched _carefully_.

7. a. Sylvia gave me a <u>thoughtful</u> answer.

   b. Sylvia answered _thoughtful_.

8. a. The judge made an <u>unfair</u> decision.

   b. The judge decided _unfairly_.

9. a. Ling gave a <u>humorous</u> response.

   b. Ling responded _humorously_.

10. a. Nathan has a <u>powerful</u> singing voice.

    b. Nathan sings _powerfully_.

Do Not Confuse *good* and *well*, or *bad* and *badly*

Remember that *good* is an adjective; it describes nouns. *Well* is an adverb; it describes verbs. (The only time *well* can be used as an adjective is when it means *healthy*, as in *I feel well today*.)

not this: You ran that race ~~good~~.
but this: You ran that race well.

not this: I cook eggs ~~good~~.
but this: I cook eggs well.

not this: How ~~good~~ do you understand grammar?
but this: How well do you understand grammar?

Bad is an adjective; it describes nouns. It also follows being verbs like *is, are, was, am, has been.* Words like *feels, looks, seems, smells, sounds,* and *tastes* are part of the group called being verbs. *Badly* is an adverb; it describes verbs.

not this: He feels ~~badly~~ about his mistake.
but this: He feels bad about his mistake. (*Feels* is a being verb; it is described by the adjective *bad.*)

not this: That soup smells ~~badly~~.
but this: That soup smells bad. (*Smells* is a being verb; it is described by the adjective *bad.*)

not this: He dances ~~bad~~.
but this: He dances badly.

Exercise 9   **Using *good* and *well*, *bad* and *badly***

Practice   Write the appropriate word in each of the following sentences.

1. If you're going to do the laundry, do it __well_____ (good, well).

2. Your dream of making a ___good_____ (good, well) salary can be achieved.

3. Thomas isn't coming with us because he doesn't feel __well_____ (good, well).

4. I wanted the car ___badly_____ (bad, badly).

5. Christa and Domingo work ___well_____ (good, well) together.

6. I used to feel ____bad_____ (bad, badly) about the accident.

7. Jorge is a driving teacher, but he drives ____badly_____ (bad, badly).

8. Ice cream goes _____well_____ (good, well) with apple pie.

9. He can't help us move because he has a ___bad_____ (bad, badly) back.

10. I think I get along ____well_____ (good, well) with my parents.

Do Not Use *more* + *-er* or *most* + *-est*

Be careful. Never write both an *-er* ending and *more*, or an *-est* ending and *most*:

not this: I want to work with someone ~~more smarter~~.
but this: I want to work with someone smarter.

not this: Alan is the ~~most richest~~ man in town.
but this: Alan is the richest man in town.

Use *than*, Not *then*, in Comparisons

When you compare things, use *than. Then* means *at a later time.*

not this: You are taller ~~then~~ I am.
but this: You are taller than I am.

not this: I'd like a car that is faster ~~then~~ my old one.
but this: I'd like a car that is faster than my old one.

When Do I Need a Comma Between Adjectives?

Sometimes you use more than one adjective to describe a noun:

I visited a cold, dark cave.
The cat had pale blue eyes.

If you look at the examples above, one uses a comma between the adjectives *cold* and *dark*, but the other doesn't have a comma between the adjectives *pale* and *blue*. Both sentences are correctly punctuated. To decide whether you need a comma, try one of these tests:

Test 1:   Try to put *and* between the adjectives. If the sentence still makes sense, put a comma between the adjectives.

> **Check for comma:** I visited a cold, dark cave. (Do you need the comma? Add *and* between the adjectives.)
> **Add *and*:** I visited a cold and dark cave. (Does the sentence still make sense? Yes. You need the comma.)
> **Correct sentence:** I visited a cold, dark cave.

> **Check for comma:** The cat had pale blue eyes. (Do you need the comma? Add *and* between the adjectives.)
> **Add *and*:** The cat had pale and blue eyes. (Does the sentence still make sense? No. You do not need the comma.)
> **Correct sentence:** The cat had pale blue eyes.

Test 2:   Try to revise the order of the adjectives. If the sentence still makes sense, put a comma between the adjectives.

> **Check for comma:** I visited a cold, dark cave. (Do you need the comma? Reverse the order of the adjectives.)
> **Reverse the order of the adjectives:** I visited a dark, cold cave. (Does the sentence still make sense? Yes. You need the comma.)
> **Correct sentence:** I visited a cold, dark cave.

> **Check for comma:** The cat had pale blue eyes. (Do you need the comma? Reverse the order of the adjectives.)
> **Reverse the order of the adjectives:** The cat had blue pale eyes. (Does the sentence still make sense? No. You don't need a comma.)
> **Correct sentence:** The cat had pale blue eyes.

You can use test 1 or test 2 to determine whether you need a comma between adjectives.

Exercise 10 **A Comprehensive Exercise on Using Adjectives and Adverbs**

Practice

Correct any errors in the use of adjectives and adverbs (including punctuation errors) in the following sentences. Some sentences do not need correcting.

1. Don is much older ~~then~~ _than_ his brother.

2. When you are searching the Internet, you can use ~~a more~~ faster way to find the information.

3. I am sure I did ~~good~~ _well_ on the history test.

4. Jessica stayed home because she didn't feel well.

5. Nathan tried to develop his photos at both Quick Shop and Dazzle Mart; Dazzle Mart did the ~~worst~~ _worse_ job.

6. Arizona has less rain than Florida.

7. Phil is the most athletic of the three cousins.

8. I bought four light pink roses from a roadside vendor.

9. The new manager of the club dressed ~~fashionable~~ _fashionably_.

10. Your answer is not ~~complete~~ _completely_ wrong; it just needs some work.

Exercise 11 **Another Comprehensive Exercise on Using Adjectives and Adverbs**

Practice

Correct any errors in the use of adjectives and adverbs (including punctuation errors) in the following sentences. Some sentences do not need correcting.

1. My brother made a complete _completely_ mess out of my apartment.

2. We entered a frightening, mysterious forest full of exotic birds.

3. The leftover chicken in the refrigerator looks bad; it has green spots on it.

4. The new recruit was told to salute quick _quickly_.

5. The man in the ambulance is real _really_ sick.

6. I ordered a lightly grilled piece of fish.

7. Sarah knows the ~~most~~ kindest ways of giving advice to unhappy people.

8. We have a choice of three old movies; I think the one with Eddie Murphy in it is the most entertaining.

9. Billy had little faith in the process; Cynthia had _less_ ~~least~~ than Billy.

10. When Sidney makes an effort, he performs well.

Exercise 12 **Editing a Paragraph for Errors in Adjectives and Adverbs**

Connect

Edit the following paragraph, correcting all the errors in the use of adjectives and adverbs. Write your corrections above the errors. There are seven errors.

Stefan is a great basketball player with three special strengths. First of all, he is the ~~most~~ boldest player I've ever seen. He takes more chances _than_ ~~then~~ anyone else, and his risk-taking brings its rewards. Last week he made several daring moves and contributed to his team's victory. Stefan's second strength is his ability to be a team player. Even though he plays so _well_ ~~good~~, he never acts as if he is smarter than anyone else. Instead, he is cooperative and supportive. He works well with others and never tries to be brilliantly on the court and steal all the glory. Stefan's third strength is determination. He is the most focused player and the ~~most~~ toughest on himself. He forces himself to practice long hours and to work on his weak spots. He never gives up. There may be better athletes _than_ ~~then~~ Stefan, but he is the most dedicated and disciplined player I know.

CHAPTER 9

Correcting Problems with Modifiers

Modifiers are words, phrases, or clauses that describe (modify) something in a sentence. All the following italicized words, phrases, and clauses are modifiers:

modifiers:

the *black* cat (word)
the cat *in the corner* (phrase)
the cat *that he adopted* (clause)

Sometimes modifiers limit another word. They make another word (or words) more specific.

the basket *in the boy's bedroom* (tells which basket)
twenty cookies (tells how many cookies)
the card *that she gave me* (tells which card)
They *seldom* visit. (tells how often)

Exercise 1 **Recognizing Modifiers**

Practice   In each of the following sentences, underline the modifiers (words, phrases, or clauses) that describe the italicized word.

1. For her birthday, Johnny gave his sister a *puppy* with an adorable face.

2. After the accident, the police were looking for a *man* driving a dark blue van.

3. The *children* waiting for Santa Claus stood at the gates of the park.

4. At the antique show, I bought a *cup*, slightly cracked in two places.

5. Ernie wanted his teacher to give him a makeup *test*.

6. We spent an hour looking for the missing *tickets*.

7. Torn in the chain-link fence, my *jeans* couldn't be mended.

8. A <u>tiny</u> *frog* covered in blue paint jumped out of the paint can.

9. Running to <u>catch the subway</u>, *Bill* tripped and fell.

10. My favorite quilted *parka*, <u>with its broken zipper and shredded lining</u>, finally had to go.

Exercise 2

Practice **Finding Modifiers in Professional Writing**

Following is an excerpt from an article by John R. Miller in the *Miami Herald*. It is a description of the office of Luther Campbell, a controversial and popular rap artist of the 1980s. The writing makes effective use of specific details, particularly through using modifiers. After you read the description, underline the modifiers that describe each italicized word or phrase.

Luther Campbell's office could belong to any successful businessman: Italian leather *chairs* and a sleekly <u>modern</u> *slab* of *something* dark and expensive for a desk. But one entire wall is bristling with enough electronics to launch a Saturn V: speakers, turntable, tuner, amplifier, CD player, tape deck, and right smack in the middle of the wall a large television hooked directly into the <u>satellite</u> *dish* that is bolted onto the roof. Two large <u>framed</u> *posters* hang behind his desk. . . . Beside the row of gold and platinum *albums* in <u>chrome frames</u> are lithographs* of <u>Luther's</u> *heroes*: the martyred* Martin and Malcolm.*

* **lithographs** means prints
* **martyred** means killed for a cause or belief
* **Martin** and **Malcolm** are Martin Luther King, Jr., and Malcolm X

CORRECTING MODIFIER PROBLEMS

Modifiers can make your writing more specific and more vivid. Used effectively and correctly, modifiers give the reader a clear picture of what you want to say, and they help you to say it precisely. But modifiers have to be used correctly. You can check for errors with modifiers as you revise your sentences.

Infobox

Three Steps in Checking for Sentence Errors with Modifiers

Step 1: Find the modifier.
Step 2: Ask, "Does the modifier have something to modify?"
Step 3: Ask, "Is the modifier in the right place, as close as possible to the word, phrase, or clause it modifies?"

If you answer no in either step 2 or step 3, you need to revise your sentence.

Review the three steps in the following example:

sample sentence: They were looking for a man walking a dog smoking a cigar.

Step 1: Find the modifier. The modifiers are *walking a dog* and *smoking a cigar.*

Step 2: Ask, "Does the modifier have something to modify?" The answer is yes. The man is walking a dog. The man is smoking a cigar. Both modifiers go with *a man.*

Step 3: Ask, "Is the modifier in the right place?" The answer is yes and no. One modifier is in the right place:

a man *walking a dog*

The other modifier is not in the right place:

a dog *smoking a cigar*

The dog is not smoking a cigar. The sentence needs to be revised.

revised sentence: They were looking for a man *walking a dog and smoking a cigar.*

Here is another example of how to apply the three steps:

sample sentence: Slathered in whipped cream and nuts, she ate the hot fudge sundae.

Step 1: Find the modifiers. The modifiers are *Slathered in whipped cream and nuts* and *hot fudge.*

Step 2: Ask, "Does the modifier have something to modify?" The answer is yes. The sundae is *slathered in whipped cream and nuts*, and the sundae is *hot fudge.*

Step 3: Ask, "Is the modifier in the right place?" The answer is yes and no. The phrase *hot fudge* is in the right place:

hot fudge sundae

But *Slathered in whipped cream and nuts* is in the wrong place:

Slathered in whipped cream and nuts, she

She is not slathered in whipped cream and nuts. The sundae is. The sentence needs to be revised.

revised sentence: She ate the *hot fudge* sundae *slathered in whipped cream and nuts.*

Caution: Be sure to put words like *almost, even, exactly, hardly, just, merely, nearly, only, scarcely,* and *simply* as close as possible to what they modify. If you put them in the wrong place, you may write a confusing sentence.

confusing sentence: Brian only wants to buy toothpaste and shampoo. (The modifier that creates confusion here is *only.* Does Brian have only one goal in life—to be a toothpaste and shampoo buyer? Or are these the only items he wants to buy? To create a clearer sentence, move the modifier.)

revised sentence: Brian wants to buy *only* toothpaste and shampoo.

The preceding examples show one common error in using modifiers. This error involves **misplaced modifiers**—words that describe something but are not where they should be in the sentence. Here is the rule to remember:

Put the modifier as close as possible to the word, phrase, or clause it modifies.

Exercise 3 **Correcting Sentences with Misplaced Modifiers**

Practice

Some of the following sentences contain misplaced modifiers. Revise any sentence that has a misplaced modifier by putting the modifier as close as possible to whatever it modifies.

1. Smashed in pieces on the pavement, he recognized his mother's favorite bowl.

revised: He recognized his mother's favorite bowl, but smashed in pieces on the pavement.

2. Suzanne scanned the library shelf and realized she had almost read every book on surfing.

revised: Suzanne scanned the library shelf and realized she had read almost every book on surfing.

3. You will remember the fun you had at the party years from now.

revised: Years from now, you will remember the fun you had at the party.

4. Speeding through the alley, a large garbage can was hit by the car.

revised: A large garbage can was hit by the car speeding through the alley.

5. Nelson read that the terrorist had been killed in the Sunday paper.

revised: In the Sunday paper, Nelson read that the terrorist had been killed.

6. I had just walked in the door when the telephone began to ring.

revised: _____

_____

7. We saw a family of squirrels on the way to the toy store.

revised: On the way to the toy store we saw a family of squirrels

8. Diane was angry at a man who dented her car named Jimmy.

revised: _____

_____

okay **9.** My coach asked me how I felt after hitting a home run.

revised: My coach asked how I felt after hitting a home run.

10. Chewing on my tulips, I spied a sneaky rabbit.

revised: I spied on a sneaky rabbit chewing on my tulips.

Correcting Dangling Modifiers

The three steps for correcting modifier problems can help you recognize another kind of error. For example, let's use the steps to check the following sentence.

sample sentence: Cruising slowly through the Everglades, two alligators could be seen.

Step 1: Find the modifier. The modifiers are *Cruising slowly through the Everglades* and *two.*

Step 2: Ask, "Does the modifier have something to modify?" The answer is yes and no. The word *two* modifies alligators. But who or what is *cruising slowly through the Everglades*? There is no person mentioned in the sentence. The alligators are not cruising.

This kind of error is called a **dangling modifier.** The modifier does not have anything to modify; it just dangles in the sentence. If you want to correct this kind of error, just moving the modifier will not work.

still incorrect: Two alligators could be seen cruising slowly through the Everglades. (There is still no person cruising, and the alligators are not cruising.)

The way to correct this kind of error is to add something to the sentence. If you gave the modifier something to modify, you might come up with several correct sentences:

revised sentences: *As we cruised slowly through the Everglades,* two alligators could be seen.

Two alligators could be seen *when the visitors were cruising slowly through the Everglades.*

Cruising slowly through the Everglades, the people on the boat saw two alligators.

Try the process for correcting dangling modifiers in another example:

sample sentence: Having struggled in the snow all day, a hot cup of coffee was welcome.

Step 1: Find the modifier. The modifiers are *Having struggled in the snow all day, hot,* and *of coffee.*

Step 2: Ask, "Does the modifier have something to modify?" The answer is yes and no. The words *hot* and *of coffee* modify *cup,* but *Having struggled in the snow all day* doesn't modify anything. Who struggled? There is nobody mentioned in the sentence. To revise, put somebody in the sentence:

revised sentences: Having struggled in the snow all day, Dan welcomed a hot cup of coffee.

After we struggled in the snow all day, a hot cup of coffee was welcome.

Remember that you cannot correct a dangling modifier just by moving the modifiers. You have to give the modifier something to modify, so you must add something to the sentence.

Exercise 4

Practice

Correcting Sentences with Dangling Modifiers

Some of the following sentences use modifiers correctly, but some have dangling modifiers. Revise the sentences that have dangling modifiers. To revise, you will have to add words or change words.

1. To get a job with that corporation, good communications skills are essential.

   revised: _Good communications skills are essential to get a job with that corporation._

2. With a solid background in mathematics, Tricia began her first year of college.

   revised: _Tricia began her first year of college with a solid background in Mathematics._

3. Working late at night, the term paper was finally completed.   ^(I finally)

   revised: _____

   _____

4. Caught in a cycle of worry and despair, life seemed to offer very little.   ^(I felt that)

   revised: _____

   _____

5. While slicing onions, a sharp knife cut into his thumb.   ^(pete was   he cat his th)

   revised: _____

   _____

6. Resolving to study harder next time, I learned from my low test score.

revised: _____

_____

7. At the age of seven, my parents got a divorce.

revised: _At the age of seven, ... when_

I was seven

8. Without a good map of the area, getting lost is likely.

revised: _Without a good map of the area,_

we are likely to get lost.

9. When fighting over a parking space, an accident between two cars occurred.

revised: _When fighting over a parking space, there_

was an accident between two cars.

10. Torn in two places, the poster could not be repaired.

revised: _____

_____

REVIEWING THE STEPS AND THE SOLUTIONS

It is important to recognize problems with modifiers and to correct these problems. Modifier problems can result in confusing or even silly sentences, and when you confuse or unintentionally amuse your reader, the reader misses your point.

Remember to check for modifier problems by using the three steps and to correct each kind of problem appropriately.

Infobox

A Summary of Modifier Problems

Checking for Modifier Problems
Step 1: Find the modifier.
Step 2: Ask, "Does the modifier have something to modify?"
Step 3: Ask, "Is the modifier in the right place?"

Correcting Modifier Problems
• If a modifier is in the wrong place (a misplaced modifier), put it as close as possible to the word, phrase, or clause it modifies.

• If a modifier has nothing to modify (a dangling modifier), add or change words so that it has something to modify.

Exercise 5 **Revising Sentences with Misplaced or Dangling Modifiers**

Practice All of the sentences below have some kind of modifier problem. Write a new, correct sentence for each one. You may move, remove, add, or change words. The first one is done for you.

1. Shot in the chest, the ambulance took the robber to the emergency room.

   revised: The ambulance took the robber, shot in the chest, to the emergency room.

2. After digging up all her flower beds, Mrs. Jabala decided to complain to the puppy's owners.

   revised: Mrs. Jabala decided to complain to the puppy's owners, after digging up all her flower beds.

3. With compassion and generosity, a donation was made to the shelter for abused women.

   revised: A donation was made with compassion and generosity to the shelter for abused women.

4. I was surprised to see a small boy riding in the front seat of the car with a cowboy hat.

   revised: _____

   _____

5. Chewing gum like a cow, the first-grade teacher reprimanded the student.

   revised: The first-grade teacher, chewing gum like a cow, reprimanded the student.

6. Soaked by the downpour, the man snug in his car felt sorry for the hurrying pedestrians.

   revised: The man snug in his car, felt sorry for the hurrying pedestrians, soaked by the down pour

7. Albert nearly finished all the chocolates in the box.

   revised: All the chocolate in the box, Albert nearly finished

8. Crusted over with rust, I decided to throw away the old lawn chair.

revised: *I decided to throw away the old lawn chair, crusted over with rust.*

9. To succeed in college, willpower and determination are essential.

revised: *Willpower and determination, to succeed in college are essential.*

10. Exploding into an array of dazzling colors, Anita watched the fireworks.

revised: *Anita watched the fireworks exploding into an array of dazzling colors.*

· Exercise 6 **Completing Sentences with Modifiers**

Collaborate

Do this exercise with a partner or a group. Below are the beginnings of sentences. Complete each sentence by adding your own words. Be sure that each new sentence is free of modifier problems. When you have completed the exercise, share your sentences with another group or with the class. The first one is done for you.

1. Scorched and dry, **the toasted English muffin tasted like a chunk of charcoal.**

2. Vanished without a trace, *The man dissapeared late afternoon.*

3. Hanging from the ceiling, *the bats were asleep.*

4. When telling a lie, *you feel bad about it.*

5. Stuck at the airport during a blizzard, *we couldn't go no where*

6. Embarrassed by the incident, *I had to hide my face.*

7. Surrounded by killer bees, *I didn't wait to go anywhere*

8. With a gigantic grin, _He made me happy_

_____

9. Looking like a movie star, _I wanted to get to_

know him .

10. Covered in mud, _I had to wash myself ._

_____

Exercise 7 **Revising for Modifier Problems**

Connect The following paragraph has some modifier problems. Correct the errors by writing above the lines. There are three errors in the paragraph.

To make friends in a new place, ^you need a sense of adventure is necessary. If you remain timid and afraid, you will not meet anyone. On the other hand, if you think of meeting new people as a challenge, the process can be fun. Striding confidently into a new school, you will impress your style the students will be impressed by your style. You may only want to disappear into a corner, but in new situations you have to make the first move. At school or at work, you need to make an effort to be outgoing and friendly. Making the first move becomes easier if you remember that getting to know people can be fun and even humorous, and making a fool of yourself once or twice does not matter. You might even meet a few other foolish people. Years from now, all those silly encounters will make great stories. By then, you will have made many new friends who will enjoy your tales.

Verbs: The Four Main Forms

Verbs are words that show some kind of action or being:

> verb
> My brother *washes* my car.

> verb
> The teddy bear *is* his oldest toy.

> verb
> Your cinnamon cake *smells* wonderful.

Verbs also tell about time:

> verb
> My brother *will wash* my car. (The time is future.)

> verb
> The teddy bear *was* his oldest toy. (The time is past.)

> verb
> Your cinnamon cake *smells* wonderful. (The time is present.)

The time of a verb is called its **tense**. You can say a verb is in the **present tense**, the **future tense**, the **past tense**, or many other tenses.

Using verbs correctly involves knowing which form of the verb to use and choosing the right verb tense.

USING STANDARD VERB FORMS

Many people use nonstandard verb forms in everyday conversation. But everyone who wants to write and speak effectively should know different levels of language, from the slang and dialect of everyday conversation to the **standard English** of college, business, and professional environments.

In everyday conversation, you might use **nonstandard forms** like the ones that follow:

Nonstandard Verb Forms

it seem	I faces	we was	you was
we goes	they don't	they talks	she work
you be	I be	he sell	it don't

But these are not correct forms in standard English. To become more familiar with standard verb forms, start with a review of the present tense.

THE PRESENT TENSE

Here are the standard verb forms of the verb *walk*:

Infobox

Standard Verb Forms in the Present Tense

I walk	he, she, it walks	you walk
you walk	we walk	they walk

Take a closer look at the standard verb forms. Only one form is different:

he, she, it *walks*

This is the only form that ends in *-s* in the present tense.

In the present tense, use an *-s* or *-es* ending on the verb only when the subject is *he*, *she*, or *it*, or the equivalent of *he*, *she*, or *it*.

examples:

He *drives* to the store on Saturdays.
Larry *walks* his dog on Saturdays. (*Larry* is the equivalent of *he*.)
The cat *chases* the birds in my garden. (The *cat* is the equivalent of *it*.)
She *reminds* me of my sister.
It *looks* like a new car.
Your engine *sounds* funny. (The word *engine* is the equivalent of *it*.)
My daughter *watches* the news on television. (The word *daughter* is the equivalent of *she*.)

Take another look at the present tense. If the verb is a standard verb, like *work*, it will follow this form in the present tense:

I *work* on the weekends.	We *work* well together.
You *work* too hard.	You two boys *work* with Joe.
He *works* for his father.	They *work* near the mall.
She *works* in a bakery.	
It *works* on solar power.	

Exercise 1 **Picking the Right Verb in the Present Tense**

Practice To familiarize yourself with standard verb forms in the present tense, underline the subject and circle the correct verb form in each of the following sentences.

1. Hoping for a good grade in Art Appreciation, Jason (attend/attends)

every lecture.

2. A meal in a fancy restaurant (cost/costs) too much for me.

3. Cynthia and her cousin (give/gives) their old clothes to charity.

4. The possibility of a robbery (frighten/frightens) me.

5. That waitress (serve/serves) us every weekend.

6. Sylvester (get/gets) a new car once a year.

7. He (wear/wears) a different shirt every day.

8. In the evening, I (sit/sits) on my patio.

9. The puppy (belong/belongs) to my neighbor.

10. He (clean/cleans) offices for a living.

Exercise 2   **More on Picking the Right Verb in the Present Tense**

Practice   To familiarize yourself with standard verb forms in the present tense, underline the subject and circle the correct verb form in each of the following sentences.

1. Your plan (sound/sounds) good to me.

2. I (buy/buys) my clothes at sales.

3. They often (travel/travels) in a camper.

4. Melanie (hesitate/hesitates) to act in a crisis.

5. Margarine (taste/tastes) like butter.

6. On the shore of the lake (stand/stands) a pavilion.

7. Tomorrow, you (speak/speaks) at the club breakfast.

8. His behavior (raise/raises) several questions.

9. A guilty conscience (tear/tears) you apart.

10. On my birthday, Tommy always (send/sends) me a card.

Exercise 3   **Writing Sentences with Verbs in the Present Tense**

Collaborate   Below are pairs of verbs. Working with a partner or a group, write one sentence using each verb. Be sure your verbs are in the present tense, and make your sentences at least five words long. When you have completed the exercise, share your sentences with another group. The first one is done for you.

1. **verbs:** listen, listens

sentence 1: Every morning on their way to work, my parents listen to a

boring radio station.

sentence 2: Sam always listens to my sad stories and silly complaints.

2. verbs: fear, fears

sentence 1: _____

_____

sentence 2: _____

_____

3. verbs: make, makes

sentence 1: I had to make myself a copy of the schedule.

sentence 2: _____

_____

4. verbs: struggle, struggles

sentence 1: _____

_____

sentence 2: _____

_____

5. verb: respect, respects

sentence 1: _____

_____

sentence 2: _____

_____

6. verbs: teach, teaches

sentence 1: _____

_____

sentence 2: _____

_____

7. verbs: sell, sells

sentence 1: _____

_____

sentence 2: _____

_____

8. verbs: confuse, confuses

sentence 1: _____

_____

sentence 2: _____

_____

9. verbs: seem, seems

sentence 1: _____

_____

sentence 2: He seems like a nice person _____

_____

10. verbs: appreciate, appreciates

sentence 1: _____

_____

sentence 2: _____

_____

Exercise 4 **Revising a Paragraph for Errors in the Present Tense**

Connect The following paragraph contains nine errors in present tense verb forms. Correct the errors in the space above the lines.

My mother puts me through the same routine every time I asks to borrow a few dollars. First, she look at me with a stern expression and questions me about my spending habits. Then she delivers a long lecture about the state of the economy. She ends her lecture by saying that money doesn't grow on trees and by bringing up my older brothers. She say Tom and Matthew never borrows money from her because they possesses a strong awareness of the value of a dollar. While my mother screams and yell, I says nothing. Finally, she reaches in her purse and gives me the money I needs. Once again, I gets the cash, and my mother gets to feel righteous.

THE PAST TENSE

The past tense of most verbs is formed by adding *-d* or *-ed* to the verb.

Infobox

Standard Verb Forms in the Past Tense

I walked	he, she, it walked	you walked
you walked	we walked	they walked

Add *-ed* to *walk* to form the past tense. For some other verbs, you add *-d*.

The zookeeper *chased* the chimpanzee.
I *trembled* with excitement.
Paul *baked* a birthday cake for his daughter.

Exercise 5 **Writing the Correct Form of the Past Tense**

Practice   To familiarize yourself with the past tense, write the correct past tense form of each verb in the blank.

1. Last year, Amy and Chris ___Cooked___ (cook) a special dinner for our anniversary.

2. The counselor ___excused___ (excuse) some of the students from class yesterday.

3. A recent letter from the bank ___informed___ (inform) me about my ATM card.

4. Yesterday's paper ___printed___ (print) a story about my old neighborhood.

5. Over the holidays, I ___Borrowed___ (borrow) a great book from Frank.

6. The chocolate bar she gave me ___contained___ (contain) nuts and raisins.

7. After recognizing my error, I ___erased___ (erase) it.

8. In high school, we seldom ___managed___ (manage) to get to sleep before midnight.

9. Visitors to last week's carnival ___enjoyed___ (enjoy) some wonderful rides and exhibits.

10. Many years ago, my grandfather ___immigrated___ (immigrate) to this country.

Exercise 6 More on Writing the Correct Form of the Past Tense

Practice   To familiarize yourself with the past tense, write the correct past tense form of each verb in the blank.

1. Last night, the two cooks ____slaved____ (slave) over a hot stove.

2. All afternoon, the little boy ____pasted____ (paste) brightly colored stickers in the book.

3. A long time ago, Mr. Chen ____reported____ (report) the news on a local television station.

4. This morning, Omar ____raced____ (race) through his breakfast.

5. Squirrels ____nested____ (nest) in our attic for several months.

6. After drinking the milk, the kitten ____purred____ (purr) loudly.

7. An old friend from my first job ____visited____ (visit) me last winter.

8. Witnesses at the scene of last night's fire ____described____ (describe) a loud explosion.

9. When I was a child, Cleavon ____encouraged____ (encourage) me to study music.

10. At the end of the play, everyone ____applauded____ (applaud) the cast.

Exercise 7 Writing Sentences with Verbs in the Present and Past Tense

Collaborate   Below are pairs of verbs. Working with a partner or a group, write a sentence using each verb. Each sentence should be five or more words long. When you have completed the exercise, share your sentences with another group. The first one is done for you.

1. **verbs:** recognizes, recognized

   sentence 1: Whenever I go to that coffee shop, the owner recognizes me.

   sentence 2: Yesterday my sister recognized a famous actor walking down our street.

2. **verbs:** place, placed

   sentence 1: I want you to place the dishes on the table.

sentence 2: *She placed the papers on my desk.*

3. verbs: mail, mailed

sentence 1: *I didn't get the mail until this morning*

sentence 2: *Joe mailed his letter two weeks ago.*

4. verbs: attacks, attacked

sentence 1: _____

_____

sentence 2: _____

_____

5. verbs: sound, sounded

sentence 1: _____

_____

sentence 2: _____

_____

6. verbs: insults, insulted

sentence 1: _____

_____

sentence 2: _____

_____

7. verbs: demand, demanded

sentence 1: _____

_____

sentence 2: _____

_____

8. verbs: dream, dreamed

sentence 1: _____

_____

sentence 2: _____

_____

9. verbs: receives, received

sentence 1: _____

_____

sentence 2: _____

_____

10. verbs: accept, accepted

sentence 1: _____

_____

sentence 2: _____

_____

Exercise 8	**Rewriting a Paragraph, Changing the Verb Tense**

Connect   Rewrite the following paragraph, changing all the present tense verbs to the past tense. Write the changes in the space above the original words.

Jennifer works at a place she hates. Her co-workers ignore her and
her boss criticizes her about the smallest details, including Jennifer's
makeup and hair style. She says Jennifer looks too sloppy to serve
customers. Jennifer also believes that the customers behave very badly.
Not one of them ever smiles or says "Thank you" when Jennifer offers
assistance. Jennifer considers her job a punishment, and she dreams of
quitting. She stays only because she needs the money.

THE FOUR MAIN FORMS OF A VERB

When you are deciding what form of a verb to use, you will probably rely on one of four verb forms: the present tense, the past tense, the present participle, or the past participle. You will use one of these forms or add a helping verb to it. As an example, look at the four main forms of the verb *walk*:

Infobox

The Four Main Forms of a Verb

Present	Past	Present Participle	Past Participle
walk	walked	walking	walked

You use the four verb forms—present, past, present participle, past participle—alone or with helping verbs to express time (tense). Forms of regular verbs like *walk* are very easy to remember.

Use the **present** form for the present tense:

They *walk* three miles every day.

The **past** form expresses past tense:

Steve *walked* to work yesterday.

The **present participle**, or *-ing* form, is used with helping verbs:

He *was walking* in a charity fund-raiser.
I *am walking* with a neighbor.
You *should have been walking* faster.

The **past participle** is the form used with the helping verbs *have, has,* or *had*:

I *have walked* down this road before.
She *has walked* to church for years.
The children *had walked* the dog before they went to school.

Of course, you can add helping verbs to the present tense:

present tense:
We *walk* in a beautiful forest.

add helping verbs:
We *will* walk in a beautiful forest.
We *must* walk in a beautiful forest.
We *can* walk in a beautiful forest.

In **regular verbs**, the four verb forms are simple: the past form is created by adding *-d* or *-ed* to the present form; the present participle is formed by adding *-ing* to the present form; and the past participle is the same as the past form.

Exercise 9
👥 Collaborate

Writing Sentences Using the Four Main Forms of a Verb

Do this exercise with a partner or a group. Below are pairs of verbs. Write a sentence for each verb. Your sentences should be at least five words long. When you have completed this exercise, share your answers with another group or with the class. The first one is done for you.

1. **verbs:** hesitate, hesitating

    sentence 1: Since I had a car accident, I hesitate before getting into a

    car.

    sentence 2: The lawyers might have been hesitating about the deal.

2. **verbs:** explained, explaining

    sentence 1: _____

sentence 2: _____

_____

3. verbs: complaining, complained (Put *have* in front of *complained*.)

sentence 1: *The lady has been complaining*
about her

sentence 2: *my parents have complained*
certain things .

4. verbs: climbed, climbing

sentence 1: _____

_____

sentence 2: _____

_____

5. verbs: accept, accepted (Put *had* in front of *accepted*.)

sentence 1: _____

_____

sentence 2: _____

_____

6. verbs: love, loved (Put *had* in front of *loved*.)

sentence 1: _____

_____

sentence 2: _____

_____

7. verbs: disappearing, disappeared (Put *has* in front of *disappeared*.)

sentence 1: _____

_____

sentence 2: _____

_____

8. verbs: confront, confronted

sentence 1: _____

_____

sentence 2: _____

_____

9. verbs: wished, wishing

sentence 1: _____

_____

sentence 2: _____

_____

10. verbs: rebel, rebelled (Put *have* in front of *rebelled.*)

sentence 1: _____

_____

sentence 2: _____

_____

IRREGULAR VERBS

The Present Tense of *be, have, do*

Irregular verbs do not follow the same rules for creating verb forms that regular verbs do. Three verbs that we use all the time—*be, have, do*—are irregular verbs. You need to study them closely. Look at the present tense forms for all three, and compare the standard present tense forms with the nonstandard ones. *Remember to use the standard forms for college or professional writing.*

present tense of *be*:

Nonstandard	Standard
~~I be *or* I is~~	I am
~~you be~~	you are
~~he, she, it be~~	he, she, it is
~~we be~~	we are
~~you be~~	you are
~~they be~~	they are

present tense of *have*:

Nonstandard	Standard
~~I has~~	I have
~~you has~~	you have
~~he, she, it have~~	he, she, it has
~~we has~~	we have
~~they has~~	they have

present tense of *do*:

Nonstandard	Standard
~~I does~~	I do
~~you does~~	you do
~~he, she, it do~~	he, she, it does
~~we does~~	we do
~~you does~~	you do
~~they does~~	they do

Caution: Be careful when you add *not* to *does*. If you're using the contraction of *does not*, be sure you write *doesn't*, instead of *don't*. Contractions should be avoided in most formal reports and business writing courses. Always check with your instructor about the use of contractions in your personal writing.

> **not this:** ~~He don't call me very often.~~
> **but this:** He doesn't call me very often.

Exercise 10 **Choosing the Correct Form of *be*, *have*, or *do* in the Present Tense**

Practice

Circle the correct form of the verb in each sentence.

1. I am sure the reporters on the scene (has/have) a deadline to meet.

2. On a day like today, I (am/be) happy to have such good friends.

3. The old washing machine still (do/does) a decent job of getting the clothes clean.

4. With a new car, we (has/have) higher car payments.

5. All my aunts and uncles (be/are) experts at telling ghost stories.

6. At the end of each month, I (am/be) confused about my lack of money.

7. I know that nobody (do/does) a better job than this cleaning service.

8. In his bedroom Peter (has/have) a big-screen television.

9. You know that David (be/is) thinking about his senior year.

10. The theater near our house (doesn't/don't) show movies after midnight.

Exercise 11 **More on Choosing the Correct Form of *be*, *have*, or *do* in the Present Tense**

Practice

Circle the correct form of the verb in each sentence.

1. Every Saturday morning I (do/does) the grocery shopping for my grandfather.

2. Cooking dinner for my family can be fun, but it (do/does) take time.

3. Other teams may brag, but I know that we (are/be) the fastest team on the court.

4. If you (has/have) any doubts about Diane's sincerity, you should talk to her.

5. I (do/does) the best I can for my family.

6. My cousin Tyra and I (has/have) a special bond.

7. When you smile that way, you (are/be) telling me a lie.

8. Deep down inside, you (has/have) a good heart.

9. When their parents have to work late, Daniella and Marc (do/does) their best to make dinner.

10. That old black dog (be/is) a gift from my brother-in-law.

Exercise 12
Connect

Revising a Paragraph with Errors in the Present Tense of *be*, *have*, and *do*

The following paragraph contains five errors in the use of the present tense forms of *be*, *have*, and *do*. Correct the errors above the lines.

My brother's plan to sell our car is making me upset and indignant.

Mike, my brother, says he be thinking about getting rid of our old Toyota.

But my parents gave that car to me and Mike so that we could use it to get

to work and school. Mike don't own the car by himself; therefore, he have

no right to sell it alone. Mike says he will split the sale money with me, but

I am still angry with him. First of all, he is not the sole owner of the car.

Second, he can't make a decision about our property without informing

me. The fact that he even considered selling the car without telling me

shows that he have no respect for my wishes. He must think I is a brain-

less, passive person. His attitude toward me is what upsets me the most.

The Past Tense of *be*, *have*, *do*

The past tense forms of these irregular verbs can be confusing. Again, compare the nonstandard forms with the standard forms. *Remember to use the standard forms for college or professional writing.*

past tense of *be*:

Nonstandard	Standard
~~I were~~	I was
~~you was~~	you were
~~he, she, it were~~	he, she, it was
~~we was~~	we were
~~you was~~	you were
~~they was~~	they were

past tense of *have*:

Nonstandard	Standard
~~I has~~	I had
~~you has~~	you had
~~he, she, it have~~	he, she, it had
~~we has~~	we had
~~you has~~	you had
~~they has~~	they had

past tense of *do*:

Nonstandard	Standard
~~I done~~	I did
~~you done~~	you did
~~he, she, it done~~	he, she, it did
~~we done~~	we did
~~you done~~	you did
~~they done~~	they did

Exercise 13 **Choosing the Correct Form of *be*, *have*, or *do* in the Past Tense**

Practice Circle the correct verb form in each sentence.

1. The man across the street (did/done) the planting for the Community Center garden.

2. The Brazilian singers at the free concert exceeded my expectations; they (was/were), without a doubt, the best part of the entertainment.

3. Janet thought you relied on an interior decorator, but I told her you (did/done) all the decorating yourself.

4. This morning Luke couldn't find his key, but I know he (have/had) it yesterday.

5. When I lived at my grandmother's house, I (was/were) not allowed to stay up late.

6. A year ago, you (was/were) a total stranger; now you are my best friend.

7. A week ago, I (had/has) a bad case of the flu.

8. When you stood at the top of the Empire State Building, you (has/had) no fear of heights.

9. At last night's lecture on AIDS, the Student Council (have/had) an information booth.

10. When she couldn't get to her job, I (did/done) her a favor and drove her to work.

Exercise 14   **More on Choosing the Correct Form of *be*, *have*, or *do***
Practice   **in the Past Tense**

Circle the correct verb form in each sentence.

1. Two hours after Melissa left, we (was/were) still unwrapping presents.

2. The sugar-free lemonade she served me (had/have) a peculiar taste.

3. My hair looks good because Lorraine (did/done) it for me last night.

4. People standing in line at the movies yesterday (had/has) to wait for at least an hour.

5. The girls in my kindergarten class (was/were) very bright and curious.

6. When he came over, he (had/have) a big bag of candy for his nephew.

7. All weekend they (was/were) waiting for the rain to stop.

8. For two months last summer I (was/were) a lifeguard for the city of Crystal Beach.

9. After she finished dinner, she (had/have) a cup of coffee with me.

10. Ted and Brian (did/done) the dishes while Ryan took out the garbage.

Exercise 15   **Revising a Paragraph with Errors in the Past Tense of *be*, *have*, and *do***
Connect   The following paragraph contains seven errors in the use of the past tense of *be*, *have*, and *do*. Correct the errors above the lines.

For no good reason, the local police gave me and my friends a hard

time last night. Frank, Rickie, and I ~~was~~ were just sitting on Rickie's truck and

drinking Pepsi in front of the Quik Mart when a patrol car pulled up. The

officer said that he ~~have~~ had a complaint about us, that we were causing a dis-

turbance, and that the store manager wanted to get rid of us. I told the offi-

cer that it ~~weren't~~ wasn't against the law to sit in front of a convenience store and

drink soda. But he said it was private property and the manager ~~have~~ had a

right to ask us to leave. The policeman done his best to roust us, and even-

tually we ~~has~~ had to leave. Because we were male and in our teens, we must

have looked threatening to the store manager. Then, when a policeman

showed up, we got angry with him even though he was just doing his job.

Most likely he and the manager ~~were~~ was upset, but my friends and I ~~was~~ were, too.

More Irregular Verb Forms

Be, have, and *do* are not the only verbs with irregular forms. There are many such verbs, and everybody who writes uses some forms of irregular verbs. When you write and you are not certain you are using the correct form of a verb, check the following list of irregular verbs.

For each verb listed, the *present,* the *past,* and the *past participle* forms are given. The present participle isn't included because it is always formed by adding *-ing* to the present form.

Irregular Verb Forms

Present	Past	Past Particple
(Today I *arise.*)	(Yesterday I *arose.*)	(I have/had *arisen.*)
arise	arose	arisen
awake	awoke, awaked	awoken, awaked
bear	bore	born, borne
beat	beat	beaten
become	became	become
begin	began	begun
bend	bent	bent
bite	bit	bitten
bleed	bled	bled
blow	blew	blown
break	broke	broken
bring	brought	brought
build	built	built
burst	burst	burst
buy	bought	bought
catch	caught	caught
choose	chose	chosen
cling	clung	clung
come	came	come
cost	cost	cost
creep	crept	crept
cut	cut	cut
deal	dealt	dealt
draw	drew	drawn
dream	dreamed	dreamed
drink	drank	drunk
drive	drove	driven
eat	ate	eaten
fall	fell	fallen
feed	fed	fed
feel	felt	felt
fight	fought	fought
find	found	found
fling	flung	flung
fly	flew	flown
freeze	froze	frozen
get	got	got, gotten
give	gave	given
go	went	gone
grow	grew	grown

Present	Past	Past Particple
hear	heard	heard
hide	hid	hidden
hit	hit	hit
hold	held	held
hurt	hurt	hurt
keep	kept	kept
know	knew	known
lay (*to put*)	laid	laid
lead	led	led
leave	left	left
lend	lent	lent
let	let	let
lie (*to recline*)	lay	lain
light	lit, lighted	lit, lighted
lost	lost	lost
make	made	made
mean	meant	meant
meet	met	met
pay	paid	paid
ride	rode	ridden
ring	rang	rung
rise	rose	risen
run	ran	run
say	said	said
see	saw	seen
sell	sold	sold
send	sent	sent
sew	sewed	sewn, sewed
shake	shook	shaken
shine	shone, shined	shone, shined
shrink	shrank	shrunk
shut	shut	shut
sing	sang	sung
sit	sat	sat
sleep	slept	slept
slide	slid	slid
sling	slung	slung
speak	spoke	spoken
spend	spent	spent
stand	stood	stood
steal	stole	stolen
stick	stuck	stuck
sting	stung	stung
stink	stank, stunk	stunk
string	strung	strung
swear	swore	sworn
swim	swam	swum
teach	taught	taught
tear	tore	torn
tell	told	told
think	thought	thought

Present	Past	Past Particple
throw	threw	thrown
wake	woke, waked	woken, waked
wear	wore	worn
win	won	won
write	wrote	written

Exercise 16 **Choosing the Correct Form of Irregular Verbs**

Practice Write the correct form of the verb in parentheses in the following sentences. Be sure to check the list of irregular verbs.

1. My year in the U.S. Marines has ___taught___ (teach) me more than you can imagine.

2. The witness told an incredible story, but he had _____ (swear) to tell the truth, under oath.

3. Last week, when the sun _____ (shine) so brightly, I got a sunburn.

4. On several occasions, the aunts' nasty remarks have _____ (hurt) the child's feelings.

5. My parents were able to buy a house because a good friend ___lent___ (lend) them some money.

6. I was so tired last night I ___lay___ (lie) down for a nap before dinner.

7. Denise and Roy were munching on taco chips and watching the game; by the second half, they had ___eaten___ (eat) all the chips.

8. The burglar heard a noise, so he ___hid___ (hide) in the closet.

9. Marisol had a painful knee injury last summer, but she ___bore___ (bear) her burden with patience.

10. Julie used to be shy, but lately she has ___become___ (become) more outgoing.

Exercise 17
Practice

More on Choosing the Correct Form of Irregular Verbs

Write the correct form of the verb in parentheses in the following sentences. Be sure to check the list of irregular verbs.

1. After the barbecue, he ___swam___ (swim) in the ocean until sundown.

2. When they broke the curfew, Alan and Cody ___strung___ (string) together a complicated story of a flat tire and a traffic jam.

3. Last year you ___led___ (lead) me to believe I was eligible for a scholarship.

4. The travel agent has ___kept___ (keep) his word about the discount air fares.

5. When you didn't call, I was sure you had ___gone___ (go) to the library without me.

6. As the policeman returned the lost kitten, the little boy ___burst___ (burst) into tears.

7. Mr. Dixon wouldn't let us ice skate on the pond; he said the pond had not ___frozen___ (freeze) solid.

8. The soldier was injured in the attack, yet he ___bleed___ (bleed) very little.

9. The runner collapsed because he hadn't ___drank___ (drink) enough fluids.

10. After yesterday's class, we ___chose.___ (choose) to go to a coffee shop for lunch.

Exercise 18
Collaborate

Writing Sentences with Correct Verb Forms

Working with a partner or a group, write two sentences that correctly use each of the following verb forms. Each sentence should be five or more words long. In writing these sentences, you may add helping verbs to the verb forms, but you may *not* change the verb form itself. When your group has completed the exercise, share your answers with another group or with the class. The first one is done for you.

1. verb: flown

sentence 1: <u>To see me, my grandfather has flown nearly a thousand miles.</u>

_____

sentence 2: <u>We usually see ducks, but they have flown south for the winter.</u>

_____

2. verb: lain

sentence 1: _____

_____

sentence 2: _____

_____

3. verb: begun

sentence 1: _____

_____

sentence 2: _____

_____

4. verb: lead

sentence 1: _____

_____

sentence 2: _____

_____

5. verb: rung

sentence 1: _____

_____

sentence 2: _____

_____

6. verb: torn

sentence 1: _____

_____

sentence 2: _____

_____

7. verb: threw

sentence 1: _____

_____

sentence 2: _____

_____

8. verb: wore

sentence 1: _____

_____

sentence 2: _____

_____

9. verb: waked

sentence 1: _____

_____

sentence 2: _____

_____

10. verb: shook

sentence 1: _____

_____

sentence 2: _____

_____

Exercise 19 **Revising a Paragraph That Contains Errors in Irregular Verb Forms**

Connect Nine of the irregular verb forms in the following paragraph are incorrect. Write the correct verb forms in the space above the lines.

I made a big mistake yesterday when I underestimated the power of the sun. Yesterday, I decided to go to the beach and lie in the sun for a while. I hadn't been outside for a while, and I had began to feel unhealthy.

I packed up my car, taking a blanket, some bottled water, and my portable CD player. I didn't take any sunscreen because it was a cloudy day and the sun shined only through the clouds. I laid in the sun for at least an hour before I felt warm. Then I started to feel drowsy and chose to take a short nap. I must have sleeped for quite a while because when I woked up, my skin was hot. By last night, I had became feverish. This morning, I flinged the sheets off my body because my skin felt so fiery. Then I begun to feel chills, as if my body had froze. I had a bad case of overexposure to the sun. If I had only knew what the sun could do to me, I would have been much more careful.

CHAPTER **11**

More on Verb Tenses

HELPING VERBS AND VERB TENSES

The main verb forms—present, past, present participle, and past participle—can be combined with *helping verbs* to create more verb tenses. Following is a list of some common helping verbs:

> **Infobox**
>
> **Some Common Helping Verbs**
>
> | | | | |
> |------|------|------|------|
> | is | was | does | have |
> | am | were | did | had |
> | are | do | has | |

These verbs change their form, depending on the subject:

> She *is* calling the ticket booth.
> I *am* calling the ticket booth

Fixed-Form Helping Verbs

Some other helping verbs always keep the same form, no matter what the subject. These are the **fixed-form helping verbs**. Following are the fixed-form helping verbs:

> **Infobox**
>
> **Fixed-Form Helping Verbs**
>
> | | | | | |
> |-------|-------|-------|--------|------|
> | can | will | may | shall | must |
> | could | would | might | should | |

Notice how the helping verb *can* is in the same form even when the subject changes:

She *can* call the ticket booth.
I *can* call the ticket booth.

The Helping Verbs *can* and *could, will* and *would*

Can is used to show the present tense:

Today, David *can* fix the washer.

Could is used to show the past tense:

Yesterday, David *could* fix the washer.

Could is also used to show a possibility or a wish:

David *could* fix the washer if he had the right tools.
Harry wishes he *could* fix the washer.

Will points to the future from the present:

Cecilia is sure she *will* win the case. (Today, in the present, Cecilia is sure she will win in the future.)

Would points to the future from the past:

Cecilia was sure she *would* win the case. (In the past, Cecilia was sure she would win in the future.)

Would is also used to show a possibility or a wish:

Cecilia *would* win the case if she prepared for it.
Cecilia wishes she *would* win the case.

Exercise 1   **Recognizing Helping Verbs**

Practice   Underline the helping verbs in the following sentences.

1. I do think the referee is right.

2. When the supervisor speaks, you should pay more attention to her.

3. Tomorrow, the weather may turn warmer.

4. Last week, I could hardly speak because I had a bad cold.

5. Now I can speak normally.

6. Does that child ever sleep?

7. If we spend money on a computer, we must select a reliable one.

8. Even though the coach has a temper, she does keep it under control.

9. Desmond went to school in our neighborhood, so he might know my sister.

10. The King of France shall arrive in a golden carriage.

Practice

Selecting *can* or *could*, *will* or *would*

In each of the following sentences, circle the correct helping verb.

1. Casey wished Juanita (will/would) call him more often.

2. Last year, I (can/could) use my husband's cell phone.

3. If the bedrooms were larger, I (will/would) buy the house.

4. When the baby smiles, you (can/could) see his resemblance to his mother.

5. When the phone rang, I (can/could) see Sherman run to answer it.

6. I am sure I (can/could) make the semifinals.

7. Last week, I felt I (can/could) solve the problem.

8. Mike knows that he (will/would) need a better job.

9. The detective believed the suspect (will/would) confess.

10. I wish you (will/would) stop worrying about the bills.

THE PRESENT PROGRESSIVE TENSE

The **progressive tense** uses the present participle (the *-ing* form of the verb) plus some form of *to be*. Following are examples of the **present progressive tense**:

Infobox			
The Present Progressive Tense			
I am walking		we are walking	
you are walking	Singular	you are walking	Plural
he, she, it is walking		they are walking	

All these forms of the present progressive tense use an *-ing* form of the verb (*walking*) plus a present form of *to be* (*am, is, are*).

Be careful not to confuse the present progressive tense with the present tense:

present tense: Terry plays tennis. (This sentence means that Terry *does* play tennis, but it does not say she is doing so at this moment.)
present progressive tense: Terry is playing tennis. (This sentence means that Terry is playing tennis at this moment.)

The present progressive tense shows us that the action is happening right now. The present progressive tense can also show future time:

Terry is playing tennis tomorrow. (This sentence means that Terry will be playing tennis in the future.)

Exercise 3
Practice

Distinguishing Between the Present Tense and the Present Progressive Tense

Circle the correct verb tense in each of the following sentences. Be sure to look carefully at the meaning of each sentence.

1. On Saturdays, we (are doing/do) the laundry.

2. My boyfriend (is playing/plays) softball right now.

3. The doctor cannot see you now; she (is reading/reads) X-rays.

4. Sometimes I (am feeling/feel) happy about my decision.

5. Every time he tells a joke, he (is making/makes) a fool of himself.

6. Occasionally, the engine (is making/makes) a strange noise.

7. Tony is busy; he (is making/makes) tortillas for dinner.

8. Late at night, the dog (is barking/barks) at every little sound.

9. That cut on your hand looks serious; I (am calling/call) the doctor.

10. Whenever it rains, Cynthia and Mike (are taking/take) the bus to school.

THE PAST PROGRESSIVE TENSE

The **past progressive tense** uses the present participle (the *-ing* form of the verb) plus a past form of *to be* (*was, were*). Following are examples of the past progressive tense:

Infobox

The Past Progressive Tense

I was walking	Singular	we were walking	Plural
you were walking		you were walking	
he, she, it was walking		they were walking	

Be careful not to confuse the past progressive tense with the past tense:

past tense: George walked carefully. (This sentence implies that George has stopped walking.)

past progressive tense: George was walking carefully when he slipped on the ice. (This sentence says that George was in the process of walking when something else happened: he slipped.)

Use the progressive tenses, both present and past, when you want to show that something was or is in progress.

Exercise 4 **Distinguishing Between the Past Tense and the Past Progressive Tense**

Practice Circle the correct verb tense in each of the following sentences. Be sure to look carefully at the meaning of each sentence.

1. I (was changing/changed) my baby's diaper when she suddenly started to scream.

2. My sister (was painting/painted) her kitchen last night.

3. After I drank the cocoa, I (was sleeping/slept) soundly.

4. James (was calling/called) me before he called Marcia.

5. Sylvia and her mother (were driving/drove) back to Texas when they heard the news on the car radio.

6. When I was seven, I (was playing/played) softball.

7. Emily (was cooking/cooked) when the stove caught fire.

8. I (was staring/stared) out the window when the teacher called on me.

9. Clifford usually drives carelessly, but he (is driving/drives) carefully right now.

10. He (is calling/calls) me all the time.

THE PRESENT PERFECT TENSE

The **present perfect tense** is made up of the past participle form of the verb plus *have* or *has* as a helping verb. Following are examples of the present perfect tense:

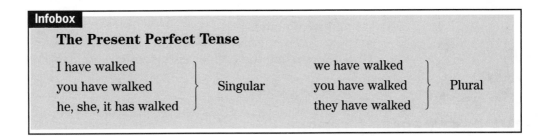

Infobox
The Present Perfect Tense

I have walked			we have walked		
you have walked	}	Singular	you have walked	}	Plural
he, she, it has walked			they have walked		

Be careful not to confuse the present perfect tense with the past tense:

past tense: Jacqueline *studied* yoga for two years. (This sentence means that Jacqueline doesn't study yoga anymore, but she did study it in the past.)

present perfect tense: Jacqueline *has studied* yoga for two years. (This sentence means that Jacqueline started studying yoga two years ago, and she is still studying it.)

The present perfect tense is used to show an action that started in the past but is still going on in the present.

Exercise 5   **Distinguishing Between the Past and Present Perfect Tenses**

Practice   Circle the correct verb tense in each of the following sentences. Be sure to look carefully at the meaning of each sentence.

1. Last week, Chief Ryman (captured/has captured) the convict who
   escaped from the Pines Correctional Institution.

2. Our neighbors (dumped/have dumped) their garbage in an empty lot for
   many years now.

3. My arthritis (was giving/has been giving) me trouble, yet I am reluctant
   to go to the doctor.

4. He (served/has served) in the navy but left to become a police officer.

5. Nancy canceled her plane reservations and (notified/has notified) the
   car rental agency.

6. Ice cream (was/has been) a popular dessert for years now.

7. We (worked/have worked) together at the Farmers' Market for six
   months and are now opening our own restaurant.

8. Lenny (contacted/has contacted) four dry cleaning stores and finally
   found one that cleans curtains.

9. I (waited/have waited) at the bus stop for an hour, and then I gave up
   and went home.

10. The cook and the cashier at the coffee shop (worked/have worked)
    here since 1997.

THE PAST PERFECT TENSE

The **past perfect tense** is made up of the past participle form of the verb with *had* as a helping verb. You can use the past perfect tense to show more than one event in the past; that is, you can use it to show when two or more events happened in the past but at different times:

past tense: Alan *cut* the grass.

past perfect tense: Alan *had cut* the grass by the time David arrived.
(Alan cut the grass *before* David arrived. Both events happened in the past, but one happened earlier than the other.)

past tense: The professor *lectured* for an hour.

past perfect tense: The professor *had lectured* for an hour when he pulled out a surprise quiz. (Lecturing came first; pulling out a surprise quiz came second. Both actions are in the past.)

The past perfect is especially useful because you write most of your essays in the past tense, and you often need to get further back into the past. Just remember to use *had* with the past participle of the verb, and you'll have the past perfect tense.

Exercise 6	**Distinguishing Between the Past and Past Perfect Tenses**
Practice	Circle the correct verb tense in the following sentences. Be sure to look carefully at the meaning of each sentence.

1. The bird (flew/had flown) out of the cage only seconds before I raced to close the cage door.

2. I needed crutches last week because I (reinjured/had reinjured) my knee playing football a month earlier.

3. Crystal won the art contest yesterday; she (worked/had worked) to win the award for years.

4. At the family dinner, I (kept/had kept) silent while my brother bragged about his new job.

5. Every Sunday, Leon (went/had gone) to lunch at his favorite Cuban restaurant.

6. Marian's mother wanted to know if we (left/had left) a package at her front door.

7. As Thomas (drove/had driven) the car with one hand, he used his other hand to point out famous landmarks.

8. My sister (finished/had finished) the coconut cake by the time I was ready for dessert.

9. He wondered if Sheila (tossed/had tossed) out the newspaper earlier in the day.

10. When the dog barked excitedly, the old man (ran/had run) to the window.

Small Reminders About Verbs

There are a few errors that people tend to make with verbs. If you are aware of these errors, you will be on the lookout for them as you edit your writing.

Used to: Be careful when you write that someone *used to* do, say, or feel something. It is incorrect to write *use to*.

not this: Wendy ~~use to~~ make pancakes for breakfast.
but this: Wendy *used to* make pancakes for breakfast.

not this: They ~~use to~~ live on my street.
but this: They *used to* live on my street.

Supposed to: Be careful when you write that someone is *supposed to* do, say, or feel something. It is incorrect to write *suppose to*.

not this: He was ~~suppose to~~ repair my watch yesterday.
but this: He was *supposed to* repair my watch yesterday.

not this: I am ~~suppose to~~ make dinner tomorrow.
but this: I am *supposed to* make dinner tomorrow.

Could have, should have, would have: Using *of* instead of *have* is another error with verbs.

not this: He ~~could of~~ sent me a card.
but this: He *could have* sent me a card.

not this: You ~~should of~~ been more careful.
but this: You *should have* been more careful.

not this: Norman ~~would of~~ enjoyed the music.
but this: Norman *would have* enjoyed the music.

Would have/had: If you are writing about something that might have been possible but that did not happen, use *had* as the helping verb.

not this: If he ~~would have~~ been friendlier, he would not be alone now.
but this: If he *had* been friendlier, he would not be alone now.

not this: I wish the plane fare ~~would have~~ cost less.
but this: I wish the plane fare *had* cost less.

not this: If David ~~would have~~ controlled his temper, he would be a free man today.
but this: If David *had* controlled his temper, he would be a free man today.

Exercise 7 **Editing a Paragraph for Small Errors in Verbs**

Connect

Correct the eight errors in *used to, supposed to, could have, should have, would have,* and *would have/had* in the following paragraph. Write your corrections in the space above the lines.

Looking back on my high school years, I realize I should have acted

differently. First, I am sorry that I didn't take my senior year seriously. I

use to cut classes all the time in my last year of high school. I believed

that senior year was my last chance to play and to live a wild life because

I would soon be working a full-time job or attending college. If I would have taken senior year more seriously, I would be having an easier time in my college classes, especially my math class. I should of paid attention to my high school math teacher when he said I was suppose to study more. He warned me that I needed to know certain basic concepts if I wanted to survive in college. I could of learned a great deal from that man. Last, I wish I would of taken a foreign language in high school. Then I could of entered college with a foundation in French or Spanish and gone into an intermediate level course. Instead, I am now required to take both Elementary and Intermediate French or Spanish in order to graduate. If I would have known in my senior year what I know now, I would be having an easier time in college.

Exercise 8   **Writing Sentences with the Correct Verb Forms**

👥 Collaborate   Do this exercise with a partner or a group. Write or complete each of the following sentences. When you have finished the exercise, be ready to share your answers with the group or with the class.

1. Complete this sentence and add a verb in the correct tense:
   He had spoken to my mother before he

   _____

   _____

2. Write a sentence that uses the words *done volunteer work* in the middle of the sentence.

   _____

   _____

3. Complete this sentence and add a verb in the correct tense:
   The painter was standing on the top rung of the ladder when he

   _____

   _____

4. Write a sentence that includes the phrases *have been* and *for three years*.

   _____

   _____

5. Complete this sentence: If Larry had taken better care of his car,

_____

_____

6. Write a sentence that contains the words *would have*.

_____

_____

7. Write a sentence that includes both these helping verbs: *can* and *could*.

_____

_____

8. Complete this sentence:
By the time the police arrived, the robbers

_____

_____

9. Write a sentence that includes the words *for many years* and *has given*.

_____

_____

10. Write a sentence that includes the words *Our family used to.*

_____

_____

Exercise 9 A Comprehensive Exercise: Editing a Paragraph for Errors in
Connect **Verb Tense**

Correct the eight errors in verb tense in the following paragraph. Write your
corrections in the space above the lines.

An experience yesterday showed me just how resourceful I can be.

Late in the afternoon, I was alone in the office, working overtime. I just

finished my work at my workstation when I smelled smoke. I have ran to

the outer office, where I saw deep gray smoke coming from a wastepaper

basket. I was approaching the basket carefully; then I saw a large flame at

the center of the smoke. The flame had already spread from the basket to a nearby cardboard box. Immediately, I took action. I did not stop to search frantically for a fire extinguisher. I did not run back to my desk to grab my briefcase or laptop. Instead, I was rushing outside to safety and had used my cell phone to call the fire department. I was calming down when the firefighters arrived. They were saying I have done the right thing by leaving a room full of paper and flammable chemicals like toner for the copy machine. In the past, I often hoped I would behave well in a crisis. Now I know I could.

CHAPTER 12

Verbs: Consistency and Voice

Remember that your choice of verb form indicates the time (tense) of your statements. Be careful not to shift from one tense to another unless you have a reason to change the time.

CONSISTENT VERB TENSE

Staying in one tense (unless you have a reason to change tenses) is called **consistency of verb tense.**

incorrect shifts in tense:

He *raced* through the yellow light, *stepped* on the gas, and *cuts* off a driver in the left lane.

A woman in a black dress *holds* a handkerchief to her face and *moaned* softly.

You can correct these errors by putting all the verbs in the same tense:

consistent present tense:

He *races* through the yellow light, *steps* on the gas, and *cuts* off a driver in the left lane.

A woman in a black dress *holds* a handkerchief to her face and *moans* softly.

consistent past tense:

He *raced* through the yellow light, *stepped* on the gas, and *cut* off a driver in the left lane.

A woman in a black dress *held* a handkerchief to her face and *moaned* softly.

Whether you correct the errors by changing all the verbs to the present tense or by changing them all to the past tense, you are making the tense *consistent*. Consistency of verb tense is important when you describe events because it helps the reader understand what happened and when it happened.

Exercise 1 Correcting Sentences That Are Inconsistent in Tense

Practice In each sentence that follows, one verb is inconsistent in tense. Cross it out and write the correct tense above it. The first one is done for you.

1. The driver was extremely apologetic: she took full responsibility for the
   looked
   fender-bender, offered to pay all costs, and ~~looks~~ very concerned.

2. When the leaves fall from the trees, my husband buys a stack of fire-
   wood, cleaned the fireplace, and builds a warm, comforting fire.

3. Annoying sales calls come at dinnertime and offer us magazine sub-
   scriptions, invite us to buy insurance, or urged us to get a burial plot.

4. Ronald and I belong to the same gym, and we ran into one another in
   the pool or meet in the weight room.

5. My father took his car to City Automotive because he likes the service
   and trusted the mechanics.

6. For three days in a row we tried calling the station, but the line was
   always busy and we lose our patience.

7. He answers my questions sarcastically and seems irritated if I wanted
   an explanation for his behavior.

8. Because the park closed at sundown, local teens lose a gathering place
   and looked for somewhere else to meet.

9. In our biology class, we went over the test grades and reviewed the test
   questions, but we run out of time for the new material.

10. Although Lucy claims she is on a budget, she spent more than I do
    when we go shopping.

Exercise 2 Editing Paragraphs for Consistency of Tense

Connect Read the following paragraphs. Then cross out any verbs that are inconsistent in
tense and write your corrections above them. Each paragraph has four errors.

1. For my children, summer vacation means freedom from school, but it
   is a difficult time for me. My two boys, Adam, age six, and Troy, age
   seven, loved being out of school. They enjoy staying up late on week

nights and sleeping late in the morning. They are thrilled not to have homework, and they expect the vacation period to be a long series of fun and games. I, on the other hand, was confronted with several questions. I have to find someone or some place willing to care for my boys while I was at my job. Summer camp is expensive, and a five-day-a-week sitter cost a fortune. I do not want to leave the boys with my mother; they get bored, and she is too old to handle them. It takes some thinking, but eventually I find ways to handle my vacation dilemma. I usually find an activities program at the local YMCA and pay a neighbor to watch the boys after the program. My sons are happy, and I am relieved that the summer problems are solved.

2. Raoul discovered a whole new side of himself when he took an art class. At first Raoul did not want to take the class at all, but he needed a humanities class in order to get his college degree. Since all the music and theater classes were closed, Raoul has no choice but to sign up for a design class. He was sure the class would be full of talented artists, and that he, a beginner, will make a fool of himself. However, the class is an introductory class, and everyone in it was on the same level as Raoul. He soon discovered that he loved working with lines and colors and creating such things as album covers and posters. Raoul's teacher praised Raoul for some outstanding work. Over the semester, Raoul developed an appreciation for art and learns the importance of design in everyday objects like billboards, magazines, and store windows.

Exercise 3 Rewriting a Paragraph for Consistent Verb Tenses

Collaborate The following paragraph has many inconsistencies in verb tenses: it shifts between past and present tenses. Working with a group, write two versions of the paragraph. Write one in the present tense, then a second one in the past tense. Split your activity; half the group can write it in one tense while the other half writes it in the other tense. After both rewrites are complete, read the new paragraphs aloud to both parts of the team, as a final check.

My first car is a compromise car. I can't afford what I want, so I have to compromise. It's an old Ford with 100,000 miles on the speedometer. The car **is** not too attractive on the outside: the paint job is dull from years of exposure to the sun, a piece of chrome has fallen off, and two of the tires **are** missing hubcaps. Mechanically, the car is a mix of good and bad. My Ford **starts** right up on the coldest mornings, but the brake linings are shot, and the car guzzles gas. As for the interior, the upholstery is torn, so I **disguise** the tear with cheap seat covers. The dash has a small crack; on the other hand, the speakers **are** in good shape. What I want **is** a shiny, fast, new sport-utility vehicle. What I have is an ancient Taurus.

But it is mine, and it runs.

PASSIVE AND ACTIVE VOICE

Verbs not only have tenses; they have voices. When the subject in the sentence is doing something, the verb is in the **active voice.** When something is done to the subject, the verb is in the **passive voice.**

active voice:

I designed the album cover. (*I*, the subject, did it.)
My friends from college raised money for the homeless shelter. (*Friends*, the subject, did it.)

passive voice:

The album cover was designed by me. (The *cover*, the subject, didn't do anything. It received the action—it was designed.)
Money for the homeless shelter was raised by my friends from college. (*Money*, the subject, didn't do anything. It received the action—it was raised.)

Notice what happens when you use the passive voice instead of the active voice:

active voice: I designed the album cover.
passive voice: The album cover was designed by me.

The sentence in the passive voice is two words longer than the one in the active voice. However, the sentence that uses the passive voice doesn't add any information, nor does it state the facts any more clearly than the one in the active voice.

Using the passive voice can make your sentences wordy, it can slow them down, and it can make them boring. The passive voice can also confuse readers. When the subject isn't doing anything, readers may have to look carefully to see who or what *is* doing something. Look at this sentence, for example:

A famous city landmark is being torn down.

Who is tearing down the landmark? In this sentence, it's impossible to find the answer to that question.

Of course, there will be times when you have to use the passive voice. For example, you may have to use it when you don't know who did something, as in these sentences:

Lana's car was stolen last week.
A bag of garbage was scattered all over my neighbor's lawn.

But in general, you should avoid using the passive voice; instead, rewrite sentences so they are in the active voice.

Exercise 4 **Rewriting Sentences, Changing the Passive Voice to the Active Voice**

Practice

In the following sentences, change the passive voice to the active voice. If the original sentence doesn't tell you who or what performed the action, add words that tell you who or what did it. The first one is done for you.

1. One of Shakespeare's plays was performed at Green River High School last night.

   rewritten: <u>Students at Green River High School performed one of Shake-</u>

   <u>speare's plays last night.</u>

2. Cecilia was promoted to assistant manager of Quality Food Mart by her boss.

   rewritten: _____

   _____

3. An offer to buy the house was made.

   rewritten: _____

   _____

4. On some weekends, the beach is closed by the lifeguards.

   rewritten: _____

   _____

5. José's father was rescued from a burning house.

   rewritten: _____

   _____

6. An agreement has been signed by the buyer and the seller.

   rewritten: _____

   _____

7. A delicious breakfast was made and eaten.

rewritten: _____

_____

8. Apologies for the cruel joke have been offered.

rewritten: _____

_____

9. Great care was put into the preparations for the party.

rewritten: _____

_____

10. A number of alternatives were considered by the disciplinary committee.

rewritten: _____

_____

Exercise 5 **Rewriting a Paragraph, Changing It to the Active Voice**

Collaborate

Do this exercise with a partner or a group. Rewrite the paragraph below, changing all verbs that are in the passive voice to the active voice. To make these changes, you may have to add words, omit words, or change the structure of sentences. Write your changes in the space above the lines. Be ready to read your new version of the paragraph to another group or to the class.

Last night an important decision was reached by the city council. A decision to add bike paths along all main roads was made. Cyclists have been made overjoyed by the news because the paths have been campaigned for, by cyclists, for years. Dangerous conditions have been suffered by the bike riders. In addition, harassment by impatient motorists has been frequently endured by cyclists. An ugly conflict between drivers and cyclists was created by the lack of bike paths. But all the bad feeling and danger have been removed by the city council. Bicycle riding will be made safer and more pleasant by bike paths.

Avoiding Unnecessary Shifts in Voice

Just as you should be consistent in the tense of verbs, you should be consistent in the voice of verbs. Do not shift from active to passive, or vice versa, without a good reason to do so.

active   **passive**
shift: *Carl wrote* the song, but the *credit was taken* by Tom.

active   **active**
rewritten: *Carl wrote* the song, but *Tom took* the credit.

passive
shift: Several *suggestions were made* by the vice president,

active
yet the *president rejected* all of them.

active
rewritten: The *vice president made* several suggestions, yet

active
the *president rejected* all of them.

Being consistent can help you to write clearly and smoothly.

Exercise 6	**Rewriting Sentences to Correct Shifts in Voice**

Practice

Rewrite the following sentences so that all the verbs are in the active voice. You may change the wording to make the sentences clear, smooth, and consistent in voice.

1. My feelings were hurt by Andrea when she called me selfish.

rewritten: _____

_____

2. A set of keys was found in the purse; the detective also discovered an old photograph in the purse.

rewritten: _____

_____

3. Lamar's attitude can be changed by you because you are honest with him.

rewritten: _____

_____

4. It was agreed by a group of neighbors that the grass needs regular cutting.

rewritten: _____

_____

5. The crowd cheered the Olympic swimmer as a record for the backstroke was broken by her.

rewritten: _____

_____

6. I was healthy all year until I was given the measles.

   rewritten: _____

   _____

7. If a secret meeting was set up by the players, they didn't tell me.

   rewritten: _____

   _____

8. The teacher expected excellence and a serious attitude was demanded from her students.

   rewritten: _____

   _____

9. Some of my classmates are money-hungry; new cars, jewelry, and fine clothes are worshiped.

   rewritten: _____

   _____

10. Minneapolis was chosen by the committee as the site of the conference; it is an accessible and friendly city.

    rewritten: _____

    _____

Exercise 7   **Editing a Paragraph for Consistency in Voice**

Connect   The following paragraph contains five unnecessary shifts to the passive voice. Correct these shifts by writing above the errors. You can add words, omit words, or change words.

> When we invited friends to dinner, Dale and I worked together and cleaned the apartment in no time. It was felt that we should fix up the apartment for our guests. We did not want them to think we lived like pigs, so we put our heads together. Soon, a plan for a quick cleanup was devised. Beds were to be made by Dale, and I would pick up all the clothes on the floor. Then the kitchen was to be cleaned while Dale vacuumed the living room. We worked fast since our friends were arriving in an hour. Just before they arrived, a reasonably clean apartment had been created by us. We were proud to show our friends the results of our hard work.

Exercise 8

Connect **A Comprehensive Exercise: Editing a Paragraph for Errors in Consistent Verb Tense and Voice**

The following paragraph has four errors related to verb tense and voice. Correct the errors in the space above the lines.

If Danielle had taken my advice, then a better choice would have been made by her. Instead, she rushed into the purchase of a car and bought a lemon. She didn't listen to my warnings about getting a mechanic to test the car before she bought it, or about shopping around for the best car deal. Danielle is too eager to have her own car, so she took the first car that caught her eye. She was impetuous and impatient for years. In all the time I have known her, Danielle has never stopped to think, and she did not think clearly yesterday. Rushing into a bad deal, she purchased a car with a cracked engine block and bad brakes. Danielle just signs the papers on the dotted line and wasted much of her money.

Making Subjects and Verbs Agree

Subjects and verbs have to agree in number. This means that a singular subject must be matched with a singular verb form and a plural subject must be matched with a plural verb form.

singular subject, singular verb
Nicole races out of the house in the morning.

plural subject,   **plural verb**
Christine, Michael, and Marie take the train to work.

singular subject, singular verb
The old *song reminds* me of Mexico.

plural subject, plural verb
Greasy *hamburgers upset* my stomach.

Caution: Remember that a regular verb has an *-s* ending in one singular form in the present tense—the form that goes with *he, she, it,* or their equivalents:

-*s* endings in the present tense:

He *takes* good care of his dog.
She *concentrates* on her assignments.
It *looks* like a nice day.
Eddie *buys* high-octane gasoline.
Nancy *seems* pleased.
The apartment *comes* with cable television.

PRONOUNS USED AS SUBJECTS

Pronouns can be used as subjects. **Pronouns** are words that take the place of nouns. When pronouns are used as subjects, they must agree in number with verbs.

Following is a list of the subject pronouns and the regular verb forms that agree with them, in the present tense:

Infobox

Subject Pronouns and Present Tense Verb Forms

Pronoun	Verb	
I	walk	
you	walk	all singular forms
he, she, it	walks	
we	walk	
you	walk	all plural forms
they	walk	

In all of the following sentences, the pronoun used as the subject of the sentence agrees in number with the verb:

singular pronoun, singular verb
I take good care of my daughter.

singular pronoun, singular verb
You sing like a professional entertainer.

singular pronoun, singular verb
She argues with conviction and courage.

plural pronoun, plural verb
We want a better deal on the apartment.

plural pronoun, plural verb
They accept my decision about moving.

Exercise 1   **Editing a Paragraph for Simple Errors in Subject-Verb Agreement**

Connect   There are six errors in subject-verb agreement in the following paragraph. If a verb does not agree with its subject, cross out the incorrect verb form and write the correct one above it.

My brother has a Saturday ritual that never varies. He always wake up at the same time, 7:00 a.m. The first thing he do is jog around the neighborhood to get his energy level up. Then he goes to the coffee shop on our street and brings home cups of freshly brewed coffee and a bag of jelly doughnuts. As he eats this breakfast, he watches cartoons on television. They are stupid, he admits, but they makes him laugh. After the cartoons are over, he gets in his car and drives to his friend Joe's house. He and Joe watches any game— football, basketball, hockey—they can find on television. Drinking Pepsi and eating potato chips, they watch the games all afternoon. When it is time for dinner, they head for a sports bar that show games on a big-screen television. My brother love his Saturdays of sports and junk food.

SPECIAL PROBLEMS WITH AGREEMENT

Agreement seems fairly simple, doesn't it? If a subject is singular, you use a singular verb form; if a subject is plural, you use a plural verb form. However, there are certain problems with agreement that will come up in your writing. Sometimes it is difficult to find the subject of a sentence; at other times it can be hard to determine whether a subject is singular or plural.

Finding the Subject

When you are checking for subject-verb agreement, you can find the real subject of the sentence by first eliminating the prepositional phrases. To find the real subject, put parentheses around the prepositional phrases. Then it will be easy to find the subject because nothing in a prepositional phrase can be the subject of a sentence.

prepositional phrases in parentheses:

A *person* (with good math skills) *is* a good candidate (for the job).

One (of the children) (from the village) (in the hills) *is* my cousin.

The *restaurant* (down the road) (from Cindy's house) *is* open all night.

Roy, (with his charm and style), *is* popular (with the ladies).

Exercise 2 **Finding the Subject and Verb by Recognizing Prepositional Phrases**

Practice Put parentheses around all the prepositional phrases in the following sentences, and identify the subject and verb by writing *S* or *V* above them.

1. A person with your talents is an asset to any company.

2. The cookies in the dairy case at the supermarket are slice-and-bake cookies for busy families.

3. With no sense of responsibility, Jeff missed the most important day of his son's life.

4. The beautiful cat on my bed is a former stray from the animal shelter.

5. The people at the end of the line are some friends of mine from Davenport.

6. A salesperson from an insurance company offered us a deal on his life insurance.

7. One of the funniest movies on my list of all-time favorites is <u>Scream</u>, a horror film with many laughs.

8. In the autumn, she carves a pumpkin into a smiling face.

9. In a panic, I searched between the pages of the newspaper for my lost credit card.

10. On his day off, Nelson drives from Parkview to Kingsbury in three hours.

Exercise 3 **Selecting the Correct Verb Form by Identifying Prepositional Phrases**

Practice In the following sentences, put parentheses around all the prepositional phrases; then circle the verb that agrees with the subject.

1. The girl with the dark eyes (is/are) giving me a signal from the other side of the room.

2. Several of the items in her closet (is/are) worth a great deal of money.

3. A realistic assessment of the city's problems (is/are) coming from the director of the budget committee.

4. The commuters on the stalled train (has/have) no idea of the length of the delay.

5. A quick meal between classes (isn't/aren't) good for your digestion.

6. The last bell of the school day (was/were) a signal for whooping and shouting among the students.

7. One of the letters on the table (is/are) a note from your mother with a check in it.

8. The oil stain under my car (makes/make) me afraid of big car repair bills.

9. One of the easiest forms of exercise (is/are) walking with a dog.

10. A representative of the airlines (has/have) announced a delay in the departure of the flight.

Changed Word Order

You are probably used to looking for the subject of a sentence in front of the verb, but not all sentences follow this pattern. Questions, sentences beginning with words like *here* or *there*, and other sentences change the word order. Therefore, you have to check carefully for subject-verb agreement:

sentences with changed word order:

      V   S
Where *are* the *packages*?

      V   S   V
When *is Mr. Hernandez giving* the exam?

      V   S

Behind the trees *is* a picnic *table*.

     V   S

There *are crumbs* on the floor.

     V   S

There *is* an *answer* to your question.

Exercise 4   **Making Subjects and Verbs Agree in Sentences with**
Practice   **Changed Word Order**

In each of the following sentences, underline the subject; then circle the correct verb form.

1. There (is/are) some unhappy people on that plane.

2. Among the travelers (was/were) a tourist from a small city in China.

3. Beneath the cherry trees (sits/sit) a bird with bright yellow feathers.

4. When (is/are) your grandparents moving to California?

5. By the edge of the road (was/were) a vegetable stand with bright

orange pumpkins.

6. Here (is/are) your copies of the lease.

7. At the back of my mind (was/were) a plan for the term paper.

8. Where (has/have) the football players gone?

9. From the top of the stadium (comes/come) a piercing scream.

10. Beyond the city limits (is/are) a popular night club and a sports club.

Exercise 5   **Writing Sentences with Subject-Verb Agreement in**
Collaborate   **Changed Word Order**

Do this exercise with a partner or a group. Complete the following, making each into a sentence. Be sure the subject and verb agree. The first one is done for you.

1. From the back of the room came three loud cheers._____

2. At the back of the dark closet hides _____

3. There are _____

4. Among the objects in the treasure chest was _____

5. Beyond the mountains is _____

6. Below the old castle stand _____

7. With every good action comes _____

8. On the edge of the bridge is _____

9. Around the concert stage sit _____

10. Here is _____

Compound Subjects

A **compound subject** is two or more subjects joined by *and, or,* or *nor.*
When subjects are joined by *and,* they are usually plural:

compound subjects joined by *and*:

  S   S   V
Bill and *Chris are* good tennis players.

      S   S   V
The *garage* and the *basement are* full of water.

     S   S V
A *restaurant* and a *motel are* across the road.

Caution: Be sure to check for a compound subject when the word order
changes.

compound subjects in changed word order:

      V   S   S
There *are* a *restaurant* and a *motel* across the road. (Two things, a restaurant and a motel, are across the road.)

      V   S   S
Here *are* your *notebook* and *pencil.* (Your notebook and pencil, two
things, are here.)

When subjects are joined by *or, either . . . or, neither . . . nor, not only
. . . but also,* the verb form agrees with the subject closest to the verb.

**compound subjects with *or, either . . . or, neither . . . nor, not only
. . . but also*:**

singular S   plural S   plural V
Christine or the *neighbors are* making dinner.

   plural S   singular S singular V
The *neighbors* or *Christine is* making dinner.

        singular S   plural S plural V
Not only my *mother* but also my *brothers were* delighted with the gift.

        plural S   singular S singular V
Not only my *brothers* but also my *mother was* delighted with the gift.

      plural S   singular S singular V
Either the *tenants* or the *landlord has* to back down.

      singular S   plural S plural V
Either the *landlord* or the *tenants have* to back down.

      plural S   singular S singular V
Neither the rose *bushes* nor the lemon *tree fits* in that corner of the yard.

      singular S   plural S plural V
Neither the lemon *tree* nor the rose *bushes fit* in that corner of the yard.

Exercise 6 Making Subjects and Verbs Agree: Compound Subjects

Practice Circle the correct form of the verb in each of the following sentences.

1. Heavy blankets or a thick quilt (is/are) essential in this cold weather.

2. After that enormous dinner, Stephen and Michelle (was/were) ready to fall asleep.

3. There (is/are) a new movie theater and a pizza place near the mall.

4. Either Ms. Lin or her uncles (subscribes/subscribe) to *Newsweek*.

5. At the bottom of the page (is/are) a photograph of the Vietnam Wall and a poem.

6. The boys or the baby sitter (is/are) at home.

7. Here (is/are) a box of toys from your kindergarten days and an old scrapbook.

8. Not only the bus driver but also the passengers (is/are) enjoying the new bus.

9. Professor Wykowski or Professor Stein (is/are) lecturing on acid rain today.

10. Washing my car and listening to my tapes (was/were) typical weekend activities for me.

Exercise 7 Recognizing Subjects and Verbs: A Review

Practice Being sure that subjects and verbs agree often depends on recognizing subjects and verbs in sentences with changed word order, prepositional phrases, and compound subjects. To review the subject-verb patterns of sentences, underline all the subjects and verbs in the following selection. Put an *S* above the subjects and a *V* above the verbs.

This excerpt is from an essay by Edna Buchanan, formerly a prize-winning journalist for the *Miami Herald* and now a famous crime novelist.

Miami's Most Dangerous Profession

Miami's most dangerous profession is not police work or fire fighting;

it is driving a cab. For taxi drivers, many of them poor immigrants,

murder is an occupational hazard. All-night gas station attendants and

convenience store clerks used to be at high risk, but steps were taken to protect them. Gas pumps now switch to self-serve after dark, with exact change only, and the attendants are locked in bullet-proof booths. Convenience stores were redesigned and drop safes were installed, leaving little cash available.

But the life of a taxi driver is just as risky as it was twenty years ago when I covered my first killing of a cabbie. Bullet-proof glass could be placed between the driver and passengers, but most owners say it is too expensive, and besides, there is no foolproof way to protect oneself totally from somebody riding in the same car.

Indefinite Pronouns

Certain pronouns, called **indefinite pronouns,** always take a singular verb.

Infobox			
Indefinite Pronouns			
one	nobody	nothing	each
anyone	anybody	anything	either
someone	somebody	something	neither
everyone	everybody	everything	

If you want to write clearly and correctly, you must memorize these words and remember that they always use singular verbs. Using your common sense isn't enough because some of these words seem plural: for example, *everybody* seems to mean more than one person—but in grammatically correct English, it takes a singular verb. Here are some examples of the pronouns used with singular verbs:

indefinite pronouns and singular verbs:

singular S   singular V
Each of my friends *is* athletic.

singular S   singular V
Everyone in the supermarket *is looking* for a bargain.

singular S   singular V
Anybody from our Spanish class *is* capable of translating the letter.

singular S   singular V
Someone from the maintenance department *is working* on the heater.

singular S   singular V
One of Roberta's nieces *is* in my sister's ballet class.

singular S   singular V
Neither of the cakes *is* expensive.

You can memorize the indefinite pronouns as the *-one, -thing,* and *-body* words—every*one,* every*thing,* every*body,* and so on, plus *each, either,* and *neither.*

Exercise 8 **Making Subjects and Verbs Agree: Using Indefinite Pronouns**

Practice Circle the correct verb in the following sentences.

1. Anybody from the southern states (knows/know) about hot summers.

2. Each of the boys (sends/send) money to Aunt Lucille.

3. (Is/Are) something the matter with the television?

4. Nothing in the refrigerator (looks/look) appetizing.

5. Neither of the dogs (barks/bark) when the doorbell rings.

6. Someone in our neighborhood (is/are) playing a radio.

7. Everything in the attic and in the basement (needs/need) to be sorted and boxed.

8. I don't think anybody in our family (wants/want) a big celebration for New Year's Eve.

9. Something in the soup or in the vegetables (smells/smell) strange.

10. One of Matthew's worst habits (is/are) worrying about insignificant details.

Exercise 9 **More on Making Subjects and Verbs Agree: Using Indefinite Pronouns**

Practice Circle the correct verb in the following sentences.

1. Here (is/are) everybody from school.

2. Nobody with good math skills (is/are) afraid of that test.

3. Everybody in my exercise class (wears/wear) black tee shirts.

4. (Has/Have) anyone from White Plains called?

5. Somebody at the movies (was/were) annoying me.

6. If you look closely, nothing in those books (talks/talk) about the subject.

7. I know that neither of the brothers (has/have) an athletic scholarship.

8. Each of the muffins (is/are) wrapped in tissue paper.

9. Anyone from the suburbs (has/have) to take the train to the city.

10. You can have rice pudding or lemon cake; either (is/are) included in the price of the dinner.

Exercise 10 **Editing for Subject-Verb Agreement in a Paragraph with**
Connect **Indefinite Pronouns**

The following paragraph has five errors in agreement of indefinite pronouns and verbs. Correct the errors in the space above the lines.

It is unfortunate that many people refuse to get involved in their community. Of course, everyone in town have some excuse for not doing volunteer work, joining a club, or participating in a community program. One of the biggest excuses is, "I'm too busy." But everyone knows, deep down, that people can always find time to do what they truly want to do. Everybody in our hectic society cope with responsibilities at home, or at work, or at school, yet sometimes the busiest people are the ones who find time to get involved in their communities. Another common excuse is, "I don't have any talents to offer a club or a volunteer group." Talent, however, is not required, for it doesn't take talent to clean up a neglected park. Anybody are capable of serving food in a soup kitchen. Somebody with no singing voice or musical skills are still welcome at a community playhouse, to build scenery or sell tickets. There are something for everybody to contribute to a community, and contributing can be fun.

Collective Nouns

Collective nouns refer to more than one person or thing.

> **Infobox**
>
> **Some Common Collective Nouns**
>
> | | | |
> |---|---|---|
> | team | company | council |
> | class | corporation | government |
> | committee | family | group |
> | audience | jury | crowd |

Collective nouns usually take a singular verb.

collective nouns and singular verbs:

singular S singular V
The *class is meeting* in the library today.

singular S singular V
The *audience was bored.*

singular S   singular V
The *jury is examining* the evidence.

A singular verb is used because the group is meeting, or feeling bored, or examining, *as one unit.*

Collective nouns take a plural verb *only* when the members of the group are acting individually, not as a unit.

collective noun with a plural verb:

plural S   plural V
The football *team are arguing* among themselves. (The phrase *among themselves* shows that the team is not acting as one unit.)

Exercise 11 **Making Subjects and Verbs Agree: Using Collective Nouns**

Practice Circle the correct verb in each of the following sentences.

1. His family (is/are) celebrating the Fourth of July with a big barbecue

at home.

2. The Classic Automobile Club (was/were) founded in 1965.

3. The board of directors (is/are) considering the cost of advertising for

a new treasurer.

4. The company with the most awards for quality (is/are) Food Service

America.

5. My team of bowlers (is/are) friendly and funny.

6. The jury (has/have) reached a verdict.

7. A group of visitors to the museum (was/were) quarreling among

themselves.

8. After the concert, the audience (was/were) screaming for an encore.

9. While the coach lectures and shouts, the team (looks/look) serious.

10. Our Student Council never (sponsors/sponsor) dances on weeknights.

MAKING SUBJECTS AND VERBS AGREE: A REVIEW

As you have probably realized, making subjects and verbs agree is not as simple as it first appears. But if you can remember the basic ideas in this section, you will be able to apply them automatically as you edit your own writing. Following is a quick summary of subject-verb agreement:

> **Infobox**
>
> ### Making Subjects and Verbs Agree: A Summary
>
> 1. Subjects and verbs should agree in number: singular subjects get singular verbs; plural subjects get plural verbs.
> 2. When pronouns are used as subjects, they must agree in number with verbs.
> 3. Nothing in a prepositional phrase can be the subject of a sentence.
> 4. Questions, sentences beginning with *here* or *there*, and other sentences can change word order.
> 5. Compound subjects joined by *and* are usually plural.
> 6. When subjects are joined by *or, either . . . or, neither . . . nor*, or *not only . . . but also*, the verb form agrees with the subject closest to the verb.
> 7. Indefinite pronouns always take singular verbs.
> 8. Collective nouns usually take singular verbs.

Exercise 12   **A Comprehensive Exercise on Subject-Verb Agreement**

Practice   This exercise covers all the rules on subject-verb agreement. Circle the correct verb form in each of the following sentences.

1. The softball team (is/are) debating the manager's decision among themselves.

2. A company in the suburbs (provides/provide) transportation to and from the city.

3. How (was/were) the cookies from the new bakery?

4. Each year, faith and optimism (grows/grow) in the renovated neighborhoods of my city.

5. Anybody with a golden retriever (knows/know) that the breed needs regular exercise.

6. Beneath the layers of tissue paper (was/were) two lace scarves.

7. Each of Isaac's friends (is/are) connected to the music business.

8. Neither Maria nor her children (like/likes) living on a farm.

9. A job applicant with experience in retailing and good computer skills (has/have) an advantage over less qualified applicants.

10. If the weather doesn't get warmer, someone (is/are) going to have an accident on the ice.

Exercise 13 **Another Comprehensive Exercise on Subject-Verb Agreement**

Practice

This exercise covers all the rules on subject-verb agreement. Circle the correct verb form in each of the following sentences.

1. There (is/are) a turkey sandwich and some macaroni salad in the refrigerator.

2. Everything in Senator Davis' speeches (seems/seem) logical to me.

3. When the days get longer, the family (has/have) summer picnics in the park.

4. In times of war, the government of the United States (has/have) called on citizens to enlist in the armed forces.

5. Nothing in his chest of toys (delights/delight) my son more than his teddy bear.

6. Yesterday there (was/were) a violent incident at the Pinetree Apartments.

7. Where in the world (is/are) your mittens?

8. Either of the girls (is/are) a good choice for class president.

9. Two weeks ago, everyone in our class (was/were) wearing heavy sweaters.

10. Sometimes the most expensive cars (needs/need) the most maintenance.

Exercise 14 **Writing Sentences with Subject-Verb Agreement: A Comprehensive**

Collaborate **Exercise**

Working with a partner or a group, write two sentences for each of the following phrases. Use a verb that fits and put it in the present tense. Be sure that the verb agrees with the subject. The first one is done for you.

1. A group of Ecuadorean students _visits my high school once a year, in the_ _fall._

A group of Ecuadorean students _corresponds with a group of high school_ _seniors from Milwaukee._

2. A box of firecrackers _____

_____

A box of firecrackers _____

_____

3. Neither Dracula nor Frankenstein _____

_____

Neither Dracula nor Frankenstein _____

_____

4. The crowd at the prizefight _____

_____

The crowd at the prizefight _____

_____

5. Everyone at the movies _____

_____

Everyone at the movies _____

_____

6. Not only the pilot but also the passengers _____

_____

Not only the pilot but also the passengers _____

_____

7. Each of his brothers _____

_____

Each of his brothers _____

_____

8. Someone with psychic powers _____

_____

Someone with psychic powers _____

_____

9. The freshman class _____

_____

The freshman class _____

_____

10. Everything in my computer files _____

_____

Everything in my computer files _____

_____

Exercise 15 **Creating Your Own Text on Subject-Verb Agreement**

👥 Collaborate

Work with a partner or a group to create your own grammar handbook. Following is a list of rules on subject-verb agreement. Write two sentences that are examples of each rule. Write an *S* above the subject of each sentence and a *V* above the verb. After you've completed this exercise, trade it for another group's exercise. Check that group's examples while they check yours. The first one is done for you.

Rule 1: Subjects and verbs should agree in number: singular subjects get singular verb forms; plural subjects get plural verb forms.

example 1:   S V
            An apple is a healthy snack. _____

_____

example 2:   S   V
            Runners need large quantities of water. _____

_____

Rule 2: When pronouns are used as subjects, they must agree in number with verbs.

example 1: _____

_____

example 2: _____

_____

Rule 3: Nothing in a prepositional phrase can be the subject of a sentence.

example 1: _____

_____

example 2: _____

_____

Rule 4: Questions, sentences beginning with *here* or *there*, and other sentences can change word order.

example 1: _____

_____

example 2: _____

_____

Rule 5: Compound subjects joined by *and* are usually plural.

example 1: _____

_____

example 2: _____

_____

Rule 6: When subjects are joined by *or, either . . . or, neither . . . nor,* or *not only . . . but also,* the verb form agrees with the subject closest to the verb.

example 1: _____

_____

example 2: _____

_____

Rule 7: Indefinite pronouns always take singular verbs.

example 1: _____

_____

example 2: _____

_____

Rule 8: Collective nouns usually take singular verbs.

example 1: _____

_____

example 2: _____

_____

Exercise 16   **A Comprehensive Exercise: Editing a Paragraph for**
Connect   **Subject-Verb Agreement**

The following paragraph has seven errors in subject-verb agreement. Correct the errors in the space above the lines.

The Lymon Company are making a change that will be very welcome to many employees. My husband, who works for the Lymon Company, came home yesterday and told me the news. The company is building a day-care center on the grounds of the factory, for the workers' children. My husband and I am delighted by the news. We has two children under the age of five, and neither a baby sitter nor local day-care centers has worked out for us. The construction of a center at my husband's workplace is a dream come true. Among his deepest desires are the wish to be near his children during the day, so he can check on them. This wish will soon come true. My husband is not the only employee at Lymon who is thrilled by the day-care plan. Everyone with small children are talking about the new child-care facilities. The facilities will make the Lymon factory a more attractive place to work. In fact, any parent with two job offers is now more likely to choose working at Lymon because child care is available. The company have made a wise decision.

CHAPTER 14

Using Pronouns Correctly: Agreement and Reference

Pronouns are words that substitute for nouns. A pronoun's **antecedent** is the word or words it replaces.

pronouns and antecedents:

antecedent   pronoun
George is a wonderful father; *he* is loving and kind.

        antecedent   pronoun
Suzanne wound the *clock* because *it* had stopped ticking.

   antecedent   pronoun
Talking on the phone is fun, but *it* takes up too much of my time.

    antecedent   pronoun
Joanne and David know what *they* want.

   antecedent   pronoun
Christopher lost *his* favorite baseball cap.

    antecedent   pronoun
The *horse* stamped *its* feet and neighed loudly.

Exercise 1 | **Identifying the Antecedents of Pronouns**

Practice

In each of the following sentences, a pronoun is underlined. Circle the word or words that are the antecedent of the underlined pronoun.

1. My best friend and her sister are looking for an apartment <u>they</u> can afford.

2. Sylvia loves fattening desserts, but I never eat <u>them</u>.

3. Taking the stairs is good for you; <u>it</u> gives you some much-needed exercise.

4. Michael, will <u>you</u> please answer me?

5. The little girl would not let go of <u>her</u> Barbie doll.

6. Last week Trina and I were exhausted; <u>we</u> had to work overtime every night.

7. The bird on my lawn seems to have hurt <u>its</u> wing.

8. The detectives are certain <u>they</u> have solved the mystery.

9. The sailors asked the captain for another day off, but <u>he</u> wouldn't give it to them.

10. The fans at last night's game lost <u>their</u> patience with the umpire.

AGREEMENT OF A PRONOUN AND ITS ANTECEDENT

A pronoun must agree in number with its antecedent. If the antecedent is singular, the pronoun must be singular. If the antecedent is plural, the pronoun must be plural.

singular antecedents, singular pronouns:

singular antecedent   singular pronoun
The *dog* began to bark wildly; *it* hated being locked up in the cellar.

singular antecedent   singular pronoun
Maria spends most of *her* salary on rent.

plural antecedents, plural pronouns:

plural antecedent   plural pronoun
Carlos and Ronnie went to Atlanta for a long weekend; *they* had a good time.

plural antecedent   plural pronoun
Cigarettes are expensive, and *they* can kill you.

SPECIAL PROBLEMS WITH AGREEMENT

Agreement of pronoun and antecedent seems fairly simple: If an antecedent is singular, use a singular pronoun. If an antecedent is plural, use a plural pronoun. There are, however, some special problems with agreement of pronouns, and these problems will come up in your writing. If you become familiar with the explanations, examples, and exercises that follow, you'll be ready to handle special problems.

Indefinite Pronouns

Certain words, called **indefinite pronouns,** are always singular. Therefore, if an indefinite pronoun is the antecedent, the pronoun that replaces it must be singular. Here are the indefinite pronouns:

Infobox			
Indefinite Pronouns			
one	nobody	nothing	each
anyone	anybody	anything	either
someone	somebody	something	neither
everyone	everybody	everything	

You may think that *everybody* is plural, but in grammatically correct English, it is a singular word. Therefore, if you want to write clearly and correctly, memorize the indefinite pronouns as the *-one, -thing,* and *-body* words: every*one,* every*thing,* every*body,* any*one,* any*thing,* and so on, plus *each, either,* and *neither.* If any of these words is an antecedent, the pronoun that refers to it is singular.

indefinite pronouns as antecedents:

indefinite pronoun antecedent   singular pronoun
Each of the women skaters did *her* best in the Olympic competition.

indefinite pronoun antecedent   singular pronoun
Everyone nominated for Father of the Year earned *his* nomination.

Avoiding Sexism

Consider this sentence:

Everybody in the cooking contest prepared _____ best dish.

How do you choose the correct pronoun to fill in this blank? You can write

Everybody in the cooking contest prepared *his* best dish.

if everybody in the contest is male. Or you can write

Everybody in the cooking contest prepared *her* best dish.

if everybody in the contest is female. Or you can write

Everybody in the cooking contest prepared *his or her* best dish.

if the contest has both male and female entrants.

In the past, most writers used *his* to refer to both men and women when the antecedent was an indefinite pronoun. Today, many writers try to use *his or her* to avoid sexual bias. If you find that using *his or her* is getting awkward and repetitive, you can rewrite the sentence and make the antecedent plural.

correct: *The entrants* in the cooking contest prepared *their* best dishes.

But you cannot shift from singular to plural:

incorrect: ~~Everybody in the cooking contest prepared their best dish.~~

Exercise 2 **Making Pronouns and Their Antecedents Agree: Simple Agreement**
Practice **and Indefinite Pronouns**

In each of the following sentences, write the appropriate pronoun in the blank. Look carefully for the antecedent before you choose the pronoun.

1. After Ellen finished the assignment, _____ felt relieved and

satisfied.

2. A few of the regular customers in my store want _____

groceries packed in boxes, not bags.

3. Someone from the men's athletic club must have lost _____

wallet.

4. Has anyone from the Girl Scouts offered _____ help to the elderly couple next door?

5. I just realized that the kitchen cabinets are greasy; I'm going to clean _____ right away.

6. Either of the little girls could have left _____ crayons on the couch.

7. One of my uncles was kind enough to offer me the use of _____ truck.

8. A single father with a large family may become overwhelmed by the stress of trying to take care of _____ children.

9. Each of the sisters believes that a degree in business administration will lead _____ to a good job.

10. Watching television can be relaxing; _____ can also be boring.

Exercise 3   **Editing a Paragraph for Errors in Agreement: Indefinite Pronouns**

Connect   The following paragraph contains six errors in agreement where the antecedents are indefinite pronouns. Correct the errors in the space above the lines.

My cousin Tina is glad she dropped out of her college sorority; she found that joining the sorority was a disappointment. Tina had expected all the girls in the sorority to be friendly and outgoing. Instead, most of them were superior and snobbish. Everyone made a point of showing off their expensive clothes and elegant jewelry. Tina felt that she could not keep up with such rich females. In addition, each of the members flaunted their family background. One of the girls bragged about their millionaire father; another said she came from a family of famous brain surgeons. Tina, whose father is a baker, was made to feel inferior. Finally, Tina left the sorority because the club was devoted to superficial activities. Tina said that every conversation focused on the next party, and if anyone brought up their need to study, the others laughed. Everyone was obsessed with their hair and their outfit for the next social event. Tina decided that she would look for a sorority with more mature, secure members.

Collective Nouns

Collective nouns refer to more than one person or thing.

Infobox

Some Common Collective Nouns

team	company	council
class	corporation	government
committee	family	group
audience	jury	crowd

Most of the time, collective nouns take a singular pronoun:

collective nouns and singular pronouns:

collective noun   singular pronoun
The *jury* in the murder trial announced *its* verdict.

collective noun   singular pronoun
The *company* I work for has been in business a long time; *it* started in Atlanta, Georgia.

Collective nouns are usually singular because the group that is announcing a verdict or starting a business is acting as one—as a unit. Collective nouns take a plural pronoun *only* when the members of the group are acting individually, not as a unit:

collective noun and a plural pronoun:

collective noun   plural pronoun
The *team* signed *their* contracts yesterday. (The members of the team signed contracts individually.)

Exercise 4 **Making Pronouns and Antecedents Agree: Collective Nouns**

Practice Circle the correct pronoun in each of the following sentences.

1. The sophomore class had (its/their) individual yearbook photos taken

yesterday.

2. That pharmaceutical corporation had a reputation for being good to

(its/their) employees.

3. The audience for the concert was enormous; (it/they) filled the stadium.

4. Impact Motors designed a new entrance to (its/their) service department.

5. A scholarship committee will examine your application and then notify

you of (its/their) decision.

6. The family lived in different parts of the country; (it/they) rarely saw

each other.

7. Several of the groups met to plan (its/their) annual children's fair.

8. Denise is furious with the telephone company; (it/they) overcharged her for some long-distance calls.

9. Our team had lost (its/their) final game of the season.

10. The rebel army began to disintegrate when the soldiers began to fight among (itself/themselves).

Exercise 5   **Editing a Paragraph for Errors in Agreement: Collective Nouns**

Connect   The following paragraph contains six errors in agreement where the antecedent is a collective noun. Correct the errors in the space above the lines.

     Yesterday Albert was very upset with our city government. Albert and his neighbors wanted the city government to close off one end of Maple Street. The residents of Maple Street, including Albert, felt that many motorists were using Maple Street as a shortcut and speeding through the formerly quiet street. The residents petitioned the government, but the government refused the residents' request, reasoning that closing the road would be expensive. Albert felt very frustrated. He shouted about the government and said they had grown out of touch with their citizens. Furthermore, Albert said, they had created a dangerous situation by allowing Maple Street to remain open. When the city government was faced with a major accident on Maple Street, they would be responsible for deaths or injuries. Their decision would have disastrous consequences, Albert said. Albert ranted on until he decided to take the neighborhood petition to the County Commission; he thought they might be more sympathetic.

Exercise 6   **Writing Sentences with Pronoun-Antecedent Agreement**

Collaborate   Working with a partner or a group, write a sentence for each of the following pairs of words, using each pair as a pronoun and its antecedent(s). The first pair is done for you.

1. men . . . their

    sentence: <u>The men at the dance were wearing their best clothes.</u>

---

2. The U.S. Navy . . . its

sentence: _____

_____

3. someone . . . his or her

sentence: _____

_____

4. millionaires . . . they

sentence: _____

_____

5. worrying . . . it

sentence: _____

_____

6. either . . . his

sentence: _____

_____

7. everything . . . its

sentence: _____

_____

8. Sal and Ryan . . . their

sentence: _____

_____

9. anyone . . . his or her

sentence: _____

_____

10. cat . . . its

sentence: _____

_____

PRONOUNS AND THEIR ANTECEDENTS: BEING CLEAR

Remember that pronouns are words that replace or refer to other words, and that those other words are called *antecedents*.

Make sure that a pronoun has one clear antecedent. Your writing will be vague and confusing if a pronoun appears to refer to more than one antecedent or if a pronoun doesn't have any specific antecedent to refer to. Such confusing language is called a problem with *reference of pronouns*.

When a pronoun refers to more than one thing, the sentence can become confusing or silly:

pronouns refer to more than one thing:

Carla told Elaine that her car had a flat tire. (Whose car had a flat tire? Carla's? Elaine's?)

Josh woke to the shrieking alarm clock, buried his head in his pillow, and threw it across the room. (What did Josh throw? The pillow? The clock? His head?)

If there is no one, clear antecedent, you must rewrite the sentence to make the reference clear. Sometimes the rewritten sentence may seem repetitive, but a little repetition is better than a lot of confusion.

unclear: Carla told Elaine that her car had a flat tire.
clear: Carla told Elaine that Carla's car had a flat tire.
clear: Carla told Elaine that Elaine's car had a flat tire.
clear: Carla told Elaine, "Your car has a flat tire."
clear: Carla told Elaine, "My car has a flat tire."

unclear: Josh woke to the shrieking alarm clock, buried his head in his pillow, and threw it across the room.
clear: Josh woke to the shrieking alarm clock, buried his head in his pillow, and threw the clock across the room.

Sometimes the problem is a little more confusing. Can you spot what's wrong with this sentence?

Linda was able to negotiate for a raise which pleased her. (What pleased Linda? The raise? Or the fact that she was able to negotiate for it?)

Be very careful with the pronoun *which*. If there is any chance that using *which* will confuse the reader, rewrite the sentence and get rid of *which*:

clear: Linda was pleased that she was able to negotiate for a raise.
clear: Linda was pleased by the raise she negotiated.

Sometimes a pronoun has nothing to refer to; it has no antecedent.

pronouns with no antecedent:

When Mary took the television to the repair shop, they said the television couldn't be repaired. (Who are "they"? Who said the television couldn't be repaired? The television service personnel? The customers? The repairmen?)

I have always been interested in designing clothes and have decided that's what I want to be. (What does *that* refer to? The only word it could refer to is *clothes*. You certainly don't want to be clothes. You don't want to be a dress or a suit.)

If a pronoun lacks an antecedent, add an antecedent or eliminate the pronoun.

add an antecedent: When Mary took the television to the repair shop and asked *the service personnel* for an estimate, they said the television couldn't be repaired.

eliminate the pronoun: I have always been interested in designing clothes and have decided I want to be a fashion designer.

To check for clear reference of pronouns, underline any pronouns that may not be clear. Then try to draw a line from that pronoun to its antecedent. Are there two or more possible antecedents? Is there no antecedent? In either case, you need to rewrite.

Exercise 7 **Rewriting Sentences for Clear Reference of Pronouns**

Practice

Rewrite the following sentences so that the pronouns have clear references. You can add, take out, or change words.

1. Oscar told Victor that he had a bad temper.

rewritten: _____

_____

2. I will never go to the Golden Palace again; they charge too much for dinner.

rewritten: _____

_____

3. Bill decided not to apply for a part-time job which worried his parents.

rewritten: _____

_____

4. My mother is a computer systems analyst, but I am not interested in it.

rewritten: _____

_____

5. My father lost his temper with Harry because he was being rude and thoughtless.

rewritten: _____

_____

6. Corinna asked her roommate if she could go to the party.

rewritten: _____

_____

7. A van skidded on the ice and hit a pickup truck, but it was not badly damaged.

rewritten: _____

_____

8. They never gave me a chance to explain when they arrested me for drunk driving.

rewritten: _____

_____

9. The manager told the assistant manager that his job was in danger of being eliminated.

rewritten: _____

_____

10. Don finally made a sale which encouraged him.

rewritten: _____

_____

Exercise 8 **Revising Sentences with Problems in Pronoun Reference: Two Ways**

Collaborate

Do this exercise with a partner or a group. Each of the following sentences contains a pronoun with an unclear antecedent. Because the antecedent is unclear, the sentence can have more than one meaning. Rewrite each sentence twice, to show two different meanings. The first one is done for you.

1. Mrs. Klein told Mrs. Yamaguchi her dog was digging up the flower beds.
rewritten:

sentence 1: _Mrs. Klein told Mrs. Yamaguchi, "Your dog is digging up the_

flower beds."

sentence 2: _Mrs. Klein told Mrs. Yamaguchi that Mrs. Klein's dog was_

digging up the flower beds.

2. Wayne's father let him bring his new motorcycle to the race.
rewritten:

sentence 1: _____

_____

sentence 2: _____

_____

3. The antique vase hit the glass tabletop, but it did not break.
rewritten:

sentence 1: _____

_____

sentence 2: _____

_____

4. She put the sandwich next to the salad and began to eat it.
rewritten:

sentence 1: _____

_____

sentence 2: _____

_____

5. Julia asked Stacy if she was invited to the wedding.
rewritten:

sentence 1: _____

_____

sentence 2: _____

_____

6. Teresa easily found a new house which made her happy.
rewritten:

sentence 1: _____

_____

sentence 2: _____

_____

7. After the children splashed water on the adults, they ran away.
rewritten:

sentence 1: _____

_____

sentence 2: _____

_____

8. Ron took the cake out of the box and gave it to me.
rewritten:

sentence 1: _____

_____

sentence 2: _____

_____

9. Arnold saw his father at his graduation.
rewritten:

sentence 1: _____

_____

sentence 2: _____

_____

10. Joe told Mike he needed a vacation.
rewritten:

sentence 1: _____

_____

sentence 2: _____

_____

Exercise 9 **Editing a Paragraph for Errors in Pronoun Reference**

Connect   The following paragraph contains five errors in pronoun reference. Correct the errors in the space above the lines.

After much confusion and indecision, I have finally made a career choice. For years, I have been trying to pick a career that would be practical and financially rewarding. In high school, they told me to look into such fields as business, accounting, or computers. I tried to commit to one of these areas, but I never felt satisfied. After much soul searching, I realized I have always loved ballet, and I decided that's what I want to be. Of course, I took years to choose a career which displeased my parents. My mother told me that her sister Edna had said her dreams of being an actress were foolish. My mother said my dreams were equally foolish. My father warned me that in ten years I would see that it was a waste of my time. But in spite of my parents' disapproval, I know I have to follow my heart.

CHAPTER 15

Using Pronouns Correctly: Consistency and Case

When you write, you write from a point of view, and each point of view gets its own form. If you write from the first person point of view, your pronouns are in the *I* (singular) or *we* (plural) forms. If you write from the second person point of view, your pronouns are in the *you* form, whether they are singular or plural. If you write from the third person point of view, your pronouns are in the *he, she,* or *it* (singular) or *they* (plural) forms.

Different kinds of writing may require different points of view. When you are writing a set of directions, for example, you might use the second person (you) point of view. For an essay about your childhood, you might use the first person (I) point of view.

Whatever point of view you use, be consistent in using pronouns. That is, do not shift the form of your pronouns without some good reason.

> **not consistent:** The last time *I* went to that movie theater, the only seat *you* could get was in the front row.
> **consistent:** The last time *I* went to that movie theater, the only seat *I* could get was in the front row.

> **not consistent:** By the time the shoppers got into the store, *they* were so jammed into the aisles that *you* couldn't get to the sales tables.
> **consistent:** By the time the shoppers got into the store, *they* were so jammed into the aisles that *they* couldn't get to the sales tables.

Exercise 1 **Consistency in Pronouns**

Practice Correct any inconsistency in point of view in each of the following sentences. Cross out each incorrect pronoun and write the correct one above it.

1. Breakfast is a meal I eat on the run because I am always late for work

and you never have time to cook a big breakfast.

2. After the students are seated at their desks, the professor circulates an

attendance sheet for you to sign.

3. Motorists must use caution when they enter the toll plaza; if they rush through the gates, you can be hit by another driver.

4. In the college snack bar, students sit at long tables, socialize with their friends, or do your homework.

5. I am very tactful when I ask my mother for money because you don't want to put her in a bad mood.

6. Although the weather was sunny, we took an umbrella in case you got caught in a shower.

7. They avoided Paul because you couldn't put up with his constant complaining.

8. When we drove into central Florida, the rain was coming down so hard you could barely see the road.

9. Every time I run into Dean, you know he has a story to tell me.

10. The first time I ate barbecued chicken, I thought it was so delicious you'd never want to eat anything else.

 **Exercise 2** **Rewriting Sentences with Consistency Problems**

Collaborate

Do this exercise with a partner or a group. Rewrite the following sentences, correcting any errors in consistency of pronouns. To make the corrections, you may have to change, add, or take out words.

1. You could tell the atmosphere was tense when we walked in and saw our friends sitting in silence.

    rewritten: _____

    _____

2. For me, Sunday is the best day of the week; I particularly like waking up as late as I want to, watching my favorite morning news shows, and lounging around in your pajamas.

    rewritten: _____

    _____

    _____

3. Children who are given too much freedom too early can become inse-cure and confused; you need limits to make you feel safe and cared for.

rewritten: _____

_____

_____

4. If you truly want to succeed in college, students must put college at the top of their schedules and devote most of your time to studying.

rewritten: _____

_____

_____

5. I won't offer to drive Brian to class because you'll lose patience waiting for Brian to show up, and I'll be in a bad mood the rest of the day.

rewritten: _____

_____

6. Sophomores who want to register for next semester have to make an appointment with your advisor before they can sign up for classes.

rewritten: _____

_____

7. The best part of my speech class is that you can relax when someone else is giving a speech.

rewritten: _____

_____

8. When I entered the studio, the singers were so friendly that you could not believe it.

rewritten: _____

_____

9. Before the painter paints new wood, he has to be sure that you have covered the wood with primer.

rewritten: _____

_____

10. There's no reason for me to apologize to Jack; he'll just carry a grudge against you anyway.

rewritten: _____

_____

Exercise 3 **Editing a Paragraph for Consistency of Pronouns**

Connect   The following paragraph has four errors in consistency of pronouns. Correct the errors in the space above the lines.

I have a perfect system for completing my holiday shopping early. First, I begin way ahead of time. As early as July, I visit the best sales and begin stockpiling gifts for members of my family. By September, I have made a list of all the people you want to buy for and what you've already bought. I circle the names of those who still need gifts. Then I visit the malls, looking specifically for gifts for the people on my list. By October, I have completed nearly all my shopping. From November on, I avoid the malls and do the remainder of my shopping by catalog. Catalog shopping is quick and easy, and it keeps you out of the stores when they are jammed with desperate shoppers trying to beat me to the bargains. When the holidays finally roll around, you can enjoy them because there is no last-minute shopping to make me crazy.

CHOOSING THE CASE OF PRONOUNS

Pronouns have forms that show number and person, and they also have forms that show **case**. Following is a list of three cases of pronouns:

Infobox

Pronouns and Their Cases

Singular Pronouns

	Subjective Case	Objective Case	Possessive Case
1st person	I	me	my (mine)
2nd person	you	you	your (yours)
3rd person	he, she, it	him, her, it	his, her (hers), its

Plural Pronouns

	Subjective Case	Objective Case	Possessive Case
1st person	we	us	our (ours)
2nd person	you	you	your (yours)
3rd person	they	them	their (theirs)

Rules for Choosing the Case of Pronouns

The rules for choosing the case of pronouns are simple:

1. When a pronoun is used as a subject, use the subjective case.
2. When a pronoun is used as the object of a verb or the object of a preposition, use the objective case.
3. When a pronoun is used to show possession, use the possessive case.

Here are some examples of the correct use of pronouns:

pronouns used as subjects:

She calls the office once a week.
Sylvia wrote the letter, and *we* revised it.
When Guy called, *I* was thrilled.

pronouns used as objects:

The loud noise frightened *me*.
The card was addressed to *him*.
Sadie's dog always traveled with *her*.

pronouns used to show possession:

The criticism hurt *her* feelings.
Our car is nearly new.
The restaurant changed *its* menu.

Exercise 4   **Choosing the Right Case of Pronouns: Simple Situations**

Practice   Circle the correct pronoun in each of the following sentences.

1. (He/Him/His) visited the city museum yesterday.

2. A week ago, Jennifer borrowed (I/me/my) best dress.

3. Dave and Brenda drove straight to Cleveland; then (they/them/their) stopped for the night.

4. (I/Me/My) need a good job for the summer.

5. Frank invited (we/us/our) to a party at the beach.

6. Cynthia asked Mark to go the dance with (she/her).

7. Paulette and Enrique are celebrating (they/them/their) fifth anniversary.

8. Uncle Tim should give the money to (we/us/our).

9. (He/Him/His) research paper was excellent.

10. Christopher scored the winning point, but (I/me/my) contributed to the victory.

PROBLEMS IN CHOOSING PRONOUN CASE

Choosing the Right Pronoun Case in a Related Group of Words

You need to be careful in choosing pronoun case when the pronoun is part of a related group of words. If the pronoun is part of a related group of words, isolate the pronoun. Next, try out the pronoun choices. Then decide which pronoun is correct and write the correct sentence. For example, which of these sentences is correct?

> Diane had a big surprise for Jack and *I*.
>
> > or
>
> Diane had a big surprise for Jack and *me*.

To choose the correct sentence, follow these steps:

Step 1: Isolate the pronoun. Eliminate the related words *Jack and*.
Step 2: Try each case.

> Diane had a big surprise for *I*.
>
> > or
>
> Diane had a big surprise for *me*.

Step 3: Decide which pronoun is correct and write the correct sentence.

> **correct sentence:** Diane had a big surprise for Jack and *me*.

The pronoun acts as an object, so it takes the objective case.

To be sure that you understand the principle, try working through the steps once more. Which of the following sentences is correct?

> Next week, my sister and *me* will start classes at Bryant Community College.
>
> > or
>
> Next week, my sister and *I* will start classes at Bryant Community College.

Step 1: Isolate the pronoun. Eliminate the related words *my sister and*.
Step 2: Try each case.

> Next week, *me* will start classes at Bryant Community College.
> Next week, *I* will start classes at Bryant Community College.

Step 3: Decide which pronoun is correct and write the correct sentence.

> **correct sentence:** Next week, my sister and *I* will start classes at Bryant Community College.

Common Errors with Case of Pronouns

In choosing the case of pronouns, be careful to avoid these common errors:

1. *Between* is a preposition. The pronouns that follow it are objects of the preposition: between *us*, between *them*, between *you and me*. It is never correct to write *between you and I*.

   examples:
   not this: What I'm telling you must be kept strictly between you and ~~I~~.
   but this: What I'm telling you must be kept strictly between you and me.

2. Never use *myself* as a replacement for *I* or *me*.

   examples:
   not this: My family and ~~myself~~ are grateful for your expressions of sympathy.

   but this: My family and I are grateful for your expressions of sympathy.

> **not this:** The scholarship committee selected Nadine and ~~myself~~.
> **but this:** The scholarship committee selected Nadine and me.

3. The possessive pronoun *its* has no apostrophe.

   examples:
   not this: The stale coffee lost ~~it's~~ flavor.
   but this: The stale coffee lost its flavor.

Exercise 5 **Choosing the Right Case of Pronouns: Problems with Pronoun Case**

Practice   Circle the correct pronoun in each of the following sentences.

1. Cristina was able to open her new store after she received a great deal

   of help from her cousins and (me/myself).

2. Basic training can be very difficult, but the program has (it's/its) benefits.

3. I told Sylvia she could come to the wedding with Freddie and (I/me).

4. When David won the lottery, he gave half of his winnings to (they/them)

   and Carlos.

5. Stuck in traffic, Dr. Chen and (he/him) used the cell phone to call the
   office.

6. My mother thinks the judges will have a hard time choosing between

   the student from Texas and (me/myself).

7. The people in the nursing home always welcome Sandra and (I/me)

   when we visit.

8. The neighbors and (we/us) spent the weekend cleaning up the streets.

9. My wife and I moved to San Diego to find more job opportunities for

   her and (I/me).

10. Ed and (I/me) watched an old movie last night.

Exercise 6 **More on Choosing the Right Case of Pronouns: Problems**
Practice **with Pronoun Case**

Circle the correct pronoun in each of the following sentences.

1. Just try to keep it a secret between you and (I/me).

2. My friends and (I/myself) want to thank you for this honor.

3. Once I started working, staying out late lost (its/it's) appeal for me.

4. We were able to settle the argument between David and (me/myself).

5. My father said he couldn't have painted the house without the help of my sister and (I/me).

6. Last week, Danny and (he/him) borrowed a van from Jesse.

7. The leadership award was a great honor for Lisa and (I/me).

8. At the dinner, Debbie and (she/her) wouldn't talk to Jim.

9. My sister arranged a wonderful treat for my girlfriend and (I/me).

10. I think the tree is diseased; it is losing too many of (its/it's) leaves.

Exercise 7 **Creating Your Own Text on Pronoun Case**

Collaborate

Working with a partner or a group, write two sentences that could be used as examples for each of the following rules. The first one is done for you.

Rule 1: When a pronoun is used as a subject, use the subjective case.

example 1: They study for tests in the math lab.

example 2: Caught in the rain, she ran for cover.

Rule 2: When a pronoun is used as the object of a verb or the object of a preposition, use the objective case. (For examples, write one sentence in which the pronoun is the object of a verb and one in which the pronoun is the object of a preposition.)

example 1: _____

example 2: _____

Rule 3: When a pronoun is used to show possession, use the possessive case.

example 1: _____

example 2: _____

Rule 4: When a pronoun is part of a related group of words, isolate the pronoun to choose the case. (For examples, write two sentences in which the pronoun is part of a related group of words.)

example 1: _____

example 2: _____

Exercise 8 **Editing a Paragraph for Case of Pronouns**

Connect

The following letter has five errors in pronoun case. Correct the errors in the space above the lines.

Dear Professor Walker,

    If you could give us an extension on the writing assignment, you would really help Steve Lopez and I. We both work at Home Warehouse, and we have had to work overtime all week. Me and Steve have been getting home after midnight, and it's been impossible for us to get our homework done. We have asked our boss for time off, but Home Warehouse has it's policy about working overtime, and Steve and myself have to follow that policy. Since we have been so busy working, we haven't started the writing assignment. If you could extend the deadline, we could do a good job on our papers, and we wouldn't tell the rest of the class about our extension. It would be a secret between Steve and I.

Sincerely,

Richard Lesniak

16 Punctuation

You probably know much about punctuation already. In fact, you probably know many of the rules so well that you punctuate your writing automatically. However, there are times when every writer wonders, "Do I need a comma here?" or "Should I capitalize this word?" The following review of the basic rules of punctuation can help you answer such questions.

THE PERIOD

Periods are used in two ways:

1. Use a period to mark the end of a sentence that makes a statement.

   examples:

   My father gave me an exciting new book.
   After the dance, we went to a coffeehouse for a snack.

2. Use a period after abbreviations.

   examples:

   Mr. Vinh
   Carlos Montoya, Sr.
   11:00 a.m.
   Dr. J. T. Mitchell

THE QUESTION MARK

Use a question mark after a direct question:

examples:

Do you have any spare change?
Wasn't that song beautiful?

If a question is not a direct question, do not use a question mark.

examples:

I wonder if it will rain tonight.
Nadine asked whether I had cleaned the kitchen.

Exercise 1 **Punctuating with Periods and Question Marks**

Practice   Add periods and question marks where they are needed in the following sentences.

1. Brian questioned whether I really believed Suzanne's story.

2. Do you think Ms Ross will ever miss a day of class?

3. If you are going to the store, can you pick up some milk?

4. Mr. Wing wants to earn a B S in chemistry.

5. I was wondering if you would like to car pool with me.

6. Norman cannot get to sleep before 3:00 a.m, so he has a hard time

   waking up in the morning.

7. Has anyone seen my umbrella?

8. We asked the teacher if she was going to give us a quiz.

9. Charles Pulaski, Jr inherited the factory from his father.

10. Why not call a plumber to fix the sink?

Exercise 2 **Punctuating with Periods and Question Marks**

👥 Collaborate   Do this exercise with a partner. First, by yourself, write a paragraph that needs periods and question marks, but leave out those punctuation marks. Then exchange paragraphs with your partner, and add the necessary periods and question marks to your partner's paragraph. Finally, you and your partner should check each other's punctuation.

Write a paragraph of at least six sentences, using the topic sentence below.

New students have many questions about college, but their questions

are soon answered. _____

_____

_____

_____

_____

_____

_____

_____

_____

THE SEMICOLON

There are two ways to use semicolons:

1. Use a semicolon to join two independent clauses.

    examples:

    Aunt Celine can be very generous; she gave me fifty dollars for my birthday.
    The ice storm was horrible; our town endured five days without electricity.

If the independent clauses are joined by a conjunctive adverb, you still need a semicolon. You will also need a comma after the conjunctive adverb if the conjunctive adverb is more than one syllable long.

    examples:

    I called the towing service; then I waited impatiently for the tow truck to arrive.
    Stephen forgot about the exam; therefore, he was not prepared for it.

2. If a list contains commas and the items on the list need to be clarified, use a semicolon to separate the items. Note how confusing the following lists would be without the semicolons.

    examples:

    The student government presidents at the conference represented Mill Valley High School, Springfield; Longfellow High School, Riverdale; Kennedy High School, Deer Creek; and Martin Luther King High School, Rocky Hills.
    The members of the musical group were Janet Reese, guitar; Richelle Dennison, drums; Sandy Simon, bass; and Lee Vickers, vocalist.

Exercise 3 **Punctuating with Semicolons**

Practice Some of the following sentences need semicolons; some do not. Add the necessary semicolons. (You may need to change some commas to semicolons.)

1. Contestants in the talent contest came from Miami, Florida; Dallas, Texas; Chicago, Illinois; Los Angeles, California; and Boston, Massachusetts.

2. A large dog bounced out of the van; the animal began to jump all over me.

3. The weather was exceptionally warm for this time of year; consequently, we decided to walk to the store instead of drive.

4. Sylvia called a number of stores but couldn't find the right kind of light bulb.

5. At the club meeting last night, these people were elected: Samantha Monceau, president; Mark Chang, first vice president; Alan Deschamps, second vice president; and Tom Robinson, treasurer.

6. For three years, my father worked at two jobs; thus he was able to make a down payment on a house.

7. A good haircut can make your hair look better and can enhance your best features.

8. Take the car; I don't need it tonight.

9. When you go hiking, you need to buy good shoes, warm socks, sturdy clothing, a comfortable hat, and a roomy backpack.

10. My brother loves late-night television; he can watch it all night.

Exercise 4 **Punctuating with Semicolons**

Connect   Add semicolons where they are needed in the following paragraph.

David's first day at work was stressful; nevertheless, he came out of the experience with a sense of accomplishment. The showroom floor where he began work was more crowded and busy than he had expected. Moreover, the customers all seemed to be in a hurry; they wanted to be helped immediately. David tried to take care of everyone but was overwhelmed by the demands of so many people. The manager of the store was encouraging; she told David things would slow down in the afternoon. By 3:00 p.m., David had learned to cope; moreover, the showroom had really emptied out. David's boss had been right; the pace was much slower in the afternoon. By the time David left, he felt less stressed and more confident. He had survived his first day at American Furniture Galleries without making any major mistakes. The worst was over; better days were ahead.

THE COMMA

There are four main ways to use a comma, and then there are other, less important ways. Memorize the four main ways. If you can learn and understand these four rules, you will be more confident and correct in your punctuation. That is, you will use a comma only when you have a reason to do so; you will not be scattering commas in your sentences simply because you think a comma might fit, as many writers do. The four main ways to use a comma are as a *lister*, a *linker*, an *introducer*, and an *inserter* (two commas).

1. **Comma as a lister.**

   Commas separate items in a series. These items can be words, phrases, or clauses.

   commas between words in a list:

   Charles was fascinated by Doreen because she was smart, sassy, and funny.

   commas between phrases in a list:

   I wanted a house on a quiet street, in a friendly neighborhood, and with a school nearby.

   commas between clauses in a list:

   In a single year my brother joined the army, he fought in the Gulf War, and he was decorated for valor.

   Note: In a list, the comma before *and* is optional, but most writers use it.

Exercise 5 **Using the Comma as a Lister**

Practice   Add commas only where they are needed in the following sentences.

   1. Skiing, snowboarding, and surfing all demand tremendous agility and fitness.

   2. The letter you lost could be in your bureau drawer, on the night stand, or behind the bookcase.

   3. I needed eggs, milk, bread, and orange juice from the supermarket.

   4. When my mother was in college, she had part-time jobs as a waitress, stock clerk, bank teller, gas station attendant, and lifeguard.

   5. The whole apartment is decorated with green, white, and yellow wallpaper.

   6. I hated my roommate, I missed my friends, and I was very homesick at summer camp.

   7. Joining a club, taking a class, and doing volunteer work are three good ways to meet people.

   8. San Diego, Philadelphia, Boston, and Chicago are cities I've visited, explored, and loved.

   9. Charlie was rude, Cindy was thoughtless, and Bill was obnoxious when they stayed at my house last month.

10. Romance can be fun, exciting, and fulfilling, but it can also be scary,

painful, and disappointing.

2. Comma as a linker

A comma and a coordinating conjunction link two independent clauses. The coordinating conjunctions are *and, but, or, nor, for, yet, so*. The comma goes before the coordinating conjunction.

comma before coordinating conjunction:

You can pick up the pizza, and I'll set the table.
The movie was long, but it was action-packed.
Diane will fly home for summer vacation, or her parents will visit her.
Our house had no basement, nor did it have much of an attic.
Norbert was thrilled by the A in Organic Chemistry, for he had studied
    really hard all semester.
Mr. Weinstein has lived in the neighborhood for a year, yet no one knows
    him very well.
The front door was open, so I went right in.

Note: Before you use a comma, be careful that the coordinating conjunction is linking two independent clauses:

no comma: Veronica wrote poetry and painted beautiful portraits.
use a comma: Veronica wrote poetry, and she painted beautiful portraits.

Exercise 6 **Using the Comma as a Linker**

Practice Add commas only where they are needed in the following sentences.

1. Christopher called me twice last night but wouldn't give a straight

    answer to my question.

2. The car has very low mileage, and it runs like a new car.

3. Steve is cutting back on his spending, for he wants to pay off his credit

    cards.

4. Anyone can check books out of the city library or use the computers in

    the reference section.

5. The sun was in my eyes, so I couldn't see the road very well.

6. Professor Rotonda never assigns papers, nor does he give essay tests.

7. A few of the players on the local softball team meet at Sloppy Joe's, and

    grab a meal after the game.

8. Carly gave my son a baby blanket, and she embroidered his name on it.

9. I always plan to clean up my bedroom, yet I never seem to get around to it.

10. Sam's cheesecake is loaded with calories, but it's too good to pass up.

3. Comma as an introducer

Put a comma after introductory words, phrases, or clauses in a sentence.

comma after an introductory word:

No, I can't afford that car.

comma after an introductory phrase:

In my opinion, that car is a lemon.

comma after an introductory clause:

When the baby smiles, I am the happiest father on earth.

Exercise 7 Using the Comma as an Introducer

Practice Add commas only where they are needed in the following sentences.

1. Sure, I'll be happy to collect your mail while you're away.

2. After you called me, I felt better about our little disagreement.

3. No one in my family has cable television, but my cousin has a satellite dish.

4. Whenever Tyrone visits, he brings a cake or cookies for my grandfather and me.

5. On my only day off, I try to sleep a little later than usual.

6. Crying loudly, the toddler held up his bruised finger.

7. On a bright sunny day in July, Amanda became a lawyer.

8. Unfortunately, you can't get tickets for that boxing match; it's sold out.

9. Before you lose your temper, count to ten.

10. With a wicked grin, my brother grabbed the last chocolate chip cookie and ran.

4. Comma as an inserter

When words or phrases that are not necessary are inserted into a sentence, put a comma on *both* sides of the inserted material.

commas around inserted material:

Her science project, a masterpiece of research, won first prize.
Selena's problem, I believe, is her fear of failure.
Julio, stuck by the side of the road, waited for the tow truck.
Artichokes, a delicious vegetable, are not always available at the local market.

Using commas as inserters requires that you decide what is essential to the meaning of the sentence and what is nonessential.

If you do not need material in a sentence, put commas around the material.
If you need material in a sentence, do not put commas around the material.

For example, consider this sentence:

The woman who was promoted to captain was Jack's wife.

Do you need the words *who was promoted to captain* to understand the meaning of the sentence? To answer this question, write the sentence without the words:

The woman was Jack's wife.

Reading the shorter sentence, you might ask, "What woman?" The words *who was promoted to captain* are essential to the sentence. Therefore, you do not put commas around them.

correct: The woman who was promoted to captain was Jack's wife.

Remember that the proper name of a person, place, or thing is always sufficient to identify it. Therefore, any information that follows a proper name is inserted material; it is not essential and gets commas on both sides.

proper names and inserted material:

Gloria Chen, who lives in my apartment building, won the raffle at Dominion High School.

Suarez Electronics, which just opened in the mall, has great deals on color televisions.

Note: Inserted material often begins with one of these *relative pronouns:* *who, which, that.* If you have to choose between *which* and *that, which* usually begins inserted material that is not essential:

The movie, which was much too long, was a comedy.

That usually begins inserted material that is essential:

The puppy that I want is a miniature poodle.

Exercise 8 **Using Commas as Inserters**

Practice   Add commas only where they are needed in the following sentences.

1. The silver and turquoise ring that I wanted cost two hundred dollars.

2. Tony Russell from my old neighborhood, is a high-powered attorney now.

3. My favorite movie, unfortunately, is not available on video.

4. Her boyfriend, thinking he could please her with flowers, brought her a dozen yellow roses.

5. The salesman's best offer, which he called a rock-bottom price, was still too high for my budget.

6. Captain Crunch, which my mother fed us every morning, is still my choice for breakfast.

7. Someone who loves tennis is still a good choice for the camp counselor's job.

8. Nicole wanted to rent *The Bodyguard*, her favorite movie, over the weekend.

9. A bad habit that really bothers me is constant complaining.

10. The teacher who helped me the most was my history teacher.

Exercise 9 **Punctuating with Commas: The Four Main Ways**

Practice   Add commas only where they are needed in the following sentences.

1. Whether it rains or shines, we'll have the Arts Fair on Saturday.

2. Even Jason, with all his good intentions, couldn't help the confused teen.

3. She blasted the radio throughout the apartment but couldn't find comfort in the music.

4. Coffee Corner, which serves great espresso, is open until midnight.

5. Aaron picked up an armchair, a coffee table, and a bookcase at his neighbor's garage sale.

6. Louis took me out to dinner last night, so I want to do something nice for him.

7. Children love to play with puppies, but small children must learn how to treat the animals.

8. Tulips look wonderful in flower beds, in bright colored pots, and in window boxes.

9. When I get a chance, I'll have to write a letter to Aunt Cecilia and thank her for the birthday present.

10. While you were sleeping, a burglar cleaned out your closet.

Exercise 10 **More on Punctuating with Commas: The Four Main Ways**

Practice   Add commas only where they are needed in the following sentences.

1. On the best summer weekends, we take our dog for long walks, or we jog near the lake.

2. My mother used to warn us against the dangers of driving too fast, drinking too much, and speaking too freely.

3. The dress that I longed for was hanging in the window of Mason's Department Store.

4. I know, of course, that you weren't invited to the party.

5. The man who won the championship title will speak tonight.

6. Richard Mannheim, who won the championship title, will speak tonight.

7. The little boy begged, and pleaded, yet, he couldn't get his mother to give him the toy.

8. Dad, do you have any spare change?

9. The chicken was not very well cooked, nor was it attractively presented.

10. Until you taught me how to swim, I was afraid of the water.

Exercise 11 👥 Collaborate   **The Four Main Ways to Use Commas: Creating Your Own Examples**

Do this exercise with a partner or a group. Below are the rules for the four main ways to use commas. For each rule, write two sentences that are examples. The first one is done for you.

Rule 1: Use a comma as a lister.

example 1: I have old photos stashed in my attic, in my closet, and in the garage.

example 2: The movie was long, dull, and pointless.

Rule 2: Use a comma as a linker.

example 1: _____

example 2: _____

Rule 3: Use a comma as an introducer.

example 1: _____

example 2: _____

Rule 4: Use a comma as an inserter (two commas).

example 1: _____

example 2: _____

Exercise 12 The Four Main Ways to Use Commas

Connect   Add commas where they are needed in the following paragraph. Do not add or change any other punctuation; just add commas.

Believe it or not, I actually enjoy cleaning my apartment. I can't say that I look forward to cleaning, but I do find some satisfaction in the chore. First of all, I find the physical exercise of washing the floors, scrubbing the sinks, and dusting the furniture to be a good way to relieve stress. Even when I am tired, the activity of cleaning seems to energize me. I also like the sense of accomplishment that comes when I have defeated the mildew and conquered the dust bunnies again. A clean living space, is I think, an achievement. After all, it takes some self-discipline to make myself grab the mop, pail, and Comet when I could be lounging around. Getting my chores done has its rewards. The part that I like best of all is being able to enjoy my sparkling new apartment—until it gets dirty again!

Other Ways to Use a Comma

Besides the four main ways, there are other ways to use a comma. Reviewing these uses will help you feel more confident as a writer.

1. **Use commas with quotations.** Use a comma to set off a direct quotation from the rest of the sentence.

   examples:
   Sylvia warned me, "Don't swim there."
   "I can give you a ride," Alan said.

   Note that the comma that introduces the quotation goes before the quotation marks. But once the quotation has begun, commas (or periods) go inside the quotation marks.

2. **Use commas with dates and addresses.** Put commas between the items in dates and addresses.

   examples:
   August 29, 1981, is the day we were married.
   I had an apartment at 2323 Clover Avenue, Houston, Texas, until I was transferred to California.

   Notice the comma after the year in the date, and the comma after the state in the address. These commas are needed when you write a date or an address within a sentence.

3. **Use commas in numbers.** Use commas in numbers of one thousand or larger.

examples:

He owed me $1,307.
That wall contains 235,991 bricks.

4. **Use commas for clarity.** Add a comma when you need it to make something clear.

examples:

She waltzed in, in a stunning silk gown.
Whatever you did, did the trick.
I don't have to apologize, but I want to, to make things right between us.
Not long after, the party ended.

Exercise 13 Other Ways to Use a Comma

Practice

Add commas where they are needed in the following sentences.

1. Professor Milovich advised me, "Whatever you choose choose carefully."

2. March 23, 1998, was the day we attended Uncle Simon's funeral.

3. "No one has a right to say that to me," the angry customer shouted.

4. He wanted $1,250 for the motorcycle, but I offered him $975 in cash.

5. Soon after, the jury adjourned for the day.

6. Rebekah is moving to Chicago, Illinois, when she finishes college.

7. A fortune teller once told me, "You have a dark stranger in your future."

8. Send the package to me at 257 Sanford Drive, Davenport, Iowa, as soon as you can.

9. "I'd rather be happy than rich," my father always said.

10. At my job in Okemos, Michigan, I made $15,000 a year.

Exercise 14 Punctuating with Commas: A Comprehensive Exercise

Practice

Add commas where they are needed in the following sentences.

1. He never apologized to my sister, nor did he pay her the money that he owed.

2. If you win, win graciously.

3. David Wong, who comes from Georgia, has never seen the Empire State Building.

4. I mailed that birthday card on April 5, 1998, but it didn't arrive until April 23, 1999.

5. Children who are afraid of the dark should not visit the Halloween Fun House.

6. Sarah offered Sam money, she gave him advice, and she listened to his complaints.

7. Dad, do you know someone who lives at 101 Ranch Road, Billings, Montana?

8. After all, you've done enough for the family that lives down the street.

9. Anton called the house yesterday and asked to speak to my sister.

10. "Let's have a party for Halloween," my little sister said, but my mother ignored her.

Exercise 15 **Punctuating with Commas: Another Comprehensive Exercise**

Practice Add commas where they are needed in the following sentences.

1. One of the greatest things about you, Josh, is your sense of humor.

2. The sunset at the beach was a mix of pink, violet, and golden streaks.

3. Sal's Pizza, which is doing a great business, is starting a take-out service.

4. Neil quit his job because he was sick of answering the phone, taking orders from customers, listening to complaints, and working until nearly midnight.

5. The woman who gave me the necklace is my godmother.

6. Whenever Luis borrows my car, he fills the tank with gas.

7. In the years to come, I'll be glad I went to college, so I don't mind working hard at college assignments now.

8. Amy and Vito spent $2,200 on living room furniture, for they wanted their new house to look elegant.

9. After Tanika heard her brother's apology, she declared, "I never knew you could be so foolish, but I have to forgive you."

10. Since you've been gone, I've started a mail-order business and hired your father-in-law.

Punctuating with Commas

👥 Collaborate

Working alone, write a paragraph that is at least six sentences long. The paragraph should require at least five commas, but leave the commas out. Then give your paragraph to a partner; let your partner add the necessary commas. Meanwhile, you punctuate your partner's paragraph. When you are both finished, check each other's answers.

Write your paragraph in the lines below, using the sentence given to you as your topic sentence.

Of all the places I remember from my childhood, one place stands out.

_____

_____

_____

_____

_____

_____

_____

_____

THE APOSTROPHE

Use the apostrophe in the following ways:

1. Use an apostrophe in contractions to show that letters have been omitted.

   examples:

do not	=	don't
she will	=	she'll
he would	=	he'd
is not	=	isn't
will not	=	won't

   Use an apostrophe to show that numbers have been omitted, too.

   example:

   the winter of 1999 = the winter of '99

   Note: Your instructor may want you to avoid contractions in formal assignments. Be sure to follow his or her instructions.

2. Use an apostrophe to show possession. If a word does not end in -s, show ownership by adding an apostrophe and -s.

   examples:

the car belongs to Maria	=	Maria's car
the key belongs to the men	=	the men's key
the hat belongs to somebody	=	somebody's hat

   If two people own something, add the 's to the second person's name.

example:

Jack and Joe own a dog   =   Jack and Joe's dog

If a word already ends in *-s* and you want to show ownership, just add an apostrophe.

examples:

The doll belongs to Dolores   =   Dolores' doll
two girls own a cat   =   the girls' cat
Mr. Ross owns a house   =   Mr. Ross' house

3. Use an apostrophe for special uses of time, and to create the plural of numbers mentioned as numbers, letters mentioned as letters, and words that normally do not have plurals.

special use of time: It took a *month's* work.
numbers mentioned as numbers: Add the *7's.*
letters mentioned as letters: Dot your *i's.*
words that normally do not have plurals: Give me some more *thank you's.*

Caution: Be careful with apostrophes. Possessive pronouns like *his, hers, theirs, ours, yours,* and *its* do not take apostrophes.

not this: I was sure the dress was ~~her's~~.
but this: I was sure the dress was hers.

not this: The movie has ~~it's~~ flaws.
but this: The movie has its flaws.

Do not add an apostrophe to a simple plural.

not this: The pudding comes in three ~~flavor's~~.
but this: The pudding comes in three flavors.

Exercise 17   **Punctuating with Apostrophes**

Practice   Add apostrophes where they are needed in the following sentences.

1. I was on my way to the mens locker room when I saw Dr. Thomas grandson at one of the weight-training machines.

2. Teresa found a house key that looked as if it belonged to her neighbors, but they said it wasnt theirs.

3. Skateboarding lost its appeal for me when I broke three ribs in a fall at the courthouse steps.

4. You cant be blamed for trying to get whats yours.

5. Maxine was sure shed be invited to Richard and Lees birthday party.

6. Iris sister pronounces her r's strangely.

7. In the summer of 99, I bought two jars of expensive moisturizing cream.

8. Its not how the company sells its products that I dislike; its the high prices.

9. Hed rather be filling out orders than listening to peoples complaints.

10. The womans generous donation was given to a womens health center.

Exercise 18 **More on Punctuating with Apostrophes**

Practice Add apostrophes where they are needed in the following sentences.

1. My aunt kept complaining about Los Angeles lack of public

transportation and its traffic jams.

2. The old farm had acres of apple trees and lush green meadows.

3. I wont go to the concert if its raining too hard.

4. Roberta insisted that the books under the seat were hers.

5. Im not interested in anybodys opinion except yours.

6. Shes tired of hearing *maybe*s instead of *certainly*s.

7. Sally is driving to her sister and brother-in-laws house for the weekend.

8. Theyre not sure whether the books are yours.

9. Arthurs going to the races at the fairgrounds tomorrow.

10. When she writes, she has a fancy way of writing her *q*s.

Exercise 19 **Punctuating with Apostrophes**

Connect Edit the following paragraph, correcting the eleven errors related to apostrophes. You need to add some apostrophes and eliminate some unnecessary apostrophes.

Its a shame how a good restaurant can lose its high standards over the years. When I was a child, my parents used to take me to Fran's Pancake House as a special treat. Frans had the best pancakes in town, but it also served a wonderful array of breakfast food, from scrambled egg's with sausage's to homemade muffins and doughnuts. My family would go to Fran's on Saturdays and wed eat so much brunch that we wouldnt eat again until dinner. The food was good and plentiful, the price's were reasonable, and the waitresses were always friendly and kind. I remember one waitress who always gave me extra butter for my pancake's. Unfortunately, time hasn't been good to the restaurant. Last week I went back

quotation marks around the titles of short works:

My father's favorite poem is "The Raven" by Edgar Allan Poe.
When I was little, I used to sing "Twinkle, Twinkle, Little Star."
I couldn't think of a good title, so I just called my essay "How I Spent My
    Summer Vacation."

If you are writing the title of a longer work like a book, movie, magazine,
play, television show, record album, or CD, underline the title.

underlining the titles of longer works:

My favorite childhood movie was <u>Star Wars</u>.
For homework, I have to read an article called "Children and Reading
    Skills" in <u>Time</u> magazine.

In printed publications such as books or magazines, titles of long works
are put in italics. But when you are writing by hand, typing, or using a
word processor, underline the titles of long works.

3. There are other, special uses of quotation marks. You use quotation marks
   around special words in a sentence.

quotation marks around special words:

When you say you are "sometimes" late, what do you mean?
People from Boston say "frappe" when they mean "milkshake."

If you are using a quotation within a quotation, use single quotation
marks:

a quotation within a quotation:

Janey said angrily, "You took my car without permission, and all you can
    say is, 'It's no big deal.'"
Aunt Mary said, "You need to teach that child to say 'please' and 'thank
    you' more often."

Exercise 22	**Punctuating with Quotation Marks**

Practice   Add quotation marks where they are needed in the following sentences.

1. Last night around nine, Samantha called to ask whether I had seen her

brother.

2. You'll never be happy, my grandmother used to say, until you find

someone to love.

3. That radio station has been playing Jingle Bells every hour.

4. Mark seemed really sincere when he said that he wanted to come to the

dance but couldn't get a ride.

5. Have you seen my brother? Samantha asked when she called around

nine last night.

6. "It's been one thing after another. I've spent the whole day handling minor emergencies," said my father.

7. "It's been one thing after another," my father said. "I've spent the whole day handling minor emergencies."

8. The toddler calls his sister "Baba" because he can't pronounce Barbara.

9. Alexander declared, "When you refused to say 'I'm sorry,' our friendship ended."

10. I think the word gone is the saddest word in the language.

| Exercise 23 | **More on Punctuating with Quotation Marks** |

Practice   Add quotation marks where they are needed in the following sentences.

1. In high school, I had to read a story called "The Black Cat."

2. "Instead of criticizing me," my sister said, "give me some encouragement."

3. Jill wondered whether she could borrow some money until payday so she could pay her overdue electric bill.

4. "I wonder if I can trouble you for a moment," my neighbor said. "I seem to have lost my keys."

5. "Absolutely not," my mother said, when I asked her if I could borrow her car.

6. Our building superintendent always says he'll get to it when we ask him to do a repair, but he never follows through.

7. "Style" is a hard word to define because it has many meanings.

8. Dave said, "I apologize. I should have said 'please' before I grabbed the last piece of cake."

9. "The computer is too slow," he complained. "It is old and outdated," he added.

10. "Without a map, you won't be able to find that house."

CAPITAL LETTERS

There are ten main situations when you capitalize.

1. Capitalize the first word of every sentence.

examples:

Sometimes we take a walk on the beach.
An apple is a healthy snack.

2. Capitalize the first word in a direct quotation if the word begins a sentence.

examples:

Jensina said, "Here is the money I owe you and a little something extra."
"Here is the money I owe you," Jensina said, "and a little something
    extra." (Notice that the second section of this quote does not begin
    with a capital letter because it does not begin a sentence.)

3. Capitalize the names of persons.

examples:

Ingrid Alvorsen and Sean Miller invited me to their wedding.
I asked Father to visit me.

Do not capitalize words like *mother, father,* or *aunt* if you put a possessive in front of them.

names with possessives:

I asked my father to visit me.
She disliked her aunt.

4. Capitalize the titles of persons.

examples:

I worked for Dr. Mabala.
She is interviewing Dean Richards.

Do not capitalize when the title is not connected to a name.

a title not connected to a name:

I worked for that doctor.
She is interviewing the dean.

5. Always capitalize nationalities, religions, races, months, days of the week, documents, organizations, holidays, and historical events or periods.

examples:

In eighth grade, I did a project on the American Revolution.
At my son's nursery school, the students presented a program to celebrate
    Thanksgiving.
Every Tuesday night, he goes to meetings at the African-American Club.

Use small letters for the seasons.

a season with a small letter:

I always look forward to the coming of winter.

6. Capitalize the names of particular places.

examples:

I used to attend Hawthorne Middle School.
My friends like to stroll through City Center Mall.

Use small letters if a particular place is not given.

small letter for no particular place:
My friends like to stroll through the mall.

7. Use capital letters for geographic locations.

examples:
Lisa wanted to attend a college in the South.
I love autumn in the Midwest.

But use small letters for geographic directions.

small letter for a geographic direction:
The easiest way to find the airport is to drive south on the freeway.

8. Capitalize the names of specific products.

examples:
I need some Tylenol for my headache.
Melanie eats a Snickers bar every day.

But use small letters for a general type of product.

small letter for a general product:
Melanie eats a candy bar every day.

9. Capitalize the names of specific school courses.

examples:
My favorite class is Ancient and Medieval History.
Alicia is taking Introduction to Computers this fall.

But use small letters for a general academic subject.

small letter for a general subject:
Before I graduate, I have to take a computer course.

10. Capitalize the first and last words in the titles of long or short works, and capitalize all other significant words in the title.

examples:
I loved the movie Sleepless in Seattle.
There is a beautiful song called "I Will Always Love You."

(Remember that the titles of long works, like movies, are underlined; the titles of short works, like songs, are placed within quotation marks.)

Exercise 24 **Punctuating with Capital Letters**

Practice   Add capital letters where they are needed in the following sentences.

1. My teachers in high school never made me take a psychology course.

2. The house I want to buy is just north of riverside drive near the springfield county garden club.

3. Felipe gave his mother a beautiful tablecloth made of irish linen.

4. "let's go see my brother," Tina said, "and borrow his truck."

5. I want to explore the west over the summer and stay away until labor day.

6. My former teacher, who is now dean Roth, told me he is looking for a new president of the spanish club.

7. Last sunday I spent the whole afternoon in front of the television, drinking pepsi and eating doritos.

8. I saw a copy of the declaration of independence at an exhibit at the hillsborough art center.

9. I once asked aunt louise if she liked being my aunt.

10. I am writing to the president of the company about the deteriorating condition of the concert hall.

Exercise 25 **Punctuating with Capital Letters: Creating Your Own Examples**

👥 Collaborate Do this exercise with a partner or a group. Below is a list giving situations when you should—or should not—use capital letters. Write a sentence at least five words long as an example for each item on the list.

1. Capitalize the names of particular places.

example: _Los Angeles is a very big city_

2. Use capital letters for geographic locations.

example: _The Amusement Park was fun._

3. Use small letters for geographic directions.

example: _I went to the zoo._

4. Capitalize historic events.

example: _____

5. Capitalize nationalities.

example: _____

6. Capitalize the names of persons.

example: _Aurthor loves to race and hike._

7. Do not capitalize words like *mother*, *father*, or *uncle* if you put a possessive in front of them.

example: _____

8. Capitalize the titles of persons.

example: _____

9. Do not capitalize when the title is not connected to a name.

example: _____

10. Capitalize the names of specific products.

example: _____

Exercise 26 **Punctuating with Quotation Marks, Underlining, and Capital Letters**

Connect

Following is a paragraph with some blank spaces. Fill in the blanks, remembering the rules for using quotation marks, underlining, and capital letters. When you have completed the exercise, be ready to share your responses with members of the class.

When I think about last year, I remember some very specific details. I remember that the song I was always listening to was called _You are the wind in the of my heart_, and the singer I admired most was _Whyteshadow_. The one movie I remember best is _____ _____, and the television program I recall watching is _____. There are several places I associate with last year, also. Among them is a store called _____, the school nearest to my home, called _____, and a place I always wanted to go to, but never visited, called _____ _____. When I think of last year, I realize that I spent many hours eating at a fast-food restaurant named _____. My favorite cold drink was _____. Today, I realize that some of my habits and tastes have changed, yet I am still very much connected to the specific places and things of the past.

NUMBERS

Spell out numbers that take one or two words to spell out.

examples:
The coat cost seventy dollars.
Bridget sent two hundred invitations.

Use hyphens to spell out numbers from twenty-one to ninety-nine.

examples:

Clarissa, twenty-three, is the oldest daughter.
I mailed sixty-two invitations.

Use numerals if it takes more than two words to spell a number.

examples:

The company sold 367 toy trains.
The price of the car was $15,629.

Use numerals to write dates, times, and addresses.

examples:

You can visit him at 223 Sailboat Lane.
I received my diploma on June 17, 1998.
We woke up at 6:00 a.m., bright and early.

Use numerals with *a.m.* and *p.m.*, but use words with *o'clock*.

example:

We woke up at six o'clock, bright and early.

ABBREVIATIONS

Although you should spell out most words rather than abbreviate them, you may use common abbreviations like *Mr.*, *Mrs.*, *Ms.*, *Jr.*, *Sr.*, and *Dr.* when they are used with a proper name. Abbreviations may also be used for references to time and for organizations widely known by initials.

examples:

I gave Dr. Lambert my medical records.
The phone rang at 3:00 a.m. and scared me out of a sound sleep.
Nancy got a job with the FBI.

Spell out the names of places, months, days of the week, courses of study, and words referring to parts of a book.

not this: I visited a friend in Philadelphia, ~~Penn.~~
but this: I visited a friend in Philadelphia, Pennsylvania.

not this: My brother skipped his ~~phys. ed.~~ class yesterday.
but this: My brother skipped his physical education class yesterday.

not this: Last week, our garbage was not picked up on ~~Weds.~~ or ~~Sat.~~, so I called the ~~Dept.~~ of Sanitation.
but this: Last week, our garbage was not picked up on Wednesday or Saturday, so I called the Department of Sanitation.

Exercise 27 **Punctuating with Numbers and Abbreviations**

Practice

Correct any errors in punctuating with numbers and abbreviations in the following sentences.

1. Mr. Zemeki's IBM computer cost over two-thousand dollars.

2. My favorite vacation was in my jr. year when I took a school trip to
Boston, Mass., to see the historical sites.

3. Can I borrow your trig. notes for the chapt. I missed?

4. Norris will be twenty-one tomorrow.

5. I signed the lease for a place at Hamilton Apts. on Feb. 1, 1997.

6. Lucinda gave fifty-seven dollars to the disaster relief fund; she made the money working for the dr. in our neighborhood clinic.

7. I asked her to give me 3 or 4 good reasons to drop my psych. class.

8. Raina is hoping to attend Cal. State U. next year, so she is taking a trip to California to explore the university.

9. Last night, I watched MTV until ten thirty-five p.m.

10. I was looking for a prof. who would do more than lecture about history.

Exercise 28

Practice

Punctuation: A Comprehensive Exercise

In the following sentences, add punctuation where it is needed and correct any punctuation errors.

1. My sister gave me a great book called The house on mango street Ill give it to you when Im finished with it.

2. Pet Haven the oldest pet supply store in town works with the local animal shelter.

3. Leo studied cooking in France thus he has been exposed to many new recipes and techniques.

4. After Lonny finished medical school he worked at Jackson memorial hospital.

5. Mr Rivera asked if there was a pharmacy nearby

6. Mr Rivera asked Is there a pharmacy nearby

7. I enjoyed my three cats antics but sometimes those cats drove me crazy.

8. You could borrow the money from your father on the other hand you could take out a bank loan.

9. Chocolate cake which is my favorite dessert is a disaster for my diet because its full of fat.

10. "If you can give me five minutes Lisa said Ill be ready to leave.

Exercise 29 Punctuation: Another Comprehensive Exercise

Practice

In the following sentences, add punctuation where it is needed and correct any punctuation errors.

1. Customers can be pushy and salespeople can be rude, but both groups need to learn patience if the marketplace is to become friendly again.

2. My car had a problem with its electrical system, so I spent two hundred [$247.00] and forty-seven dollars on repairs.

3. My mother always used to sing a song by James Taylor called "You've [G F] got a friend."

4. Jeff and I were married on Jan. [January] 23, 1990, in Tallahassee, [Florida] Fla. but moved farther south a year later.

5. One movie that I will never forget is Schindlers List.

6. Sure, you can borrow my hair dryer, mom, but remember to bring it back.

7. Last night, I washed and ironed all of Agnes' summer dresses her ruffled yellow one, her blue pinafore, and her pink sundress.

8. When you call Rafael remind him to buy soda, potato chips, dip and salsa for the mens softball game tomorrow.

9. I woke up at 6 a.m., so I had time to eat breakfast before I went to Miami-Dade [C] community [C] college.

10. Unless he does some work on that beat up house, he wont be able to sell it.

Exercise 30 Adding Punctuation to Paragraphs

Connect

The following paragraphs come from an article in *People* magazine. They tell the true story of two people on the *Titanic*, the famous ship that sank when it hit an iceberg in 1912.

As you read the paragraphs, you will notice that they are missing some punctuation (twenty-three punctuation marks). Add the necessary punctuation.

Isidor and Ida Strauss: Inseparable in Life, Then in Death

Ida Strauss refused at least two opportunities to escape the sinking

Titanic, choosing instead to die with her husband of fifty-one years, a well

known philanthropist* who owned Macy's department store News that the couple had shared their fate came as no surprise to their six children and many friends. When they were apart, they wrote to each other every day, says Joan Adler, director of the Strauss historical society "She called him my darling papa. He called her my darling momma." For years they even celebrated their different birthdays on the same day.

As the *Titanic* went down, Ida sixty-three refused the pleas of officers to climb into a lifeboat, insisting instead that her maid take her place and handing the young woman her fur coat (I wont need this anymore, she said). She was finally cajoled* into boarding the second to last lifeboat, only to clamber* out again as Isidor sixty-seven stepped away. Last seen clasped in an embrace Ida and Isidor are memorialized in a Bronx cemetery with a monument inscribed, "Many waters cannot quench love, neither can the floods drown it"

* **philanthropist:** a person who donates money to charity
* **cajoled:** persuaded
* **clamber:** climb

CHAPTER

17

Spelling

No one is a perfect speller, but there are ways for anyone to become a better speller. If you can learn a few spelling rules, you can answer many of your own spelling questions.

VOWELS AND CONSONANTS

To understand the spelling rules, you need to know the difference between vowels and consonants. **Vowels** are the letters *a*, *e*, *i*, *o*, *u*, and sometimes *y*. **Consonants** are all the other letters.

The letter *y* is a vowel when it has a vowel sound.

examples:

silly (The *y* sounds like *ee*, a vowel sound.)
cry (The *y* sounds like *i*, a vowel sound.)

The letter *y* is a consonant when it has a consonant sound.

examples:

yellow (The *y* has a consonant sound.)
yesterday (The *y* has a consonant sound.)

SPELLING RULE 1: DOUBLING A FINAL CONSONANT

Double the final consonant of a word if all three of the following are true:

1. the word is one syllable, or the accent is on the last syllable;
2. the word ends in a single consonant preceded by a single vowel, and
3. the ending you are adding starts with a vowel.

examples:

begin	+	ing	=	beginning
shop	+	er	=	shopper
stir	+	ed	=	stirred
occur	+	ed	=	occurred
fat	+	est	=	fattest
pin	+	ing	=	pinning

Exercise 1 **Doubling a Final Consonant**

Practice   Add -*ed* to the following words by applying the rule for doubling final consonants.

1. refer   _____   6. expel   _____

2. scatter _____   7. abandon _____

3. plan   _____   8. wonder   _____

4. trick   _____   9. suffer   _____

5. offer   _____   10. prefer _____

SPELLING RULE 2: DROPPING THE FINAL e

Drop the final *e* before you add an ending that starts with a vowel.

examples:

observe	+	ing	=	observing
excite	+	able	=	excitable
fame	+	ous	=	famous
create	+	ive	=	creative

Keep the final *e* before an ending that starts with a consonant.

examples:

love	+	ly	=	lovely
hope	+	ful	=	hopeful
excite	+	ment	=	excitement
life	+	less	=	lifeless

Exercise 2 **Dropping the Final e**

Practice   Combine the following words and endings by following the rule for dropping the final *e*.

1. move   +   able   _____

2. time   +   less   _____

3. shape   +   ly   _____

4. come   +   ing   _____

5. shape   +   ing   _____

6. advertise +   ment   _____

7. terminate +   ion   _____

8. defense   +   ive   _____

9. tame   +   ness   _____

10. debate   +   able   _____

SPELLING RULE 3: CHANGING THE FINAL *y* TO *i*

When a word ends in a consonant plus *y*, change the *y* to *i* when you add an ending.

examples:

try	+	es	=	tries
silly	+	er	=	sillier
rely	+	ance	=	reliance
tardy	+	ness	=	tardiness

Note: When you add *-ing* to words ending in *y*, always keep the *y*.

examples:

cry	+	ing	=	crying
rely	+	ing	=	relying

Exercise 3   **Changing the Final *y* to *i***

Practice   Combine the following words and endings by applying the rule for changing the final *y* to *i*.

1. copy   +   er   _____

2. pretty   +   ness _____

3. buy   +   er   _____

4. mercy   +   less _____

5. copy   +   ing   _____

6. carry   +   ed   _____

7. annoy   +   ance _____

8. pity   +   ful   _____

9. cry   +   es   _____

10. dismay +   ed   _____

SPELLING RULE 4: ADDING *-s* OR *-es*

Add *-es* instead of *-s* to a word if the word ends in *ch, sh, ss, x,* or *z*. The *-es* adds an extra syllable to the word.

examples:

box	+	es	=	boxes
witch	+	es	=	witches
class	+	es	=	classes
clash	+	es	=	clashes

Exercise 4 Adding *-s* or *-es*

Practice   Add *-s* or *-es* to the following words by applying the rule for adding *-s* or *-es*.

1. vanish _____   6. stretch _____

2. church _____   7. wander _____

3. trespass _____   8. clock _____

4. bunch _____   9. fizz _____

5. fox _____   10. retreat _____

SPELLING RULE 5: USING *ie* OR *ei*

Use *i* before *e* except after *c*, or when the sound is like *a*, as in *neighbor* and *weigh*.

examples of *i* before *e*:
relief   niece   friend   piece

examples of *e* before *i*:
conceive   sleigh   weight   receive

Exercise 5 Using *ie* or *ei*

Practice   Add *ie* or *ei* to the following words by applying the rules for using *ie* or *ei*.

1. d e c __ __ v e   6. t h __ __ f

2. r e c __ __ p t   7. v __ __ n

3. t r __ __ d   8. c h __ __ f

4. b e l __ __ f   9. p e r c __ __ v e

5. f r __ __ g h t   10. a c h __ __ v e

Exercise 6 Spelling Rules: A Comprehensive Exercise

Practice   Combine the following words and endings by applying the spelling rules.

1. tax   +   s *or* es   _____

2. guy   +   s *or* es   _____

3. fly   +   s *or* es   _____

4. beauty   +   ful   _____

5. deserve   +   ing   _____

6. home   +   less   _____

7. care   +   ful   _____

8. care   +   ing   _____

9. defer   +   ed   _____

10. scan   +   er   _____

Exercise 7 **Spelling Rules: Another Comprehensive Exercise**

Practice Combine the following words and endings by applying the spelling rules.

1. steady   +   ness   _____

2. ship   +   ment   _____

3. ship   +   ed   _____

4. regret   +   ing   _____

5. catch   +   s *or* es   _____

6. pass   +   s *or* es   _____

7. handy   +   er   _____

8. weigh   +   s *or* es   _____

9. marry   +   ed   _____

10. murmur   +   ed   _____

Exercise 8 **Creating Examples for the Spelling Rules**

Collaborate Working with a partner or a group, write examples for the following rules.

Spelling Rule 1: Doubling the Final Consonant
Double the final consonant of a word if all three of the following are true:

1. the word is one syllable, or the accent is on the last syllable;
2. the word ends in a single consonant preceded by a single vowel; and
3. the ending you are adding starts with a vowel.

example:

1. Write a word that is one syllable (or is accented on the last syllable), and

   that ends in a consonant preceded by a single vowel: _____

2. Write an ending that starts with a vowel: _____

3. Combine the word and the ending: inferred _____

Spelling Rule 2: Dropping the Final *e*
Drop the final *e* before you add an ending that starts with a vowel.

example:

1. Write a word that ends with an *e:* _____

2. Write an ending that starts with a vowel: _____

3. Combine the word and the ending: _____

Spelling Rule 3: Changing the Final *y* to *i*
When a word ends in a consonant plus *y*, change the *y* to *i* when you add an ending.

examples:

1. Write a word that ends in a consonant plus *y*: _____

2. Write an ending: _____

3. Combine the word and the ending: _____

Spelling Rule 4: Adding *-s* or *-es*
Add *-es* instead of *-s* to a word if the word ends in *ch*, *sh*, *ss*, *x*, or *z*. The *-es* adds an extra syllable to the word.

examples:

1. Write a word that ends in *ch*, *sh*, *ss*, *x*, or *z*: _____

2. Add *-es* to the word: _____

Spelling Rule 5: Using *ie* or *ei*
Use *i* before *e* except after *c*, or when the sound is like *a*, as in *neighbor* and *weigh*.

examples:

1. Write three words that use *i* before *e*: _____,

_____, _____

2. Write one word that uses *ei*: _____

Exercise 9 **Editing a Paragraph for Spelling**

Connect

Correct the twelve spelling errors in the following paragraph. Write your correction in the space above each error.

I have never been able to spell. I beleive my spelling problems come from several difficultys. First of all, I don't know how to use a dictionary. Whenever I had a spelling problem in grade school, my teachers refered me to a dictionary. But if I didn't know how to spell that word, how did I know where to look it up? After several trys, I always gave up. Second, I am a person who doesn't have much patience, especially when I write. I am someone who dislikes writing and who rushs through my assignments. I don't take the time to correct errors, and I don't spend much time

lookking for spelling mistaks. I am so releived to have finished the paper,
I don't want to spend any more time on it. Third, I don't believe that
spelling is very important. I figure that the purpose of puting words on
paper is makeing a point. Therefore, if you get my point, the spelling
shouldn't matter. Unfortunatly, most people believe that spelling does
matter, and so I guess I have to spend some time learning this skill.

HOW DO YOU SPELL IT? ONE WORD OR TWO?

Sometimes you can be confused about certain words. You are not sure whether
to combine them to make one word or to spell them as two words. The lists
below show some commonly confused words.

Words That Should Not Be Combined

a lot	even though	good night
all right	every time	living room
dining room	in front	no one
each other	high school	

Words That Should Be Combined

another	nevertheless
bathroom	newspaper
bedroom	playroom
bookkeeper	roommate
cannot	schoolteacher
downstairs	southeast, northwest, etc.
good-bye, goodbye, or good-by	throughout
grandmother	worthwhile
nearby	yourself

Words Whose Spelling Depends on Their Meaning

one word: *Already* means "before."
He offered to do the dishes, but I had *already* done them.

two words: *All ready* means "ready."
My dog was *all ready* to play Frisbee.

one word: *Altogether* means "entirely."
That movie was *altogether* too confusing.

two words: *All together* means "in a group."
My sisters were *all together* in the kitchen.

one word: *Always* means "every time."
My grandfather is *always* right about baseball statistics.

two words: *All ways* means "every path" or "every aspect."
We tried *all ways* to get to the beach house.
He is a gentleman in *all ways*.

one word: *Anymore* means "any longer."
I do not want to exercise *anymore*.

two words: *Any more* means "additional."
Are there *any more* pickles?

one word: *Anyone* means "any person at all."
Is *anyone* home?

two words: *Any one* means "one person or thing in a special group."
I'll take *any one* of the chairs on sale.
He offered to give *any one* of the students a ride home.

one word: *Apart* means "separate."
Liam stood *apart* from his friends.

two words: *A part* is "a piece or section."
I read *a part* of the chapter.

one word: *Everyday* means "ordinary."
Tim was wearing his *everyday* clothes.

two words: *Every day* means "each day."
Sam jogs *every day*.

one word: *Everyone* means "all the people."
Everyone has bad days.

two words: *Every one* means "all the people or things in a specific group."
My father asked *every one* of the neighbors for a donation to the Red Cross.

Exercise 10 **How Do You Spell It? One Word or Two?**

Practice   Circle the correct word in each of the following sentences.

1. It was an (altogether/all together) beautiful ceremony; I was happy to see my family (altogether/all together) at the wedding.

2. Celeste went to (highschool/high school) with (everyone/every one) of the contestants in the cooking contest.

3. The decorator painted the (diningroom/dining room) a pale green, but he painted (apart/a part) of the (bedroom/bed room) a bright orange.

4. If Mr. Han (cannot/can not) write the letter, you should write it (yourself/your self).

5. Sue and Anna live (nearby/near by), and they see (eachother/each other) often.

6. I told my (roommate/room mate) I had (already/all ready) called the (highschool/high school).

7. When my brother left, he said (goodnight/good night) but not (good-bye/good bye).

8. When I woke up, I did my (everyday/every day) chores, just the way I (always/all ways) do.

9. (Throughout/Through out) the night, Paul listened for the sound of a door opening (downstairs/down stairs).

10. An article in the (newspaper/news paper) said the accident victim was going to be (alright/all right).

Exercise 11   **How Do You Spell It? One Word or Two?**

Connect   The following paragraph contains ten errors in word combinations. Correct the errors in the space above each line.

My highschool education helped me to grow emotionally and intellectually. Even though I was not the best student, I know that I learned something from everyone of my classes. My history class taught me that the past is an all together fascinating subject, and my history teacher showed me what being a school teacher is all about. In my art class, I saw that people in every culture want to add beauty to their lives in always and at all times. My consumer math class helped me to be a better bookkeeper. My biology class was my toughest class, and at first I hated it. Never the less, I learned from it. My instructor showed me that I can not treat a laboratory like a play room. An other thing she did was give me a new respect for the environment. She taught me that noone has a right to abuse our natural resources. I will always be grateful to her and to all my high school teachers for introducing me to new skills and ideas.

A LIST OF COMMONLY MISSPELLED WORDS

Below is a list of words you use often in your writing. Study this list and use it as a reference.

1. absence	9. actually	17. American
2. absent	10. advertise	18. answer
3. accept	11. again	19. anxious
4. accommodate	12. all right	20. apology
5. ache	13. a lot	21. apparent
6. achieve	14. almost	22. appetite
7. acquire	15. always	23. appreciate
8. across	16. amateur	24. argue

25. argument
26. asked
27. athlete
28. attempt
29. August
30. aunt
31. author
32. automobile
33. autumn
34. avenue
35. awful
36. awkward
37. balance
38. basically
39. because
40. becoming
41. beginning
42. behavior
43. belief
44. believe
45. benefit
46. bicycle
47. bought
48. breakfast
49. breathe
50. brilliant
51. brother
52. brought
53. bruise
54. build
55. bulletin
56. bureau
57. buried
58. business
59. busy
60. calendar
61. cannot
62. career
63. careful
64. catch
65. category
66. caught
67. cemetery
68. cereal
69. certain
70. chair
71. cheat
72. chicken
73. chief
74. children
75. cigarette
76. citizen
77. city

78. college
79. color
80. comfortable
81. committee
82. competition
83. conscience
84. convenient
85. conversation
86. copy
87. cough
88. cousin
89. criticism
90. criticize
91. crowded
92. daily
93. daughter
94. deceive
95. decide
96. definite
97. dentist
98. dependent
99. deposit
100. describe
101. desperate
102. development
103. different
104. dilemma
105. dining
106. direction
107. disappearance
108. disappoint
109. discipline
110. disease
111. divide
112. doctor
113. doesn't
114. don't
115. doubt
116. during
117. dying
118. early
119. earth
120. eighth
121. eligible
122. embarrass
123. encouragement
124. enough
125. environment
126. especially
127. etc.
128. every
129. exact
130. exaggeration

131. excellent
132. except
133. excite
134. exercise
135. existence
136. expect
137. experience
138. explanation
139. factory
140. familiar
141. family
142. fascinating
143. February
144. finally
145. forehead
146. foreign
147. forty
148. fourteen
149. friend
150. fundamental
151. general
152. generally
153. goes
154. going
155. government
156. grammar
157. grateful
158. grocery
159. guarantee
160. guard
161. guess
162. guidance
163. guide
164. half
165. handkerchief
166. happiness
167. heavy
168. height
169. heroes
170. holiday
171. hospital
172. humorous
173. identity
174. illegal
175. imaginary
176. immediately
177. important
178. independent
179. integration
180. intelligent
181. interest
182. interfere
183. interpretation

184. interrupt
185. iron
186. irrelevant
187. irritable
188. island
189. January
190. jewelry
191. judgment
192. kindergarten
193. kitchen
194. knowledge
195. laboratory
196. language
197. laugh
198. leisure
199. length
200. library
201. listen
202. loneliness
203. lying
204. maintain
205. maintenance
206. marriage
207. mathematics
208. meant
209. measure
210. medicine
211. million
212. miniature
213. minute
214. muscle
215. mysterious
216. naturally
217. necessary
218. neighbor
219. nervous
220. nickel
221. niece
222. ninety
223. ninth
224. occasion
225. o'clock
226. often
227. omission
228. once

229. operate
230. opinion
231. optimist
232. original
233. parallel
234. particular
235. peculiar
236. perform
237. perhaps
238. permanent
239. persevere
240. personnel
241. persuade
242. physically
243. pleasant
244. possess
245. possible
246. potato
247. practical
248. prefer
249. prejudice
250. prescription
251. presence
252. president
253. privilege
254. probably
255. professor
256. psychology
257. punctuation
258. pursue
259. quart
260. really
261. receipt
262. receive
263. recognize
264. recommend
265. reference
266. religious
267. reluctantly
268. remember
269. resource
270. restaurant
271. rhythm
272. ridiculous
273. right

274. sandwich
275. Saturday
276. scene
277. schedule
278. scissors
279. secretary
280. seize
281. several
282. severely
283. significant
284. similar
285. since
286. sincerely
287. soldier
288. sophomore
289. strength
290. studying
291. success
292. surely
293. surprise
294. taught
295. temperature
296. theater
297. thorough
298. thousand
299. tied
300. tomorrow
301. tongue
302. tragedy
303. trouble
304. truly
305. twelfth
306. unfortunately
307. unknown
308. until
309. unusual
310. using
311. variety
312. vegetable
313. Wednesday
314. weird
315. which
316. writing
317. written
318. yesterday

18 Words That Sound Alike / Look Alike

WORDS THAT SOUND ALIKE / LOOK ALIKE

Words that sound alike or look alike can be confusing. Here is a list of some of these confusing words. Study this list, and make a note of any words that give you trouble.

a, an, and

A is used before a word beginning with a consonant or consonant sound.

> Jason bought *a* car.

An is used before a word beginning with a vowel or vowel sound.

> Nancy took *an* apple to work.

And joins words or ideas.

> Pudding *and* cake are my favorite desserts.
> Fresh vegetables taste delicious, *and* they are nutritious.

accept, except

Accept means "to receive."
> I *accept* your apology.

Except means "excluding."
> I'll give you all my books *except* my dictionary.

addition, edition

An *addition* is something that is added.

> My father built an *addition* to our house in the form of a porch.

An *edition* is an issue of a newspaper or one of a series of printings of a book.

> I checked the latest *edition* of the *Daily News* to see if my advertisement is in it.

advice, advise

Advice is an opinion offered as a guide; it is what you give someone.

> Betty asked for my *advice* about finding a job.

Advise is what you do when you give an opinion offered as a guide.

> I couldn't *advise* Betty about finding a job.

affect, effect

Affect means "to influence something."

> Getting a bad grade will *affect* my chances for a scholarship.

Effect means "a result" or "to cause something to happen."

> Your kindness had a great *effect* on me.
> The committee struggled to *effect* a compromise.

allowed, aloud

Allowed means "permitted."

> I'm not *allowed* to skateboard on those steps.

Aloud means "out loud."

> The teacher read the story *aloud.*

all ready, already

All ready means "ready."

> The dog was *all ready* to go for a walk.

Already means "before."

> David had *already* made the salad.

altar, alter

An *altar* is a table or place in a church.

> They were married in front of the *altar.*

Alter means "to change."

> My plane was delayed, so I had to *alter* my plans for the evening.

angel, angle

An *angel* is a heavenly being.

> That night, I felt an *angel* guiding me.

An *angle* is the space within two lines.

> The road turned at a sharp *angle.*

are, our

Are is a verb, the plural of *is.*

> We *are* friends of the mayor.

Our means "belonging to us."

> We have *our* family quarrels.

beside, besides

Beside means "next to."

> He sat *beside* me at the concert.

Besides means "in addition."

> I would never lie to you; *besides,* I have no reason to lie.

brake, break

Brake means "stop," or "a device for stopping."

> That truck *brakes* at railroad crossings.
> When he saw the animal on the road, he hit the *brakes*.

Break means "to come apart," or "to make something come apart."

> The eggs are likely to *break*.
> I can *break* the seal on that package.

breath, breathe

Breath is the air you take in, and it rhymes with "death."

> I was running so fast, I lost my *breath*.

Breathe means "to take in air."

> He found it hard to *breathe* at high altitudes.

buy, by

Buy means "to purchase something."

> Sylvia wants to *buy* a shovel.

By means "near," "by means of," or "before."

> He sat *by* his sister.
> I learn *by* taking good notes in class.
> *By* ten o'clock, Nick was tired.

capital, capitol

Capital means "a city" or "wealth."

> Albany is the *capital* of New York.
> Jack invested his *capital* in real estate.

A *capitol* is a building.

> The city has a famous *capitol*.

cereal, serial

A *cereal* is a breakfast food or a type of grain.

> My favorite *cereal* is Cheerios.

Serial means "in a series."

> Look for the *serial* number on the appliance.

choose, chose

Choose means "to select." It rhymes with *snooze*.

> Today I am going to *choose* a new sofa.

Chose is the past tense of *choose*.

> Yesterday I *chose* a new rug.

close, clothes, cloths

Close means "near" or "intimate." It can also mean "to end or shut something."

> We live *close* to the train station.
> James and Margie are *close* friends.
> Noreen wants to *close* her eyes for ten minutes.

Clothes are wearing apparel.

> Eduardo has new *clothes*.

Cloths are pieces of fabric.

> I clean the silver with damp *cloths* and a special polish.

coarse, course

Coarse means "rough" or "crude."

> The top of the table had a *coarse* texture.
> His language was *coarse*.

A *course* is a direction or path. It is also a subject in school.

> The hurricane took a northern *course*.
> In my freshman year, I took a *course* in drama.

complement, compliment

Complement means "complete" or "make better."

> The colors in that room *complement* the style of the furniture.

A *compliment* is praise.

> Trevor gave me a *compliment* about my cooking.

conscience, conscious

Your *conscience* is your inner moral guide.

> His *conscience* bothered him when he told a lie.

Conscious means "aware" or "awake."

> The accident victim was not fully *conscious*.

council, counsel

A *council* is a group of people.

> The city *council* meets tonight.

Counsel means "advice" or "to give advice."

> I need your *counsel* about my investments.
> My father always *counsels* me about my career.

decent, descent

Decent means "suitable" or "proper."

> I hope Mike gets a *decent* job.

Descent means "the process of going down, falling, or sinking."

> The plane began its *descent* to the airport.

desert, dessert

A *desert* is dry land. To *desert* means "to abandon."

> To survive trip across the *desert*, people need water.
> He will never *desert* a friend.

Dessert is the sweet food we eat at the end of a meal.

> I want ice cream for *dessert*.

do, due

Do means "perform."

   I have to stop complaining; I *do* it constantly.

Due means "owing" or "because of."

   The rent is *due* tomorrow.
   The game was canceled *due* to rain.

does, dose

Does is a form of *do*.

   My father *does* the laundry.

A *dose* is a quantity of medicine.

   Whenever I had a cold, my mother gave me a *dose* of cough syrup.

fair, fare

Fair means "unbiased." It can also mean "promising" or "good."

   The judge's decision was *fair*.
   Jose has a *fair* chance of winning the title.

A *fare* is a fee for transportation.

   My subway *fare* is going up.

farther, further

Farther means "at a greater physical distance."

   His house is a few blocks *farther* down the street.

Further means "greater" or "additional." Use it when you are not describing a physical distance.

   My second French class gave me *further* training in French conversation.

flour, flower

Flour is ground-up grain, an ingredient used in cooking.

   I use whole wheat *flour* in my muffins.

A *flower* is a blossom.

   She wore a *flower* in her hair.

forth, fourth

Forth means "forward."

   The pendulum on the clock swung back and *forth*.

Fourth means "number four in a sequence."

   I was *fourth* in line for the tickets.

hear, here

Hear means "to receive sounds in the ear."

   I can *hear* the music.

Here is a place.

   We can have the meeting *here*.

heard, herd

Heard is the past tense of *hear*.

> I *heard* you talk in your sleep last night.

A *herd* is a group of animals.

> The farmer has a fine *herd* of cows.

hole, whole

A *hole* is an empty place or opening.

> I see a *hole* in the wall.

Whole means "complete" or "entire."

> Silvio gave me the *whole* steak.

its, it's

Its means "belonging to it."

> The car lost *its* rear bumper.

It's is a shortened form of *it is* or *it has*.

> *It's* a beautiful day.
> *It's* been a pleasure to meet you.

knew, new

Knew is the past tense of *know*.

> I *knew* Teresa in high school.

New means "fresh," "recent," "not old."

> I want some *new* shoes.

know, no

Know means "to understand."

> They *know* how to play soccer.

No is a negative.

> Carla has *no* fear of heights.

Exercise 1   **Words That Sound Alike/Look Alike**

Practice   Circle the correct word in each of the following sentences.

1. David has traveled (farther/further) than I have, and he is so clever at finding bargains that he rarely pays full (fair/fare).

2. The jury was (conscience/conscious) of the prosecutor's hints that the (cereal/serial) killer had no conscience/conscious.

3. I'm nearly deaf; you must come over (hear/here) so I can (hear/here) you.

4. The Oakwood Student (Council/Counsel) meets on the (forth/fourth) floor of the library building.

5. When I (heard/herd) the trucks outside my window, they sounded like a (heard/herd) of cattle running down the street.

6. (Does/Dose) Olivia ever (complement/compliment) you on your appearance or even say you have a (decent/descent) hairstyle?

7. Cristina and Amy are such (close/clothes/cloths) friends that they wear each other's (close/clothes/cloths).

8. My little nephew insisted on helping me cook; he spilled (flour/flower) all over the kitchen floor and poured a (hole/whole) gallon of milk down the sink.

9. Some people believe that a guardian (angel/angle) is right (beside/besides) them when they are in trouble.

10. I had an elaborate dinner (all ready/already) for her arrival, but she said she had (all ready/already) eaten.

 **Exercise 2** Collaborate

Words That Sound Alike/Look Alike

Working with a partner or a group, write one sentence for each of the words below. When you have completed this exercise, exchange it with another group's exercise for evaluation.

1. a. its _____

   b. it's _____

2. a. are _____

   b. our _____

3. a. accept _____

   b. except _____

4. a. brake _____

   b. break _____

5. a. buy _____

   b. by _____

6. a. choose _____

   b. chose _____

7. a. desert _____

   b. dessert _____

8. a. conscience _____

   b. conscious _____

9. a. cereal _____

   b. serial _____

10. a. forth _____

   b. fourth _____

Exercise 3   **Correcting Errors in Words That Sound Alike/Look Alike**

Connect   The following paragraph has eight errors in words that sound alike or look alike. Correct the errors in the space above each error.

I am not sure how to chose a career. I want a job that pays well, so that I can live a comfortable life and retire with enough capitol to maintain my lifestyle. Of coarse, I also want to work in a place where I am aloud to express myself. It would be awful just to sit and stare at a computer screen all day. If I were trapped in a tiny office all day, I don't think I could breath. On the other hand, it may be foolish to expect too much of a job. A good job is hard to find, and maybe I should settle for financial security even if the work is boring. I think I should get some advise about my career because my choice will affect my entire future. Besides, some wise council can help me stop worrying about the hole issue.

MORE WORDS THAT SOUND ALIKE/LOOK ALIKE

lead, led

When *lead* rhymes with *need*, it means "to give direction, to take charge." When *lead* rhymes with *bed*, it is a metal.

The marching band will *lead* the parade.
Your bookbag is as heavy as *lead*.

Led is the past form of *lead* when it means "to take charge."

The cheerleaders *led* the parade last year.

loan, lone

A *loan* is something you give on the condition that it be returned.

When I was broke, I got a *loan* of fifty dollars from my aunt.

Lone means "solitary, alone."

> A *lone* shopper stood in the checkout line.

loose, lose

Loose means "not tight."

> In the summer, *loose* clothing keeps me cool.

To *lose* something means "to be unable to keep it."

> I'm afraid I will *lose* my car keys.

moral, morale

Moral means "upright, honorable, connected to ethical standards."

> I have a *moral* obligation to care for my children.

Morale is confidence or spirit.

> After the game, the team's *morale* was low.

pain, pane

Pain means "suffering."

> I had very little *pain* after the surgery.

A *pane* is a piece of glass.

> The girl's wild throw broke a window *pane*.

pair, pear

A *pair* is a set of two.

> Mark has a *pair* of antique swords.

A *pear* is a fruit.

> In the autumn, I like a *pear* for a snack.

passed, past

Passed means "went by." It can also mean "handed to."

> The happy days *passed* too quickly.
> Janice *passed* me the mustard.

Past means "a time before the present." It can also mean "beyond" or "by."

> The family reunion was like a trip to the *past*.
> Rick ran *past* the tennis courts.

patience, patients

Patience is calm endurance.

> When I am caught in a traffic jam, I should have more *patience*.

Patients are people under medical care.

> There are too many *patients* in the doctor's waiting room.

peace, piece

Peace is calmness.

> Looking at the ocean brings me a sense of *peace*.

A *piece* is a part of something.

> Norman took a *piece* of coconut cake.

personal, personnel

Personal means "connected to a person." It can also mean "intimate."

> Whether to lease or own a car is a *personal* choice.
> That information is too *personal* to share.

Personnel are the staff in an office.

> The Digby Electronics Company is developing a new health plan for its *personnel*.

plain, plane

Plain means "simple," "clear," or "ordinary." It can also mean "flat land."

> The restaurant serves *plain* but tasty food.
> Her house was in the center of a windy *plain*.

A *plane* is an aircraft.

> We took a small *plane* to the island.

presence, presents

Your *presence* is your attendance, your being somewhere.

> We request your *presence* at our wedding.

Presents are gifts.

> My daughter got too many birthday *presents*.

principal, principle

Principal means "most important." It also means "the head of a school."

> My *principal* reason for quitting is the low salary.
> The *principal* of Crestview Elementary School is popular with students.

A *principle* is a guiding rule.

> Betraying a friend is against my *principles*.

quiet, quit, quite

Quiet means "without noise."

> The library has many *quiet* corners.

Quit means "stop."

> Will you *quit* complaining?

Quite means "truly" or "exactly."

> Victor's speech was *quite* convincing.

rain, reign, rein

Rain is wet weather.

> We have had a week of *rain*.

To *reign* is to rule; *reign* is royal rule.

> King Arthur's *reign* in Camelot is the subject of many poems.

A *rein* is a leather strap in an animal's harness.

> When Charlie got on the horse, he held the *reins* very tight.

right, rite, write

Right means "a direction (the opposite of left)." It can also mean "correct."

To get to the gas station, turn *right* at the corner.
On my sociology test, I got nineteen out of twenty questions *right*.

A *rite* is a ceremony.

I am interested in the funeral *rites* of other cultures.

To *write* is to set down words.

Brian has to *write* a book report.

sight, site, cite

A *sight* is something you can see.

The truck stop was a welcome *sight*.

A *site* is a location.

The city is building a courthouse on the *site* of my old school.

Cite means "to quote an authority." It can also mean "to give an example."

In her term paper, Christina wanted to *cite* several computer experts.
When my father lectured me on speeding, he *cited* the story of my best
friend's car accident.

stair, stare

A *stair* is a step.

The toddler carefully climbed each *stair*.

To *stare* is to give a long, fixed look.

I wish that woman wouldn't *stare* at me.

stake, steak

A *stake* is a stick driven into the ground.

The gardener put *stakes* around the tomato plants.

A *steak* is a piece of meat or fish.

I like my *steak* cooked medium rare.

stationary, stationery

Stationary means "standing still."

As the speaker presented his speech, he remained *stationary*.

Stationery is writing paper.

For my birthday, my uncle gave me some *stationery* with my name
printed on it.

than, then

Than is used to compare things.

My dog is more intelligent *than* many people.

Then means "at that time."

I lived in Buffalo for two years; *then* I moved to Albany.

their, there, they're

Their means "belonging to them."

> My grandparents donated *their* old television to a women's shelter.

There means "at that place." It can also be used as an introductory word.

> Sit *there*, next to Simone.
> *There* is a reason for his happiness.

They're is a short form of *they are*.

> Jaime and Sandra are visiting; *they're* my cousins.

thorough, through, threw

Thorough means "complete."

> I did a *thorough* cleaning of my closet.

Through means "from one side to the other." It can also mean "finished."

> We drove *through* Greenview on our way to Lake Western.
> I'm *through* with my studies.

Threw is the past form of *throw*.

> I *threw* the moldy bread into the garbage.

to, too, two

To means "in a direction toward." It is also a word that can go in front of a verb.

> I am driving *to* Miami.
> Selena loves *to* write poems.

Too means "also." It also means "very" or "excessively."

> Anita played great golf; Adam did well, *too*.
> It is *too* kind of you to visit.

Two is the number.

> Mr. Almeida owns *two* clothing stores.

vain, vane, vein

Vain means "conceited." It also means "unsuccessful."

> Victor is *vain* about his dark, curly hair.
> The doctor made a *vain* attempt to revive the patient.

A *vane* is a device that moves to indicate the direction of the wind.

> There was an old weather *vane* on the barn roof.

A *vein* is a blood vessel.

> I could see the *veins* in his hands.

waist, waste

The *waist* is the middle part of the body.

> He had a leather belt around his *waist*.

Waste means "to use carelessly." It also means "thrown away as useless."

> I can't *waste* my time watching trashy television shows.
> That manufacturing plant has many *waste* products.

wait, weight

Wait means "to hold oneself ready for something."

I can't *wait* until my check arrives.

Weight means "heaviness."

He tested the *weight* of the bat.

weather, whether

Weather refers to the conditions outside.

If the *weather* is warm, I'll go swimming.

Whether means "if."

Whether you help me or not, I'll paint the hallway.

were, we're, where

Were is the past form of *are*.

Only last year, we *were* scared freshmen.

We're is the short form of *we are*.

Today *we're* confident sophomores.

Where refers to a place.

Show me *where* you used to play basketball.

whined, wind, wined

Whined means "complained."

Polly *whined* about the weather because the rain kept her indoors.

Wind (when it rhymes with *find*) means "to coil or wrap something" or "to turn a key."

Wind that extension cord or you'll trip on it.

Wind (when it rhymes with *sinned*) is air in motion.

The *wind* blew my cap off.

If someone *wined* you, he treated you to some wine.

My brother *wined* and dined his boss.

who's, whose

Who's is a short form of *who is* or *who has*.

Who's driving?
Who's been stealing my quarters?

Whose means "belonging to whom."

I wonder *whose* dog this is.

woman, women

Woman means "one female person."

A *woman* in the supermarket gave me her extra coupons.

Women means "more than one female person."

Three *women* from Missouri joined the management team.

wood, would

Wood is the hard substance in the trunks and branches of trees.

> I have a table made of polished *wood*.

Would is the past form of *will*.

> Albert said he *would* think about the offer.

your, you're

Your means "belonging to you."

> I think you dropped *your* wallet.

You're is the short form of *you are*.

> *You're* not telling the truth.

Exercise 4   **Words That Sound Alike/Look Alike**

Practice   Circle the correct word in each of the following sentences.

1. I told the salesman I (wood/would) rather have a (wood/would) fence (than/then) a metal one.

2. (Were/We're/Where) is the cake you (were/we're/where) supposed to bring to the birthday party?

3. Carl is (waiting/weighting) for me to decide (weather/whether) I want to go to the movies.

4. During the (rain/reign/rein) of Queen Elizabeth I, England suffered (thorough/through/threw) many political and religious conflicts.

5. The photographer insisted that the model remain (stationary/stationery) while he took some extra photographs.

6. I'm bringing my son, and (to/too/two) of my sisters are bringing (their/there) children, (to/too/two).

7. The (principal/principle) I live by is "Don't (waist/waste) time worrying."

8. My grandson had (quiet/quit/quite) a temper tantrum when I told him to be (quiet/quit/quite) and (quiet/quit/quite) interrupting me.

9. It's better to tell the (plain/plane) truth (than/then) to lie.

10. I work on a construction (sight/site/cite) near (to/too/two) of the city's most famous landmarks.

Exercise 5 **Words That Look Alike/Sound Alike**

Collaborate

Working with a partner or a group, write one sentence for each of the words below. When you have completed this exercise, exchange it with another group's completed exercise for evaluation.

1. a. stair _____

    b. stare _____

2. a. vain _____

    b. vane _____

    c. vein _____

3. a. were _____

    b. we're _____

    c. where _____

4. a. whose _____

    b. who's _____

5. a. your _____

    b. you're _____

6. a. stake _____

    b. steak _____

7. a. personal _____

    b. personnel _____

8. a. peace _____

    b. piece _____

9. a. moral _____

    b. morale _____

10. a. loose _____

    b. lose _____

Exercise 6 **Correcting Errors in Words That Sound Alike/Look Alike**

Connect

The following paragraph has eight errors in words that sound alike or look alike. Correct the errors in the space above each error.

Every April, my college has a celebration called The Rites of Spring.

Students, faculty, and administrators, to, enjoy this time too welcome a new and hopeful season. The art department sponsors a giant outdoor exhibit of photography, pottery, and would carving. Students in the horticulture program display the spring blossoms we've all been weighting for, for so long. Creative students read poetry on a stage backed with flowers. Everyone enjoys the music provided by the music department. The combination of art, music, poetry, and flowers makes this celebration a special time. It is the first campus activity to be held outdoors after months of bad whether. And even if it reins, the festival goes on—indoors. A time to celebrate spring is good for the moral of everyone: teachers, students, and administrative personal.

Exercise 7 **Words That Sound Alike/Look Alike: A Comprehensive Exercise**

Practice Circle the correct word in each of the following sentences.

1. I think Antonia needs to be more (conscious/conscience) of the (hole/whole) situation.

2. (Its/It's) too bad you forgot to bring (a/an) pencil with (a/an) eraser.

3. I'm not sure what (affect/effect) the (weather/whether) will have on his plans.

4. David asked Maria to (advice/advise) him about what (close/clothes/cloths) to wear.

5. My brother never thought I would get (thorough/through/threw) Algebra I; (beside/besides), he never believed I would get an A.

6. Bill (knew/new) I would never (desert/dessert) him in bad times.

7. The dog jumped on (its/it's) hind legs when it (heard/herd) me unwrap the stake/steak.

8. The weather (vain/vane/vein) was tilted at a strange (angel/angle).

9. Children are not (aloud/allowed) in that movie unless (their/there/they're) accompanied by an adult.

10. My grandmother started (wait/weight) training at a gym; she is an exceptional (woman/women).

Exercise 8
Practice

Words That Sound Alike/Look Alike: Another Comprehensive Exercise

Circle the correct word in each of the following sentences.

1. She was (all ready/already) to wax the car, but Damian had

   (all ready/already) done it.

2. Tom wrecked his (forth/fourth) (pair/pear) of shoes by walking in

   puddles; in (addition/edition), he got mud on his slacks.

3. On my way to work, I (passed/past) a big dog that did nothing but

   (stair/stare) at me.

4. Can you tell me (whose/who's) (cereal/serial) is spilled all over the floor?

5. The (patience/patients) at the children's clinic were thrilled with the

   gaily wrapped (presence/presents).

6. My sister needs a (brake/break) from her job; she does nothing

   (accept/except) work.

7. Vanessa gave me a (loan/lone) so I could (buy/by) gas for my car.

8. My coat was made of a (coarse/course) fabric that felt like a

   (peace/piece) of a blanket.

9. I'm paying you a (complement/compliment) when I say (your/you're)

   a (fare/fair) boss.

10. We (know/no) he will never (quiet/quit/quite) the team as long as he

    is healthy.

Exercise 9
Connect

Correcting Words That Sound Alike/Look Alike:
A Comprehensive Exercise

The following paragraph has eleven errors in words that sound alike or look alike. Correct the errors in the space above each line.

Horror movies scare me so much that I can hardly breath. I remember

one night when I was home alone, watching an old Dracula movie on tele-

vision. By the middle of the movie I was so terrified that I couldn't leave

my chair, even during a commercial brake. Once the movie was over and I

went to bed, I began to here strange noises outside. Soon the noises

seemed to be moving closer, and I was certain that a loan vampire was walking up the stares and wood soon arrive at my bedroom door. There was nothing I could do. I couldn't drive a steak through his heart, which was the way the hero killed the vampire in the movie. All I could do was weight for my doom. After what seemed like hours, I fell asleep. The next morning, I told myself that horror movies our silly and fake and that I should never loose any sleep over another movie. Unfortunately, every time I see a scary movie, I forget my own advise.

CHAPTER 19

Using Prepositions Correctly

Prepositions are usually short words that often signal a kind of position, possession, or other relationship. The words that come after the preposition are part of a **prepositional phrase.** You use prepositions often because there are many expressions that contain prepositions.

Sometimes it is difficult to decide on the correct preposition. The following pages explain kinds of prepositions and their uses, and list some common prepositions.

PREPOSITIONS THAT SHOW TIME

At a specific time means "then."

> I will meet you *at* three o'clock.
> *At* 7:00 p.m., he closes the store.

By a specific time means "no later than" that time.

> You have to finish your paper *by* noon.
> I'll be home *by* 9:30.

Until a specific time means "continuing up to" that time.

> I talked on the phone *until* midnight.
> I will wait for you *until* 7:00 p.m.

In a specific time period is used with hours, minutes, days, weeks, months, or years.

> *In* a week, I'll have my diploma.
> My family hopes to visit me *in* August.

> **Note**: Write *in* the morning, *in* the afternoon, *in* the evening, but *at* night.

For a period of time means "during" that time period.

> James took music lessons *for* five years.
> I studied *for* an hour.

Since means "from then until now."

> I haven't heard from you *since* December.
> Juanita has been my friend *since* our high school days.

On a specific date means "at that time."

> I'll see you *on* March 23.
> The restaurant will open *on* Saturday.

During means "within" or "throughout" a time period.

> The baby woke up *during* the night.
> Robert worked part-time *during* the winter semester.

PREPOSITIONS THAT INDICATE PLACE

On usually means "on the surface of," "on top of."

> Put the dishes *on* the table.
> They have a house *on* Second Avenue.

In usually means "within" or "inside of."

> Put the dishes *in* the cupboard.
> They have a house *in* Bolivia.

At usually means "in," "on," or "near to."

> I'll meet you *at* the market.
> The coffee shop is *at* the corner of Second Avenue and Hawthorne Road.
> Jill was standing *at* the door.

EXPRESSIONS WITH PREPOSITIONS

angry about: You are *angry about* a thing.

> Suzanne was *angry about* the dent in her car.

angry with: You are *angry with* a person.

> Richard became *angry with* his mother when she criticized him.

approve of, disapprove of: You *approve* or *disapprove of* a thing, or of a person or group's actions.

> I *approve of* the new gun law.
> I *disapprove of* smoking in public places.

argue about: You *argue about* some subject.

> We used to *argue about* money.

argue for: You *argue for* something you want.

> The Student Council *argued for* more student parking.

argue with: You *argue with* a person.

> When I was a child, I spent hours *arguing with* my little sister.

arrive at: You *arrive at* a place.

> We will *arrive at* your house tomorrow.

between, among: You use *between* with two. You use *among* with three or more.

> It will be a secret *between* you and me.
> We shared the secret *among* the three of us.

bored by, bored with: You are *bored by* or *bored with* something. Do *not* write *bored of*.

> The audience was *bored by* the long movie.
> The child become *bored with* her toys.
> **not this:** ~~I am bored of school.~~

call on: You *call on* someone socially or to request something of a person.

> My aunt *called on* her new neighbors.
> Our club will *call on* you to collect tickets at the door.

call to: You *call to* someone from a distance.

> I heard him *call to* me from the top of the hill.

call up: You *call up* someone on the telephone.

> When she heard the news, Susan *called up* all her friends.

differ from: You *differ from* someone, or something *differs from* something.

> Roberta *differs from* Cheri in hair color and height.
> A van *differs from* a light truck.

differ with: You *differ with* (disagree with) someone about something.

> Theresa *differs with* Mike on the subject of food stamps.

different from: You are *different from* someone; something is *different from* something else. Do *not* write *different than*.

> Carl is *different from* his older brother.
> The movie was *different from* the book.
> **not this:** ~~The movie was different than the book.~~

grateful for: You are *grateful for* something.

> I am *grateful for* my scholarship.

grateful to: You are *grateful to* someone.

> My brother was *grateful to* my aunt for her advice.

interested in: You are *interested in* something.

> The children were *interested in* playing computer games.

look at: You *look at* someone or something.

> My sister *looked at* my haircut and laughed.

look for: You *look for* someone or something.

> David needs to *look for* his lost key.

look up: You *look up* information.

> I can *look up* his address in the phone book.

made of: Something or someone is *made of* something.

> Do you think I'm *made of* money?
> The chair was *made of* plastic.

need for: You have a *need for* something.

> The committee expressed a *need for* better leadership.

object to: You *object to* something.

> Lisa *objected to* her husband's weekend plans.

obligation to: You have an *obligation to* someone.

>I feel an *obligation to* my parents, who supported me while I was in college.

opportunity for: You have an *opportunity for* something; an *opportunity* exists *for* someone.

>The new job gives her an *opportunity for* a career change.
>A trip to Korea is a wonderful *opportunity for* Mimi.

pay for: You *pay* someone *for* something.

>I have to *pay* the plumber *for* the repairs to my sink.

pay to: You *pay* something *to* someone.

>Brian *paid* fifty dollars *to* the woman who found his lost dog.

popular with: Something or someone is *popular with* someone.

>Jazz is not *popular with* my friends.

prefer . . . to: You *prefer* something *to* something.

>I *prefer* jazz *to* classical music.

prejudice against: You have a *prejudice against* someone or something.

>My father finally conquered his *prejudice against* women drivers.

>**Note:** Remember to add *-ed* when the word becomes an adjective.

>He is *prejudiced against* scientists.

protect against: Something or someone *protects against* something or someone.

>A good raincoat can *protect* you *against* heavy rain.

protect from: Something or someone *protects from* something or someone.

>A good lock on your door can *protect* you *from* break-ins.

qualification for: You have a *qualification for* a position.

>Andre is missing an important *qualification for* the job.

qualified to: You are *qualified to* do something.

>Tim isn't *qualified to* judge the paintings.

quote from: You *quote* something *from* someone else.

>The graduation speaker *quoted* some lines *from* Shakespeare.

reason for: You give a *reason for* something.

>He offered no *reason for* his rude behavior.

reason with: You *reason with* someone.

>Sonny tried to *reason with* the angry motorist.

responsible for: You are *responsible for* something.

>Luther is *responsible for* the mess in the kitchen.

responsible to: You are *responsible to* someone.

>At the restaurant, the waiters are *responsible to* the assistant manager.

rob of: You *rob* someone *of* something.

>His insult *robbed* me *of* my dignity.

similar to: Someone or something is *similar to* someone or something.

Your dress is *similar to* a dress I had in high school.

succeed in: You *succeed in* something.

I hope I can *succeed in* getting a job.

superior to: Someone or something is *superior to* someone or something.

My final paper was *superior to* my first paper.

take advantage of: You *take advantage of* someone or something.

Maria is going to *take advantage of* the fine weather and go to the beach.

take care of: You *take care of* someone or something.

Rick will *take care of* my cat while I'm away.

talk about: You *talk about* something.

We can *talk about* the trip tomorrow.

talk over: You *talk over* something.

The cousins met to *talk over* the plans for the anniversary party.

talk to: You *talk to* someone.

I'll *talk to* my father.

talk with: You *talk with* someone.

Esther needs to *talk with* her boyfriend.

tired of: You are *tired of* something.

Sylvia is *tired of* driving to work.

wait for: You *wait for* someone or something.

Jessica must *wait for* Alan to arrive.

wait on: You use *wait on* only if you wait on customers.

At the diner, I have to *wait on* too many people.

Exercise 1 **Choosing the Correct Preposition**

Practice Circle the correct preposition in each of the following sentences.

1. Susan told me that she would have the room ready (by/in) an hour.

2. We drove around Manchester (for/since) two hours.

3. We could find a good used car (at/in) Olsen Auto Market.

4. Dennis has a studio apartment (in/on) Orchard Street.

5. I couldn't find the cold pills (in/on) the bathroom drawer.

6. Magda and Pierre stayed up (by/until) midnight, talking about old times.

7. When Eddie gets upset, it is impossible to reason (for/with) him.

8. My boss said I was responsible (for/to) the mess in the kitchen.

9. The shipment of oranges will arrive (at/to) the warehouse next week.

10. The ceremony was so long that I became bored (of/with) it.

Exercise 2 **More on Choosing the Correct Preposition**

Practice   Circle the correct preposition in each of the following sentences.

1. Every time my sister sees a spider, she thinks she has to call (to/up) an exterminator.

2. Nora differs (from/with) Andy on the issue of capital punishment.

3. Nancy hasn't had a cigarette (in/on) a month.

4. I saw him riding (in/on) a car yesterday; he waved at me from the back seat.

5. If I finish college, I will be more likely to succeed (at/in) the business world.

6. When Eddie loses his temper, it is impossible to reason (for/with) him.

7. The management told me I needed additional qualifications (for/to) the position of assistant manager.

8. We can divide the cooking (among/between) the four of us.

9. Yvette is a good swimmer, but she prefers tennis (over/to) swimming.

10. My little brother was sitting in a tree and calling (on/to/up) his friends below.

Exercise 3 **Writing Sentences Using Expressions with Prepositions**

Collaborate   Do this exercise with a partner or a group. Below are pairs of expressions with prepositions. Write a sentence that contains each pair. The first one is done for you.

1. a. argue with   b. object to

   sentence: <u>In college, I used to argue with my roommate whenever he would</u>

   <u>object to my loud music.</u>

2. a. angry about   b. complain to

   sentence: _____

   _____

3. a. grateful for   b. succeed in

   sentence: _____

   _____

4. a. succeed in   b. capable of

sentence: _____

_____

5. a. interested in   b. bored by

sentence: _____

_____

6. a. call on   b. qualified to

sentence: _____

_____

7. a. prejudice against   b. superior to

sentence: _____

_____

8. a. grateful to   b. opportunity for

sentence: _____

_____

9. a. pay for   b. pay to

sentence: _____

_____

10. a. responsible to   b. different from

sentence: _____

_____

Exercise 4 **Writing Sentences Using Expressions with Prepositions**

Collaborate   Do this exercise with a partner. Review the list of expressions with prepositions in this chapter. Select five expressions that you think are troublesome for writers. Write the expressions below. Then exchange lists with your partner. Your partner will write a sentence for each expression on your list; you will write sentences for his or her list. When you have completed the exercises, check each other's sentences.

1. expression: _____

sentence: _____

2. expression: _____

    sentence: _____

3. expression: _____

    sentence: _____

4. expression: _____

    sentence: _____

5. expression: _____

    sentence: _____

Exercise 5   **Using Prepositions Correctly**

Connect   The following paragraph has seven errors in prepositions. Correct the errors in the space above each error.

    I usually don't go to horror movies because I hate scenes filled with blood. However, I recently saw a horror movie that changed my opinion of frightening films. I went because my best friend persuaded me to take a chance on a movie that is very popular for all age groups and all kinds of audiences. My friend said the movie was excellent and swore I would not object at any of the violent scenes. Even though I entered the theater with a real prejudice on this kind of film, I was pleasantly surprised. I found myself interested on the plot and characters, and I was happy to note that the horror in the film didn't come from blood and gore. It came from the suspense and mystery on the movie. The use of darkness, shadows, and eerie music created most of the thrills. I am grateful for my friend for taking me to this movie, and I have learned that some horror movies are different than others.

Exercise 6   **Recognizing Prepositional Phrases in a Famous Speech**

Collaborate   Do this exercise with a group. Following is part of a famous speech by Winston Churchill, a prime minister of Great Britain during World War II. When Churchill gave this speech in 1940, the Nazis had just defeated the British troops at Dunkirk, France. In this speech, Churchill explained the events at Dunkirk and then rallied the nation to keep fighting.

To do this exercise, have one member of your group read the speech aloud while the other members listen. Then underline all the prepositional phrases in it. Be ready to share your answers with another group.

We shall not flag* nor fail. We shall go on to the end. We shall fight in France and on the seas and oceans; we shall fight with growing confidence and growing strength in the air.

We shall defend our island whatever the cost may be; we shall fight on beaches, on landing grounds, in fields, in streets and on the hills. We shall never surrender, and even if, which I do not for a moment believe, this island or a large part of it were subjugated* and starving, then our empire beyond the seas, armed and guarded by the British Fleet, would carry on the struggle until in God's good time the New World, with all its power and might, steps forth to the liberation and rescue of the Old.

* **flag:** to lose energy
* **subjugated:** conquered by the enemy
* **the fleet:** a group of warships

Writing in Steps
The Process Approach

INTRODUCTION

Learning by Doing

Writing is a skill, and like any skill, it improves with practice. Through a menu of activities, this part of the book gives you the opportunity to improve your writing. Some activities can be done alone; some ask that you work with a partner or with a group. You can do some in the classroom; some can be done at home. The important thing to remember is that *good writing takes practice*; you can learn to write well by writing.

Steps Make Writing Easier

Writing is easier if you *don't try to do everything at once*. Producing a piece of effective writing demands that you think, plan, focus, and draft; then rethink, revise, edit, and proofread. You can become frustrated if you try to do all these things at the same time.

To make the task of writing easier, this section breaks the process into four major steps:

Thought Lines

In this step, you *think* about your topic, and you gather ideas. You *react* to your own ideas and add more ideas to your first thoughts. Or you react to other people's ideas as a way of generating your own writing material.

Outlines

In this step, you learn to *plan* your writing. You examine your own ideas and begin to *focus* them around one main idea. Planning involves combining, dividing, and sometimes even discarding the ideas you started with. It involves more thinking about the point you want to make and devising the best way to express it.

Rough Lines

In this step, your thinking and planning begin to shape themselves into a piece of writing. You complete a *draft* of your work—a rough version of the finished product. And then you think again, as you examine the draft and check it. Checking it begins the process of *revision*, "fixing" the draft so that it takes the shape you want it to and expresses your ideas clearly.

Final Lines

In this step, you give the final draft of your writing one last, careful *review*. When you prepare the final copy of your work, you *proofread* and concentrate on identifying and correcting any mistakes in word choice, spelling, mechanics, or punctuation you may have overlooked. This step is the *final check* of your work to make sure your writing is the best that it can be.

These four steps in the writing process—*thought lines*, *outlines*, *rough lines*, and *final lines*—always overlap. You may be changing your plan (the *outlines* stage) even as you work on the *rough lines* of your paper, and there is no rule that says you cannot move back to an earlier step when you need to. Thinking of writing as a series of steps helps you to see the process as a *manageable task*. You can avoid doing everything at once and becoming overwhelmed by the challenge.

Once you learn these four steps, you can put them to use. As you work through the writing chapters of this book, you will work with examples of each of the four steps and practice them.

CONTENTS
Writing in Steps: The Process Approach   247

20

Writing a Paragraph: Generating Ideas— Thought Lines

The paragraph is the basic building block of most writing. A **paragraph** is a group of sentences focusing on one idea or one point. Keep this concept in mind: *one idea for each paragraph.* Focusing on one idea or one point gives a paragraph *unity.* If you have a new point, start a new paragraph.

You may ask, "Doesn't this mean my paragraph will be short? How long should a paragraph be, anyway?" To convince a reader of one main point, you need to make the point, support it, develop it, explain it, and describe it. There will be shorter and longer paragraphs, but for now, you can assume that your paragraph will be between seven and twelve sentences long.

This chapter will guide you through the first step of the writing process, the *thought lines,* where you generate ideas for your paragraph.

BEGINNING THE THOUGHT LINES

Suppose your instructor asks you to write a paragraph about family. To write effectively, you need to know your *purpose* and your *audience.* In this case, you already know your purpose—to write a paragraph that makes some point about family. You also know your audience, since you are writing this paragraph for your instructor and your classmates. Often, your purpose is to write a specific type of paper for a class. However, you may have to write with a different purpose for a particular audience. Writing instructions for a new employee at your workplace, writing a letter of complaint to a manufacturer, and composing a short autobiographical essay for a scholarship application are examples of different purposes and audiences.

Freewriting, Brainstorming, Keeping a Journal

Once you have identified your purpose and audience, you can begin by finding some way to *think* on paper. To gather ideas, you can use the techniques of freewriting, brainstorming, or keeping a journal.

Freewriting Give yourself ten minutes to write whatever comes into your mind on the subject. If you can't think of anything to write, just write, "I can't think of anything to write" over and over until you think of something else. The main goal of **freewriting** is to *write without stopping*. Don't stop to tell yourself, "This is stupid," or "I can't use any of this in a paper." Just write. Let your ideas flow. Write freely. Here's an example:

Freewriting About Family

Family. Family. Whose family? What is a family? What does she want me to write about? I'm not married. I don't have a family. Sure, my mother. I guess I have a big other fami-ly, too. Cousins, aunts, uncles. But my basic family is my mother and brother Tito. Is that a family? She's a good mom. Always takes care of me. Family ties. Family matters. How a family treats children.

Brainstorming Brainstorming is like freewriting because you write whatever comes into your head, but it is a little different because you can *pause to ask yourself questions* that will lead to new ideas. When you brainstorm alone, you "interview" yourself about a subject. Or you can brainstorm within a group.

If you are brainstorming about family, alone or with a partner or group, you might begin by listing ideas and then add to the ideas by asking and answering questions. Here's an example:

Brainstorming About Family

Family.
Family members.

Who is your favorite family member?
I don't know. Uncle Ray, I guess.

Why is he your favorite?
He's funny. Especially at those family celebrations.

What celebrations?
Birthdays, anniversaries, dinners. I hated those dinners when I was little.

Why did you hate them?
I had to get all dressed up.

What else did you hate about them?
I had to sit still through the longest, most boring meals.

Why were they boring?
All these grown-ups talking. My mother made me sit there, politely.

Were you angry at your mother?
Yes. Well, no, not really. She's strict, but I love her.

If you feel that you are running out of ideas in brainstorming, try to form a question out of what you've just written. For example, if you write, "Families are changing," you could form these questions:

What families? How are they changing? Are the changes good? Why? Why not?

Forming questions helps you keep your thoughts flowing, and you will eventual-ly arrive at a suitable focus for your paragraph.

Keeping a Journal A **journal** is a notebook of your personal writing, a notebook in which you write regularly and often. *It is not a diary, but it is a place to record your experiences, reactions, and observations*. In it, you can write about what you've done, heard, seen, read, or remembered. You can include sayings that you'd like to remember, news clippings, snapshots—anything that you'd like to recall or consider. Journals are a great way to practice your writing and a great source of ideas for writing.

If you were asked to write about family, for example, you might look through entries in your journal in search of ideas, and you might see something like this:

Journal Entry About Family

I was at Mike's house last night. We were just sitting around, talking and listening to CDs. Then we were bored, so we decided to go to the movies. When we left, we walked right past Mike's mother in the kitchen. Mike didn't even say good-bye or tell her where we were going. Mike is so rude to his mother. He can't stand her. Lots of my friends hate their parents. I'm lucky. I'm close to my mother.

Finding Specific Ideas

Whether you freewrite, brainstorm, or consult your journal, you end up with something on paper. Follow these first ideas; see where they can take you. You are looking for specific ideas, each of which can focus the general one you started with. At this point, you do not have to decide which specific idea you want to write about. You just want to narrow your range of ideas.

You might ask, "Why should I narrow my ideas? Won't I have more to say if I keep my topic big?" But remember that a paragraph has one idea. You want to say one thing clearly, and you want to use convincing details that support your main idea. If you write one paragraph on the broad topic of family, for example, you will probably make only general statements that say very little and bore your reader.

General ideas are big, broad ones. Specific ideas are narrow. If you scanned the freewriting example on family, you might underline many specific ideas that could be topics.

Family. Family. Whose family? What is a family? What does she want me to write about? I'm not married. I don't have a family. Sure, <u>my mother</u>. I guess I have a <u>big other family</u>, too. Cousins, aunts, uncles. But <u>my basic family</u> is my mother and brother Tito. Is that a family? <u>She's a good mom</u>. <u>Always takes care of me</u>. Family ties. Family matters. How a family treats children.

Consider the underlined parts. Many of them are specific ideas about family. You could write a paragraph about one underlined item or about several related items.

Another way to find specific ideas is to make a list after brainstorming, underlining specific ideas. Here is an underlined list about family:

Family.
Family members.
<u>Uncle Ray</u>.
He's funny. Especially at those <u>family celebrations. Birthdays, anniversaries, dinners. I hated those dinners when I was little.</u>
<u>I had to get all dressed up.</u>
I had to sit still through the <u>longest, most boring meals</u>. All these grown-ups, talking. My mother made me sit there, politely.
<u>She's strict, but I love her.</u>

These specific ideas could lead you to specific topics.

If you reviewed the journal entry on family, you would be able to underline many specific ideas:

> I was at Mike's house last night. We were just sitting around, talking and listening to CDs. Then we were bored, so we decided to go to the movies. When we left, we walked right past Mike's mother in the kitchen. <u>Mike didn't even say good-bye or tell her where we were going. Mike is so rude to his mother. He can't stand her. Lots of my friends hate their parents. I'm lucky. I'm close to my mother.</u>

Remember, following the steps in gathering ideas can lead you to specific ideas. Once you have some specific ideas, you can pick one idea and develop it.

Exercise 1 **Brainstorming Questions and Answers**

Practice

Following are several general topics. For each one, brainstorm by writing three questions and answers related to the topic that could lead you to specific ideas. The first topic is done for you.

1. general topic: home computers

Question 1. Do I need my home computer?

Answer 1. Sure. I use it all the time.

Question 2. But what do I use it for?

Answer 2. Games. Surfing the Internet.

Question 3. So I don't use it for anything serious, do I?

Answer 3. It helps me do research and type my papers.

2. general topic: sports injuries

Question 1. _____

Answer 1. _____

Question 2. _____

Answer 2. _____

Question 3. _____

Answer 3. _____

3. general topic: childhood fears

Question 1. _____

Answer 1. _____

Question 2. _____

Answer 2. _____

Question 3. _____

Answer 3.   _____

4. general topic: violent movies

Question 1. _____

Answer 1.   _____

Question 2. _____

Answer 2.   _____

Question 3. _____

Answer 3.   _____

5. general topic: employment

Question 1. _____

Answer 1.   _____

Question 2. _____

Answer 2.   _____

Question 3. _____

Answer 3.   _____

Exercise 2 **Finding Specific Ideas in a List**

Practice Following are general topics; each general topic is followed by a list of words or phrases about the general topic. It is the kind of list you could make after brainstorming. Underline the words or phrases that are specific and could lead you to a specific topic. The first list is done for you.

1. general topic: sleeping habits

— how people sleep

— <u>snoring all night</u>

— everyone sleeps

— <u>why people toss and turn</u>

— ways of sleeping

2. general topic: pets

— litter box training

— all kinds of pets

  – obedience school

  – adopting a shelter dog

  – animals and people

3. general topic: exercise

  – finding good running shoes

  – physical activity

  – benefits of a health club

  – exercising with a friend

  – getting exercise

4. general topic: shoppers

  – people in stores

  – bargain hunters

  – buyers of merchandise

  – last-minute shoppers

  – shopaholics

5. general topic: health

  – anatomy and physiology

  – getting enough vitamins

  – cold remedies

  – staying well

  – doctors

Exercise 3 **Finding Specific Ideas in Freewriting**

Practice
Following are two samples of freewriting. Each is a written response to a different topic. Read each sample, and then underline any words or phrases that could become the focus of a paragraph.

Freewriting on the Topic of Cooking

What do I know about cooking? I'm a guy. I never cook. My mom cooks really well. My girlfriend cooks, too. She can't cook like my mother. I did cook, once. It was a disaster. Nearly set my apartment on fire when I tried to cook a turkey. I love turkey. My mother makes a great turkey dinner. Home cooking. Nothing like it. It's great. That's cooking. Home cooking is better than a restaurant any day.

Freewriting on the Topic of Jobs

My first job. My boss was Mr. Silvero. Now, I have a woman boss. Male vs. female bosses, pro and con. My first job was a summer job when I was still in high school. High school jobs. They don't pay much. Good experience, though. Mr. Silvero taught me a lot.

Exercise 4 **Finding Topics Through Freewriting**

👥 Collaborate

Begin this exercise alone; then complete it with a partner or group. First, pick one of the topics and freewrite on it for ten minutes. Then read your freewriting to your partner or group. Ask your listener(s) to jot down any words or phrases that lead to a specific subject for a paragraph. Your listener(s) should read the jotted-down words or phrases to you. You will be hearing a collection of specific ideas that came from *your* writing. As you listen, underline the words in your freewriting.

Freewriting Topics (pick one):

    a. sports

    b. money

    c. crime

Freewriting on _____ (name of topic chosen)

_____

_____

_____

_____

_____

_____

_____

Selecting an Idea

After you have a list of specific ideas, you must pick one and try to develop it by adding details. To pick an idea about family, you could survey the ideas you gathered through freewriting. Review the following freewriting, in which the specific ideas are underlined:

Family. Family. Whose family? What is a family? What does she want me to write about? I'm not married. I don't have a family. Sure, <u>my mother</u>. I guess I have a <u>big other family</u>, too. Cousins, aunts, uncles. But <u>my basic family</u> is my mother and brother Tito. Is that a family? <u>She's a good mom</u>. <u>Always takes care of me</u>. Family ties. Family matters. How a family treats children.

Here are the specific ideas (the underlined ones) in a list:

— my mother	— She's a good mom.
— a big other family	— always takes care of me
— my basic family	

Looking at these ideas, you decide to write your paragraph on this topic: My Mother.

Now you can begin to add details.

Adding Details to an Idea

You can develop the one idea you picked in a number of ways:

1. *Check your list* for other ideas that seem to fit the one you've picked.

2. *Brainstorm*—ask yourself more questions about your topic, and use the answers as details.

3. *List any new ideas* you have that may be connected to your first idea.

One way to add details is to go back and check your list for other ideas that seem to fit with the topic of My Mother. You find these entries:

She's a good mom. Always takes care of me

Another way to add details is to brainstorm some questions that will lead you to more details. These questions do not have to be connected to each other; they are just questions that could lead you to ideas and details.

Question: What makes your mom a good mom?
Answer: She works hard.

Question: What work does she do?
Answer: She cooks, cleans.

Question: What else?
Answer: She has a job.

Question: What job?
Answer: She's a nurse.

Question: How is your mother special?
Answer: She had a rough life.

Another way to add details is to list any ideas that may be connected to your first idea of writing about your mother. The list might give you more specific details:

- makes great chicken casserole
- good-looking for her age
- lost her husband
- went to school at night

If you tried all three ways of adding details, you would end up with this list of details connected to the topic of My Mother:

— She's a good mom.	— She had a rough life.
— always takes care of me	— makes great chicken casserole
— She works hard.	— good-looking for her age
— She cooks, cleans.	— lost her husband
— She has a job.	— went to school at night
— She's a nurse.	

You now have details that you can work with as you move into the next stage of writing a paragraph.

This process may seem long, but once you have worked through it several times, it will become nearly automatic. When you think about ideas before you try to shape them, you are off to a good start.

Infobox

Beginning the Thought Lines: A Summary

The thought lines stage of writing a paragraph enables you to gather ideas. This process begins with four steps:

1. *Think on paper and write down any ideas that you have about a general topic.* You can do this by freewriting, brainstorming, or keeping a journal.

2. *Scan your writing for specific ideas that have come from your first efforts.* List these ideas.

3. *Pick one specific idea.* This idea will be the topic of your paragraph.

4. *Add details to your topic.* You can add details by reviewing your early writing, by questioning, and by thinking further.

FOCUSING THE THOUGHT LINES

Once you have a topic and some ideas about the topic, your next step is to *focus* your topic and ideas around some point. Two techniques that you can use are

- marking a list of related ideas
- mapping related ideas

Marking Related Ideas

To develop a marked list, take another look at the list developed under the topic My Mother. The same list is shown below, but this time you'll notice that some of the items have been marked with letters that represent categories for related items:

H marks ideas about your mother at home.
J marks ideas about your mother's job.
B marks ideas about your mother's background.

Here is the list:

H	She's a good mom.	B	She had a rough life.
H	always takes care of me	H	makes great chicken casserole
H & J	She works hard.		good-looking for her age
H	She cooks, cleans.	B	lost her husband
J	She has a job.	B	went to school at night
J	She's a nurse.		

You have probably noticed that one item, *She works hard*, is marked with two letters, H and J, because your mother works hard both at home and on the job. One item on the list, *good-looking for her age*, is not marked. Perhaps you can come back to this item later, or perhaps you will decide you do not need it in your paragraph.

To make it easier to see what ideas you have and how they are related, try *grouping related ideas*, giving each list a title, like this:

my mother at home

  — She's a good mom.   always takes care of me
  — She works hard.   She cooks, cleans.
  — makes great chicken casserole

my mother at her job

  — She has a job.   She's a nurse.
  — She works hard.

my mother's background

  — She had a rough life.   lost her husband
  — went to school at night

Mapping

Another way to focus your ideas is to mark your first list of ideas and then cluster the related ideas into separate lists. You can *map* your ideas like this:

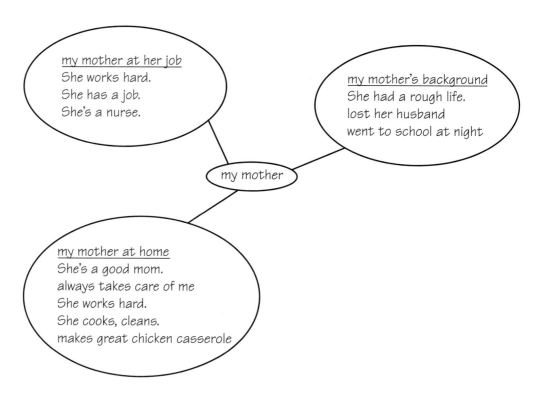

Whatever way you choose to examine and group your details, you are working toward a focus, a point. You are asking and beginning to answer the question, "Where do the details lead?" The answer will be the main idea of your paragraph, which will be stated in the topic sentence.

Exercise 5 **Grouping Related Items in Lists of Details**

Practice

Following are lists of details. In each list, circle the items that seem to fit in one group; then underline the items that seem to belong to a second group. Some items may not belong in either group. The first list is done for you.

1. topic: my favorite aunt

<u>always cheerful</u>	(unusual appearance)
<u>tells jokes</u>	(orange hair)
gives me compliments	an accountant
<u>laughs at her troubles</u>	(outrageous hats)
(dresses in wild colors)	drives a jeep

2. topic: a snowstorm

traffic jam	heating bills
little driving visibility	slick roads
icicles gleaming on trees	dazzling white hills
children home from school	exquisite snowflakes
beautiful snowdrifts	roads closed

3. topic: reasons to quit smoking

nicotine patch	stained teeth
tobacco smell on clothes	emphysema
lung cancer	nicotine gum
heart disease	teenage smokers
bad breath	no-smoking areas

4. topic: my first job

long hours	on my feet too long
had my own spending money	restaurant waitress
rude customers	ugly uniform
boss was nice	friendly co-workers
too many job responsibilities	forced to work weekends

5. topic: my mother's house

brick patio	wooden floors
apple tree in the yard	my favorite house
border of roses	cozy kitchen
attic bedroom	nasty landlord
old-fashioned bathroom	near my school

Forming a Topic Sentence

Grouping details leads you to a focus for your paragraph. That focus is stated in the topic sentence. To form a topic sentence, do the following:

1. Review your details and see if you can form some general idea that will summarize the details.

2. Write that general idea in one sentence.

The sentence that summarizes the details is the **topic sentence.** It makes a general point, and the more specific details you have gathered will support this point.

To form a topic sentence about your mother, you can ask yourself questions about the details. First, there are many details about your mother. You can ask yourself, "What kinds of details do I have?" You have details about your mother's background, about her job, and about her role as a mother. You might then ask, "Can I summarize those details?" You might then summarize those details to get the topic sentence:

My mother survived difficult times to become a good parent and worker.

Check the sentence against your details. Does it cover your mother's background? Yes, it mentions that she survived *rough times.* Does it cover her job? Yes, it says she is a *good worker.* Does it cover her role as a mother? Yes, it says she is a *good parent.* The topic sentence is acceptable; it is a general idea that summarizes the details.

Hints About Topic Sentences

1. Be careful. *Topics are not the same as topic sentences. A topic is the subject you will write about. A topic sentence states the main idea you have developed on a topic.* Consider the differences between the following topics and topic sentences:

   topic: my mother
   topic sentence: My mother survived difficult times to become a good parent and worker.

   topic: effects of drunk driving
   topic sentence: Drunk driving hurts the victims, their families, and their friends.

Exercise 6 **Turning Topics into Topic Sentences**

 Collaborate

Do this exercise with a partner or a group. The following list contains some topics and some topic sentences. Have someone read the list aloud. As the list is read, decide which items are topics. Put an *X* next to those items. On the lines following the list, rewrite the topics into topic sentences.

1. _____ One way to lose weight

2. _____ Why fish make good pets

3. _____ Poor planning wrecked my wedding

4. _____ How to change a tire easily and safely

5. _____ My father is my best friend

6. _____ I learned compassion at my job

7. _____ A great city to visit

8. _____ Speeding is foolish and selfish

9. _____ A bad cold

10. _____ Voice mail can be irritating.

Rewrite the topics. Make each one into a topic sentence.

_____

_____

_____

_____

_____

_____

2. *Topic sentences do not announce;* they make a point. Look at the following sentences and notice the differences between the sentences that announce and the topic sentences:

announcement: The subject of this paper will be my definition of a bargain.
topic sentence: A bargain is a necessary item that I bought at less than half the regular price.

announcement: I will discuss the causes of depression in teenagers.
topic sentence: Depression in teenagers can be caused by stress at home, work, or school.

Exercise 7 **Turning Announcements into Topic Sentences**

👥 Collaborate Do this exercise with a partner or a group. The following list contains some topic sentences and some announcements. Have someone read this list aloud. As the list is read, decide whether items are announcements. Put an *X* next to those items. On the lines following the list, rewrite the announcements, making them topic sentences.

1. _____ I learned to be a good tennis player by practicing regularly.

2. _____ How to become a good dancer is the subject of this paper.

3. _____ The pressures on teenagers will be explained.

4. _____ Working mothers feel stressed at home, at work, and at social gatherings.

5. _____ I will explain the reasons for attending a college near your home.

6. _____ Buying at thrift shops can save you money and give you quality merchandise.

7. _____ Why our school needs a bigger parking lot is the issue to be discussed.

8. _____ The three characteristics of a good friend are the topic of this essay.

9. _____ A real leader is responsible, confident, and generous.

10. _____ This essay will tell you why people watch soap operas.

Rewrite the announcements. Make each one a topic sentence.

_____

_____

_____

_____

_____

_____

3. *Topic sentences should not be too broad* to develop in one paragraph. A topic sentence that is too broad may take many pages of writing to develop. Look at the following broad sentences and then notice how they can be narrowed.

too broad: Television violence is bad for children. (This sentence is too broad because "television violence" could include anything from bloody movies to the nightly news, and "children" could mean anyone under eighteen. Also, "is bad for children" could mean anything from "causes nightmares" to "provokes children to commit murder.")

a narrower topic sentence: Violent cartoons teach preschoolers that hitting and hurting are fun.

too broad: Education changed my life. (This sentence is so broad that you would have to talk about your whole education, and your whole life, to support it.)

a narrower topic sentence: Studying for my high school equivalency diploma gave me the confidence to try college.

Exercise 8 **Revising Topic Sentences That Are Too Broad**

Collaborate Do this exercise with a partner or a group. Following is a list of topic sentences. Some are too broad to support in one paragraph. Have someone read this list aloud. As the list is read, decide which sentences are too broad. Put an *X* next to those sentences. On the line following the list, rewrite those sentences, focusing on a limited idea—a topic sentence—that could be supported in one paragraph.

1. _____ Working can be very frustrating.

2. _____ Getting children to go to bed is the hardest part of baby-sitting.

3. _____ College was a big change for me.

4. _____ Television has too much influence on people.

5. _____ Divorce can be very hard on children.

6. _____ Beer advertising on television makes drinking seem like a way to be popular.

7. _____ My brother grew up when he started working.

8. _____ A college math class forced me to learn how to study.

9. _____ Christopher developed self-confidence when he joined a boxing club.

10. _____ When parents argue, teenagers can feel torn and confused.

Rewrite the broad sentences. Make each one more limited.

_____

_____

_____

_____

_____

_____

4. *Topic sentences should not be too narrow* to develop in one paragraph. A topic sentence that is too narrow can't be supported by details. It may be a fact, which can't be developed. A topic sentence that is too narrow leaves you with nothing more to say.

   too narrow: We had fog yesterday.
   a better, expanded topic sentence: Yesterday's fog made driving difficult.

   too narrow: I moved to Nashville when I was twenty.
   a better, expanded topic sentence: When I moved to Nashville at age twenty, I learned to live on my own.

Exercise 9 **Revising Topic Sentences That Are Too Narrow**

 Collaborate

Do this exercise with a partner or a group. Following is a list of topic sentences. Some of them are too narrow to be developed in a paragraph. Have someone read the list aloud. As the list is read, decide which sentences are too narrow. Put an *X* next to those sentences. On the lines following the list, rewrite those sentences as broader topic sentences that could be developed in a paragraph.

1. _____ Jack's truck is a new Ford.

2. _____ A station wagon is a more practical car than a sport-utility vehicle.

3. _____ Our house is in a valley near some farms.

4. _____ Living in the center of town has three advantages.

5. _____ The sun on the beach was hot.

6. _____ Christine gave me a tie.

7. _____ Mr. Rodriguez' offer of a ride was generous and thoughtful.

8. _____ When Dana made me a cake, she showed me her love.

9. _____ Levar's haircut cost fifty dollars.

10. _____ Betty asked to borrow $100, but I had reasons for refusing her request.

Rewrite the narrow sentences. Make each one broader.

_____

_____

_____

_____

_____

_____

Once you have a topic sentence, you have completed the thought lines stage of writing. This stage begins with free, unstructured thinking and writing. As you work through the thought lines process, your thinking and writing will become more focused.

Infobox

Focusing the Thought Lines: A Summary

The thought lines stage of writing a paragraph enables you to develop an idea into a topic sentence and related details. You can *focus* your thinking by working in steps.

1. Try marking a list of related details or mapping to group your ideas.

2. Write a topic sentence that summarizes your details.

3. Check your topic sentence. Be sure that it makes a point and focuses the details you have developed. Be sure that it is a sentence (not a topic), is not too broad or too narrow, and is not an announcement.

Exercise 10 **Recognizing and Writing Good Topic Sentences**

Practice Some of the following are good topic sentences. Others are not: they are topics (not topic sentences), or announcements, or they are too broad, or too narrow. Put an *X* next to the ones that are not good topic sentences and rewrite them in the lines following the list.

1. _____ How you can get the best deal on textbooks

2. _____ Hitchhiking is a dangerous form of transportation.

3. _____ Education has always been difficult for me.

4. _____ On Fridays, my bank stays open late.

5. _____ Sources of protein in a healthy diet

6. _____ Too many people are committing violent crimes.

7. _____ Several risks associated with skydiving will be the subject of this paper.

8. _____ Vitamin C can be found in many popular foods.

9. _____ A new way to meet people

10. _____ A twenty-four-hour pharmacy is a neighborhood asset.

Rewrite the faulty topic sentences:

_____

_____

_____

_____

_____

_____

_____

Exercise 11 **Writing Topic Sentences for Lists of Details**

Practice Following are lists of details that have no topic sentences. Write an appropriate topic sentence for each one.

1. **topic sentence:** _____

_____

Walking is good exercise.
Walking saves money spent on gas for a car.

Walkers don't get stuck in traffic.
Walkers get to enjoy their surroundings.
Cars pollute the air, but walkers don't.
Walking is less stressful than driving.

2. topic sentence: _____

_____

Professor Spinetti is a patient teacher.
He is willing to answer questions.
He gives extra help after class.
He has many office hours for student conferences.
He demands students' best work.
Professor Spinetti is very strict about deadlines.
He gives many assignments.

3. topic sentence: _____

_____

coffee mugs
soup mugs
mugs with sayings on them
plastic mugs
mugs with cartoon characters
beer mugs
china mugs
mugs with college names
glass mugs

4. topic sentence: _____

_____

Don says he is my friend.
Calls me at midnight to talk
Talks behind my back
Likes to tell me his problems
Always wants to do things on weekends
Borrows my money and car
Gives me advice
Never offers to pay for anything

5. topic sentence: _____

_____

Spends time with his children every weekend
Tries to be home to tuck them in at night
Works overtime to support his family.
Shares household chores with his wife
Arrives at work early
Volunteers for work projects so he may be promoted
Gives his wife love and respect

Writing a Paragraph: Devising a Plan— Outlines

Once you have a topic sentence, you can begin working on an *outline* for your paragraph. The **outline** is a *plan* that helps you stay focused in your writing. The outline begins to form when you write your topic sentence and list the related details beneath it.

CHECKING YOUR DETAILS

You can now look at your list and ask yourself an important question: "Do I have enough details to support my topic sentence?" Remember, your goal is to write a paragraph of seven to twelve sentences.

Consider this topic sentence and list of details:

> **topic sentence:** Fresh fruit is a good dessert.
> **details:** tastes good
> healthy
> easy

Does the list contain enough details for a paragraph of seven to twelve sentences? Probably not.

Adding Details When There Are Not Enough

To add details, try brainstorming. Ask yourself some questions:

- – What fruit tastes good?
- – What makes fruit a healthy dessert?
- – Why is it easy? How can you serve it?

By brainstorming, you may come up with these details:

> **topic sentence:** Fresh fruit is a good dessert.
> **details:** tastes good
> a ripe peach or a juicy pineapple tastes delicious
> crunchy apples always available and satisfying
> plump strawberries are great in summer

healthy
low in calories
rich in vitamins and fiber
easy
served as it is
in a fruit salad
mixed with ice cream or sherbet
no cooking necessary

Keep brainstorming until you feel you have enough details for a seven-to-twelve-sentence paragraph. Remember, it is better to have too many details than to have too little, for you can always edit the extra details later.

Exercise 1 **Adding Details to Support a Topic Sentence**

Do this exercise with a partner or a group. The following topic sentences have some—but not enough—details. Write sentences to add details to each list.

1. topic sentence: Renting a movie on video has many advantages over seeing a movie in a theater.

details:
1. You don't have to get dressed up to see a video at home.
2. You can stop the video to get a snack or answer the phone.

3. _____

_____

4. _____

_____

5. _____

_____

6. _____

_____

2. topic sentence: My car is full of items that need to be cleaned or thrown out.

details:
1. The floor mats are covered in dust and leaves.

2. There is an empty Kleenex box on the back seat.

3. _____

_____

4. _____

_____

    5. _____

       _____

    6. _____

       _____

    7. _____

       _____

3. topic sentence: People go to the mall for a number of reasons.

details:

    1. Some people go to buy one specific piece of clothing and then leave.
    2. Others are there to enjoy the air conditioning on a hot day.

    3. _____

       _____

    4. _____

       _____

    5. _____

       _____

    6. _____

       _____

4. topic sentence: I listen to some kind of music nearly all day.

details:

    1. I hear soft background music at the supermarket.

    2. I jog with a Walkman that plays a cassette of world music.

    3. When I wake up, my son is singing a song from *Sesame Street*.

    4. _____

       _____

    5. _____

       _____

    6. _____

       _____

7. _____

_____

5. topic sentence: Not all fast-food restaurants offer the same kinds of food.

details: 1. Some offer pizza.

2. Others sell deli subs.

3. _____

_____

4. _____

_____

5. _____

_____

6. _____

_____

Eliminating Details That Do Not Relate to the Topic Sentence

Sometimes, what you thought were good details don't relate to the topic sentence because they don't fit or support your point. Eliminate details that don't relate to the topic sentence. For example, the following list contains details that don't relate to the topic sentence. Those details are crossed out.

topic sentence: My neighbors are making my home life unbearable.
details: play their albums loud at 3 a.m.
I can't sleep
leave garbage all over the sidewalk
~~come from Philadelphia~~
sidewalk is a mess
insects crawl all over their garbage
~~I carefully bag my garbage~~
they argue loudly and bang on the walls
my privacy is invaded
park their van in my parking space

Exercise 2 **Eliminating Details That Do Not Fit**

Practice Following are topic sentences and lists of details. Cross out the details that do not fit the topic sentence.

1. topic sentence: Some professional athletes set a bad example for the children who admire them.
details: One basketball player choked a coach.
I think basketball has become more of a business than a sport.

A baseball player spit at an umpire.
Several football players have been charged with abusing their wives or girlfriends.
I used to collect autographs of famous players.
Some hockey players are notorious for fighting on the ice.
Children see this behavior and think it is acceptable.

2. topic sentence: Caps are worn by all kinds of people in all kinds of places.

details: Truckers wear caps when they drive.
Men on tractors wear caps with the name of the tractor company.
Caps are inexpensive.
Children in Little League wear baseball caps.
There are caps to protect fishermen from the sun.
Servers in some restaurants have to wear caps.
Some ladies wear baseball caps covered in sequins to match their fancy clothes.
College bookstores sell caps with the name of the college on them, for students.
Years ago, businessmen used to wear hats to work.
Teens wear caps when they're having a bad hair day.

3. topic sentence: Daniella is known for bringing something whenever she visits.

details: If she visits someone in the hospital, she always brings flowers.
Fresh flowers are really expensive.
Daniella brings dessert when you invite her for dinner.
She brings me candy when she stops by.
When Celeste had a baby, Daniella brought the baby a knitted blanket.
I invited her to a picnic, and she came with an extra bag of ice.
Daniella always takes an extra pencil to class for the person who forgot one.

4. topic sentence: When I was ten, my six-year-old brother made a hobby out of teasing me.

details: Jimmy liked to pull my hair and run away.
He called me "chicken."
Sometimes he would sing, "Little chicken, little chicken" to me.
Jimmy was my mother's favorite.
In my father's car, Jimmy would kick me.
When I fought back, Jimmy blamed me for the fight.
My father drove an old Toyota.
Jimmy borrowed my games and books without telling me.
He never gave them back.

5. topic sentence: The new movie theater was very glamorous.
details: The exterior was made to look like a rock and roll drive-in restaurant.

Neon lights were shaped like guitars and musical notes.
Rock music blasted outside the ticket booths.
The ticket prices were reasonable.
The movies showing were the same as the ones at the theater down the block.
The concessions area sold gourmet pizza as well as popcorn and candy.
It also had a coffee bar with cappuccino.

From List to Outline

Take another look at the topic sentence and list of details on the topic of My Mother:

topic sentence: My mother survived difficult times to become a good parent and worker.
details: She's a good mom.
Always takes care of me.
She works hard.
She cooks, cleans.
makes a great chicken casserole
She has a job.
She's a nurse.
She had a rough life.
lost her husband
went to school at night

After you scan the list, you will be ready to develop the outline of a paragraph.

The outline is a plan for writing, and it can be a kind of draft in list form. It sketches what you want to write and the order in which you want to present it. An organized, logical list will make your writing unified because each item on the list will relate to your topic sentence.

When you plan, keep your topic sentence in mind:

My mother <u>survived difficult times</u> to become <u>a good parent</u> and <u>worker</u>.

Notice that the key words are underlined and lead to key phrases:

- survived difficult times
- a good parent
- a good worker

Can you put the details together so that they connect to one of these key phrases?

survived difficult times

- She had a rough life, lost her husband, went to school at night

a good parent

- She's a good mom, Always takes care of me, She cooks, cleans, makes a great chicken casserole

a good worker

- She works hard, She has a job, She's a nurse

With this kind of grouping, you have a clearer idea of how to organize a paragraph. You may have noticed that the details grouped under each phrase explain or give examples that are connected to the topic sentence. You may also have noticed that the detail "She works hard" is placed under the phrase "a good worker." It could also be placed under "a good parent," so it would be your decision where to place it.

Now that you have grouped your ideas with key phrases and examples, you can write an outline:

An Outline for a Paragraph on My Mother

topic sentence:	My mother survived difficult times to become a good parent and worker.

details: **difficult times**	She had a rough life. She lost her husband. She went to school at night.
a good parent	She's a good mom and always takes care of me. She cooks and cleans. She makes a great chicken casserole.
a good worker	She works hard at her job. She's a nurse.

As you can see, the outline combines some details from the list. Even with these combinations, the details are very rough in style. As you reread the list of details, you may notice places that need more combining, places where ideas need more explaining, and places that are repetitive. Keep in mind that an outline is merely a rough organization of your paragraph.

As you work through the steps of designing an outline, you can check for the following:

✔ Checklist

A Checklist for an Outline

✔ **Unity:** Do all the details relate to the topic sentence? If they do, the paragraph will be unified.

✔ **Support:** Do I have enough supporting ideas? Can I add to those ideas with more specific details?

✔ **Coherence:** Are the ideas listed in the right order? If the order of the points is logical, the paragraph will be coherent.

Coherence

Check the sample outline again, and you'll notice that the details are grouped in the same order as in the topic sentence: first, details about your mother's difficult life; then, details about your mother as a parent; finally, details about your mother as a worker. Putting details in an order that matches the topic sentence is a logical order for this paragraph. It makes the paragraph *coherent.*

Determining the Order of Details

Putting the details in logical order makes the ideas in the paragraph easier to follow. The most logical order for a paragraph depends on the subject of the paragraph. If you are writing about an event, you might use **time order** (such as telling what happened first, second, and so forth); if you are arguing some point, you might use **emphatic order** (such as saving your most convincing idea for last); if you are describing a room, you might use **space order** (such as describing from left to right or from top to bottom).

Exercise 3 **Coherence: Putting Details in the Right Order**

Practice These outlines have details that are in the wrong order. In the space provided, number the sentences so that they are in the proper order: *1* would be the number for the first sentence, and so on.

1. topic sentence: My last day at my job was sadder than I had expected.

(Put the sentences in time order, from first to last.)

_____ Everyone went through his or her morning routine as usual.

_____ I spent my afternoon feeling hurt and insulted.

_____ At lunch time, no one even asked me out for a farewell lunch.

_____ When I first came in, no one acted as if they remembered it was my last day.

_____ Just as we were closing the store, my boss and co-workers surprised me with a big cake and other treats.

_____ I left feeling grateful for their thoughtfulness.

_____ I was also sad to leave these kind people.

2. topic sentence: My son looked as if he had fallen into a mud pit.

(Put the sentences in space order, from head to foot.)

_____ Jackie's white sneakers were covered in a gray-green muck.

_____ His shorts were wet with slime.

_____ His eyelashes were covered with mud.

_____ Jackie's hair was flat and matted with dirt.

_____ Mud and twigs clung to his socks.

_____ His yellow tee shirt had thick blotches of dirt.

3. topic sentence: Driving without a seat belt is foolish and dangerous.

(Put the sentences in emphatic order, from the least important reason to the most important.)

_____ You can be killed.

_____ If the police see you without your belt, you can get a ticket.

_____ You can be bumped and bruised in a minor fender-bender.

_____ You can be severely hurt in a more serious accident.

4. topic sentence: The speech was long, boring, and confusing.

(Put the sentences in the same order as in the topic sentence.)

_____ The speaker jumped from topic to topic.

_____ One minute he was talking about pollution; then he was telling a joke.

_____ He spoke in a monotone.

_____ He was putting me to sleep.

_____ I checked my watch after thirty minutes.

_____ He went on for another forty minutes.

Where the Topic Sentence Goes

The outline format helps you organize your ideas. The topic sentence is written above the list of details. This position helps you remember that the topic sentence is the main idea and that the details that support it are written under it. You can easily check each detail on your list against your main idea. You can also check the unity (relevance) and coherence (logical order) of your details.

When you actually write a paragraph, the topic sentence does not necessarily have to be the first sentence in the paragraph. Read the following paragraphs, and notice where each topic sentence is placed.

Topic Sentence at the Beginning of the Paragraph

<u>Dr. Chen is the best doctor I have ever had</u>. Whenever I have to visit him, he gives me plenty of time. He does not rush me through a physical examination and quickly hand me a prescription. Instead, he takes time to chat with me and encourages me to describe my symptoms. He examines me carefully and allows me to ask as many questions as I want. After I am dressed, he discusses his diagnosis, explains what medicine he is prescribing, and tells me exactly how and when to take the medication. He tells me what results to expect from the medication and how long it should take for me to get well. Dr. Chen acts as if he cares about me. I believe that is the most important quality in a doctor.

Topic Sentence in the Middle of the Paragraph

The meal was delicious, from the appetizer of shrimp cocktail to the dessert of strawberry tarts. Marcel had even taken the time to make home-baked bread and fresh pasta. <u>Marcel had worked hard on this dinner, and his hard work showed</u>. Everything was served on gleaming china placed on an immaculate tablecloth. There were fresh flowers in a cut glass bowl at the center of the table, and there was a polished goblet at every place setting. The pale green napkins had been carefully ironed and folded into precise triangles.

Topic Sentence at the End of the Paragraph

> I woke up at 5:00 a.m. when I heard the phone ringing. I rushed to the phone, thinking the call was some terrible emergency. Of course, it was just a wrong number. Then I couldn't get back to sleep because I was shaken by being so suddenly awakened and irritated by the wrong number. The day got worse as it went along. My car stalled on the freeway, and I had to get towed to a repair shop. The repair cost me $250. I was three hours late for work and missed an important training session with my boss. On my way out of work, I stepped into an enormous puddle and ruined a new pair of shoes. <u>Yesterday was one of those days when I should have stayed in bed.</u>

Be sure to follow your own instructor's directions about placement of the topic sentence.

Exercise 5   **Identifying the Topic Sentence**

Practice   Underline the topic sentence in each of the following paragraphs.

1. Last week I had just gotten out of bed when I had an unpleasant surprise. I was in the kitchen, making myself some instant coffee, when I ran my hand through my tangled hair. I suddenly realized that one of my earrings, a small gold ball, was gone. Since I knew I had been wearing it when I went to bed, I figured it was somewhere in the apartment. I crawled on the floor, checked the corners and crannies, and shook out the bedsheets and pillows. I looked everywhere. I couldn't find it. The next day, I looked again, but I again found nothing except dust and crumbs. Finally, I was forced to give up. Then, yesterday, I was again making coffee. As I spooned the last of the coffee granules out of the jar, a small gold ball appeared at the bottom. It was my earring. I have now realized that sometimes objects get lost in the strangest places.

2. Larry is addicted to cookies. He keeps a bag of chocolate chip cookies in his car, and he has been known to drive with one hand on the wheel and one in the cookie bag. At the food court in the mall, he will skip the tacos and burgers and head straight for the freshly baked cookies. Everyone at the local bakery knows Larry. For his birthday, the staff makes

Larry a giant cookie, the size of a flat cake, and writes "Happy Birthday" on it, in icing. The local Girl Scouts also know Larry well, for he is their biggest buyer of Girl Scout cookies.

3. I was going to give my father a tie for Father's Day, but then I realized he has very little use for ties. He used to wear ties to work, but now his office doesn't require them. When he dresses up, he wears a sports coat but no tie. Most men don't wear ties anymore. My boyfriend, for example, works in the construction business, so he doesn't wear a tie to work. Also, he refuses to go to any restaurant or club that requires ties. My brother rarely wears ties, either. He is a college student and never dresses up. In fact, I'm not sure he owns a tie. He probably borrows one of my father's old ties if he needs one.

CHAPTER 22

Writing a Paragraph: Writing, Revising, and Editing the Drafts— Rough Lines

An **outline** is a draft of a paragraph in list form. Once you have an outline, you are ready to write the list in paragraph form—to "rough out" a draft of your assignment.

ROUGH LINES

The *rough lines* stage of writing is the time to draft, revise, edit, and draft again. You may write several **drafts** or versions of the paragraph in this stage. Writing several drafts is not an unnecessary chore or a punishment. It is a way of taking pressure off yourself. By revising in steps, you are telling yourself, "The first try doesn't have to be perfect."

Review the outline on the topic of My Mother. You can create a first draft of this outline in the form of a paragraph. (*Remember that the first line of each paragraph is indented.*) In the draft of the following paragraph, the first sentence of the paragraph is the topic sentence.

A First Draft of a Paragraph on My Mother

```
    My mother survived difficult times to become a good parent
and worker. She had a rough life. She lost her husband. She went
to school at night. She's a good mom and always takes care of
me. She cooks and cleans. She makes a great chicken casserole.
She works hard at her job. She's a nurse.
```

Revising and Editing the Draft

Once you have a first draft, you can begin to think about revising and editing it. **Revising** means rewriting the draft to change the structure, the order of the sentences, and the content. **Editing** includes making changes in the choice of words, in the selection of the details, in the punctuation, and in the patterns and kinds of sentences. It may also include adding **transitions**—words, phrases, or sentences that link ideas.

One easy way to begin the revising and editing process is to read your work aloud to yourself. As you do so, listen carefully to your words and concentrate

280

on their meaning. Each question in the following checklist will help you focus on a specific part of revising and editing. The name (or key term) for each part is in parentheses.

✔ Checklist

A Checklist for Revising the Draft of a Paragraph (with key terms)

✔ Am I staying on my point? (unity)

✔ Should I eliminate any ideas that do not fit? (unity)

✔ Do I have enough to say about my point? (support)

✔ Should I add any details? (support)

✔ Should I change the order of my sentences? (coherence)

✔ Is my choice of words appropriate? (style)

✔ Is my choice of words repetitive? (style)

✔ Are my sentences too long? Too short? (style)

✔ Should I combine any sentences? (style)

✔ Am I running sentences together? (grammar)

✔ Am I using complete sentences? (grammar)

✔ Can I link my ideas more smoothly? (transitions)

If you apply the checklist to the draft of the paper on My Mother, you will probably find these rough spots:

- The sentences are very short and choppy.
- Some sentences could be combined.
- Some words are repeated often.
- Some ideas need more details for support.
- The paragraph needs transitions: words, phrases, or sentences that link ideas.

Consider the following revised draft of the paragraph, and notice the changes, underlined, that have been made in the draft:

A Revised Draft of a Paragraph on My Mother

`topic sentence:`	My mother survived difficult times
`sentences combined,`	to become a good parent and worker. Her
`transition`	hard times began when she lost her hus-
`details added`	band. At his death, she was only nineteen
`details added, transition`	and had a baby, me, to raise. She sur-
	vived by going to school at night to
`details added, transition`	train for a career. Even though she lives
	a stressful life, she is a good mom. She
`details added`	always takes care of me. She listens to
	my problems, encourages me to do my best,
`details added`	and praises all my efforts. She cleans
	our apartment until it shines, and she

(continued)

| | makes dinner every night. She makes a |
| transition details added | great chicken casserole. In addition, she works hard at her job. She is a nurse at a home for elderly people, where she is on her feet all day and is still kind and cheerful. |

When you are revising your own paragraph, you can use the checklist to help you. Read the checklist several times; then reread your draft, looking for answers to the questions on the list. If your instructor agrees, you can work with your classmates. You can read your draft to a partner or group. Your listener(s) can react to your draft by applying the questions on the checklist and by making notes about your draft as you read. When you are finished reading aloud, your partner(s) can discuss their notes about your work.

Exercise 1 **Revising a Draft for Unity**

Practice

Some of the sentences in the following paragraph do not fit the topic sentence. (The topic sentence is the first sentence in the paragraph.) Cross out the sentences that do not fit.

When a toy becomes a fad, some parents teach their children the wrong lessons. Every year, it seems that one particular toy is the rage, and every child just has to have it immediately. When I was little I had a Cabbage Patch Doll. Some parents camp out all night in front of a toy store so they can be sure to get the latest toy for their son or daughter. Such behavior teaches children that it is really important to have the newest toy, and that their parents are supposed to give them everything the children want. Toys cost too much-these days. Some parents take their children to the toy store, and the children see their mother or father pushing, shouting, and shoving to get the newest toy. The children learn that it is acceptable to hurt others to get what you want. The children see the same thing when their parents cut off other drivers on the highways. Trying to please their children, parents can end up teaching them to be greedy, selfish, and overly aggressive.

Exercise 2 **Adding Support to a Draft**

Collaborate

Do this exercise with a partner or a group. The following paragraph needs more details to support its point. Add the details in the blank spaces provided.

Our trip to Florida was a disappointment. First of all, the weather was terrible. (Add two sentences of details.) _____

_____

_____

_____.

In addition, the amusement park we visited was too crowded for us to enjoy. For example, the parking lots were so full, we had to wait thirty minutes for a parking space. (Add one sentence of details about the crowding.) _____

_____.

Worst of all, I got sick on our trip. (Add two sentences of detail.) _____

_____

_____

_____. I'm glad I got to see Florida, but I wish my visit had been more enjoyable.

Exercise 3   **Revising a Draft for Coherence**

Practice   In the following paragraph, one sentence is in the wrong place. Move it to the right place in the paragraph by drawing an arrow from the sentence to its proper place.

Damien's gift to his mother was dazzling. He handed her an elegantly wrapped box. Inside the tissue paper was a beautiful silver and turquoise necklace. On top of the box was a blue silk rose tied with shiny blue ribbon. The ribbon covered blue wrapping paper dotted with silver stars. When she tore off the wrapping paper and opened the lid of the box, Damien's mother saw a nest of silver and blue tissue paper. She plunged her hands into the soft tissue paper to discover her gift.

Exercise 4   **Revising a Draft for Style**

Collaborate   Do this exercise with a partner or a group. The following paragraph is repetitive in its word choice. Replace each underlined word with a word that is less repetitive. Write the new word above the underlined one.

There are some drinks that go with certain seasons. On a cold winter day, for example, I don't want a <u>cold</u> glass of lemonade or iced tea. I want something hot to drink, like cocoa or cappuccino. In contrast, when the weather is <u>hot</u>, I can't imagine drinking hot coffee. Summer is the time I crave orange juice straight from the refrigerator or Pepsi in a glass full of crushed ice. The <u>cold</u> touch of an ice-filled glass against my forehead is one of the joys of a hot day. Similarly, warming my hands on the <u>hot</u> surface of a mug of coffee makes winter feel comfortable. So whether the weather is <u>hot</u> or <u>cold</u>, there are beverages that make the temperature feel better!

<table>
<tr><td>**Exercise 5**</td><td>**Revising a Draft by Combining Sentences**</td></tr>
<tr><td>Practice</td><td></td></tr>
</table>

The following paragraph has many short, choppy sentences that are underlined. Wherever you see two or more underlined sentences clustered next to each other, combine them into one clear, smooth sentence. Write your revised version of the paragraph in the spaces above the lines. To review ways to combine sentences, see Chapter 5.

José loves mysteries. <u>He visits every used bookstore in our town. He looks for mysteries he hasn't read yet.</u> He is a member of the Mystery Book Club. <u>On weekends, he works with a drama group. The group stages mystery plays. The plays are staged at local restaurants.</u> The plays are part of a dinner theater show that involves the audience in solving the mystery. <u>In addition to reading mysteries and acting in them, José enjoys watching mysteries on television. He sees them at the movies. He enjoys them on video.</u> Some day, José will write a mystery of his own. I am sure it will be excellent because José already knows everything there is to know about dark crimes, dangerous secrets, and suspenseful endings.

<table>
<tr><td>**Exercise 6**</td><td>**Revising a Draft by Correcting Run-Together Sentences**</td></tr>
<tr><td>Practice</td><td></td></tr>
</table>

The following paragraph has some run-together (run-on) sentences. Correct the run-ons by writing in the spaces above the lines. To review ways to correct run-on sentences, see Chapter 3.

I love to watch the dogs in my neighborhood when they are being taken for a walk. One large boxer I know walks calmly and slowly, his head held proudly. Other dogs are so emotional they can hardly suppress their excitement. One terrier pulls at his leash he has to sniff every tree and inspect every inch of sidewalk. A big black Labrador jumps up to greet every passerby. Then there are the happy dogs every day I see a big golden retriever smiling, with her tennis ball in her mouth. She knows she is on her way to the park to play "fetch." A tiny Yorkshire terrier trots proudly as she displays a tiny pink satin bow in her topknot. I love dogs but I do not have a pet of my own. Therefore, I rely on the dogs in my neighborhood to bring me amusement, entertainment, and joy.

Exercise 7 **Editing a Paragraph for Complete Sentences**

Practice The following paragraph has some incomplete sentences (sentence fragments). Correct the fragments by writing in the spaces above the lines. To review ways to correct sentence fragments, see Chapter 6.

Food can be a source of disagreement in my family. My mother insists on serving large, elaborate meals even when nobody is very hungry. She becomes angry and hurt by our indifference to all her hard work. My father also likes to cook. Such food as barbecued ribs and grilled fish. My sister, who is a vegetarian, refuses to eat either my mother's or my father's cooking. Instead, she buys her own food. Preferring to eat yogurt and organic vegetables. When I come to visit with a bag full of gourmet meats, salads, and cakes, I cause an argument. My mother is upset. Because I didn't let her do the cooking. While my sister won't eat the meat, the nonorganic salads full of pesticides, or the cakes full of refined sugar. Meanwhile, my father wants to know why we couldn't have a barbecue.

Writing a Paragraph: Polishing, Proofreading, and Preparing Final Copy—Final Lines

The final lines of your paragraph are the result of careful thinking, planning, and revising. After many drafts, and when you are satisfied with the result, read the final draft to polish and proofread. You can avoid too many last-minute corrections if you check your last draft carefully for the following:

- spelling errors
- punctuation errors
- mechanical errors
- word choice
- a final statement

CORRECTING THE FINAL DRAFT OF A PARAGRAPH

Take a look at the following final draft of the paragraph on My Mother. The draft has been corrected directly above the crossed-out material. You will notice corrections in spelling, punctuation, mechanics, and word choice. You'll see that the slang term "mom" has been changed to "mother." At the end, you'll notice that a final statement has been added to unify the paragraph.

A Corrected Draft of a Paragraph on My Mother

My mother survived difficult ~~time's~~ **times** to become a good

parent ~~parrent~~ and worker. Her hard times began when she lost her

husband. At his death, ~~She~~ **she** was only nineteen and had a baby,

me, to raise. ~~she~~ **She** survived by going to school at ~~nite~~ **night** to

train for a career. Even though she lives a stressful **still**

life, she is a good ~~mom~~ **mother**. She ~~always take~~ **always takes** care of me. She **today**

listens to my ~~prolems~~ **problems**, ~~encourage~~ **encourages** me to do my best, and

praises all my efforts. She cleans our apartment until it

shine, and she makes dinner every night. She makes a ~~great~~ *delicious*
~~shine~~ *shines*

chicken casserole. In addition, she works hard at her job.

She is a nurse at a home for elderly people, where she is on

her feet ~~allday~~ *all day* and is still kind and cheerful. At work or at

home, my mother is an inspiration to me.

Exercise 1 **Correcting the Errors in the Final Lines of a Paragraph**

Practice

Proofread the following paragraph, looking for errors in word choice, spelling, punctuation, and mechanics. Correct the fourteen errors by crossing out each mistake and writing the correction above it.

My sister is so involved in her nighttime soap opera that she is missing out on reel life. She has to watch her show every Wensday night. if she is not going to be home that night, she set's her VCR to tape the show. But lately she wont even go out on Wednesdays because she dont want to miss the latest episode of the soap opera. She has started to ware her hair like on of the characters on the show, and I think she is starting to sound like that character, to. When some of the actors from that show made an appearance at a local mall, my sister was the first on their to see them. She is the president of the local fan club. I think the show is stuppid and silly, but I don't care if she watchs it. I am just worry that it is taking over her life.

Exercise 2 **More on Correcting the Errors in the Final Lines of a Paragraph**

Practice

Proofread the following paragraph, looking for errors in word choice, spelling, punctuation, and mechanics. Correct the fifteen errors by crossing out each mistake and writing the correction above it.

An old ghost story used to terriffy me. I first heard it one halloween when some older boy's were swapping tales on a dark playground. The story was about an old building in the neighborhood. Supposably a man was murdered in the basement, many year ago. The story said that you could still here the man groaning on dark nights. In addition, the story claimed that no one had ever lived in the house since the murder.

that story haunted me for year's. I was afraid to passed that building, expesially at night. Then the building was demolished. A disco was built in it's place. I was happy because I figured that nobody could hears the groans of the Ghost over the noise of the disco, so the spirit had probally moved on. Finely, I stopped being afraid.

Giving Your Paragraph a Title

When you prepare the final copy of your paragraph, you may be asked to give it a title. The title should be short and should fit the subject of the paragraph. For example, an appropriate title for the paragraph on your mother could be "My Wonderful Mother" or "An Inspiring Mother." Check with your instructor to see if your paragraph needs a title. (In this book, the paragraphs do not have titles.)

Exercise 3 **Creating a Title**

With a partner or group, create a title for the following paragraph.

Title: _____

My family left New Jersey when I was seven years old, and I am very happy living in Florida. However, sometimes I feel homesick for the North. At Christmas, especially, I wish I could see the snow fall and then run outdoors to make a snowman. In December, it feels strange to string outdoor lights on palm trees. I also miss the autumn, when the leaves on the trees turn fiery red and gold. Sometimes my aunt in New Jersey sends me an envelope of autumn leaves, and I remember the crackle of leaves beneath my feet and the smell of the burning leaves in the fall bonfires. Life is different in Florida, where we enjoy sunshine all year. We are spared the icy gray days of a Northern winter, the slush of melting snow, and the gloomy rain of early spring. I now live in a place that is always warm and bright, but sometimes I miss the changing seasons of my first home.

Reviewing the Writing Process

In four chapters, you have worked through *four important steps* in writing. As you become more familiar with the steps and with working through them, you will be able to work more quickly. For now, try to remember the four steps:

Infobox

The Steps of the Writing Process

Thought Lines: gathering ideas, thinking on paper through freewriting, brainstorming, or keeping a journal

Outlines: planning the paragraph by grouping details, focusing the details with a topic sentence, listing the support, and devising an outline

Rough Lines: drafting the paragraph, then revising and editing it

Final Lines: preparing the final version of the paragraph, with one last proofreading check for errors in preparation, spelling, punctuation, and mechanics

Following are the outlines, rough lines, and final lines versions of the paragraph on My Mother. Notice how the assignment evolved through the stages of the writing process.

An Outline for a Paragraph on My Mother

topic sentence:	My mother survived difficult times to become a good parent and worker.
details:	She had a rough life.
	She lost her husband.
	She went to school at night.
	She's a good mom and always takes care of me.
	She cooks and cleans.
	She makes a great chicken casserole.
	She works hard at her job.
	She's a nurse.

A Revised Draft of a Paragraph on My Mother

My mother survived difficult times to become a good parent and worker. Her hard times began when she lost her husband. At his death, she was only nineteen and had a baby, me, to raise. She survived by going to school at night to train for a career. Even though she lives a stressful life, she is a good mom. She always takes care of me. She listens to my problems, encourages me to do my best, and praises all my efforts. She cleans our apartment until it shines, and she makes dinner every night. She makes a great chicken casserole. In addition, she works hard at her job. She is a nurse at a home for elderly people, where she is on her feet all day and is still kind and cheerful.

A Final Version of a Paragraph on My Mother
(Changes from the draft are underlined.)

My mother survived difficult times to become a good parent and worker. Her hard times began when she lost her husband. At his death, she was only nineteen and had a baby, me, to raise. She survived by going to school at night to train for a career. Even though she <u>still</u> lives a stressful life <u>today</u>, she is a good <u>mother</u>. She always takes care of me. She listens to my problems, encourages me to do my best, and praises all my efforts. She cleans our apartment until it shines, and she makes dinner every night. She makes a <u>delicious</u> chicken casserole. In addition, she works hard at her job. She is a nurse at a home for elderly people, where she is on her feet all day and is still kind and cheerful. <u>At work or at home, my mother is an inspiration to me.</u>

Lines of Detail: A Walk-Through Assignment

Write a paragraph about a friend. To write this paragraph, follow these steps:

Step 1: For fifteen minutes, freewrite or brainstorm about a friend.

Step 2: Survey your freewriting or brainstorming and underline any specific ideas you can find. Put these ideas in a list.

Step 3: Pick one idea from your list; it will be your topic. Try to develop it by adding details. Get details by going back to your list for other ideas that fit your topic, by brainstorming for more ideas, and by listing new ideas.

Step 4: Group your related ideas by marking a list of your ideas and then putting all the ideas with the same mark into one category, all the ideas with the next mark into another category, and so on, or by mapping.

Step 5: Write a topic sentence and list your ideas below it.

Step 6: Draft your paragraph by writing the topic sentence and all the ideas on your list in paragraph form. Revise, draft, and edit until you are satisfied with your paragraph.

Step 7: Proofread your final draft; then prepare your good copy of your paragraph.

Writing Your Own Paragraph

When you write on any of these topics, be sure to go through the stages of the writing process in preparing your paragraph.

1. This assignment involves working with a group. First, pick a topic from the following list:

> bad drivers
> keeping secrets
> powerful music

Next, join a group of other students who picked the same topic you did. Brainstorm in a group. Discuss questions that could be asked to get ideas for your paragraph.

For the drivers topic, sample questions could include "What kind of driver is the worst?" or "How can you avoid being a bad driver?"

For the secrets topic, sample questions could include "When is it permissible to reveal a secret?" or "Have you ever asked someone to keep your secret?"

For the music topic, sample questions could include "When is music most powerful? At sad occasions or at happy ones?"

As you brainstorm, write the questions down. Keep them flowing. Don't stop to answer them. Don't stop to say, "That's silly," or "I can't answer that." Try to gather at least twelve questions.

Twelve Brainstorming Questions:

1. _____

2. _____

3. _____

4. _____

5. _____

6. _____

7. _____

8. _____

9. _____

10. _____

Once you have the questions, split up. Begin the thought lines step by answering as many questions as you can. You may also add more questions or freewrite. Then pick a specific topic, list the related details, and write a topic sentence.

Work through the outlines stage by developing an outline with sufficient details.

After you've written a draft of your paragraph, read it to your writing group, the same people who met to brainstorm. Ask each member of your group to make one positive comment and one suggestion for revision.

Finally, revise and edit your draft, considering the group's ideas for improvement. When you are satisfied with your revised draft, prepare a final copy of the paragraph.

2. Following are some topic sentences. Select one and use it to write a paragraph.

Parents should always remember that children need _____ and

_____.

Learning a new language is hard because _____.

The two things that surprised me about college were _____ and

_____.

Some people enjoy _____ because it is an escape from

their problems.

3. This assignment requires you to interview a partner. Your final goal is to write a paragraph that will inform the class about your partner. Your paragraph should use this topic sentence:

_____ (fill in your partner's name) has had three

significant experiences.

Step 1: Before you write the paragraph, prepare to interview a classmate. Make a list of six questions you want to ask. They can be questions such as "Have you ever had any interesting experiences?" or "Have you ever been in danger?" Write at least six questions *before* you begin the interview. List the questions below, leaving room to fill in short answers later.

Interview Form

1. **Question:** _____

   Answer: _____

2. **Question:** _____

   Answer: _____

3. **Question:** _____

   Answer: _____

4. **Question:** _____

   Answer: _____

5. **Question:** _____

   Answer: _____

6. **Question:** _____

   Answer: _____

Additional questions and answers: _____

_____

_____

_____

Step 2: As you interview your partner, ask the questions on your list and jot down brief answers. Ask any additional questions you can think of as you are talking; write down the answers in the additional lines at the end of the interview form.

Step 3: Change places. Let your partner interview you.

Step 4: Split up. Use the list of questions and answers about your partner as the thought lines part of your assignment. Work on the outline and draft steps.

Step 5: Ask your partner to read the draft version of your paragraph, to write any comments or suggestions for improvement below the paragraph, and to mark any spelling or grammar errors in the paragraph itself.

Step 6: Revise your draft. When you have completed a final version of your paragraph, read the paragraph to the class.

4. Select one of the following topics. Narrow an aspect of the topic and write a paragraph on it. If you choose the topic of old movies, for example, you might want to narrow it by writing about your favorite old movie.

clothing styles	sports heroes	lies
holidays	college rules	habits
old movies	the Internet	recycling
working out	doctors	fears

5. Look carefully at photograph A. Use the details of the photograph to write a paragraph with this topic sentence:

A photograph can reveal the different personalities of kindergartners.

You can create a personality for each child and support your choice by describing the child's facial expression, physical stance, and relation to the other children.

Photograph A

6. Study photograph B. Are the students in this photo dressed like the students at your college? Or are they dressed differently? Use the details of the photo to write a paragraph answering these questions.

Photograph B

Name: _____ Section: _____

Peer Review Form for a Paragraph

After you have written a draft version of your paragraph, let a writing partner read it. When your partner has completed the following form, discuss it. Then repeat the same process for your partner's paragraph.

The topic sentence of this paragraph is _____

_____

_____

The detail that I liked best begins with the words _____

_____

The paragraph has (enough/too many/too few) [circle one] details to support the topic sentence.

A particularly good part of the paragraph begins with the words _____

_____

I have questions about _____

Other comments on the paragraph: _____

_____

_____

_____

_____

_____

_____

_____

_____

_____

_____

_____

Reviewer's Name: _____

Writing a Paragraph: Focus on Coherence and Unity

Whenever you write, you want to be certain that your writing has a *clear and logical organization*. If it does, it has **coherence**. You also want to be sure that your writing *makes a point* and that *all your details relate to the point*. If it does, your writing will have **unity**. You can check for coherence and unity during the stages of the writing process.

Thought Lines

Focus on Coherence and Unity

Suppose your instructor asks you to write on this topic:

My Last _____

You might begin by *freewriting*:

Freewriting on My Last _____

My last _____. My last what? Last chance? Last dance? My last chance at passing algebra. My last cup of coffee. My last day of high school. That was wild. Seniors are crazy sometimes. Coffee—I love coffee. Quit it suddenly. Last cup of morning coffee. Needed my morning coffee.

You scan your freewriting and realize that you have three possible topics: My Last Day of High School, My Last Chance at Passing Algebra, and My Last Cup of Coffee. Since you do not have any details on passing algebra, and the last day of high school seems like a topic that many students might write about, you decide to be original and work with My Last Cup of Coffee.

| **Exercise 1** | **Finding Topics in Freewriting** |

Practice

Each of the freewriting examples that follow contains more than one possible topic for a paragraph. In the spaces below each freewriting, write the possible topics, and write the one that you think would be the best topic for a paragraph.

Briefly explain why it would be the best topic: Is it the one with the most details? Is it the most original topic? Or is it the one that would be the easiest to develop with specific details?

1.   **Freewriting on This Topic: My Only** _____

My only. Only the lonely. Only what? My only friend in middle school. My only win at gambling. Those silly Lotto cards you scratch off and see the amount underneath. What a surprise. I never win anything. My only regret is _____ _____. I don't know. I regret I didn't study more in high school. Don't look back. Never regret. Move ahead.

possible topics: _____

your choice of the best topic: _____

reason for your choice: _____

2.   **Freewriting on This Topic: My Best** _____

My best dress. A beautiful satin dress. Emerald green. My best day. The best day ever. Hard to tell. I guess the day I met Antonio. Antonio was so hand-some. I miss him now. It's hard to break up. The day we met, he was so funny. I thought he was wild. A friend. My best friend. I could write about my best friend. Friends are special. Hard to find a true friend. I trust my best friend.

possible topics: _____

your choice of the best topic: _____

reason for your choice: _____

Listing Ideas

Now that you have a specific topic, you can scan your freewriting for all your ideas on that topic. You can put all those ideas into a list:

My Last Cup of Coffee
- I love coffee.
- Quit it suddenly.
- Last cup of morning coffee.
- Needed my morning coffee.

Adding Specific Details by Brainstorming

To add ideas to your list, try brainstorming. Add questions that will lead you to more details. You can start with questions that are based on the details you already have. See where the questions—and their answers—lead you.

Question: Why do you love coffee?
Answer: I love the taste.

Question: Is that the only reason?
Answer: It picks me up. Gives me energy. My whole family drinks it. People come over for coffee.

Question: Why did you quit it suddenly?
Answer: I figured quitting suddenly would be the best way. Don't drag it out.

Question: **Why was your last cup drunk in the morning? Why not the after-noon or evening?**

Answer: My first cup in the morning was the one I needed the most. To wake up.

Question: **Were there any other times you needed it?**

Answer: I needed it all day.

Question: **Can you be more specific?**

Answer: I craved coffee around 10:00 a.m., and then again around 3:00 or 4:00 p.m., and also after dinner.

Question: **How did you feel after you quit?**

Answer: I felt terrible at first. Now I feel great.

As you can see, questions can lead you to more details and can help you to decide whether you will have enough details to develop a paragraph on your topic, or whether you need to choose another topic. In this case, the details in the answers are sufficient for writing a paragraph.

Exercise 2

 Collaborate

Brainstorming for Details

Following are topics and lists of details. With a partner or group, brainstorm at least five questions and answers, based on the existing details, that could add more details. The first one is partly done for you.

1. topic: A Power Failure

— The electricity went off.
— It was a very hot day.
— We had no air conditioning or fans.
— The ice in the refrigerator was melting.
— I tried to cool off.
— I couldn't do a lot of things because there was no electricity.

Brainstorming Questions and Answers:

Question 1: How long did the power stay off?

Answer 1:   About four hours.

Question 2: What was the temperature?

Answer 2:   Ninety degrees.

Question 3: _____

Answer 3:   _____

Question 4: _____

Answer 4:   _____

Question 5: _____

Answer 5:   _____

2. topic: Riding the School Bus

- The students were loud.
- They were mean to the driver.
- I had to wait for the bus in the dark.
- The driver was always yelling.
- I made friends on the bus.

Brainstorming Questions and Answers:

Question 1: _____

Answer 1: _____

Question 2: _____

Answer 2: _____

Question 3: _____

Answer 3: _____

Question 4: _____

Answer 4: _____

Question 5: _____

Answer 5: _____

3. topic: A Special Gift

- Dave gave it to me.
- It was a framed picture.
- He was very thoughtful.
- The picture was special.
- He really surprised me.
- It happened a long time ago.

Brainstorming Questions and Answers:

Question 1: _____

Answer 1: _____

Question 2: _____

Answer 2: _____

Question 3: _____

Answer 3: _____

Question 4: _____

Answer 4: _____

Question 5: _____

Answer 5: _____

Focusing the Thought Lines

To begin focusing your topic and details around some point, list your topic and all the details you have gathered so far. The list below includes all the details gathered from freewriting and brainstorming.

My Last Cup of Coffee

- I love coffee.
- Quit it suddenly.
- Last cup of morning coffee.
- Needed my morning coffee.
- I love the taste of coffee.
- It picks me up.
- Gives me energy.
- My whole family drinks it.
- People come over for coffee.
- I figured quitting suddenly would be the best way.
- Didn't want to drag it out.
- My first cup in the morning was the one I needed the most.
- To wake up.
- I needed it all day.
- I craved coffee around 10:00 a.m., and then again around 3:00 or 4:00 p.m., and also after dinner.
- I felt terrible at first.
- Now I feel great.

Coherence: Grouping the Details and Selecting a Logical Order

If you survey the list, you can begin to group the details:

Why I Love Coffee

- I love the taste.
- It picks me up.
- Gives me energy.
- My whole family drinks it.

When I Needed Coffee

- My first cup in the morning was the one I needed most.
- To wake up.
- I needed it all day.
- I craved coffee around 10:00 a.m., and then again around 3:00 or 4:00 p.m., and also after dinner.

How I Quit

- Last cup of morning coffee.
- Figured quitting suddenly would be the best way.
- Didn't want to drag it out.

How I Felt After Quitting

- I felt terrible at first.
- Now I feel great.

Looking at these groups, you notice that two, Why I Love Coffee and When I Needed Coffee, are background. Another group, How I Quit, tells about the moment of quitting. And the last group tells how you felt *after* you had your last cup. These groups seem to lead to a *logical order* for the paragraph: a *time order*. A logical order will give your paragraph coherence.

Unity: Selecting a Topic Sentence

To give the paragraph unity, you need a point—a topic sentence. Surveying your topic and detail, you might decide on this topic sentence:

My last cup of coffee was in the morning.

To be sure that your paragraph has *unity*, check your topic sentence. It should (1) make a point, and (2) relate to all your details.

Does it make a point? No. It says your last cup of coffee was in the morning. That isn't much of a point. It is too narrow to develop into a paragraph. Does the topic sentence relate to all your details? No. You have details about why you love coffee, when you needed it, how you quit, and how you felt afterward. But with your topic sentence, you can talk only about the morning you quit.

You need a better topic sentence. To find it, ask yourself questions like

Did I learn anything from this experience?
Did the experience hurt me?
Did it help me?
Was it a sad experience?
Was it a joyful one?
Were the results good or bad?
Is there a lesson in this experience?

Surveying your details, you might realize that they tell of someone who drank a great deal of coffee, and who feels better after he or she quit. You might decide on a better topic sentence:

My last cup of coffee was the beginning of better health.

This topic sentence relates to many of the details you have. You can mention why you love coffee and when you drank it so that you can give some background on how hard it was to quit. You can explain quitting and discuss how you felt afterward. This topic sentence will give your paragraph unity.

To check your topic sentence for unity, ask the following questions:

✔ Checklist

Unity and the Topic Sentence: A Checklist

✔ Does the topic sentence make a point?

✔ Is the point broad enough to cover all the details?

✔ Do the details relate to the topic sentence?

If the answer to these questions is yes, you are helping to unify your paragraph.

Now that you have a topic sentence and a list of details, you are ready to begin the outlines stage of writing.

Exercise 3 **Grouping Details**

Practice

Below are topics and lists of details. Group the details of each list, writing them under the appropriate headings. Some details may not fit under any of the headings.

1. topic: Time for Myself
  details: In my free time I can get exercise.
        I need time to relieve emotional stress.

Time for myself allows me to clean my apartment.
A day off is a day to do errands.
I have a minute to think about myself and my goals and needs.
I can catch up on my sleep.
I can put my worries aside.

List details about physical benefits: _____

_____

_____

_____

List details about practical benefits: _____

_____

_____

_____

List details about psychological benefits: _____

_____

_____

_____

2. topic: A True Friend
  details: Salvatore always lent me money.
        He never criticized my decisions.
        He gave me encouragement about my dream of going to college.
        Salvatore wouldn't let others gossip about me.
        Salvatore cheered me up when I was sad.
        Salvatore didn't lie to me.

List details about what Salvatore did: _____

_____

_____

_____

List details about what Salvatore didn't do: _____

_____

_____

_____

3. topic: A Pleasant Holiday
  details: We had a great picnic on Labor Day.
           I boiled two dozen eggs for deviled eggs.
           Charlie marinated chicken the night before.
           We told old stories as we ate.
           At the picnic, we danced to the radio.
           Before the picnic, Teresa set up the picnic table outside.
           Charlie grilled the chicken in the yard while we socialized.
           I brought my special deviled eggs and potato salad.
           Everyone brought his or her best recipes.
           Everyone sang as we cleaned up and got ready to leave.
           We left with a promise to do it again.

List details about the time before the picnic: _____

_____

_____

_____

List details about the time during the picnic: _____

_____

_____

_____

_____

List details about the time after the picnic: _____

_____

_____

_____

Exercise 4   **Deciding on a Logical Order**

Practice   Below are topic sentences and lists of details. The lists are not in any logical order. In the space below each list, decide which order would be most appropriate for organizing the list: (1) time order (what happened first, second, etc.), (2) space order (from top to bottom, left to right, inside to out, etc.), or (3) emphatic order (saving the most important details for last).

    1. topic sentence: My mother left my father for several reasons.
           details: They had little in common.
               He wanted an exciting life; she wanted a family.
               They couldn't communicate.
               He couldn't show his feelings.
               She was shy.
               He was beginning to abuse her physically.
               He hit her, twice, when he was drinking.

They married too young.
She was seventeen.
He was nineteen.

The order that would work best: _____

2. topic sentence: The appearance of the airplane impressed me.
   details: The seats were freshly upholstered.
   The carpet was clean.
   The exterior paint on the plane was new.
   The wings gleamed.
   The cute animal painted on the tail of the plane seemed friendly.
   The colors of the interior were bright and cheerful.
   The overhead luggage bins were roomy.

The order that would work best: _____

3. topic sentence: My visit to the dentist was extremely frustrating.
   details: All he did was take X-rays and schedule an appointment with a specialist.
   I had a toothache.
   I had to sit in the waiting room for an hour.
   I called and convinced the dentist's receptionist to squeeze me in, without an appointment.
   I had to sit alone in an examining room for forty minutes.
   I told the dentist I was in pain.

The order that would work best: _____

4. topic sentence: The restaurant was a romantic place for a wedding reception.
   details: Beyond the hall, a large dining room contained a dance floor.
   The dining room tables had lovely flower arrangements.
   Tiny white lights sparkled in the trees on the outdoor patio.
   The fragrance of orange blossoms filled the patio.
   A marble entrance hall gleamed.
   The dining room wallpaper was a pale silk.
   Paintings in gilded frames covered the walls of the hall.
   The dining room opened onto an outdoor patio.

The order that would work best: _____

Exercise 5 **Creating Topic Sentences**

Collaborate Do this exercise with a partner or a group. Following are lists of details. For each list, write two appropriate topic sentences.

1. topic sentence 1: _____

_____

topic sentence 2: _____

_____

details: I love anything made with chocolate.
I love chocolate candy, devil's food cake, and
brownies.
There is a creamy taste to chocolate.
Chocolate also gives me a burst of energy.
Chocolate is fattening.
It has oils that can be bad for your cholesterol level.
It has little nutritional value.

2. topic sentence 1: _____

_____

topic sentence 2: _____

_____

details: I was poor in algebra in high school.
I was afraid to take it in college.
It was a required course.
When I took my college algebra course, I was
nervous.
I failed the first two tests.
I worked with a tutor.
I studied on my own.
I did all the homework problems.
I still failed the third test.
I was frustrated.
Yet I kept working.
Suddenly, my studying paid off.
I began to understand algebra.
Now I am getting B's and C's in the class.

3. topic sentence 1: _____

_____

topic sentence 2: _____

_____

details: My old television broke.
The repair would have cost over $150.
I figured the television wasn't worth repairing.
I could get a new one for a little more money.
My friend offered to sell me his color television for
$230.

It seemed like a good deal.

His television was only a year old.

I walked around the stores.

I saw a new model of his television on sale for $219.

Outlines

Focus on Coherence and Unity

Once you have a topic sentence and a list of details, you can write them in outline form. Below are both the list of details and a draft outline for the paragraph on My Last Cup of Coffee. As you read the outline, you will notice that some of the items on the earlier list have been combined and the details have been grouped into logical categories.

A List of Details on My Last Cup of Coffee

- I love coffee.
- Quit it suddenly.
- Last cup of morning coffee.
- Needed my morning coffee.
- I love the taste of coffee.
- It picks me up.
- Gives me energy.
- My whole family drinks it.
- People come over for coffee.
- I figured quitting suddenly would be the best way.
- Didn't want to drag it out.
- My first cup in the morning was the one I needed the most.
- To wake up.
- I needed it all day.
- I craved coffee around 10 a.m., and then again around 3:00 or 4:00 p.m., and also after dinner.
- I felt terrible at first.
- Now I feel great.

Draft Outline on My Last Cup of Coffee
Paragraph Focus: Coherence and Unity

topic sentence:	My last cup of coffee was the beginning of better health.
details: **why I love coffee**	I love the taste of coffee. Coffee picks me up and gives me energy. My whole family drinks it. People come over for coffee.
when I needed it	My first cup in the morning was the one I needed the most. I needed it to wake up. I needed it around 10:00 a.m., and again around 3:00 or 4:00 p.m., and after dinner.
how I quit	I had my last cup of morning coffee. I quit suddenly. I figured quitting suddenly would be the best way. I didn't want to drag it out.
how I felt after quitting	I felt terrible at first. Now I feel great.

Once you have a draft outline, you can review it for unity and coherence. Use the checklist below as a guide.

✔ **Checklist**

A Checklist for Coherence and Unity in the Outline

✔ Do all the details relate to the topic sentence? (unity)

✔ Are the details in a clear and logical order? (coherence)

When you review the draft outline, you may notice two problems:

1. The details about your family drinking coffee and about people coming over for coffee do not relate to the topic sentence. The topic sentence is about you, not your family. These details do not fit.

2. The details about how you quit could be in a better order: Why you quit suddenly should be explained *before* the details about your last cup.

Even though you checked for unity when you wrote a topic sentence, and you arranged your details in logical categories, you need to stay focused on unity and coherence in each stage of the writing process. Following is a revised outline on My Last Cup of Coffee. This version is more unified and coherent.

A Revised Outline on My Last Cup of Coffee
Paragraph Focus: Coherence and Unity

```
topic sentence: My last cup of coffee was the beginning of better
                health.
details:       ⌠ I love the taste of coffee.
why I love     ⌡ Coffee picks me up and gives me energy.
coffee         ⌠ My first cup in the morning was the one I needed
               │ most.
when I needed it⟨ I needed it to wake up.
               │ I needed coffee all day.
               │ I needed it around 10:00 a.m., and again around
               ⌡ 3:00 or 4:00 p.m., and after dinner.
               ⌠ I quit suddenly.
how I quit     │ I figured quitting suddenly would be the best way.
               │ I didn't want to drag it out.
               ⌡ I had my last cup of morning coffee.
how I felt     ⌠ I felt terrible at first.
after quitting ⌡ Now I feel great.
```

Exercise 6 **Finding Details That Do Not Fit**

Practice

Following are outlines. In each outline, there are details that do not relate to the topic sentence. Cross out the details that do not fit.

1. topic sentence: For several reasons, I avoid buying clothes that need ironing.

details: I am a very busy person.

I don't have time to iron.

Ironing a cotton shirt can take ten minutes.

A week's worth of shirts can take me more than an hour.

My sister-in-law is always ironing.

Even if I find time to iron the clothes that need ironing, they are not worth the time.

After I wear them for ten minutes, they are wrinkled.

They look as though I have not ironed them.

A steam iron works best.

I never wear my clothes that need ironing.

I figure that, if I wear them, I will have to iron them again, soon.

2. topic sentence: My son needs to control his temper.

        details: Jimmy is an angry five-year-old.

He can suddenly lose his temper.

I think he inherited his temper from me.

But I have learned to control my temper.

When he gets upset, Jimmy sometimes punches his sister Gloria.

Other times, he throws objects, like a toy or stuffed animal.

Sometimes he kicks the wall.

Jimmy has not done much harm yet, but he has to stop his tantrums before he hurts someone.

There is a course called Dealing with Your Child's Anger.

I might take it.

Jimmy could hurt himself, too.

3. topic sentence: Friday nights are my favorite time of the week.

        details: I get paid on Fridays.

I have money to spend.

I do not have any night classes on Friday.

On Friday night, I have the whole weekend to look forward to.

I can do my homework on Sunday.

I always meet my friends at a club on Fridays.

My best friend is a real night person.

We listen to music and have a meal at the club.

I feel rich, carefree, and excited.

Exercise 7 **Recognizing Details That Are Out of Order**

Practice   Each of the following outlines has one detail that is out of order. Indicate where it belongs by drawing an arrow from it to the place where it should go.

1. topic sentence: My brother's carelessness cost me my job yesterday.

        details: Tom was supposed to drive me to work.

I got up on time, but he overslept.

I had to rush him through breakfast so he would not be late.

He had forgotten to put the spare tire in the car.
We got in the car, and the gas gauge was on "Empty."
The night before, Tom had forgotten to put gas in the car.
We made it to the gas station, riding on gas fumes.
Getting gas made me fifteen minutes late for work.
A mile past the gas station, we had a flat tire.
I was ready to scream.
"No problem," said Tom.
Then he looked embarrassed.
Waiting for the tow truck took an hour.
I was so late, my boss fired me.

2. topic sentence: Davey's Halloween costume was perfect.
details: My sister turned her two-year-old into a tiny Godzilla.
He had slippers that looked like rubber claws.
His mask was a smiling green lizard face.
Around his neck was a scarf of rubbery, bumpy green material, like lizard skin.
He wore a green jump suit with brown dots.
Attached to it was a long dinosaur tail.
His socks were speckled black and green.

3. topic sentence: Listening to the words "I dare you" can be foolish and dangerous.
details: Accepting a dare shows weakness.
It means you let others tell you what to do.
It means you cannot make up your own mind.
Some people play dangerous games and die.
Accepting a dare can be dangerous.
Some people race cars, on a dare, and dent their cars or hurt their engines.
Some people climb to the top of walls and break legs or arms.

Exercise 8 **Putting Details in the Correct Order**

👥 Collaborate Do this exercise with a partner or a group. In each of the outlines below, the list of details is in the wrong order. Number the details in the correct order, writing *1* next to the detail that should be listed first, and so on.

1. topic sentence: Samantha's plan for giving a surprise birthday party showed her talent for organizing.

details: _____ She invited Tyrone, the guest of honor, for a quiet dinner at her house on the day she wanted to have the party.

_____ Two weeks before the party, she mailed the invitations, each clearly marked "Surprise Party."

_____ Once she knew Tyrone would come for dinner, she made a list of people to invite.

_____ On the day of the party, she called each guest.

_____ In her call, she reminded them to be early.

_____ When her guests arrived, she hid them all on the gaily decorated back porch.

_____ Tyrone entered the porch and saw all his friends in a room decorated for a party.

_____ When Tyrone arrived, Samantha led him to the porch.

_____ The guests and Tyrone had a wonderful time.

2. topic sentence: Getting my son to preschool in the morning is a chore.

details: _____ I have to go back to his bedroom at least twice.

_____ He says "Yes" when I ask him if he's awake, but he buries his head under the covers.

_____ I come in early and wake him gently.

_____ He races to my car but resists wearing his seat belt.

_____ He won't wear the clothes I put out for him.

_____ He comes to breakfast wearing one green and one blue sneaker and a torn sweatshirt.

_____ At breakfast, he can't decide what to eat.

_____ I finally give him Cheerios, but he plays with them.

_____ Once he is out of bed, we fight about his clothes.

_____ I finally give up and let him wear whatever he wants; meanwhile, I make breakfast.

_____ It gets late, so we rush to leave.

3. topic sentence: Yesterday, I began learning how to make my own decisions.

details: _____ Enrique was out of town yesterday.

_____ I was offered a new job at a higher salary than my current job.

_____ I was forced to think for myself.

_____ I usually get my boyfriend Enrique to make all my decisions.

_____ The job offer was good for one day only.

_____ I considered the advantages of the new job

_____ I thought about the drawbacks of the new position.

_____ At first I was very anxious about thinking for myself and couldn't concentrate.

_____ Then I calmed down and began to think.

_____ Once I had made my own decision, I felt wonderful.

Rough Lines

Focus on Coherence and Unity

Once you have a good outline, you can write a first draft of your paragraph. Below is a first draft created from the outline on My Last Cup of Coffee.

A First Draft on My Last Cup of Coffee
Paragraph Focus: Coherence and Unity

My last cup of coffee was the beginning of better health. I love the taste of coffee. Coffee picks me up and gives me energy. My first cup of coffee in the morning was the one I needed most. I needed it to wake up. I needed coffee all day. I needed it around 10:00 a.m., and again around 3:00 or 4:00 p.m., and after dinner. I quit suddenly. I figured quitting suddenly would be the best way. I didn't want to drag it out. I had my last cup of morning coffee. I felt terrible at first. Now I feel great.

Once you have a first draft, you can begin to think about revising and editing. To check your draft for unity and coherence, use the following checklist:

✔ Checklist

A Checklist for Coherence and Unity in the Draft of a Paragraph

✔ Am I sticking to my point? (unity)

✔ Should I take out any ideas that do not fit? (unity)

✔ Should I add any ideas that make my point easier to follow? (coherence)

✔ Should I change the order of my sentences? (coherence)

✔ Can I link my ideas more smoothly? (coherence)

If you apply the checklist to the draft of the paragraph on My Last Cup of Coffee, you will probably find these rough spots:

- One major idea is missing from the paragraph: Why did you decide to give up coffee? How was it hurting your health?
- Some of the sentences are very choppy.
- The paragraph needs transitions to link ideas.

Transitions

Transitions are *words*, *phrases*, or even *sentences* that link ideas. Sometimes they tell the reader what he or she has just read and what is coming next. Every kind of writing has its own transitions. You choose a transition based on the kind of ideas you are linking. Following is a list of some common transitions and their uses:

Infobox

Some Common Transitions and Their Uses

To join two ideas: again, also, and, another, besides, furthermore, in addition, likewise, moreover, similarly

To show a contrast or a different opinion: although, but, however, in contrast, instead, nevertheless, on the contrary, on the other hand, or, otherwise, still, yet

To show a cause-and-effect connection: accordingly, as a result, because, consequently, for, so, therefore, thus

To give an example: for example, for instance, in the case of, like, such as, to illustrate

To show time: after, always, at the same time, before, finally, first (second, third, etc.), meanwhile, next, often, recently, shortly, soon, subsequently, then, until, when, while

To show a similarity: all, both, each, like, similarly

To show a position in space: above, ahead of, alongside, among, around, away, below, beneath, beside, between, beyond, by, close, down, far, here, in front of, inside, near, nearby, next to, on, on top of, outside, over, there, toward, under, underneath, up

---

There are many other transitions you can use, depending on what you need to link your ideas. Take a look at the paragraph below and notice all the underlined words, phrases, and sentences. They are all transitions.

A Paragraph with Transitions Underlined

Buying a used car instead of a new one can offer you several advantages. <u>First</u>, a used car is likely to be cheaper than a new one. <u>While</u> it is glamorous to drive out of the car dealer's lot in a shiny new car, it is not so glamorous to face hefty car payments. <u>A second reason to buy a used car also has to do with money</u>. The cost of insuring a used car should be cheaper than the cost of insuring a new one. Insurance for any car costs a great deal, <u>so</u> you should think about saving as much as you can. <u>Another reason</u> relates to safety. People used to be afraid to buy used cars <u>because</u> they thought the car might be unsafe. <u>However</u>, today you can buy a used car with a limited warranty and feel a little safer. It is true that a new car offers you a more exciting deal; <u>on the other hand</u>, a used one saves you money. <u>Both</u> the new and the used car can offer you safe driving, <u>but</u> the older one will allow you to sleep at night, free of worries about car and insurance payments.

Revising the Draft for Transitions and Added Ideas

When you read the revised draft of the paragraph that follows, you will notice the added transitions. The transitions make the ideas easier to follow and the style smoother.

You will also notice that a new idea has been added: an explanation of how coffee was damaging your health. Since the topic sentence of the paragraph is about *better health* after *quitting coffee,* you need to explain the negative effects of coffee. The added idea and its details make the paragraph more coherent.

These changes and other revisions for more specific details and sentence combining are underlined in the following revised draft:

A Revised Draft on My Last Cup of Coffee
Paragraph Focus: Coherence and Unity

	My last cup of coffee was the beginning
transition added	of better health. <u>It was hard for me to stop drinking coffee because I love the taste of</u>
transitions added, sentences combined	<u>coffee, and coffee picks me up and gives me energy.</u> <u>In addition,</u> I needed coffee. My first cup of coffee in the morning was the
transition added	one I needed most. <u>Then</u> I needed coffee all day. I needed it around 10:00 a.m., again around 3:00 or 4:00 p.m., and after dinner.
transition added, new ideas	<u>My needing coffee led to health problems. I began to feel jumpy if I didn't get my coffee soon enough, and I had terrible</u>
transition added	<u>headaches.</u> <u>So</u> I decided to quit. I decided
transition added	quitting suddenly would be the best way <u>since</u>
detail added	I didn't want to drag it out. <u>Last Monday,</u> I
detail added	had my last cup of morning coffee. <u>It tasted</u>
transition added	<u>wonderful.</u> <u>Then</u> I began to feel terrible <u>as</u>
detail added	<u>my body began to function without coffee. For</u>
details added, transition added	<u>days, I felt miserable without coffee. Finally, I began to improve.</u> Now I feel great.

When you are checking the draft of your own paragraph, pay particular attention to coherence and unity. Even though you check for them in the thought lines and outlines steps of writing, be aware that problems in clear and logical organization (coherence) and in sticking to a point (unity) can turn up in the rough lines step. Careful revision will help you eliminate such problems.

Exercise 9 **Recognizing Transitions**

Practice   Underline all the transitions—words, phrases, and sentences—in the paragraphs below.

1. My two brothers have very different ways of coping with stress. Alonzo, my older brother, first pretends there is nothing stressful happening. Then he gradually admits he is feeling stressed but continues to act as if he is not bothered. Meanwhile, his stress is building until he is very stressed out. Finally, Alonzo collapses under the stress. Marcus, my younger brother, handles stress in an entirely different manner. Unlike Alonzo, Marcus recognizes stress as soon as it appears. At the same time, he begins to cope by worrying, whining, and predicting disaster. Next he calms himself down by overeating and overspending. Subsequently, he is even more stressed because he has gained weight and spent too much money. While Marcus and Alonzo handle stress in opposite ways, they both handle it in unhealthy ones.

2. Marcia's plan for passing her history course was a disaster from start to finish. As the semester began, Marcia was determined to pass history this time since she had already failed it once. Moreover, she needed this course in order to graduate. Therefore, Marcia started the course intending to do well. However, her plan was to cram for all the tests, and her idea of working hard on the assigned papers was to work hard only on the night before they were due. By mid-semester, Marcia was again failing history. At the same time, she was reluctant to talk to her instructor. Marcia waited until the week of final exams to talk to her instructor. First, she asked the teacher if there was any extra credit Marcia could do. When the instructor said it was too late in the term for extra credit, Marcia angrily told the instructor that the course was too difficult. Furthermore, Marcia said, the instructor covered the material too quickly.

After this meeting had hurt Marcia's relationship with her teacher, Marcia's only option was to study hard for the final exam. She studied, but her last-minute studying wasn't enough to give her a passing grade. The next time Marcia takes this course, she will have a better plan for success.

Exercise 10 **Adding the Appropriate Transitions**

Practice In the paragraphs below, transitions are shown in parentheses. Circle the appropriate transitions.

1. Sam deserves an award for Father of the Year. (First/Thus), he takes an active role in raising his two sons, Daniel, three, and James, two. (Meanwhile/For example), he takes them to preschool every morning and arranges his work schedule so that he can be home when they finish school. (Consequently/In addition), he himself is in school so that he can get a better job and can earn more money for his boys. He works nights and goes to school in the morning. He is struggling to be a chef. Sam is a caring father to his own boys, (and/in contrast) he is a father to his sister's baby, Troy. (After/Until) Troy's father died, Sam became a substitute father. He spends time with Troy every week and acts as Troy's advisor and role model. Sam is a loving, dedicated parent to these boys. He manages to be a good parent even though he is short of time and money. (Therefore/Furthermore), I think he deserves an award for his outstanding role as a father.

2. People should concentrate on the road (while/after) they are driving. I have seen drivers who are driving with one hand, or no hands, (because/thus) they are eating a burger, doing their hair, or reading a map. These people are an accident waiting to happen. Other people drive out of their driveways and immediately use their cell phones. If the call was so important, why didn't they make it (after/before) they got in their car? Instead, they are so busy calling that they pay no attention to their driving. (Meanwhile/Until), they are drifting out of their lane or turning

without signaling. They can hurt themselves; (otherwise/furthermore),
they can hurt me. I pay attention when I drive, and I don't want to be the
victim of drivers who can't keep their attention on the road.

Exercise 11 **Using Transitions**

Collaborate Do this exercise with a partner or a group. Write a sentence for each item below.
Be ready to share your answers with another group or with the entire class.

1. Write a sentence with *thus* in the middle of the sentence.

_____

2. Write a sentence that begins with *Recently*.

_____

3. Write a sentence with *for example* in the middle of the sentence.

_____

4. Write a sentence that begins with *Underneath*.

_____

5. Write a sentence with *otherwise* in the middle of the sentence.

_____

6. Write a sentence with *yet* in the middle of the sentence.

_____

7. Write a sentence with *on the other hand* in the middle of the sentence.

_____

8. Write a sentence that begins with *When*.

_____

9. Write a sentence that begins with *In front of*.

_____

10. Write a sentence with *recently* in the middle of the sentence.

_____

Final Lines

Focus on Coherence and Unity

Before you prepare your final copy of your paragraph, check it again for coherence and unity, and for any places where grammar, word choice, and style need revision. Check also for any errors in spelling and punctuation.

Following is the final version of the paragraph on My Last Cup of Coffee. (See draft on page 312.) As you review the final version, you will notice several changes:

- Some specific details have been added.
- The word "needed" has been changed to "craved," to avoid too much repetition.
- In one sentence, the word "it" has been replaced with a more specific word.
- A contraction, "didn't," has been changed to "did not," for a more formal tone.
- A final point, about breaking a dependency on coffee, has been added to reinforce the topic sentence.

The paragraph did not need a final revision for coherence or unity, but it needed some changes to make the details sharper and the meaning clearer.

A Final Version of a Paragraph on My Last Cup of Coffee
Paragraph Focus: Coherence and Unity (Changes from draft on p. 312 are underlined.)

	My last cup of coffee was the beginning of better health. It was hard for me to stop drinking coffee because I love the taste of
detail added	coffee, and coffee picks me up <u>emotionally</u> and gives me energy. In addition, I needed coffee. My first cup of coffee in the morning was the one I needed most. Then I needed it all day.
word changed	I <u>craved</u> it around 10 a.m., again around 3:00
word added	or 4:00 p.m., and after dinner, <u>too</u>. My needing coffee led to health problems. I began to
no contraction	feel jumpy if I <u>did not</u> get my coffee soon enough, and I had terrible headaches. So I decided to quit. I figured quitting suddenly
no contraction,	would be the best way since I <u>did not</u> want to
word changed	drag <u>the process</u> out. Last Monday, I had my last cup of morning coffee. It tasted wonderful. Then I began to feel terrible as my body
details added	began to function without coffee. <u>I was nervous and irritable. My head throbbed with pain.</u> For days, I felt miserable without cof-
details added	fee. Finally, I began to improve. <u>Now I feel</u>
final point added	<u>healthy, calm, and energetic, and I no longer depend upon coffee for my good feelings.</u>

Exercise 12 **Correcting Errors in Final Lines**

Practice

Proofread the following paragraph. Correct any errors in spelling, punctuation, or word choice. There are fourteen errors. Write your corrections in the space above each error.

My last glimpse of my old house was a sad yet happy ocassion. I was

leaving a place were I had spent my hole childhood, so the place had

many pleasant memories. I remebered the time I had a suprise birthday party an the time I got a new kitten. I also looked back on the softball game's we use to play in front of the house. We have some good times. On the other hand, I remembered the bad time's. I thought of the day my brother was kill, and I recalled my mother face when she heard the news. From then on, our house was a sad house. Therefore, as I drove away from the old house and took one last look, I was glad to leave. I look forward to starting over in a new home.

Lines of Detail: A Walk-Through Assignment

For this assignment, write a paragraph on My First _____. (You fill in the blank. Your topic will be based on how you complete step 1 below.)

Step 1: To begin the thought lines part of writing this paragraph, complete the following questionnaire. It will help you think of possible topics and details.

Collaborative Questionnaire for Gathering Topics and Details

Answer the following questions as well as you can. Then read your answers to a group. The members of the group should then ask you follow-up questions, based on your answers. For example, if your answer is "I felt nervous," a group member might ask, "Why were you nervous?" or "What made you nervous?" Write your answers on the lines provided; the answers will add details to your list.

Finally, tear out the page and ask each member of your group to circle one topic or detail that could be developed into a paragraph. Discuss the suggestions.

Repeat this process for each member of the group.

Questionnaire:

1. Have you ever been interviewed for a job? When? _____

_____

Write four details you remember about the interview:

a. _____

b. _____

c. _____

d. _____

Additional details to add after working with the group:

_____

_____

_____

2. Do you remember your first day of school (in elementary school, middle school, high school, or college)? Write four details about that day.

a. _____

b. _____

c. _____

d. _____

Additional details to add after working with the group:

_____

_____

_____

3. Do you remember your first visit to a special place? Write four details about that place.

a. _____

b. _____

c. _____

d. _____

Additional details to add after working with the group:

_____

_____

_____

Step 2: Select a topic from the details and ideas on the questionnaire. Brainstorm and list ideas about the topic.

Step 3: Group your ideas. You may want to group them in time order, or from least important to most important.

Step 4: Survey your grouped ideas and write a topic sentence. Check that your topic sentence makes a point and is broad enough to relate to all the details.

Step 5: Write an outline of your paragraph, putting the grouped details below the topic sentence. Check your outline. Be sure that all the details relate to the topic sentence and that the details are in a clear and logical order.

Step 6: Write a first draft of your paragraph. Then revise and edit: check that you are sticking to your point, that all your details relate to your point, that your ideas are easy to follow, and that you are using effective transitions.

Step 7: In preparing the final copy of your paragraph, check for errors in punctuation, spelling, and word choice.

Writing Your Own Paragraph

When you write on any of the following topics, follow the stages of the writing process in preparing your paragraph.

1. Write about the best or the worst day of your life. Begin by freewriting. Then read your freewriting, looking for both the details and the focus of your paragraph.

   If your instructor agrees, ask a writing partner or a group to (a) listen to your freewriting, (b) help you focus it, (c) help you add details by asking you questions.

2. Interview a family member or friend who is older than you. Ask the person about a significant event in his or her childhood. Ask questions as the person speaks. You can ask questions like, "Why do you think you remember this incident?" or "How did you feel at the time?" Take notes. If you have a tape recorder, you can tape the interview. But take notes as well.

   When you have finished the interview, review the information with the person you've interviewed. Would he or she like to add anything? If you wish, ask follow-up questions.

   Next, on your own, find a point to the story. Use that point in your topic sentence. In this paragraph, you will be writing about another person, not about yourself.

3. Write about a time when you were afraid. Begin by brainstorming questions about what frightened you, why you were afraid, how you dealt with the situation, and so forth. In the outlines stage, focus on some point about the incident: Did you learn from it? Did it change you? Did it hurt or help you? Answering such questions can help you come to a point.

4. Write about a time when you felt very lucky. Include details about the time before, during, and after your good luck.

5. Following are some topic sentences. Complete one of them and use it to write a paragraph.

   When _____, I became angry because _____.

   Saying good-bye to _____ was one of the hardest things I have ever done.

   One day at _____ taught me _____.

   My greatest success came when I _____.

   The longest day of my life was the day I _____.

6. To write on this topic, begin with a partner. Ask your partner to tell you about a day that turned out unexpectedly. It can be a day that included a good or bad surprise.

   As your partner speaks, take notes. Ask questions. When your partner has finished speaking, review your notes. Ask your partner if he or she has anything to add.

   On your own, outline and draft a paragraph on your partner's day. Read your draft to your partner, adding comments and suggestions.

Check the final draft of your paragraph for errors in punctuation, spelling, and word choice.

Your partner can work through this same process to write a paragraph about a day that turned out unexpectedly for you.

7. Write a paragraph that tells a story based on photograph A. In the photo, an elementary school student is dribbling a basketball between his legs as a physical education teacher or coach watches. Create an incident from this photo. Is the adult scolding or praising the child? Has the child broken a rule or performed well? Is the adult angry or pleased? You can include what happened before, during, and after the scene in the photo.

8. Write a paragraph that tells a story based on photograph B. The photo shows a couple in a narrow alley. Create an incident from this photo. You can imagine the relationship of the man and woman, what they are saying, what happened before they were in the alley, and what will happen next.

Photograph A

Photograph B

Name: _____ **Section:** _____

Peer Review Form for a Paragraph: Focus on Coherence and Unity

After you have written a draft of your paragraph, let a writing partner read it. When your partner has completed the following form, discuss the responses. Then repeat the same process for your partner's paragraph.

The topic sentence for this paragraph is _____

_____

The order used in this paragraph is (a) time order, (b) space order, (c) emphatic order, (d) other

[choose one]. If you chose "other," briefly describe the order: _____

_____

One effective transition is _____

(Write the words of a good transition.)

The part of the paragraph that I like best begins with the words _____

_____

I think this paragraph is (a) easy to follow, (b) a little confusing [choose one].

I have questions about _____

I would like to see something added about _____

_____

I would like to take out the part about _____

_____

Other comments on the paragraph: _____

_____

_____

_____

_____

_____

_____

Reviewer's Name: _____

WRITING FROM READING

Binge Nights: The Emergency on Campus
Michael Winerip

Michael Winerip is a staff writer for the New York Times Magazine. *In an article on binge drinking among college students, he tells the story of Ryan Dabbieri, a twenty-two-year-old senior at the University of Virginia.*

Words You May Need to Know

tailgating party (paragraph 2): a party held outside the stadium, usually in the parking lot, before a game

"fourth-year fifth" (4): a tradition among some seniors at the University of Virginia of drinking a fifth of liquor for the last home football game

blood alcohol level (5): a measure of the concentration of alcohol in a person's blood; a blood alcohol level of .25 is over three times the state of Virginia's limit for legal intoxication

1   Researchers consider a person who has had five drinks on one occasion during the previous two weeks to be a binge drinker. By that definition, Ryan Dabbieri, a 22-year-old University of Virginia senior, was a binger although he did not think of himself that way. "I didn't drink a lot," said Ryan, an electrical engineering major. "Maybe once a week, I'd do five, maybe six or seven drinks in two hours. What I drank was pretty typical."

2   He was looking forward to the November 29 Virginia Tech game, the season finale. At a tailgating party that afternoon, Ryan drank bourbon with several friends. "I was pouring and I was very excited about the game and, apparently, I was pouring two or three times as big shots for myself as everyone else," he recalled. "I didn't realize it. I remember maybe three shots. I can't remember after that, but my friends said I actually drank five or six big shots in ten, fifteen minutes."

3   The police did not bother tailgaters, but as fans poured into the stadium, there was security everywhere, looking for alcohol. "I was pretty out of it," Ryan said. "One of my friends said, 'You'll have to sober up to get in.' I tightened up to get through; then once I was in, I sort of fell apart." The rest he has since pieced together from friends and doctors.

4   When he began throwing up in the stands, the two women he was with decided they had better get him out of there. It was a lot of work lugging him back to the car—six feet, one inch, and 165 pounds worth of dead weight. As they passed, people made sly comments about "doing your fourth-year fifth." His friends planned to drive him home and put him to bed, but one of them was a lifeguard trained in first aid, and when Ryan didn't come to, they took him to the hospital as a precaution. At the emergency room, they got a wheelchair and

rolled him in, and about then, he stopped breathing. When doctors realized it, they raced to put him on a respirator. They estimated his breathing had stopped for four minutes and did a brain scan to check for damage.

5   His blood alcohol level was .25.

6   He came to the next morning in the intensive care unit, but was still so drunk, he didn't realize why he was in the hospital. When he tried to talk, the tube in his throat prevented him, and on a piece of paper he wrote, "What happened?" That evening, he said, "I woke up and my dad was standing there. He'd come in from Atlanta. My parents are divorced, and I don't see him often, so it was a big shock to me—that's when I realized I'd almost died."

7   He says the experience was hardest for his friends, who saved his life. "They were by my side the whole time, scared to death I would die," he said. "Being unconscious, I missed all the emotion of it."

8   "I don't see myself drinking again," he added. "I'm lucky not to be dead."

Exercise 13 **Recognizing Transitions in "Binge Nights: The Emergency on Campus"**

Practice

Michael Winerip uses many transitions—words and phrases—to tell the story of Ryan Dabbieri. Read the following paragraph from "Binge Nights." Then reread it, underlining all the words or phrases that tell *when* or *where* something is taking place.

When he began throwing up in the stands, the two women he was with decided they had better get him out of there. It was a lot of work lugging him back to the car—six feet, one inch, and 165 pounds of dead weight. As they passed, people made sly comments about "doing your fourth-year fifth." His friends planned to drive him home and put him to bed, but one of them was a lifeguard trained in first aid, and when Ryan didn't come to, they took him to the hospital as a precaution. At the emergency room, they got a wheelchair and rolled him in, and about then, he stopped breathing. When doctors realized it, they raced to put him on a respirator. They estimated his breathing had stopped for four minutes and did a brain scan to check for damage.

WRITING FROM READING "Binge Nights: The Emergency on Campus"

When you write on any of the following topics, be sure to work through the stages of the writing process in preparing your paragraph.

1. Write about your own close call: a time when you were in danger but were rescued or saved yourself. To begin the assignment, freewrite on your memories of the experience.

2. Write about a time when a happy occasion turned into an emergency. If your instructor agrees, you may want to begin the assignment by asking a writing partner to interview you, asking questions such as the following:

> Why was this time particularly happy?
> What caused the emergency?
> How did you feel during the emergency?
> How did you feel when the emergency was over?

3. Write about doing something you later regretted. In your topic sentence, you may want to consider the lesson you learned from your actions.

4. Write a paragraph summarizing Ryan Dabbieri's experience with binge drinking. Be sure that your topic sentence makes some point about his experience.

5. Ryan Dabbieri says his experience was especially hard on his friends. Write about a time when something you did was hard on your friend(s).

6. Write a paragraph using one of the topic sentences below:

I saw the dangers of binge drinking when _____.

A person I know has a habit that recently put him/her in danger.

_____ (write *I* or a person's name) gave in to peer pressure

when _____.

When I saw _____, I saw how dangerous some traditions

can be.

The Baby Myna
Ved Mehta

Ved Mehta, blind since the age of four, grew up in India but was educated at Oxford University in England and Harvard University in the United States. He became a writer of essays and short stories and received many awards. In this selection from his autobiography, Mehta tells a story of his childhood.

Words You May Need to Know

frenetically (paragraph 5): frantically
surreptitiously (13): secretly
defiant (26): rebellious, disobedient
abrasive (26): rough
treble notes (26): high-pitched notes

harmonium (26): an organlike
  keyboard instrument
enticing (28): tempting, attractive
hillocks (29): little hills

1 One day, Sher Singh returned from leave in his village in the Kangara District, in the hills, with a baby myna for me. "I have brought you a friend," he said. "It's a baby myna. It's one of the only birds in the world that can talk. It's just the right age to learn to talk."

2 I was excited. I went with Sher Singh to the Mozang Chowk and bought a wire cage with a door, a metal floor, and a little swing. The cage had a hook at the top, and I hung it in my room. (We were temporarily living in our own house, at 11 Temple Road.) I got a couple of brass bowls—one for water, the other for grain—and filled them up and put them in the cage. I got a brush for cleaning out the cage. I named the myna Sweetie. The name came to me just out of the sky.

3 "How do you catch a baby myna?" I asked Sher Singh.

4 "It's difficult, Vedi Sahib. There are very few of them around, and you have to know where a baby myna is resting with her mother. You have to slip up on them in the middle of the night, when they are sleeping in their nest, and throw a cover over them and hope that you catch the baby, because only a baby myna can learn to talk. Sometimes the mother myna will nip at your finger, and there are people in my village who are constantly getting their fingers nipped at because they have been trying to catch a baby myna."

5 At first, Sweetie was so small that she could scarcely fly even a few inches. I would sit her on my shoulder and walk around the room. She would dig her nervous, trembling claws through my shirt and into my shoulder as she tried to keep her balance, fluttering around my ear and sending off little ripples of air. But Sweetie grew fast, and soon she was flying around my room. Before I opened her cage to fill up the bowls or clean the floor, I would have to shut the door. She would often nip at my fingers and escape from the cage. She would go and perch on the mantelpiece. When I ran to the mantelpiece to catch her, she would fly up to the curtain rod. When I climbed up onto the windowsill and

shook the curtain, she would fly back to the mantelpiece. Sometimes she would be so silent that I would wonder if she was still in the room. Other times, I would hear her flying all around the room—now she would be by the window, now by the overhead light, her wings beating against the pane and the lampshade. I would make kissing sounds, as I had heard Sher Singh make them. I would call to her—"Sweetie! Sweetie!" I would whistle affectionately. I would run frenetically from one end of the room to the other. I would scream with rage. But she wouldn't come to me. I would somehow have to summon Sher Singh through the closed door, and then give him a cue to come in when I thought she wasn't near the door, and he would have to prance around the room and somehow catch her with his duster.

6   "She's a real hill girl, all right, flying around like that," he would say.

7   When we had finally got her back in the cage, I would scold her roundly, but it didn't seem to do much good.

8   "Vedi Sahib, you'll lose her, like your eyes, if you don't keep her always in the cage," Sher Singh said.

9   "But then how can I feed her? How can I clean out her cage?"

10   "I will do all that, Vedi Sahib. And, because I can see, I can watch her."

11   "But I like looking after her," I said.

12   "You'll lose her, Vedi Sahib," he said. "And mind your finger. She's getting big."

13   I devised a way of filling her bowls and cleaning some of the cage's floor by surreptitiously sticking my fingers between the wires. But now and again I would want to feel her on her swing or take her out and hold her, and then she would nip at my finger and sometimes draw blood. She would escape and give me a real run around the room.

14   Every time I passed Sweetie's cage, I would say "Hello, Sweetie," and wait for her to talk. But she would only flutter in the cage or, at most, make her swing squeak.

15   "Are you sure Sweetie can talk?" I asked Sher Singh.

16   "All baby mynas from Kangara can learn to talk," he said.

17   "Are you sure she is from Kangara?"

18   "Only mynas from Kangara have a black patch on the throat. You can feel it, and you can ask anyone—it's as black as coal."

19   I took Sweetie out of her cage. I held her tight in one hand and tried to feel the patch on her throat with the other. She screamed and tried to bite my finger, but I finally found the patch. It was a little soft, downy raised circle that throbbed with her pulse.

20   "What do mynas sound like when they talk?" I later asked Sher Singh.

21   "They have the voice of the Kangara, of a Kangara hill girl."

22   "What is that?"

23   "The Punjab hills, the leaves in the wind, the waterfall on a mountainside—you know, Vedi Sahib, it's the sound of a peacock spreading its wings in Kangara at dawn."

24   One day, I passed her cage and said, "Hello, Sweetie."

25   "Hello, Sweetie," she answered.

26   I jumped. I don't know how I had expected her voice to sound, but it was thin, sharp, and defiant—at once whiny and abrasive—like three treble notes on the harmonium played very fast. Her words assaulted my ears—"Sweetie" was something that film stars called each other on the screen, and sounded very naughty.

27   I had scarcely taken in the fact that Sweetie could really speak when she repeated "Hello, Sweetie." She kept on repeating it, hour after hour. "Hello, Sweetie" would suddenly explode into the air like a firecracker.

28   Try as I would, I couldn't teach her to say anything else. All the same, there was something thrilling and comforting in having my own film star in the cage, and I got so used to her enticing outbursts that I missed them when she kept quiet or was dozing.

29   Every evening, at the time when my big sisters and my big brother went to play hockey or some other game with their school friends, it was Sher Singh's duty to take me for a walk to Lawrence Gardens. There I would ride the merry-go-round—a big, creaky thing with wooden seats and a metal railing—while Sher Singh ran alongside. It would revolve and lurch, tipping this way and that way, filling me with terror and excitement. On the ground, I would throw off my shoes and run up and down the hillocks. They were covered with damp, soft grass and occasional patches of dead grass. The grass would caress, tickle, and prick my feet. All around, there were the light, cheerful sounds of sighted children running and playing and of birds flying and perching and calling. In the distance, there was the solitary, mournful song of a nightingale.

30   I felt sorry that Sweetie, shut up in the house, couldn't enjoy the company of other birds, and one evening I insisted that we take her along in her cage and let her enjoy the fresh air and the life of Lawrence Gardens, even if it was only through the wires of her cage.

31   "But don't let her out of the cage," Sher Singh said. "She is a spirit from the hills. She will fly back to Kangara."

32   "Fly all the way back to Kangara! She would die without food or water. Besides, she is my friend. She wouldn't leave me."

33   "Vedi Sahib, you know how loyal Kangara servants are?"

34   "No one could be more loyal than you, Sher Singh."

35   "Well, Kangara mynas are as disloyal as Kangara servants are loyal. You can love a beloved myna all you want to, give her all the grain to eat you want to, give her all the water to drink you want to, and at the first opportunity she will nip at your finger and fly away. But you can kick a servant from Kangara and he will still give you first-class service."

36   "Why is that?"

37   "Because servants from Kangara, like mynas, have breathed the Himalayan air and are free spirits. A Kangara servant is a servant by choice—but no myna is in a cage by choice."

38   I couldn't follow exactly what Sher Singh was saying, but I laughed. Anyway, I insisted that we take Sweetie with us.

39   At Lawrence Gardens, I had no intention of taking Sweetie out of her cage, but when she heard the other birds she set up such a racket that children and servants who usually took little notice of me wandered toward us to find out what I was doing to the poor myna. They said all kinds of things:

40   "She is lonely."

41   "He's keeping her a prisoner."

42   "Tch, tch! He can't play with other children, so he won't let his myna play with other birds."

43   "She'll fly away to Kangara!" I cried.

44   People laughed, hooted, and jeered. "She's so small she probably can't even fly up to that tree."

45   "Why are you pointing? He doesn't know how high that tree is."

46   I suddenly got an idea. I had with me a ball of strong, fortified string that Brother Om used for flying kites. I took Sweetie out of the cage and, while I held her screaming and biting in my hands, I had Sher Singh tie up her legs with the string. Then I caught hold of the ball and let her go, and the people about us clapped and cheered. I started giving her string, and she flew high up and pulled and tugged. I gave her more string and let her lead me where she would around the grass. I thought it was a wonderful game. Before I knew what had happened, her weight at the end of the string was gone, and the limp string had fluttered down on me.

47   "She's bitten through the string! Look, she's bitten through the string!" everyone shouted, running away.

48   "Sher Singh, catch her! Catch her!" I cried. "Bring Sweetie back!"

49   "I think I see her!" he called, running off.

50   A few minutes later, Sher Singh came back. "She's nowhere to be found, Vedi Sahib. She's gone, Sahib—gone straight back to Kangara. You will now have to get along without Sweetie."

51   Sher Singh and I looked for her all over Lawrence Gardens, calling "Sweetie! Sweetie!" until it was dark and everyone had left. Then Sher Singh and I walked home with the empty cage.

Exercise 14   **Recognizing the Steps in "The Baby Myna"**

Practice   Ved Mehta explains several stages in his ownership and loss of Sweetie. Complete the exercise below by rereading "The Baby Myna" and focusing on the steps.

   1. There were several stages in Sweetie's flying around the room.

      a. At first, she could barely fly a short distance.

      b. Then she would escape from the cage when Mehta tried to feed her.

      c. At that time, Mehta had to ask _____ to catch Sweetie.

   d. Finally, Mehta devised a way to feed her and clean her cage without her escaping.

   e. But he would sometimes want to _____

   and she would again _____ .

2. He followed several steps in getting her to talk.

   a. Every time he passed her cage, he said, _____

   b. Then he asked Sher Singh if Sweetie _____

   c. As part of his answer, Sher Singh told Mehta to feel _____

   _____

   d. Finally, one day, Sweetie said _____ and kept

   saying it, hour after hour.

3. On the day he lost Sweetie, Mehta took several steps that led to the loss.

   a. First, he took her to Lawrence Gardens in her cage.

   b. Then she began to set up a racket when she heard other birds.

   c. The children in the gardens convinced Mehta to let Sweetie out of

   her cage by saying things like _____

   _____ and _____

   _____

   d. To keep Sweetie in his possession while she was out of her cage,

   Mehta did this: _____

   e. Sweetie got free when she _____

Exercise 15 **Recognizing Mehta's Use of Sense Words in "The Baby Myna"**

Practice As Mehta tells his story of Sweetie, he does not write much about what someone or something *looks* like; instead, he relies on many words that describe a *sound* or *touch*. Complete this exercise using the exact words of the story.

   1. Write some exact words that describe what Mehta's hand feels when

   Mehta holds Sweetie: _____

   _____

   2. Write some exact words to describe what Sweetie's voice sounds like:

   _____

3. Write some exact words that Mehta uses to describe the grass against his feet: _____

_____

4. Write some exact words to describe what Sweetie, perched on Mehta's shoulder, felt like to Mehta: _____

_____

_____

5. Write the exact words that describe the feeling of the patch on Sweetie's throat: _____

_____

WRITING FROM READING "The Baby Myna"

When you write on any of the following topics, be sure to work through the stages of the writing process in preparing your paragraph.

1. Write a paragraph about an incident with an animal. The incident may have happened to you, or you may have seen it happen to someone else. As a way of starting, list all the details of the incident and then put them in time order.

2. Write about a time when you tried to hold on to someone or something that wanted to be free. To begin, you can freewrite all your memories of this situation.

3. As Ved Mehta tells his story, we become aware of how his blindness affects what he does. For instance, because he is blind, he has a hard time catching Sweetie when she flies in his room. On the other hand, Mehta, being blind, seems very aware of every sound and of the textures of objects, animals, and nature. Write a paragraph about what it means to have a specific disability. To begin this assignment, you might want to interview a friend who is disabled.

4. Write about a time in your childhood when other children pressured you to do something. To begin, you can ask a writing partner to interview you, asking questions like the following:

> Did you give in to their pressure?
> If so, why? Was it out of fear?
> If you didn't give in, why didn't you?
> How did you feel during and after the incident?

After the interview, you can interview your partner so he or she can collect ideas for his or her paragraph.

5. Write a paragraph about how you tried to train a pet. Focus on one specific skill or behavior (such as fetching a ball, walking on a leash) that you were trying to develop in your pet.

6. Write about a time you saw an animal in a cage. Focus on what you think the animal was feeling or on your own reaction to the scene.

7. Write a paragraph about what Ved Mehta learned from his experience of owning, training, and losing Sweetie.

I Fell in Love, Or My Hormones Awakened
Judith Ortiz Cofer

Judith Ortiz Cofer, daughter of a Puerto Rican mother and a mainland Unit-ed States father, was born in Puerto Rico. When she was four years old, Cofer and her family moved to the United States. There she earned both bachelor's and master's degrees in English, and later she completed further studies at Oxford University in England. Cofer has taught English in the South and is a well-known poet. This excerpt from her autobiography tells of the bittersweet experience of first love.

Words You May Need to Know

Marlon Brando (paragraph 1): a movie star who, in the 1950s and 1960s, often played rebels and loners

L&M's (4): a brand of cigarettes

adulation (6): adoration, excessive devotion

extravaganza (7): an elaborate drama

Paterson (7): a city in New Jersey

seamstress (8): a woman whose occupation is sewing

Michelangelo (8): an Italian sculptor and painter in sixteenth-century Italy

gluttonously (9): greedily

relished (9): enjoyed

ruddy (9): having a fresh, healthy color

sergeant-at-arms (9): an officer whose job is to keep order

disdain (9): arrogance, contempt

phantom (11): ghostly

1   I fell in love, or my hormones awakened from their long slumber in my body, and suddenly the goal of my days was focused on one thing: to catch a glimpse of my secret love. And it had to remain secret, because I had, of course, in the great tradition of tragic romance, chosen to love a boy who was totally out of my reach. He was not Puerto Rican; he was Italian and rich. He was also an older man. He was a senior at the high school when I came in as a fresh-man. I first saw him in the hall, leaning casually on a wall that was the border line between girlside and boyside for underclassmen. He looked extraordinarily like a young Marlon Brando—down to the ironic little smile. The total of what I knew about the boy who starred in every one of my awkward fantasies was this: that he was the nephew of the man who owned the supermarket on my block; that he often had parties at his parents' beautiful home in the suburbs which I would hear about; that his family had money (which came to our school in many ways)—and this fact made my knees weak; and that he worked at the store near my apartment building on weekends and in the summer.

2   My mother could not understand why I became so eager to be the one sent out on her endless errands. I pounced on every opportunity from Friday to late Saturday afternoon to go after eggs, cigarettes, milk (I tried to drink as much of it as possible although I hated the stuff)—the staple items that she would order from the "American" store.

3   One day I did see him. Dressed in a white outfit like a surgeon: white pants and shirt, white cap, and (gross sight, but not to my love-glazed eyes) blood-smeared butcher's apron. He was helping to drag a side of beef into the freezer storage area of the store. I must have stood there like an idiot because I remember that he did see me; he even spoke to me! I could have died. I think he said, "Excuse me," and smiled vaguely in my direction.

4   After that, I *willed* occasions to go to the supermarket. I watched my mother's pack of cigarettes empty ever so slowly. I wanted her to smoke them fast. I drank milk and forced it on my brother (although a second glass for him had to be bought with my share of Fig Newton cookies, which we both liked, but we were restricted to one row each). I gave my cookies up for love and watched my mother smoke her L&M's with so little enthusiasm that I thought (God, no!) that she might be cutting down on smoking or maybe even giving up the habit. At this crucial time!

5   I thought I had kept my lonely romance a secret. Often I cried hot tears on my pillow for the things that kept us apart. In my mind there was no doubt that he would never notice me (and that is why I felt free to stare at him—I was invisible). He could not see me because I was a skinny Puerto Rican girl, a freshman that did not belong to any group he associated with.

6   At the end of the year I found out that I had not been invisible. I learned one little lesson about human nature—adulation leaves a scent, one that we are all equipped to recognize, and no matter how insignificant the source, we seek it.

7   In June the nuns at our school would always arrange for some cultural extravaganza. In my freshman year, it was a Roman banquet. Our young, energetic Sister Agnes was in the mood for spectacle. She ordered the entire student body (it was a small group of under 300 students) to have our mothers make togas out of sheets. Then, as the last couple of weeks of school dragged on, the city of Paterson becoming a concrete oven, and us wilting in our uncomfortable uniforms, we labored like frantic Roman slaves to build a splendid banquet hall in our small auditorium.

8   On the night of the banquet, my father escorted me in my toga to the door of our school. I felt foolish in my awkwardly draped sheet (blouse and skirt underneath). My mother had no great skill as a seamstress. The best she could do was hem a skirt or a pair of pants. That night I would have traded her for a peasant woman with a golden needle. I saw other Roman ladies emerging from their parents' cars looking authentic in sheets of material that folded over their bodies like the garments on a statue by Michelangelo. How did they do it? How was it that I always got it just slightly wrong, and worse, I believed that other people were just too polite to mention it. "The poor little Puerto Rican girl," I could hear them thinking. But in reality, I must have been my worst critic, self-conscious as I was.

9   All during the program I was in a state of controlled hysteria. My secret love sat across the room from me looking supremely bored. I watched his every

move, taking him in gluttonously. I relished the shadow of his eyelashes on his ruddy cheeks, his pouty lips smirking sarcastically at the ridiculous sight of our little play. Once he slumped down in his chair, and our sergeant-at-arms nun came over and tapped him on his shoulder. He drew himself up slowly, with disdain. I loved his rebellious spirit. I believed myself still invisible to him in my "nothing" status as I looked upon my beloved. But towards the end of the evening, he looked straight across the room and into my eyes! How did I survive the killing power of those dark pupils? I trembled in a new way. I was not cold—I was burning! Yet I shook from the inside out, feeling light-headed, dizzy.

10   The room began to empty, and I headed for the girls' lavatory. I wanted to relish the miracle in silence. I did not think for a minute that anything more would follow. I was satisfied with the enormous favor of a look from my beloved. I took my time, knowing that my father would be waiting outside for me, impatient. The others would ride home. I would walk home with my father. I wanted as few witnesses as possible. When I could no longer hear the crowds in the hallway, I emerged from the bathroom, still under the spell of those mesmerizing eyes.

11   The lights had been turned off in the hallway, and all I could see was the lighted stairwell, at the bottom of which a nun would be stationed. My father would be waiting just outside. I nearly screamed when I felt someone grab me by the waist. But my mouth was quickly covered by someone else's mouth. I was being kissed. My first kiss and I could not even tell who it was. I pulled away to see that face not two inches away from mine. It was he. He smiled down at me. Did I have a silly expression on my face? My glasses felt crooked on my nose. I was unable to move or speak. More gently, he lifted my chin and touched his lips to mine. This time I did not forget to enjoy it. Then, like the phantom lover that he was, he walked away into the darkened corridor and disappeared.

12   I don't know how long I stood there. My body was changing right there in the hallway of a Catholic school. My cells were tuning up like musicians in an orchestra, and my heart was a chorus. It was an opera I was composing, and I wanted to stand still and just listen. But, of course, I heard my father's voice talking to the nun. I was in trouble if he had had to ask about me. I hurried down the stairs, making up a story on the way about feeling sick. That would explain my flushed face, and it would buy me a little privacy when I got home.

Exercise 16	**Recognizing the Time Order of "I Fell in Love, Or**
Practice	**My Hormones Awakened"**

"I Fell in Love, Or My Hormones Awakened" tells a story that covers many months. Judith Ortiz Cofer is careful to indicate exactly what happened at what time. In the following spaces, list the incidents that happened at the following times.

1. One day in the supermarket, Cofer finally _____

_____

2. In June, Sister Agnes had all the high school students working on _____

_____

3. On the night of the banquet, Cofer looked at the other girls in their

togas and felt _____

4. During the banquet, Cofer watched _____

5. Then she realized he was _____

6. She stayed in the girls' lavatory because she _____

_____

7. In the hallway, she received _____

8. Afterward, alone in the hallway, she felt _____

_____

9. Then she heard _____

10. As she hurried down the stairs, she made up a story about _____

_____

Exercise 17
Practice

Recognizing Time Transitions in "I Fell in Love, Or My Hormones Awakened"

Cofer's story describes incidents that cover one school year. She uses many transitions to indicate time to be sure that her writing is coherent and smooth. In the following paragraph, underline all the words or phrases that are time transitions.

All during the program I was in a state of controlled hysteria. My secret love sat across the room from me looking supremely bored. I watched his every move, taking him in gluttonously. I relished the shadow of his eyelashes on his ruddy cheeks, his pouty lips smirking sarcastically at the ridiculous sight of our little play. Once he slumped down in his chair, and our sergeant-at-arms nun came over and tapped him on his shoulder. He drew himself up slowly, with disdain. I loved his rebellious spirit. I believed myself still invisible to him in my "nothing" status as I looked upon my beloved. But towards the end of the evening, he looked straight across the room and into my eyes! How did I survive the killing power of those dark pupils? I trembled in a new way. I was not cold—I was burning! Yet I shook from the inside out, feeling light-headed, dizzy.

WRITING FROM READING "I Fell in Love, Or My Hormones Awakened"

When you write on any of the following topics, be sure to work through the stages of the writing process in preparing your paragraph.

1. Judith Ortiz Cofer says that her first experience with love taught her "one little lesson about human nature—adulation leaves a scent, one that we are all equipped to recognize, and no matter how insignificant the source, we seek it." Write a paragraph explaining what she means by these words and how she learned the lesson. You can begin by discussing her words with a group. First, remember that "adulation" means adoration or excessive devotion, and the source of the adulation is the person giving this excessive devotion and adoration. Then you might consider such questions as the following:

   Who is giving adulation? To whom?
   Who recognizes the "scent" of the adulation? That is, who recognizes that he/she is being given this adulation?
   Who feels insignificant?
   Who seeks out the source of the adulation?

2. Write a paragraph about a time when you suddenly felt older, more grown up. To begin, list all the details of the incident and then put them in time order.

3. Write a paragraph about a time when you were infatuated. To begin, you can freewrite, focusing on how you felt at each stage of the infatuation.

4. Write a paragraph about a time when someone was infatuated with you. To begin, you can freewrite about how you felt at each stage of the infatuation.

5. Write a paragraph from the boy's point of view in "I Fell in Love, Or My Hormones Awakened." That is, imagine what he was feeling at different stages of the story: when he saw Judith at the supermarket, when he looked at her at the Roman banquet, and when he kissed her.

6. Write a paragraph about a secret—yours or someone else's—and how it was revealed. To begin, you can ask a writing partner to interview you, asking such questions as the following:

   Why did you or someone else feel the need to keep something secret?
   How was the secret revealed?
   Who revealed it?
   Why was it revealed?
   What were the effects of revealing it?

   After your interview, interview your partner so that he or she can collect ideas for his or her paragraph.

7. Cofer writes about a time when she felt insignificant. Write a paragraph about a time when you felt insignificant. Be sure to include the circumstances that led to your feeling that way: Did you feel like an outsider in your community? Did you feel physically unattractive, awkward, or unintelligent? Also discuss the result of such feelings: Were you able to overcome them? If so, how?

CHAPTER 25

Writing a Paragraph: Focus on Support and Details

Whenever you write, you want to be sure that your point has sufficient support. **Support** means that *you have enough to say about your point*, and that *you include enough specific details* to make your point effectively. You can check for sufficient support and specific details at each stage of the writing process.

Thought Lines

Focus on Support and Details

Suppose your instructor asks you to write about this topic: An Outdoor Place. You might begin by *brainstorming*:

Sample Brainstorming on an Outdoor Place
Paragraph Focus: Support and Details

Question: **What place?**
Answer: Outside somewhere.

Question: **Like the outside of a building?**
Answer: Maybe.

Question: **The beach?**
Answer: That would be OK. But everybody will write on that.

Question: **How about a park?**
Answer: Yes. A park would be good.

Question: **How about the park near your workplace—the city park?**
Answer: I could do that. I go there at lunchtime.

You scan your brainstorming and realize you have three possible topics: the outside of a building, the beach, or a city park. You decide that you can write the most about the city park, so you brainstorm further:

Brainstorming on a Specific Topic: A City Park
Paragraph Focus: Support and Details

Question: **What does the park look like?**
Answer: It's small.

Question: **How small?**
Answer: Just the size of an empty lot.

Question: **What's in it?**
Answer: Some trees. Benches.

Question: **Any swing sets or jungle gyms?**
Answer: No, it's not that kind of park. Just a green space.

Question: **Why do you like this park?**
Answer: I just like it. It's near the store where I work. I go there at lunchtime.

Question: **But <u>why</u> do you go there?**
Answer: It's nice and green. It's not like the rest of the city.

Question: **What's the rest of the city like?**
Answer: The rest of the city is dirty, gray, and noisy.

By asking and answering questions, you can (1) choose a topic, and (2) begin to develop ideas on that topic. Each answer can lead you to more questions and thus to more ideas.

Exercise 1 **Identifying Topics in Brainstorming**

Practice

Following are examples of early brainstorming. In each case, the brainstorming is focused on selecting a narrow topic from a broad one. Imagine that the broad topic is one assigned by your instructor. Survey each example of brainstorming and list all the possible narrower topics within it.

    1. broad topic: Describe a party you attended.
    brainstorming:

Question: **What kind of party?**
Answer: I don't know. I don't go to many parties.

Question: **When you were younger, you had a birthday party, didn't you?**
Answer: Yes, that was fun. It was when I was six.

Question: **Did you have friends come over, or just family?**
Answer: Some friends from my first-grade class came.

Question: **Or could you write about another party?**
Answer: Maybe the office party last week.

Question: **Was it fun?**
Answer: Yes, but I don't know what I'd write about it.

Question: **How about another kind of party?**
Answer: Maybe I could write on my sister's graduation party.

possible topics: _____

_____

2. broad topic: Write about an attractive person.
brainstorming:

Question: **Who is attractive?**
Answer: Maybe a movie star.

Question: **Male or female?**
Answer: I don't know. Maybe I could write about a model.

Question: **What does attractive mean?**
Answer: Beautiful. Handsome. Maybe it means attractive inside. Because of an attractive personality or warmth.

Question: **So who is attractive inside?**
Answer: My sister Lupe. She's not beautiful, but she's beautiful inside.

possible topics: _____

_____

Exercise 2 Collaborate

Developing Ideas Through Further Brainstorming

Following are examples of brainstorming. Each example brainstorms a single, narrow topic. Working with a group, write four further questions and answers based on the ideas already listed.

1. topic: my bed
brainstorming:

Question: **What can you say about your bed?**
Answer: It's comfortable.

Question: **Why is it comfortable?**
Answer: I sleep in it.

Question: **Everybody sleeps in beds. Why is <u>yours</u> so comfortable?**
Answer: It's broken in.

Question: **What do you mean?**
Answer: The mattress fits my body.

Question: **How?**
Answer: It's soft enough to fit around me.

Four additional questions and answers:

_____

_____

_____

_____

_____

_____

_____

_____

2. topic: my favorite meal, a burger and fries
brainstorming:

Question: **Why do you like burgers and fries so much?**
Answer: I like crispy fries and juicy burgers.

Question: **Why? Is it the taste?**
Answer: Sure.

Question: **What do you like about the taste of a burger?**
Answer: I guess I like the pickles and onions and the chewy taste of ground meat.

Question: **What else?**
Answer: I like beef.

Four additional questions and answers:

_____

_____

_____

_____

_____

_____

_____

_____

Focusing the Thought Lines

To begin focusing your topic and details around some point, list the topic and all the details you've gathered so far. The following list includes all the details you've gathered from both sessions of brainstorming on A City Park.

topic: A City Park

- park near my workplace
- I go there at lunchtime.
- It's small.
- just the size of an empty lot
- Some trees. Benches.
- a green space
- I like it.
- It's near the store where I work.
- It's nice and green.
- It's not like the rest of the city.
- The rest of the city is dirty, gray, and noisy.

Grouping the Details

If you survey the list, you can begin to group the details:

What It Looks Like

- It's small.
- just the size of an empty lot
- It's nice and green.
- a green space
- Some trees. Benches.

Location

- park near my workplace
- It's near the store where I work.

How I Feel About It

- I like it.
- I go there at lunchtime.
- It's not like the rest of the city.
- The rest of the city is dirty, gray, and noisy.

Surveying the details, you notice that they focus on the look and location of a place you like. You decide on this topic sentence:

A small city park is a nice place for me because it is not like the rest of the city.

You check your topic sentence to decide whether it covers all your details. Does it cover what the park looks like and its location? Yes. The words "small" and "city" relate to what it looks like and its location. Does it cover how you feel about the park? Yes. It says the park is "a nice place for me because it is not like the rest of the city."

Now that you have a topic sentence and a list of details, you are ready to begin the outlines step of writing.

Exercise 3 **Grouping Details**

Practice   Following are topics and lists of details. Group the details of each list, writing them under the appropriate headings. Some details may not fit under any of the headings.

1. topic: A Beautiful Flower Arrangement
   details: The roses smelled sweet and feminine.
            The small white carnations made the red roses seem brighter.
            The ferns had the scent of the woods.
            The vase was shaped like a tall column.
            There were small pink chrysanthemums among the roses.
            The vase was blue and white china.
            A huge white silk ribbon circled the vase.

List details about what the flowers looked like: _____

_____

_____

List details about the vase: _____

_____

_____

List details about the smell of the flowers: _____

_____

_____

2. **topic:** An Antique Book
   details: It had a green leather cover.
   The title of the book was pressed into the cover in faded gold letters.
   The pages were yellow.
   The book smelled musty.
   Several pages were loose.
   Two pages had stains.
   The corners of the leather cover were frayed.
   The title page was missing.

List details about the cover of the book: _____

_____

_____

List details about the inside of the book: _____

_____

_____

3. **topic:** An Irritating Person
   details: My friend James interrupts me when I speak.
   He never returns the clothes he borrows.
   He talks nonstop.
   He never picks up the check when we go out to eat.
   He always wants sympathy.
   He rarely shows up when his friends need a favor.
   He is always unhappy.

List details about James' speech habits: _____

_____

List details about the way James treats his friends: _____

_____

_____

_____

List details about James' emotions and mental attitude: _____

_____

Exercise 4 **Writing Appropriate Topic Sentences**

Collaborate Do this exercise with a partner or a group. Following are lists of details. For each list, write two appropriate topic sentences.

1. topic sentence 1: _____

_____

_____

topic sentence 2: _____

_____

_____

details: The living room of the old house had faded, peeling wallpaper.
The fireplace was full of dirt and dust.
The carpet was spotted with mildew.
The wooden floor in the hall was rotted.
The stairs creaked and groaned.
The upstairs bedrooms were shabby.
Yet all the rooms were spacious.
The price of the house was a bargain.
The architecture was elegant.

2. topic sentence 1: _____

_____

_____

topic sentence 2: _____

_____

_____

details: I approached the dentist's office with cold, shaking hands.
I could feel sweat trickling down my back.
My jaw was clenched.
My stomach churned.
I imagined the tortures of the dentist's drill.
I pictured the size of the needle.

3. topic sentence 1: _____

_____

_____

topic sentence 2: _____

_____

_____

details: Ice crystals covered the frozen dinner.
The ice made the meatballs look gray.
The meal came out of the carton as a solid block of ice.

As it cooked in the microwave, the frozen dinner began to look edible.
The meatballs began to darken.
The noodles separated into golden strips.
When the microwave timer went off, I tasted the dinner.
It was a wet, icy mess inside.

4. topic sentence 1: _____

_____

_____

topic sentence 2: _____

_____

_____

details: When I am anxious, my boyfriend listens.
Last week, I was worried about losing my job.
He was very patient while I talked and talked about being unemployed.
When I am happy, he shares my happiness.
I recently got an A on a history test.
Edward took me out to dinner, to celebrate.
He said he was proud of me.

Outlines

Focus on Support and Details

Once you have a topic sentence, a list of details, and some grouping of the details, you can write them in outline form. Following is a draft outline for a paragraph on A City Park. As you read it, you will notice that the grouping of the details has led to three areas in the outline: location of the park, what it looks like, and how I feel about it. You will also notice that some repetitive details have been eliminated or combined.

Draft Outline for a Paragraph on A City Park
Paragraph Focus: Support and Details

```
topic sentence: A small city park is a nice place for me because
                it is not like the rest of the city.
details:
location         { It is near the store where I work.
                 ┌ It is just the size of an empty lot.
what it looks    │ It is nice.
like             ┤ It is a green space.
                 └ It has some trees and benches.
                 ┌ I like it.
how I feel       │ I go there at lunchtime.
about it         ┤ It is not like the rest of the city.
                 └ The rest of the city is dirty, gray, and noisy.
```

Once you have a draft outline, you can review it for support and details. Use the following checklist as a guide:

✔ Checklist

A Checklist for Support and Details in an Outline

✔ Do I have enough to say to support my point?

✔ Do I have specific details?

If you look at the draft outline, you'll notice that it has some problems:

- There is not enough to say about the park's location.
- The details are not very specific. Words like "nice" do not say much, and "nice" is used twice, in the topic sentence and in the details.

To make your word choice more precise, you can brainstorm:

Question: You say, "A small city park is a nice place." What do you mean by "nice"?

Answer: I don't know.

Question: Do you mean "pretty"? Or "comfortable"? Or "pleasant"?

Answer: "Pleasant" is good.

Question: OK. So you can change your topic sentence to say, "A small city park is a <u>pleasant</u> place," etc. But what are you going to do with your list of details, where you say, "It is nice"?

Answer: I can change the words to "It is pleasant."

Question: No. That's repetitive. And here you're describing what the park <u>looks</u> like. So you need a word that describes the appearance of the park.

Answer: OK. I'll use "attractive."

Adding Support

The outline on A City Park has only one sentence about location: "It is near the store where I work." Some writers would simply leave the one sentence and tell themselves they will add more support later. But leaving supporting ideas for later can be risky. Later, you may have forgotten what you wanted to say. Thus an incomplete outline can lead to an undeveloped paragraph. Below is an outline that lacks support:

An Incomplete Outline

```
topic sentence: Every minute of the dance was an adventure.
       details: We tried new food at dinner.
                We made new friends.
                We learned some exciting dances.
```

You might write this outline and tell yourself you will add more support later. Later, however, you might be in a hurry, or tired, or out of ideas. So you put together this paragraph:

An Incomplete Paragraph

```
        Every minute of the dance was an adventure. At dinner,
we tried new food. Then we made new friends. Finally, we
learned some exciting new dances.
```

Consider the outline below, which contains more support:

```
topic sentence: Every minute of the dance was an adventure.
       details: We entered a room decorated like a French
                cafe.
                We tried new food at dinner.
                For the first time, I tasted chicken cooked
                in wine.
                My boyfriend ate snails.
                We made new friends.
                Two people at our table turned out to be vis-
                iting from Panama.
                They shared our interest in computer games.
                We learned some exciting dances.
                A great dancer introduced us to a romantic
                tango and a French dance.
```

It would probably be easier to write a developed paragraph from the developed outline than from the skimpy one.

A Revised Outline

Below is the revised outline for a paragraph on A City Park. When you read it, you will notice some more specific details and support.

A Revised Outline on A City Park
Paragraph Focus: Support and Details
(Changes from the draft outline on page 345 are underlined.)

```
topic sentence:      A small city park is a pleasant place for me
                     because it is not like the rest of the city.
details:             It is near the store where I work.
location           { It is only a ten-minute walk from the store.
                   ( It is attractive.
what it looks      { It is a green space.
like               ( It has some trees and benches.
                   ( I like it.
how I feel         { I go there at lunchtime.
about it           { It is not like the rest of the city.
                   ( The rest of the city is dirty, gray, and noisy.
```

Exercise 5 **Using Specific Words**

Practice   In the following sentences, replace the underlined word(s) with a more specific word or words. Write the new word(s) in the space above the old one(s).

1. He's a <u>good</u> friend.

2. That movie was <u>interesting</u>.

3. This chicken tastes <u>funny</u>.

4. That's a <u>bad</u> road.

5. Jim gave me a <u>funny</u> look when I asked him about the car accident.

6. I had a <u>good</u> time at the concert.

7. My new sneakers cost <u>a lot</u>.

8. He gave me a <u>nice</u> card for my birthday.

9. She has a <u>nice</u> personality.

10. That hat looks <u>funny</u> on you.

Exercise 6 **Finding Specific Words to Match General Terms**

Collaborate

Following are general terms. On the numbered lines, list four specific words or phrases connected to each general term. After you have completed your lists, exchange your paper with a partner. Add two more specific terms to each of your partner's lists. Be prepared to read your lists to the class, and add all the terms you hear from other lists. The first item is done for you.

1. general term: car
specific words or phrases:

1. convertible   4. jalopy

2. sedan   5. limousine

3. station wagon   6. sports car

extras: racing car, taxi

2. general term: cake
specific words or phrases:

1. _____   4. _____

2. _____   5. _____

3. _____   6. _____

extras: _____

3. general term: gardening tool
specific words or phrases:

1. _____   4. _____

2. _____   5. _____

3. _____   6. _____

extras: _____

4. general term: fish
   specific words or phrases:

1. _____   4. _____

2. _____   5. _____

3. _____   6. _____

extras: _____

5. general term: clothes
   specific words or phrases:

1. _____   4. _____

2. _____   5. _____

3. _____   6. _____

extras: _____

Exercise 7 **Adding Details to an Outline**

👥 Collaborate Do this exercise with a partner or a group. Below are very skimpy outlines. Add a detail to each blank line.

1. topic sentence: Wedding presents fall into several categories.
       details: There are gifts for the kitchen.

   _____

   _____

   There are gifts for the bathroom.

   _____

   _____

   There are gifts for the couple to enjoy in their leisure time.

   _____

   _____

2. topic sentence: I have three reasons for disliking my art teacher.
       details: First, he is impatient.
                He expects me to learn a new technique immediately.
                He becomes irritated when I ask questions about a technique.
                Second, he is inconsiderate.
                He is always late for class, keeping us waiting.

He talks so fast that the class cannot follow his explanations.
Third, he is unfair.

_____

_____

3. topic sentence: Borrowing money can lead to problems.
    details: It can hurt friendships.
       Someone who does not pay a debt on time is not a good friend anymore.
       It can cause stress.

_____

       It can lead to more debt.

_____

_____

4. topic sentence: Birds make good pets.
    details: They are easy to care for.

_____

_____

       They bring cheerfulness into your home.

_____

_____

       They do not need a large space in order to be happy.

_____

Exercise 8 **Revising an Outline**

Practice

Below is a draft outline. Read it, and then underline all the words that could be more specific.

  topic sentence: It took me two years to find a good job.
    details: First, I had a job at a gas station.
       That job was OK, but it was not fulfilling.
       I just sat in a glass booth and collected people's money.
       A year later, I found a job as a waiter.
       I made good money on tips, but the hours were from 7:00 p.m. to 1:00 a.m.
       I also found the work repetitive and boring.
       I wanted a job where I could help people.
       Last week, I found a job at a hospital.
       My co-workers are very nice.

Best of all, I am able to use my talent for relating to
others.
I call this a good job.

Rough Lines

Focus on Support and Details

Once you have a good outline, you can write a first draft of your paragraph.
Below is a first draft created from the outline of the paragraph on A City Park.

A First Draft of a Paragraph on A City Park
Paragraph Focus: Support and Details (from outline on page 347)

```
     A small city park is a pleasant place for me because it is
not like the rest of the city. The park is near the store where
I work. It is only a ten-minute walk from the store. It is just
the size of an empty lot. It is attractive. It is a green space.
It has some trees and benches. I like it. I go there at
lunchtime. It is not like the rest of the city. The rest of the
city is dirty, gray, and noisy.
```

Once you have the first draft, you can begin to think about revising and editing. To check your draft for support and details, use the following checklist:

> **✔ Checklist**
>
> ### A Checklist for Support and Details in the Draft of a Paragraph
>
> ✔ Do I have enough ideas to support my topic sentence?
>
> ✔ Do I have enough details?
>
> ✔ Are my details specific?
>
> ✔ Do my details include words that appeal to the *senses*?

If you apply the checklist to the draft paragraph on A City Park, you will probably notice these rough spots:

- The details need to be more specific.
- The details need to use some sense words.

Using Sense Words in Your Details

One way to make your details vivid is to use *sense words*—words that relate to
the five senses. As you revise your details, ask yourself the following:

What does it *look* like?
What does it *sound* like?
What does it *smell* like?
What does it *taste* like?
What does it *feel* like?

Of course, you cannot use all of the five senses in every paragraph you write, but
you can be aware of sense words. Sometimes *brainstorming* can be a way to

help you find sense words. For example, if you were thinking about describing a department store during the December holiday season, you might brainstorm for details, like this:

Question: **What does the store look like?**
Answer: All decorated.

Question: **How is it decorated?**
Answer: Glittering garlands. White lights.

Question: **What else do you see?**
Answer: Shoppers. They look anxious and stressed.

Question: **What else about the shoppers?**
Answer: Many are carrying heavy shopping bags, the ones with rope handles.

Question: **What do you hear?**
Answer: Holiday songs.

Question: **Can you be specific?**
Answer: "Rudolph the Red-Nosed Reindeer."

Question: **What do you smell?**
Answer: Perfume. All those salesclerks try to spray me with samples of perfume.

Question: **What else?**
Answer: Sometimes I smell cinnamon or holly-scented candles.

Sense details make your writing vivid. Try to include such details in your paragraphs. Often you can brainstorm sense details easily if you focus your thinking.

Infobox

Using Sense Words

For the sense of	think about
sight	colors, light and dark, shadows or brightness
hearing	noise, silence, or the kinds of sounds you hear
smell	fragrances, odors, scents, aromas, or perfume
taste	bitter, sour, sweet, or compare the taste of one thing with the taste of another
touch	the feel of things against your fingertips or skin: hardness, softness, roughness, or smoothness

---

Revising the Draft for More Specific Details and Sense Words

Below is a revised draft of the paragraph on A City Park. When you read it you will notice the added specific details and sense words. You will also notice that some short, choppy sentences have been combined, and that one sentence of details has been added at the end of the paragraph.

A Revised Draft of a Paragraph on A City Park
Paragraph Focus: Support and Details

---

sentences combined

A small city park is a pleasant place for me because it is not like the rest of the city. The park is near the store where I work;

(continued)

	<u>in fact, it is only a ten-minute walk.</u> It is just the size of an empty lot. It is attrac-
specific details, sense words	tive with its <u>small green lawn, maple trees, and weathered wooden benches.</u> <u>I like it, so</u>
sentences combined	<u>I visit it at lunchtime.</u> It is not like the rest of the city, which is dirty, gray, and
sense words and specific details	<u>filled with the noise of screeching brakes, rumbling trucks, and blaring horns.</u> The park
sentence added, more sense words	is a clean, quiet spot, <u>where the sun filters through the leaves of trees.</u>

Although it is important to work on specific details and sense words in each stage of your writing, it is easiest to focus on revising for details in the drafting stage, when you have a framework for what you want to say. With that framework, you can concentrate on the most vivid way to express your ideas.

Exercise 9   **Interviewing for Specific Answers**

To practice being specific, interview a partner. Ask your partner to answer the questions below. Write his or her answers in the spaces provided. When you have finished, change places. Be as specific as you can in your answers.

1. What is the title of your favorite song? _____

_____

2. When you eat pizza, what toppings do you put on the pizza? _____

_____

3. What vegetable do you refuse to eat? _____

_____

4. What is the silliest dog's name you've ever heard? _____

_____

5. If you bought a new car, what color would it be? _____

_____

6. What noise irritates you the most? _____

_____

7. Name one article of your clothing that you think cost too much.

_____

8. What one item do you *always* take to class? _____

_____

9. Who is the most overrated athlete? _____

_____

10. If you could have any pet in the world, what would it be? _____

_____

Exercise 10
Practice

Using Sense Words

Write sense words for the following items.

1. Write three words or phrases to describe the taste of chocolate

pudding: _____

_____

2. Write three words or phrases to describe the smells in a bakery:

_____

_____

3. Write three words or phrases to describe the sounds of an amusement

park: _____

_____

4. Write three words or phrases to describe the texture of a kitten's fur:

_____

_____

5. Write three words or phrases to describe what a circus clown looks like:

_____

_____

Exercise 11
Collaborate

Brainstorming Sense Words for a Paragraph

With a partner or group, brainstorm the following topic sentences for paragraphs. For each topic sentence, list five questions and answers that could help you create details with sense words.

1. topic sentence: Her desk was clean and beautifully organized.
brainstorming:

Question 1: _____

Answer 1: _____

Question 2: _____

Answer 2:   _____

Question 3: _____

Answer 3:   _____

Question 4: _____

Answer 4:   _____

Question 5: _____

Answer 5:   _____

2. **topic sentence:** The basement had become a garbage dump.
   brainstorming:

Question 1: _____

Answer 1:   _____

Question 2: _____

Answer 2:   _____

Question 3: _____

Answer 3:   _____

Question 4: _____

Answer 4:   _____

Question 5: _____

Answer 5:   _____

3. **topic sentence:** The restaurant was so crowded that I did not enjoy
   being there.
   brainstorming:

Question 1: _____

Answer 1:   _____

Question 2: _____

Answer 2:   _____

Question 3: _____

Answer 3:   _____

Question 4: _____

Answer 4: _____

Question 5: _____

Answer 5: _____

Exercise 12 **Revising for Specific Details or Sense Words**

Practice In the following paragraph, replace each underlined word or phrase with more specific details or sense words. Write your changes in the space above each underlined item.

My boyfriend cooked his first Thanksgiving dinner last week, and it was a great success. Michael is a cook at an Italian restaurant, but he had never cooked a traditional Thanksgiving dinner. However, when his mother got the flu, Michael volunteered to cook for his family for the holiday. He had <u>a lot of</u> people to feed, so he began early. At <u>an early time</u> on Thanksgiving morning, Michael made <u>some desserts</u>. Then he set the table. He used a <u>pretty</u> tablecloth and a <u>nice</u> centerpiece with some <u>good</u> dishes. When he was done, the tablecloth looked <u>pretty</u> and the centerpiece was <u>nice</u>. Later, he cooked the fifteen-pound turkey, the sausage and onion stuffing, and <u>some vegetables</u>. By the time the family sat down to dinner, they were thrilled by <u>all the good smells</u>. They loved <u>the taste of the turkey</u> and the <u>texture</u> of the mashed potatoes. All across the room, people eating <u>made sounds of pleasure</u>. By the time people had finished the meal, they felt <u>full</u> but happy.

Final Lines

Focus on Support and Details

Before you prepare the final copy of your paragraph, check it again for any problems in support and details, and for any places where grammar, word choice, and style need revision. Check also for any errors in spelling and punctuation.

Following is the final version of the paragraph on A City Park. As you review it, you'll notice several changes:

- The name of the park has been added, to make the details more specific.
- There were too many repetitions of "it" in the paragraph, so "it" has frequently been changed to "the park," or "Sheridan Park," and so on.

- An introductory sentence has been added to make the beginning of the paragraph smoother.
- A transition has been added.

A Final Lines Version of a Paragraph on A City Park
Paragraph Focus: Support and Details (Changes from draft on p. 352 are underlined.)

introductory sentence added	<u>Everyone has a place where he or she can relax.</u> A small city park is a pleasant place for me because it is not like the rest of the
specific detail added	city. <u>Sheridan Park</u> is near the store where I work; in fact, it is only a ten-minute walk.
word changed	<u>The park</u> is just the size of an empty lot. <u>In</u>
transition added	<u>spite of this tiny size,</u> Sheridan Park is
word changed	attractive with its small green lawn, maple trees, and weathered wooden benches. I like it,
words changed	so I visit <u>the place</u> at lunchtime. <u>The park</u> is not like the rest of the city, which is dirty, gray, and filled with the noise of screeching brakes, rumbling trucks, and blaring horns. The park is a clean, quiet spot, where the sun filters through the leaves of trees.

Exercise 13 **Correcting Errors in the Final Lines**

Practice

Proofread the following paragraph. Correct any errors in spelling, punctuation, or word choice. There are ten errors. Write your corrections in the space above each error.

Yesterday I found a brochure for a vaccation in the Bahamas, and I immediately entered a beautiful fantasy. I pictured turquoise water's and pale sand's I could see myself stroling down the beach where the sand would feel like sugar between my toes. I imagine the soft rhythmn of the tide and the louder beat of reggae music. In my dream, an island girl brout me a foamy drink filled with pineapple mango papaya, and guava juice. I sipped the drink from a bowl carved out of half a coconut. I felt that I was drinking in paradise, but unfortunately, my paradise was onely a dream.

Lines of Detail: A Walk-Through Assignment

For this assignment, write a paragraph about your classroom, the one in which you take this class.

Step 1: To begin, freewrite on your classroom for ten minutes. In your freewriting, focus on how you would *describe* your classroom.

Step 2: Next, read your freewriting to a partner or a group. Ask your listener(s) to write down any ideas in your freewriting that could lead to a specific topic for your paragraph. (For example, maybe your freewriting has several ideas about what you feel when you are in the classroom, or how others behave, or how the furniture and decor of the room create a mood.)

Step 3: With a specific topic in mind, list all the ideas in your freewriting that might fit that main topic.

Step 4: Now, brainstorm. Write at least ten questions and answers based on your list of ideas.

Step 5: Group all the ideas you've found in freewriting and brainstorming. Survey them, and write a topic sentence for your paragraph. Your topic sentence may focus on the atmosphere of the classroom, the look of the classroom, how you feel in the classroom, the activity in the classroom, and so forth.

Step 6: Write an outline. Be sure that your outline has enough supporting points for you to write a paragraph of seven to twelve sentences.

Step 7: Write and revise your paragraph. Check each draft for support, and work on using specific details and sense words.

Step 8: Share your best draft with a partner or the group. Ask for suggestions or comments. Revise once more.

Step 9: Prepare the final copy of your paragraph, checking for errors in punctuation, spelling, or word choice.

Writing Your Own Paragraph

When you write on any of the following topics, be sure to follow the stages of the writing process in preparing your paragraph.

1. Write about a memorable meal. It can be a meal that you remember because it was great, or one that you remember because it was terrible. In describing the meal, try to use sense words that connect to smell, sight, and texture (touch), and even sound, as well as taste.

2. Write about your most comfortable piece of clothing. In your topic sentence, focus on what makes it so comfortable.

3. Interview a partner so that you and your partner can gather details and write separate paragraphs with the title, "My Dream Car."

    First, prepare a list of at least six questions to ask your partner. Write down your partner's answers and use these answers to ask more questions. For example, if your partner says she wants a fast car, ask her how fast she would like to drive. If your partner says he would like a sport-utility vehicle, ask him what kind.

    When you have finished the interview, switch roles. Let your partner interview you.

    Finally, give your partner his or her interview responses, take your own responses, and use them as the basis for gathering as many details as you can. In this way, you are working through the thought lines stage of your paragraph. Then go on to the other stages. Be prepared to read your completed paragraph to your partner.

4. Write a paragraph that describes one of the following:

> the contents of your wastebasket
> the contents of your refrigerator
> people riding the subway
> people in the express lane at the supermarket
> children riding the school bus
> a toddler in a car seat or stroller
> the contents of your medicine cabinet
> what you ate for breakfast

Be sure to focus your paragraph with a good topic sentence.

5. Write a paragraph about the messiest room you've ever seen.

6. Imagine a place that would bring you a sense of peace. In a paragraph, describe that place.

7. Following are some topic sentences. Complete one of them and use it to write a paragraph.

> The happiest place I know is _____.

> _____ is the most comfortable place in my home.

> Whenever I visit _____, I feel a sense of _____.

> Between classes, the halls of the college seem _____.

> I like to spend time alone at _____ because _____.

8. Write about the sensations of being caught in rush hour traffic. You might begin by brainstorming all the details you recall.

9. Look carefully at photograph A, of two men playing in a soccer match. Write a paragraph describing what you see. You can include details about the physical appearance of the men or the way their bodies are positioned. You can describe their clothes, shoes, or facial expressions. You can also focus on the feeling created by this photo: Is it excitement? Tension? Struggle?

10. Write a paragraph about photograph B, of a dog and a rooster sitting on a chair together. Pay attention to the animals' expressions as well as to the other details. You may want to imagine what the dog and the rooster are thinking.

Photograph A

Photograph B

Name: _____   **Section:** _____

Peer Review Form for a Paragraph: Focus on Support and Details

After you have written a draft version of your paragraph, let a writing partner read it. When your partner has completed the following form, discuss the responses. Then repeat the same process for your partner's paragraph.

The part of this paragraph that I like best begins with the words _____

_____

This paragraph uses some sense words and phrases. Among these sense words and phrases

are _____

_____

The part of the paragraph that could use more specific details or sense words begins with the

words _____

The topic sentence of this paragraph is _____

_____

_____

I think there is (enough/too little) [circle one] support for the topic sentence.

I have questions about _____

_____

Other comments on the paragraph: _____

_____

_____

_____

_____

_____

_____

_____

_____

Reviewer's Name: _____

WRITING FROM READING

I Wish
Lillian Gwin

When Lillian Gwin wrote this, in 1970, she was a high school senior at Flan-dreau Indian School in South Dakota, a high school run by the Bureau of Indian Affairs. Her writing won a contest and was published in an anthology of prose and poetry by young Native Americans. Gwin, a member of the Gros Ventre–Arika tribe, writes of her sadness in the white man's world and her hopes for the future.

Words You May Need to Know

tanning: converting an animal hide or skin into leather

deer hide: deer skin

muck: filth, dirt

I wish I could see the campsite of my ancestors and hear the laughter of children playing Indian games, and men talking about the last hunt, or see the women sitting quietly on the ground tanning a fresh deer hide. I wish I could sit by a clear pool of water, see my reflection in its purity, and let my horse drink. Instead, I look into the pond at a shoe, a piece of paper, cans, old tires, and I say to myself, "My great-grandfather wouldn't have watered his horse in this muck!" I sometimes wish I could ride, ride, ride, and never see another white man's building. But at night when I lie down on the white man's bed, I look out the window and up to the stars twinkling merrily, and I know that the Great Spirit, who put them there, also planned the Indians' new pathway. I promise myself that I will face the white man's tomorrow with a prayer in my heart for the unity of man. He would want it that way.

Exercise 14

Practice

Identifying Sense Words and Specific Words in "I Wish"

Lillian Gwin uses many sense words and specific words. To become aware of her writing techniques, reread "I Wish" and complete the following exercise.

1. Gwin uses several words or phrases that describe what someone can see. Write the exact words of two examples of sight words or phrases from her writing.

   a. _____

   b. _____

2. Gwin also uses several words or phrases describing what someone can hear. Write the exact words of two examples of sound words or phrases from her writing.

   a. _____

   b. _____

3. Instead of writing that she sees "junk" in a pond, Gwin uses very specific words to describe what is in the pond. Write the specific words:

_____

_____

4. Instead of saying, "I wish I could run away from white society," Gwin uses very specific words to make the same point. Write the specific words:

_____

_____

WRITING FROM READING "I Wish"

When you write on any of the following topics, be sure to work through the stages of the writing process in preparing your paragraph.

1. Lillian Gwin uses many details to describe a world she dreams about. Write a paragraph in which you use many details to describe an environment or lifestyle you dream about.

2. Write a description of a place in nature. It might be a beach, a forest, a field, a mountain, a lake, and so on. In your description, try to be very specific and to use sense words.

3. Imagine yourself in another time and place. Write a paragraph giving details about your life in that time and place.

4. Write a paragraph called "I Wish." Write about whatever you wish for. Concentrate on using specific details and sense words.

5. Interview someone who is much older than you. Ask the person to describe a part of his or her life that is gone now. It could be something like a family routine, or a way of traveling, shopping, working, or enjoying leisure time. Ask questions and take notes, looking for specific details. Write a paragraph about this person's description.

6. Write a paragraph about a situation that saddened you and about how you learned to cope with the situation. Describe the situation with specific details and sense words.

Death Row (from *The Chamber*)
John Grisham

John Grisham, a Mississippi lawyer, is a best-selling author of legal thrillers. Many of his novels, including A Time to Kill, The Firm, *and* The Rainmaker, *have been made into movies. In this selection from his novel* The Chamber, *he describes Sam, a convicted murderer on death row at the State Penitentiary in Parchman, Mississippi.*

Words You May Need to Know

the Delta (paragraph 1): in Mississippi, a flat plain of land between branches of a river
linger (1): remain, stay on in a place
boundless (3): unlimited

ventilation (3): facilities for providing fresh air
dank (3): unpleasantly moist or humid
penal facility (3): prison

1   A loud thunderstorm rolled across the Delta before dawn, and Sam was awakened by the crack of lightning. He heard raindrops dropping hard against the open windows above the hallway. Then he heard them drip and puddle against the wall under the windows not far from his cell. The dampness of his bed was suddenly cool. Maybe today would not be so hot. Maybe the rain would linger and shade the sun, and maybe the wind would blow away the humidity for a day or two. He always had these hopes when it rained, but in the summer a thunderstorm usually meant soggy ground which under a glaring sun meant nothing but more suffocating heat.

2   He raised his head and watched the rain fall from the windows and gather on the floor. The water flickered in the reflected light of a distant yellow bulb. Except for this faint light, the Row was dark. And it was silent.

3   Sam loved the rain, especially at night and especially in the summer. The State of Mississippi, in its boundless wisdom, had built its prison in the hottest place it could find. And it designed its Maximum Security Unit along the same lines as an oven. The windows to the outside were small and useless, built that way for security reasons, of course. The planners of this little branch of hell also decided that there would be no ventilation of any sort, no chance for a breeze getting in or the dank air getting out. And after they built what they considered a model penal facility, they decided they would not air condition it. It would sit proudly beside the soybeans and cotton, and absorb the same heat and moisture from the ground. And when the land was dry, the Row would simply bake along with the crops.

4   But the State of Mississippi could not control the weather, and when the rains came and cooled the air, Sam smiled to himself and offered a small prayer of thanks. A higher being was in control after all. The state was helpless when it rained. It was a small victory.

5   He eased to his feet and stretched his back. His bed consisted of a piece of foam, six feet by two and a half, four inches thick, otherwise known as a mattress. It rested on a metal frame fastened securely to the floor and wall. It was covered with two sheets. Sometimes they passed out blankets in the winter. Back pain was common throughout the Row, but with time the body adjusted and there were few complaints. The prison doctor was not considered to be a friend of death row inmates.

6   He took two steps and leaned on his elbows through the bars. He listened to the wind and thunder, and watched the drops bounce along the windowsill and splatter on the floor. How nice it would be to step through that wall and walk through the wet grass on the other side, to stroll around the prison grounds in the driving rain, naked and crazy, soaking wet with water dropping from his hair and beard.

Exercise 15   **Identifying Sense Words and Specific Details in "Death Row"**

Practice

In describing death row, Grisham uses many sense words and specific words. To become more aware of his writing techniques, reread "Death Row" and complete the following exercise.

1. Grisham uses many words or phrases that describe sounds. Write the exact words of two examples of sound words or phrases from his writing:

   a. _____

   b. _____

2. Grisham uses several words or phrases that describe how something feels to the touch (temperature, texture, etc.). Write the exact words of two examples of touch words or phrases from his writing:

   a. _____

   b. _____

3. Grisham uses several words or phrases that describe what Sam can see. Write the exact words of two examples of sight words or phrases from his writing:

   a. _____

   b. _____

4. Instead of saying that Sam had a small, uncomfortable bed, Grisham uses very specific words to describe the bed. Write those exact words:

   _____

   _____

   _____

5. Instead of saying that Sam would like to be free, Grisham uses very specific words to describe Sam's wish. Write those exact words:

_____

_____

_____

_____

WRITING FROM READING "Death Row"

When you write on any of the following topics, be sure to work through the stages of the writing process in preparing your paragraph.

1. To begin this paragraph, sit in one room for fifteen minutes. During that time, list what you see, hear, smell, feel, and even taste. Use this list as the basis for a paragraph describing morning, afternoon, or night in the room.

2. Describe a time when you felt free. Begin your assignment by brainstorming. Prepare at least seven questions like "Where was I at the time?," "What was I seeing?," and so on. Use the questions, answers, and follow-up questions and answers to gather ideas. Focus your questions and answers on sense words and specific words.

3. Write a paragraph that uses one of the following topic sentences. Be sure that you support the topic sentence with specific words and sense words.

Topic sentences:
Even in a depressing place, a person can feel hope.

Nature can bring pleasure when a person is feeling low.

Hope kept me going when _____.

4. Grisham writes about what one person, a prisoner in a cell, sees, hears, and feels. Write a paragraph describing what one of the following people sees, hears, and feels (and perhaps even smells or tastes):
a baby in a playpen
a toll collector in a tollbooth
a puppy or kitten left alone in the kitchen
an umpire at a baseball game
a truck driver on an interstate highway
a model on the runway at a fashion show

5. Write about a time when you were confined in one place for longer than you wanted to be. To begin this assignment, have a writing partner interview you. Your partner should begin with at least six questions like "How did you feel?," "What did the place look like?," and "Why were you there?"

Your partner should write down your answers and use these answers to form more questions. For example, if you say you felt bored, your partner might ask, "What bored you?"

When you have been interviewed, switch roles. Interview your partner, with your own prepared list of questions.

At the end of both interviews, give your partner his or her responses and take your own. Use them as the basis for the thought lines part of your paragraph. Focus on using specific words and sense words.

A Different Mirror
Ronald Takaki

Ronald Takaki, born in Honolulu, is a historian known for his books on history, race, and multiculturalism. The following excerpt is from his book A Different Mirror. *In the book, Takaki argues that in studying America's history, we must study all the groups that have created America, so that we "see ourselves in a different mirror." This excerpt focuses on specific details that support the idea of America's diversity.*

Words You May Need to Know

ethnic diversity: variety of people, races, and cultures
discerned: recognized, perceived
Ellis Island: an island off the shore of New York City where many immigrants first landed in America
Angel Island: an island off San Francisco
Chinatown, Harlem, South Boston, the Lower East Side (of New York City): places associated with a variety of ethnic groups and races

derived: originated from
Forty-Niners: People who joined the Gold Rush of 1849, when gold was discovered in California
vaqueros: cowboys

The signs of America's ethnic diversity can be discerned across the continent: Ellis Island, Angel Island, Chinatown, Harlem, South Boston, the Lower East Side, places with Spanish names like Los Angeles and San Antonio or Indian names like Massachusetts and Iowa. Much of what is familiar in America's cultural landscape actually has ethnic origins. The Bing cherry was developed by an early Chinese immigrant named Ah Bing. American Indians were cultivating corn, tomatoes, and tobacco long before the arrival of Columbus. The term *okay* was derived from the Choctaw word *oke*, meaning "it is so." There is evidence indicating that the name *Yankee* came from Indian terms for the English—from *eankke* in Cherokee and *Yankwis* in Delaware. Jazz and blues as well as rock and roll have African-American origins. The "Forty-Niners" of the Gold Rush learned mining techniques from the Mexicans; American cowboys acquired herding skills from Mexican vaqueros and adopted their range terms—such as *lariat* from la *reata*, *lasso* from *lazo*, and *stampede* from *estampida*. Songs like "God Bless America," "Easter Parade," and "White Christmas" were written by a Russian-Jewish immigrant named Israel Baline, more popularly known as Irving Berlin.

Exercise 16
Practice

Recognizing Takaki's Use of Specific Details

To illustrate his point about the diversity of America's history, Ronald Takaki gives many specific examples of the sources of our language and heritage. Fill in those examples below.

1. What fruit did a Chinese immigrant develop?

_____

2. Where did the term *Yankee* come from?

_____

3. Who taught the "Forty-Niners" mining techniques?

_____

4. What kinds of music have African-American origins?

_____

5. Who first grew corn, tomatoes, and tobacco?

_____

6. What American word grew out of the Choctaw word *oke*?

_____

7. What was the background of the person who wrote "God Bless America"?

_____

8. Name one American state that has an Indian name.

_____

9. Name one American city that has a Spanish name.

_____

10. What American word came from the Mexican word *estampida*?

_____

WRITING FROM READING "A Different Mirror"

When you write on any of the following topics, be sure to work through the stages of the writing process in preparing your paragraph.

1. Interview three people in your class. Ask each to tell you about his or her family background. Before you begin, prepare a list of at least six questions, such as "Were you born in this country?" or "Do you know how long your family has been in America?" Use the answers as the basis for a paragraph on diversity in your classroom. You may discover a wide range of backgrounds or a similarity of backgrounds. In either case, you have details for a paragraph about your classmates and their origins.

2. Write a paragraph about the many foods that are considered typically American but that really originated in another country or culture. Give specific examples.

3. Takaki gives examples of words Americans use, like *Yankee*, that originated in another language. Write a paragraph on words or expressions that Americans use that originated in another language. (For example, many Americans who are not Spanish use the word *adios*.)

4. Write a paragraph on the place names in America that came from one or more other languages. You might write about only Spanish place names, for example, and group them into states and cities. Or you could write about place names from several languages and group them into Spanish names, American Indian names, French names, and so forth.

5. Write a paragraph about what one ethnic group has contributed to American life and culture. You can use specific examples of contributions to language, music, dance, food, clothing, customs, and so forth.

CHAPTER **26**

Writing from Reading

WHAT IS WRITING FROM READING?

One way to find topics for writing is to draw from your ideas, memories, and observations. Another way is to write from reading you've done. You can react to something you've read; you can agree or disagree with it. You can summarize what you've read. Many college assignments ask you to write about an assigned reading such as an essay, a chapter in a textbook, or an article in a journal. This kind of writing requires an active, involved attitude toward your reading. Such reading is done in steps:

1. Preread.
2. Read.
3. Reread with a pen or pencil.

Attitude

Before you begin the first step of this reading process, you have to have a certain *attitude*. That attitude involves thinking of what you read as half of a conversation. The writer has opinions and ideas; he or she makes points just as you do when you write or speak. The writer supports his or her points with specific details. If the writer were speaking to you in conversation, you would respond to his or her opinions or ideas. You would agree, disagree, or question. You would jump into the conversation, linking or contrasting your ideas with those of the other speaker.

The right attitude toward reading demands that you read in the same way you converse: you *become involved*. In doing this, you "talk back" as you read, and later, you may react in your own writing. Reacting as you read will keep you focused on what you are reading. If you are focused, you will remember more of what you read. With an active, involved attitude, you can begin the step of prereading.

Prereading

Before you actually read an assigned essay, a chapter in a textbook, or an article in a journal, magazine, or newspaper, take a few minutes to look it over, and be ready to answer the following questions:

> **✔ Checklist**
>
> ### A Prereading Checklist
>
> ✔ How long is this reading?
>
> ✔ Will I be able to read it in one sitting, or will I have to schedule several time periods to finish it?
>
> ✔ Are there any subheadings in the reading? Do they give any hints about the reading?
>
> ✔ Are there any charts? Are there graphs? Is there boxed information? Are there any photographs or illustrations with captions? Do the photos or captions give any hints about the reading?
>
> ✔ Is there any introductory material about the reading or the author? Does the introductory material give me any hints about the reading?
>
> ✔ What is the title of the reading? Does the title hint at the point of the reading?
>
> ✔ Are there any parts of the reading underlined or emphasized in some other way?
>
> ✔ Do the emphasized parts hint at the point of the reading?

Why Preread?

Prereading takes very little time, but it helps you immensely. Some students believe it is a waste of time to scan an assignment; they think they should jump right in and get the reading over with. However, spending just a few minutes on preliminaries can save hours later. And most importantly, prereading helps you become a *focused reader*.

If you scan the length of an assignment, you can pace yourself. And if you know how long a reading is, you can alert yourself to its plan. For example, a short reading has to come to its point soon. A longer essay may take more time to develop its point and may use more details and examples.

Subheadings, charts, graphs, and boxed or other highlighted materials are important enough that the author wants to emphasize them. Looking over that material *before* you read gives you an overview of the important points the reading will contain.

Introductory material or introductory questions will also help you know what to look for as you read. Background on the author or on the subject may hint at ideas that will come up in the reading. Sometimes the title of the reading will give you the main idea.

You should preread so that you can start reading the entire assignment with as much knowledge about the writer and the subject as you can get. When you then read the entire assignment, you will be reading *actively*, for more knowledge.

Forming Questions Before You Read

If you want to read with a focus, it helps to ask questions before you read. Form questions by using the information you gained from prereading.

Start by noting the title and turning it into a question. If the title of your assigned reading is "Causes of the Civil War," ask, "What were the causes of the Civil War?"

You can turn subheadings into questions. If you are reading an article about self-esteem, and one subheading is "Influence of Parents," you can ask, "How do parents influence a person's self-esteem?"

You can also form questions from graphics and illustrations. If a chapter in your economics textbook includes a photograph of Wall Street, you can ask, "What is Wall Street?" or "What is Wall Street's role in economics?" or "What happens on Wall Street?"

You can write down these questions, but it's not necessary. Just forming questions and keeping them in the back of your mind helps you read actively and stay focused.

An Example of the Prereading Step

Take a look at the article that follows. Don't read it; *preread* it.

Part-Time Job May Do Teenagers More Harm Than Good
Gary Klott

Gary Klott is a personal finance consultant for the National Newspaper Syndicate. In this article, he explores the effects of part-time jobs on high school students.

Words You May Need to Know

extracurricular activities (paragraph 2): activities outside the regular academic course, like clubs and sports

assume (3): suppose, take for granted
menial (4): of a low level, degrading
instant gratification (4): immediate satisfaction

1   Given today's high cost of auto insurance, dating, video games, music CDs and designer clothing, it shouldn't come as any surprise that a growing number of high school students are taking part-time jobs during the school year. Most parents have done little to discourage their children from working after school. In fact, many parents figure that part-time jobs can help teach their children about responsibility and the value of a dollar and better prepare them for life in the adult workaday world. But there is growing evidence to suggest that parents ought to sharply restrict the number of hours their children work during the school year.

2   Academic studies over the past decade have found that high school students who work—particularly those who work long hours during the school week—tend to do less well in school, miss out on the benefits of extracurricular activities and have more behavioral problems. Most recently, a study of 12th-graders by Linda P. Worley, a high school counselor in Marietta, Georgia, indicated that grades suffer when students work more than ten hours during the school week. The highest grade-point averages were found for students who worked only on weekends, 3.07, and for those who baby-sat or did yard work,

3.13. Students who didn't work at all had an average GPA of 3.02, while those who worked up to ten hours a week earned an average GPA of 2.95. Students working ten to twenty hours a week averaged 2.77, twenty to thirty hours per week 2.53 and thirty or more hours 2.10.

3   Even if a student manages to maintain good grades, parents shouldn't automatically assume that long work hours aren't harming their child's education. Several studies found that many students kept up their grades by choosing easier courses. A 1993 study of 1,800 high school sophomores by researchers at Temple University and Stanford University found that students who worked more than twenty hours a week spent less time on homework, cut class more often, cheated more on tests and assignments, had less interest in formal education, had a higher rate of drug and alcohol use, and had lower self-esteem.

4   Researchers also note that some of the perceived benefits of afterschool jobs are often overrated. For example, many of the jobs high school students take on are menial and provide few skills that will prove useful after high school. And many students learn the wrong lessons about the value of a dollar since they tend to spend all of their job earnings on cars, clothes, and other purchases that provide instant gratification without saving a penny.

By prereading the article, you might notice the following:

- The title of the article is "Part-Time Job May Do Teenagers More Harm Than Good."
- The article is short and can be read in one sitting.
- The author writes about money, and he writes for newspapers.
- The introductory material says the article is about teenagers with part-time jobs.
- There are several vocabulary words you may need to know.

You might begin reading the article with these questions in mind:

- Why are part-time jobs harmful to teens?
- What are the harmful effects?
- Why is a writer who writes about money saying that it is bad for teens to make money?
- Should teens have full-time jobs instead of part-time jobs?

Reading

The first time you read, try to *get a sense of the whole piece* you are reading. Reading with questions in mind can help you do this. If you find that you are confused by a certain part of the reading selection, go back and reread that part. If you do not know the meaning of a word, check the vocabulary list to see if the word is defined for you. If it isn't defined, try to figure out the meaning from the way the word is used in the sentence.

     If you find that you have to read more slowly than usual, don't worry. People vary their reading speed according to what they read and why they are reading it. If you are reading for entertainment, for example, you can read quickly; if you are reading a chapter in a textbook, you must read more slowly. The more complicated the reading selection, the more slowly you will read it.

An Example of the Reading Step

Now read "Part-Time Job May Do Teenagers More Harm Than Good." When you've completed your first reading, you will probably have some answers to the prereading questions that you formed.

Answers to Prereading Questions

Part-time jobs can hurt teens' grades and other areas of their lives such as their behavior and attitudes.

The writer, who writes about money, says part-time jobs give students bad spending habits.

Full-time work would be worse than part-time work.

Rereading with Pen or Pencil

The second reading is the crucial one. At this point, you begin to think on paper as you read. In this step, you make notes or write about what you read. Some students are reluctant to do this because they are not sure what to note or write. *Think of making these notes as a way of learning, thinking, reviewing, and reacting.* Reading with a pen or pencil in your hand keeps you alert. With that pen or pencil, you can

- mark the main point of the reading.
- mark other points.
- define words you don't know.
- question parts of the reading that seem confusing.
- evaluate the writer's ideas.
- react to the writer's opinions or examples.
- add ideas, opinions, or examples of your own.

There is no single system for marking or writing as you read. Some readers like to underline the main idea with two lines and to underline other important ideas with one line. Some students like to put an asterisk (a star) next to important ideas, while others like to circle key words.

Some people use the margins to write comments like "I agree!" or "Not true!" or "That's happened to me." Sometimes readers put questions in the margin; sometimes they summarize a point in the margin, next to its location in the essay. Some people list important points in the white space above the reading, while others use the space at the end of the reading.

Every reader who writes as he or she reads has a personal system; what these systems share is an attitude. *If you write as you read, you concentrate on the reading selection, get to know the writer's ideas, and develop ideas of your own.*

As you reread and make notes, don't worry too much about noticing the "right" ideas. Instead, think of rereading as the time to jump into a *conversation* with the writer.

An Example of Rereading with Pen or Pencil

For "Part-Time Job May Do Teenagers More Harm Than Good," your marked article might look like the following:

Part-Time Job May Do Teenagers More Harm Than Good

Gary Klott

I agree!

Given today's high cost of auto insurance, dating, video games, music CDs and designer clothing, it shouldn't come as any surprise that a growing number of high school students are taking part-time jobs during the school year. Most parents have done little to discourage their children from work-

what parents believe

ing after school. In fact, many parents figure that part-time jobs can help teach their children about responsibility and the value of a dollar and better prepare them for life in the adult workaday world. But there is growing evidence to sug-

what parents should do

gest that parents ought to sharply restrict the number of hours their children work during the school year.

*

Academic studies over the past decade have found that high school students who work—particularly those who work long hours during the school week—tend to do less well in school, miss out on the benefits of extracurricular activities and have more behavioral problems. Most recently, a study of 12th-

example

graders by Linda P. Worley, a high school counselor in Marietta, Georgia, indicated that grades suffer when students work more than ten hours during the

the more you work, the lower the grades

school week. The highest grade-point averages were found for students who worked only on weekends, 3.07, and for those who baby-sat or did yard work, 3.13. Students who didn't work at all had an average GPA of 3.02, while those who worked up to ten hours a week earned an average GPA of 2.95. Students working ten to twenty hours a week averaged 2.77, twenty to thirty hours per week 2.53 and thirty or more hours 2.10.

Even if a student manages to maintain good grades, parents shouldn't automatically assume that long work hours aren't harming their child's education. Several studies found that many students kept up their grades by

other harm to education

choosing easier courses. A 1993 study of 1,800 high school sophomores by researchers at Temple University and Stanford University found that students who worked more than twenty hours a week spent less time on homework, cut class more often, cheated more on tests and assignments, had less interest in formal education, had a higher rate of drug and alcohol use, and had

self-respect, pride

lower self-esteem.

Researchers also note that some of the perceived benefits of afterschool jobs are often overrated. For example, many of the jobs high school students take on are menial and provide few skills that will prove useful after high school.

bad spending habits

And many students learn the wrong lessons about the value of a dollar since they tend to spend all of their job earnings on cars, clothes, and other purchases that provide instant gratification without saving a penny.

What the Notes Mean

In the sample above, much of the underlining indicates sentences or phrases that seem important. The words in the margin are often summaries of what is underlined. In the first paragraph, for example, the words "what parents believe" and "what parents should do" are like subtitles in the margin.

An asterisk in the margin signals an important idea. When "example" is written in the margin, it notes that a point is being supported by a specific example. Sometimes, what is in the margin is the reader's reaction, like "I agree!" One item in the margin is a definition. The word "self-esteem" is circled and defined in the margin as "self-respect, pride."

The marked-up article is a flexible tool. You can go back and mark it further. You may change your mind about your notes and comments and find other, better, or more important points in the article.

You write as you read to involve yourself in the reading process. Marking what you read can help you in other ways, too. If you are to be tested on the reading selection or are asked to discuss it, you can scan your markings and notations at a later time for a quick review.

Exercise 1

Practice

Reading and Making Notes for a Selection

Following is a paragraph from "Part-Time Job May Do Teenagers More Harm Than Good." First, read it. Then reread it and make notes:

1. Underline the first eight words of the most specific example in the paragraph.

2. Circle the phrase "formal education" and define it in the margin.

3. At the end of the paragraph, summarize its main point.

Paragraph from "Part-Time Job May Do Teenagers More Harm Than Good"

Even if a student manages to maintain good grades, parents shouldn't automatically assume that long work hours aren't harming their child's education. Several studies found that many students kept up their grades by choosing easier courses. A 1993 study of 1,800 high school sophomores and juniors by researchers at Temple University and Stanford University found that students who worked more than twenty hours a week spent less time on homework, cut class more often, cheated more on tests and assignments, had less interest in formal education, had a higher rate of drug and alcohol use and had lower self-esteem.

Main point of the paragraph (in your own words): _____

_____

_____

WRITING A SUMMARY OF A READING

There are a number of ways you can write about what you have read. You may be asked for a summary of an article or chapter, or for a reaction to it, or to write about it on an essay test. For each of these, this chapter will give you guidelines so you can follow the stages of the writing process.

A *summary* of a reading gives the important ideas in brief form and in your own words. It includes (1) the writer's main idea, (2) the ideas used to explain the main idea, and (3) some examples or details.

Thought Lines

Marking a List of Ideas

When you preread, read, and make notes on the reading selection, you have already begun the thought lines stage of a summary. You can think further, on paper, by *listing the points* (words, phrases, sentences) you've already marked on the reading selection.

To find the main idea for your summary and the ideas and examples connected to the main idea, you can *mark related ideas on your list*. For example, the list below was made from "Part-Time Job May Do Teenagers More Harm Than Good." Three symbols are used to mark the following:

S   the effects of part-time jobs on **schoolwork**
O   **other** effects of part-time jobs
P   what **parents** think about part-time jobs

Some items on the list don't have a mark since they do not relate to any of the categories.

A Marked List of Ideas for a Summary of "Part-Time Job May Do Teenagers More Harm Than Good"

	high cost of car insurance, dating, video games, music CDs, and designer clothing
P	parents think part-time jobs teach responsibility, money and job skills
	parents should restrict teens' work hours
S	working students do less well in school
S	study of 12th-graders by Linda P. Worley said grades suffer if students work more than ten hours in school week
S	students who work long hours choose easier courses
S	they spend less time on homework
S	they cut class more
S	they cheat more
S	they are less interested in school
O	they use drugs and alcohol more
O	they have lower self-esteem
	some perceived benefits are overrated
O	students spend money foolishly

The marked list could then be reorganized, like this:

the effects of part-time jobs on school work

— working students do less well in school
— study of 12th-graders by Linda P. Worley said grades suffer if students work more than ten hours in the school week
— students who work long hours choose easier classes
— they spend less time on homework
— they cut class more
— they cheat more
— they are less interested in school

other effects of part-time jobs

— if they work over twenty hours, they use drugs and alcohol more
— they have lower self-esteem
— working students spend money foolishly

what many parents think about part-time jobs

— parents think part-time jobs teach responsibility, money and job skills

Thought Lines

Selecting a Main Idea

The next step in the process is to select the idea you think is the writer's *main* point. If you look again at the list of ideas, you see one category that has only one item: what many parents think about part-time jobs. In this category, the only item is that parents think part-time jobs teach responsibility, money, value and job skills.

Is this item the main idea of the article? If it is, then all the other ideas support it. But the other ideas contradict this point.

It is not the main idea, but it *is* connected to the main idea. The author is saying that parents *think* part-time jobs are good for high school students, but they may not be, especially if students work long hours.

You can write a simpler version of this main idea:

Parents should know that working long hours at part-time jobs is not good for teens.

Once you have a main idea, check it to see whether it fits with the other ideas in your organized list. *Do the ideas in the list connect to the main idea?* Yes: The ideas about the effects of jobs on schoolwork show the negative impact of part-time work. So do the ideas about the other effects. And the part about what parents *think* can be used to contrast their beliefs with what jobs *really* do to teens.

Once you have a main point that fits an organized list, you can move to the outlines stage of a summary.

Exercise 2
Practice

Marking a List of Ideas and Finding the Main Idea for a Summary

Following is a list of ideas from the article "Binge Nights: The Emergency on Campus" by Michael Winerip (pages 323–24). Read the list, and then mark each item with one of these symbols:

L **lessons learned** from the experience
P **personal background** on the binge drinker
S **steps** leading to the emergency
E the life-and-death **emergency**

After you've marked all the ideas, survey them and think of one main idea. Try to focus on a point that connects to what Ryan Dabbieri, the binge drinker, learned.

1. _____ Ryan Dabbieri was a twenty-two-year-old senior at the University of Virginia.

2. _____ Ryan did not think he was a binge drinker.

3. _____ About once a week, he would drink five to seven drinks in two hours.

4. _____ Before one big football game, he drank five or six very big shots of bourbon in fifteen minutes, at a party.

5. _____ At the stadium, he straightened up, to get by security.

6. _____ Inside, he passed out.

7. _____ His friends carried him outside.

8. _____ They couldn't revive him.

9. _____ In the emergency room, he stopped breathing for four minutes.

10. _____ His friends were terrified.

11. _____ The doctors did a scan for brain damage.

12. _____ Ryan's father flew in from Atlanta.

13. _____ Ryan awoke the next day in intensive care.

14. _____ Ryan says he won't drink again.

15. _____ He says he is lucky to be alive.

Main idea: _____

_____

_____

Outlines

Summary

Below is an outline for a summary of "Part-Time Job May Do Teenagers More Harm Than Good." As you read it, you'll notice that the main idea of the thought lines stage has become the topic sentence of the outline, and that most of the other ideas have become details.

**Outline for a Summary of "Part-Time Job May
Do Teenagers More Harm Than Good"**

```
topic sentence:  Parents should know that working long hours at
                 part-time jobs is not good for teens.

details:         Working students do less well in school.
                 A study of 12th-graders by Linda P. Worley showed
                 this.
effects on       It showed that grades suffer if students work
schoolwork       more than ten hours in the school week.
                 Students who work long hours choose easier
                 courses.
                 They spend less time on homework.
                 They cut class more.
                 They are less interested in school.
                 They use drugs and alcohol more.
other effects    They have lower self-esteem.
                 They spend money foolishly.
```

In the outline, the part about what many parents think about part-time jobs has been left out. Since it was an idea that contrasted with the topic sentence, it did not seem to fit. That kind of selecting is what you do in the outlines stage of writing a summary. In the rough lines stage, you may change your mind and decide to use the idea later.

Rough Lines

Attributing Ideas in a Summary

The first draft of your summary paragraph is your first try at *combining* all the material into one paragraph. The draft is much like the draft of any other paragraph, with one exception: *When you summarize another person's ideas, be sure to say whose ideas you are writing.* That is, *attribute* the ideas to the writer. Let the reader of your paragraph know

1. the author of the selection you are summarizing
2. the title of the selection you are summarizing.

You may want to *attribute ideas by giving your summary paragraph a title,* such as

```
A Summary of "Part-Time Job May Do Teenagers More Harm
Than Good" by Gary Klott
```

Note that you put the title of Klott's article in quotation marks.

Or you may want to *put the title and author into the paragraph itself.* Below is a draft version of a summary of "Part-Time Job May Do Teenagers More Harm Than Good" with the title and the author incorporated into the paragraph.

**A Draft of a Summary of "Part-Time Job May
Do Teenagers More Harm Than Good"**

```
   "Part-Time Job May Do Teenagers More Harm Than Good" by Gary
Klott says that parents should know that working long hours at
```

(continued)

part-time jobs is not good for teens. Working students do less well in school. A study of 12th-graders by Linda P. Worley showed that grades suffer if students work more than ten hours during the school week. Students who work long hours choose easier courses, spend less time on homework, cut class more often, and cheat more. They are less interested in school. They use drugs and alcohol more and have less self-esteem. They spend money foolishly.

When you look this draft over and read it aloud, you may notice a few problems:

- The draft is very choppy; it needs transitions.
- In some places, the word choice could be better.
- The beginning of the paragraph could use an introduction.
- Linda P. Worley did a study about grades and working students. But the other information about effects on schoolwork came from other studies. This difference should be made clear.
- The paragraph ends abruptly.

Final Lines

Summary

Look carefully at the final lines version of the summary. Notice how the idea about what parents think has been added as an introduction, and how transitions and word choice have improved the summary. Also notice how one phrase, "Other studies indicate that," clarifies the ideas in the summary, and how an added conclusion clinches the paragraph.

A Final Version of a Summary of "Part-Time Job May Do Teenagers More Harm Than Good" (Changes from the draft are underlined.)

Many parents think part-time jobs teach their children responsibility, money and job skills, but they may be wrong. An article called "Part-Time Job May Do Teenagers More Harm Than Good" by Gary Klott says that parents should know that working long hours at part-time jobs is not good for teens. First of all, working students do less well in school. A study of 12th-graders by Linda P. Worley showed that grades suffer if students work more than ten hours during the school week. Other studies indicate that students who work long hours choose easier courses, spend less time on their homework, and are likely to cheat and cut classes. In addition, such students are less interested in school. They have problems outside of school, too—they use drugs and alcohol more than other students and have less self-esteem. Finally, they do not learn financial responsibility from their jobs since they spend money foolishly. Parents must consider all these drawbacks before they allow their teens to work long hours.

Writing summaries is good writing practice, and it also helps you develop your reading skills. Even if your instructor does not require you to turn in a polished summary of an assigned reading, you may find it helpful to summarize what you have read. In many classes, midterms or other exams cover many assigned readings. If you make a short summary of each reading as it is assigned, you will have a helpful collection of focused, organized material to review.

WRITING A REACTION TO A READING

A summary is one kind of writing you can do after reading, but there are other kinds. Your instructor might ask you to *react by writing about some idea you got from your reading.* If you read "Part-Time Job May Do Teenagers More Harm Than Good," your instructor might have asked you to react by writing about this topic:

> Gary Klott says that parents may have the wrong idea about their children's jobs. Write about another part of teen life that parents may not understand.

You might begin to gather ideas by freewriting.

Thought Lines

Reaction to a Reading: Freewriting

You can freewrite in a reading journal, if you wish. This is a special kind of journal in which you write about selections that you have read. To freewrite, you can

- write key points made by the author.
- write about whatever you remember from the reading selection.
- write down any of the author's ideas that you think you might want to write about someday.
- list questions raised by what you've read.
- connect the reading selection to other things you've read, heard, or experienced.
- write any of the author's exact words that you might like to remember, putting them in quotation marks.

A freewriting that reacts to "Part-Time Job May Do Teenagers More Harm Than Good" might look like this:

Freewriting for a Reaction to a Reading

"Part-Time Job May Do Teenagers More Harm Than Good"—Gary Klott

Jobs can be bad for teens. Authors says parents should stop teens from working too many hours. But how? Most parents are afraid of their teens. Or they don't want to interfere. They figure teens want to be independent. I know I wanted to be independent when I was in high school. Did I? I'm not so sure. I think I wanted some attention from my folks. Maybe parents don't know this. Why didn't I say anything?

Thought Lines

Selecting a Topic, Listing and Developing Ideas

Once you have your freewriting, you can survey it for a topic. You might survey the freewriting above and decide you can write about how parents do not know their teens want attention. To gather ideas, you begin a list:

teens want attention and parents don't know

   — sometimes teens look independent
   — they act smart
   — no real self-confidence
   — friends aren't enough
   — I wanted my father's approval
   — teens can't say what they need
   — to get attention, they break rules
   — I would have liked some praise

Next you survey the list. Then you organize, expand, and develop this list until you have a main point, the topic sentence, and a list of details. You decide on this topic sentence:

Some parents are unaware that their teenage children need attention.

With a topic sentence and a list of details, you are ready to begin the outlines stage of writing.

Outlines

Reaction to a Reading

An outline might look like the one following. As you read it, notice that the topic sentence and ideas are *your* opinions, not the ideas of the author of "Part-Time Job May Do Teenagers More Harm Than Good." You used his ideas to come up with your own. Also notice how it builds on the ideas on the list and organizes them in a clear order.

An Outline of a Reaction to a Reading

topic sentence:	Some parents are unaware that their teenage children need attention.
details: **what parents see**	{ Teens act independent. They act smart. They break rules. Parents think that rule-breaking means teens want to be left alone.
what teens want	{ Teens do it to get attention. Teens can't say what they need. They have no real self-confidence. Their friends aren't enough.
personal example	{ I wanted my father's approval. I would have liked some praise.

Rough Lines

Reaction to a Reading

If your outline gives you enough good ideas to develop, you are on your way to a paragraph. If you began with the ideas above, for example, you could develop them into a paragraph like this:

A Draft of a Reaction to a Reading

> Some parents are unaware that their teenage children need attention. Teens act independent and smart. They break their parents' rules, and their parents think teenage rule-breaking is a sign the children want to be left alone. Teens break rules to get attention. They can't say what they need; therefore, they act out their needs. Teens have no real self-confidence. Friends aren't enough. I wanted my father's approval. I would have liked some praise.

Final Lines

Reaction to a Reading

When you read the draft version of the paragraph, you probably noticed some places where it could be revised:

- The word choice could be better.
- There is too much repetition of words like "need" or "needs" or "their parents" or "children."
- The paragraph needs many transitions.
- Since the ideas are reactions related to a point by Gary Klott, he needs to be mentioned.
- The ending is a little abrupt.

Following is the final version of the same paragraph. As you read it, notice how the changes make it a clearer, smoother, more developed paragraph.

A Final Version of a Reaction to a Reading
(Changes from the draft are underlined.)

> Gary Klott says that many parents do not understand the impact of their teenagers' part-time jobs. There is another part of teen life that parents may not understand. Some parents are unaware that their teenage children need attention. Teens act independent and self-assured. They break their parents' rules, and their parents think the rule-breaking is a sign the children want to be left alone. However, adolescents break rules to get attention. They can't say what they crave; therefore, they act out their needs. Teens have no real self-confidence. While friends help adolescents develop self-confidence, friends aren't enough. My own experience is a good example of what adolescents desire. I wanted my father's approval. I would have liked some praise, but I couldn't ask for what I needed. My father was a parent who was unaware.

WRITING ABOUT AGREEMENT OR DISAGREEMENT

Thought Lines

Agree or Disagree Paragraph

Another way to write about a reading selection is to find a point in it and *agree or disagree with that point*. To begin writing about agreement or disagreement, you can review the selection and jot down any statements that provoke a strong reaction in you. You are looking for statements with which you can agree or disagree based on your experience. If you reviewed "Part-Time Job May Do Teenagers More Harm Than Good," you might list these statements as points of agreement or disagreement:

Points of Agreement or Disagreement from a Reading

"grades suffer when students work more than ten hours during the school week." — agree

high school students who work many hours "had less interest in formal education" — disagree

Then you might *pick one of the statements and react to it in writing*. If you disagreed with the statement that high school students who work many hours "had less interest in formal education," you might begin by brainstorming:

Brainstorming for a Disagree Paragraph

Question: Why do you disagree that high school students who work long hours have less interest in formal education?

Answer: It is not always true. I worked long hours and I was still interested in getting a good education.

Question: If you were interested in school, why were you so focused on your job?

Answer: To make money.

Question: Then wasn't money more important than school?

Answer: No. I was working to make money to pay for college. Working was the only way I could afford college.

Question: Do you think it looked as if you didn't care about education?

Answer: Yes, sure.

Question: Why?

Answer: I used to be so tired from working I would fall asleep in class.

Once you have some ideas from brainstorming, you can list them, group them, and add to them by more brainstorming. Your topic sentence can be a way of stating your disagreement with the original point:

Although Gary Klott says that high school students who work long hours tend to lose interest in school, my experience was just the opposite.

With a topic sentence and details, you can work on the outlines stage of your paragraph.

Outlines

Agree or Disagree Paragraph

An outline might look like the following. Notice that the topic sentence is your opinion, and that the details are from your experience.

Outline of a Disagree Paragraph

topic sentence:	Although Gary Klott says that high school students who work long hours may lose interest in school, my experience was just the opposite.
details: **my experience**	While I was in high school, I worked long hours. I was very interested in getting a good education. I wanted to graduate from college. To save money for college, I was working long hours. Working was the only way I could pay for college.
why I appeared uninterested	It probably looked as if I didn't care about school. I was tired from working. I fell asleep in class.

Rough Lines

Agree or Disagree Paragraph

Once you have a good outline, you can develop it into a paragraph:

A Draft of a Disagree Paragraph

Although Gary Klott says that high school students who work long hours lose interest in school, my experience was just the opposite. When I was in high school, I worked long hours. I endured my job and even increased my hours because I was interested in getting a good education. I wanted to graduate from college. I was working long hours to save money for college. Working was the only way I could pay tuition. I know that, to my teachers, it probably looked as if I didn't care about school. I was tired from working. I fell asleep in class.

Final Lines

Agree or Disagree Paragraph

When you surveyed the draft of the paragraph, you probably noticed some places that need revision:

- The paragraph could use more specific details.
- Some sentences could be combined.
- It needs a last sentence, reinforcing the point that students who work long hours may be very interested in school.

As you read the final lines version of the paragraph, notice how the revisions improve the paragraph.

A Final Version of a Disagree Paragraph
(Changes from the draft are underlined.)

```
        Although Gary Klott says that high school students who work
long hours lose interest in school, my experience was just the
opposite. When I was in high school, I worked long hours. Some-
times I worked twenty-five hours a week at a fast-food restau-
rant. I endured my job and even increased my hours because I was
interested in getting a good education. I wanted to graduate from
college. I was working long hours to save money for college since
working was the only way I could pay tuition. I know that, to my
teachers, it probably looked as if I didn't care about school.
I was so tired from working I came to school in a daze. I fell
asleep in class. But my long, hard hours at work made me deter-
mined to change my life through education.
```

WRITING FOR AN ESSAY TEST

Another kind of writing from reading involves the essay test. Most essay questions require you to write about an assigned reading. Usually, an essay test requires you to write from memory, not from an open book or notes. Such writing can be stressful, but breaking the task into steps can eliminate much of the stress.

Before the Test: The Steps of Reading

If you work though the steps of reading days before the test, you are halfway to your goal. Prereading helps to keep you focused, and your first reading gives you a sense of the whole selection. The third step, rereading with a pen or pencil, can be particularly helpful when you are preparing for a test. Most essay questions will ask you to either summarize or react to a reading selection. In either case, you must be familiar with the reading's main idea, supporting ideas, examples, and details. If you note these by marking the selection, you are teaching yourself about the main point, supporting ideas, and structure of the reading selection.

Shortly before the test, review the marked reading assignment. Your notes will help you to focus on the main point and the supporting ideas.

During the Test: The Stages of Writing

Answering an essay question for a test may seem very different from writing at home. After all, on a test, you must rely on your memory and write within a time limit, and these restrictions can make you feel anxious. However, by following the stages of the writing process, you can meet that challenge calmly and confidently.

Thought Lines

Before you begin to write, think about these questions: Is the instructor asking for a summary of a reading selection? Or is he or she asking you to react to a specific idea in the reading by describing or developing that idea with examples or by agreeing or disagreeing? For example, in an essay question about the article "Part-Time Job May Do Teenagers More Harm Than Good" by Gary Klott, you might be asked (1) to explain why Klott thinks a part-time job can be bad for a teenager (a summary), (2) to explain what Klott means when he says that students who work long hours may keep their grades up but still miss out on the best education (a reaction, in which you develop and explain one part of the reading), or (3) to agree or disagree that afterschool jobs teach the wrong lesson about the value of money (a reaction, so you have to be aware of what Klott said on this point).

Once you have thought about the question, list or freewrite your first ideas. At this time, do not worry about how "right" or "wrong" your writing is; just write your first thoughts.

Outlines

Your writing will be clear if you follow a plan. Remember that your audience for this writing is your instructor and that he or she will be evaluating how well you stick to the subject, make a point, and support it. Your plan for making a point about the subject and supporting that point can be written in a brief outline.

First, reread the question. Next, survey your list or freewriting. Does it contain a main point that answers the question? Does it contain supporting ideas and details?

Next, write a main point, and then list supporting ideas and details under the main point. Your main point will be the topic sentence of your answer. If you need more support, try brainstorming.

Rough Lines

Write your point and supporting ideas in paragraph form. Remember to use effective transitions and to combine short sentences.

Final Lines

You will probably not have time to copy your answer, but you can review it, proofread it, and correct any errors in spelling, punctuation, or word choice. This final check can produce a more polished answer.

Organize Your Time

Some students skip steps: they immediately begin writing their answer to an essay question, without thinking or planning. Sometimes they find themselves stuck in the middle of a paragraph, panicked because they have no more ideas. At other times, they find themselves writing in a circle, repeating the same point over and over. Occasionally, they even forget to include a main idea.

You can avoid these hazards by spending time on each of the stages. Planning is as important as writing. For example, if you have half an hour to write an essay, you can divide your time like this:

5 minutes thinking, freewriting, listing
10 minutes planning, outlining
10 minutes drafting
5 minutes reviewing, proofreading

Writing from Reading: A Summary of Options

Reading can give you many opportunities for your own writing. You can summarize a writer's work, use it as a springboard for your own related writing, or agree or disagree with it. You can use the ideas you read about to answer an essay question. However you decide to write from reading, you must still work through the same writing process. Following the steps of thought lines, outlines, rough lines, and final lines will help you develop your work into a polished paragraph.

Lines of Detail: A Walk-Through Assignment

Here are three ideas from "Part-Time Job May Do Teenagers More Harm Than Good":

1. Students who work long hours miss out on extracurricular activities at school.

2. Parents should prevent their teenage children from working long hours.

3. Teens who work spend their money foolishly.

Pick *one* of these ideas, with which you agree or disagree. Write a paragraph explaining why you agree or disagree. To write your paragraph, follow these steps:

Step 1: Begin by listing at least three reasons or examples why you agree or disagree. Make your reasons or examples as specific as you can, using your experiences or the experiences of friends and family.

Step 2: Read your list to a partner or group. With the help of your listener(s), add reasons, examples, and details.

Step 3: Once you have enough ideas, transform the statement you agreed or disagreed with into a topic sentence.

Step 4: Write an outline by listing your reasons, examples, and details below the topic sentence. Check that your list is in a clear and logical order.

Step 5: Write a draft of your paragraph. Check that you have attributed Gary Klott's statement, you have enough specific details, you have combined any choppy sentences, and you have used good transitions. Revise your draft until the paragraph is smooth and clear.

Step 6: Before you prepare the final copy, check your draft for errors in spelling, punctuation, and word choice.

WRITING FROM READING "Part-Time Job May Do Teenagers More Harm Than Good"

When you write on any of the following topics, be sure to work through the stages of the writing process in preparing your paragraph.

1. Klott talks about high school students who work to pay for car insurance, dates, video games, music CDs, and designer clothes. However, students might not have to work so hard if they learned to do without things they don't really need: the latest clothes, the newest CD, their own car, and so forth. Write a paragraph about the many things high school students buy that they don't really need.

2. Work can interfere with high school. Write about something else that interferes with high school. You can write about social life, extracurricular activities, sports, family responsibilities, or any other part of a student's life that can prevent him or her from focusing on school.

    As you plan this paragraph, think about details that could fit these categories:

    Why students choose this activity/responsibility over school

    The effects on students' schoolwork

    How to balance school and other activities or responsibilities.

3. Many parents believe that a part-time job is good for high school students, but a job can sometimes be harmful. Write a one-paragraph letter to parents warning them about some other part of teen life (not jobs) that parents may think is good but that may be harmful. You can write about the dangers of a teenager's being popular, or having a steady boyfriend or girlfriend, or always being number one in academics.

    Once you've chosen the topic, brainstorm with a partner or group: ask questions, answer them, and add details. After you've brainstormed, work by yourself and proceed through the stages of preparing your letter to parents.

4. Some parents have misconceptions (incorrect ideas) about their teenage children; for instance, they may believe that the teen with a part-time job is automatically learning how to handle money. On the other hand, teenage children have misconceptions about their parents. Write about some misconception that teens have about their parents. You might, for instance, write about teens' mistaken belief that

    the best parents are the ones who give their children the most freedom,

    or

    parents who love you give you everything you want,

    or

    parents do not remember what it is like to be young.

    To begin, freewrite on one mistaken idea that teens might have about their parents. Focus on your own experiences, memories, and so on—as a teen or as a parent of teenagers. Use your freewriting to find details and a focus for your paragraph.

5. Klott writes about parents' need to restrict teens' work hours. Write about a family rule that you hated when you were a child or a teen. Include your feelings about that rule today.

Name: _____   Section: _____

Peer Review Form for Writing from Reading

After you have written a draft of your paragraph, let a writing partner read it. When your partner has completed the following form, discuss the comments. Then repeat the same process for your partner's paragraph.

This paragraph [circle one] (1) summarizes, (2) agrees or disagrees, (3) reacts to an idea connected to a reading selection.

I think this paragraph should include [circle one] (1) both the title and the author of the reading selection, (2) the author of the reading selection, (3) neither the title nor the author of the reading selection.

The topic sentence of this paragraph is _____

_____

_____

The best part of this paragraph begins with the words _____

_____

One suggestion to improve this paragraph is to _____

_____

_____

Other comments on the paragraph: _____

_____

_____

_____

_____

_____

_____

_____

_____

_____

_____

Reviewer's Name: _____

WRITING FROM READING

To practice the skills you've learned in this chapter, follow the steps of prereading, reading, and rereading with a pencil as you read the following selections.

New Directions
Maya Angelou

Maya Angelou was born Marguerite Johnson in St. Louis, Missouri, in 1928. She survived many hardships to become one of the most famous and beloved writers in America. Although she is best known for her autobiographical books, Angelou is also a political activist, singer, and performer on stage and screen. Her achievements include best-selling books, literary awards, and the reciting of her poetry at the inauguration of President William Clinton. In this essay, Angelou tells the story of a woman who cut a new path for her life.

Words You May Need to Know

burdensome (paragraph 1): troublesome, heavy
conceded (2): admitted
domestic (3): a household worker
meticulously (4): very carefully
cotton gin (4): a factory with a machine for separating cotton fibers from seeds
brazier (6): a container that holds live coals, covered by a grill, used for cooking
savors (6): food that smells and tastes good

lint (6): cotton fibers
specters (6): ghosts
balmy (9): mild and soothing
hives of industry (9): a place swarming with busy workers
looms (11): rises in front of us
assess (11): evaluate, judge
ominous (11): threatening
resolve (11): determination
unpalatable (11): not acceptable

1   In 1903 the late Mrs. Annie Johnson of Arkansas found herself with two toddling sons, very little money, a slight ability to read and add simple numbers. To this picture add a disastrous marriage and the burdensome fact that Mrs. Johnson was a Negro.

2   When she told her husband, Mr. William Johnson, of her dissatisfaction with their marriage, he conceded that he too found it to be less than he expected, and had been secretly hoping to leave and study religion. He added that he thought God was calling him not only to preach but to do so in Enid, Oklahoma. He did not tell her that he knew a minister in Enid with whom he could study and who had a friendly, unmarried daughter. They parted amicably, Annie keeping the one-room house and William taking most of the cash to carry himself to Oklahoma.

3   Annie, over six feet tall, big-boned, decided that she would not go to work as a domestic and leave her "precious babes" to anyone else's care. There was no possibility of being hired at the town's cotton gin or lumber mill, but maybe there was a way to make the two factories work for her. In other words, "I looked up the road I was going and back the way I come, and since I wasn't

satisfied, I decided to step off the road and cut me a new path." She told herself that she wasn't a fancy cook but that she could "mix groceries well enough to scare hungry away and from starving a man."

4   She made her plans meticulously and in secret. One early evening to see if she was ready, she placed stones in two five-gallon pails and carried them three miles to the cotton gin. She rested a little, and then, discarding some rocks, she walked in the darkness to the sawmill five miles farther along the dirt road. On her way back to her little house and her babies, she dumped the remaining rocks along the path.

5   That same night she worked into the early hours boiling chicken and frying ham. She made dough and filled the rolled-out pastry with meat. At last she went to sleep.

6   The next morning she left her house carrying the meat pies, lard, an iron brazier, and coals for a fire. Just before lunch she appeared in an empty lot behind the cotton gin. As the dinner noon bell rang, she dropped the savors into boiling fat and the aroma rose and floated over to the workers who spilled out of the gin, covered with white lint, looking like specters.

7   Most workers had brought their lunches of pinto beans and biscuits or crackers, onions and cans of sardines, but they were tempted by the hot meat pies which Annie ladled out of the fat. She wrapped them in newspapers, which soaked up the grease, and offered them for sale at a nickel each. Although business was slow, those first days Annie was determined. She balanced her appearances between the two hours of activity.

8   So, on Monday if she offered hot fresh pies at the cotton gin and sold the remaining cooled-down pies at the lumber mill for three cents, then on Tuesday she went first to the lumber mill presenting fresh, just-cooked pies as the lumbermen covered in sawdust emerged from the mill.

9   For the next few years, on balmy spring days, blistering summer noons, and cold, wet, and wintry middays, Annie never disappointed her customers, who could count on seeing the tall, brown-skin woman bent over her brazier, carefully turning the meat pies. When she felt certain the workers had become dependent on her, she built a stall between the two hives of industry and let the men run to her for their lunchtime provisions.

10   She had indeed stepped from the road which seemed to have been chosen for her and cut herself a brand-new path. In years that stall became a store where customers could buy cheese, meal, syrup, cookies, candy, writing tablets, pickles, canned goods, fresh fruit, soft drinks, coal, oil, and leather soles for worn-out shoes.

11   Each of us has the right and the responsibility to assess the roads which lie ahead, and those over which we have traveled, and if the future road looms ominous or unpromising, and the roads back uninviting, then we need to gather our resolve and, carrying only the necessary baggage, step off that road into another direction. If the new choice is also unpalatable, without embarrassment, we must be ready to change that as well.

Exercise 3 **Completing a List Outline of "New Directions"**

Practice   After you've read "New Directions," read the following exercise. Then reread "New Directions," looking for the details that will complete this outline.

Maya Angelou tells the story of a woman whose determination and hard work helped her make a new direction for her life.

Mrs. Annie Johnson's husband left her to become _____

_____ in Enid, Oklahoma.

She was left with little money, two _____

_____ , and a one-room house.

She decided not to work as _____ ;

instead, she planned to use her cooking skills.

To test her plan, she practiced walking a total of _____

miles, from her home to the cotton gin and sawmill, and back again.

To practice carrying a heavy load, she carried _____

_____ .

The same night, she cooked chicken and ham and made pastry.

The next morning, she carried her meat pies and cooking equipment to the cotton gin and sawmill.

Although the men had brought their lunch, they were attracted by _____

_____ .

For years, Annie Johnson sold the pies in two locations, in all weather.

Eventually, she _____ and let the

men come to her.

Later, she sold not only food but also _____

_____

_____

She is proof that we must all _____

_____

_____

WRITING FROM READING "New Directions"

When you write on any of the following topics, be sure to work through the steps of the writing process in preparing your paragraph.

1. Using the ideas and examples you gathered in Exercise 3, write a summary of "New Directions."

2. Write about someone who had many strikes against him or her but who succeeded. Be sure that you include some of the difficulties this person faced.

3. Maya Angelou says, "Each of us has the right and responsibility to assess the roads which lie ahead, and those over which we have traveled," and if an old road or a future road looks dark, we must "step off that road into another direction."

   Write a paragraph that agrees or disagrees with that statement.

   Begin by working with a group. First, discuss what you think the statement means. Then ask at least six questions about the statement. You may ask such questions as, "Does everyone have the courage or talent to choose a new road?" or "What keeps some people from choosing a new direction?" or "Do you know anyone who has done what Angelou advises?"

   Use the questions and answers to decide whether you want to agree or disagree with Angelou's statement.

4. There is an old saying, "When the going gets tough, the tough get going," and Mrs. Annie Johnson's story seems to prove the saying is true. She was faced with poverty, lack of job opportunities, and the care of two children, and yet through hard work, creativity, and determination, she triumphed.

   Write a paragraph that tells a story and proves the truth of another old saying. You can use a saying like "Take time to stop and smell the roses," or "You never know what you can do until you try," or any other saying.

   Begin by freewriting about old sayings and what they mean to you. Then pick one that connects to your experience or the experience of someone you know. Use that saying as the focus of your paragraph.

Home Away from Home
Beth Nieman

Beth Nieman is a home day-care provider in Phoenix, Arizona. In this essay, she explains what parents should understand about her role in their children's lives.

Words You May Need to Know

accredited (paragraph 2): certified to meet requirements
seminars (2): meetings for exchanging information and study
breezily (3): carelessly, casually
held in reserve (4): saved

ideal (6): perfect
displeasure (6): disapproval
specifications (7): requirements
upscale (8): upper-class
aired (9): expressed

1   I'm a home day-care provider—the person who opens my home and family to other people's children for 20 to 50 hours a week while they are at work. I provide food, toys, activities, companionship and encouragment to the youngsters in their parents' absence. I know from the smiles on the little ones' faces that they enjoy themselves while in my care, and they've come to expect me to be kind and helpful. However, I'm not always sure what their parents expect from me.

2   I try hard to be professional. I'm accredited by the National Association for Family Child Care, and I attend seminars on everything from safety and nutrition to planning kids' crafts and summer activities. I encourage the children's efforts, no matter how small. I help Junior to help himself, to take responsibility for his belongings, to learn counting and the alphabet, to feed himself and to share. In return, I am offered a small hand as we cross the street. I'm asked to tie a shoe, dress a doll or examine an invisible wound. We share a laugh, a story . . . a childhood.

3   Parents should understand that I, like themselves, need to earn a living. As a self-employed person, it's up to me to keep myself busy. I am legally permitted to have a certain number of children in my home, and if I don't have them, I'll feel it in the wallet. Therefore, when a mother fails to arrive as scheduled, or breezily calls two hours late on Monday morning and announces that little Arlene won't be coming to day care this week because her great-aunt from Rhode Island has just arrived and will be caring for her instead (for free), I have two choices. I can swallow hard and say, "Oh, OK. Well, thanks for letting me know" (which is what I used to do), or I can have parents sign a contract at the beginning of our business relationship, stating that they will pay me a fixed amount per week each Monday, whether they bring their child or not. This is what my son's preschool does, because the school doesn't have a paying customer temporarily to fill my son's slot if he can't go to school due to family vacation or illness.

4   That brings to mind another problem. It's just not reasonable for parents to expect me to care for a sick child. I don't have the facilities or an extra person

to handle the job, and it starts an exhausting cycle among myself and the children of passing germs back and forth. When I call parents and say that their child is feverish or vomiting or has diarrhea, I expect the mother or father to come and get him, not ask, "Well, what do you want me to do?" I realize that illness is unpleasant and inconvenient, but it is for me, too, and for the other children in my care. Surely I can't be expected to send the other kids home when one child is sick. I would like to suggest to parents that they make some backup arrangements or a few vacation days should be held in reserve should someone need to stay home with a sick child.

5   I had to laugh the other day when a friend dropped by at lunchtime. She looked around the table and smiled to see the little ones eating their nutritionally balanced lunches, complete with milk to drink and fruit for dessert. "You've really got it made," she said. "I would love to be able to work from home the way you do. I work with greedy, selfish people all day long, and I hate it!" Just as I was about to respond, a fight broke out. "That's my bunch of grapes!" "I had it first!" "Aaaugh!" "She hit me!"

6   "OK, OK," laughed my friend. "Point taken." Yes, I work in conditions that are sometimes less than ideal. I vacuum two or three times daily. I wipe noses and bottoms, repair broken toys and hurt feelings, and occasionally I'm spit on by my clients (though usually not intentionally). It's surprising, though, what an odd idea parents sometimes have of what I do all day long (though they are most emphatic in saying that they, themselves, could never do it). I'm sure they don't mean to be hurtful when they remark with displeasure at a fresh bandage ("What happened? Weren't you watching him?"), a ketchup stain ("This was a new outfit!"—then why did she wear it to day care?) or glance around, silently disapproving of the scattered toys, cookie crumbs and books (or so I imagine). It is always delightful to hear a compliment or a word of thanks at the end of a 10-hour day instead of a complaint.

7   I bring these issues to light because I've had the distinct impression that I'm thought to be a nanny, "the help," if you will. I'm not. I am a self-employed businesswoman. If I'm selected as a day-care provider, the child will receive excellent care and individual attention, will watch no television, will be served nutritious meals and have a variety of activities, both active and quiet, that are appropriate for his age. If I were a nanny, employed to watch a child to exact specifications, that would be one thing. But working parents can't afford to spend that much money on day care and bring their children to a group caregiver instead. At my house, I make the rules, set the policies, decide what I will and will not do. I would like my clients to respect my needs and accept the fact that outside of hiring Alice from "The Brady Bunch," they're going to have to meet me halfway. I'll try to be flexible, too. Otherwise, I'll be out of business! There are, after all, plenty of home day-care providers to choose from.

8   Sometimes I envy these mothers. I see someone drive up to my home in a car much newer than the one I drive (Is it paid for?). Their work clothes are fab-

ulous compared with my home-issue sweats and tennis shoes (Do you have to dry-clean that?). Most parents have a more upscale address than I do. But I wonder who really does have it all? I am inclined to think it's me. The person who answers my child's questions is me; I have lots of time to hug him, tell him stories and listen to his naptime prayers.

9   I have thought of escaping to corporate America on days when yet another area on my rug absorbs a spill, yet another complaint is aired by a picky eater, or a parent arrives 30 minues late and doesn't call me. But I have learned one very important lesson as a day-care provider that prevents me from leaving my children with sitters while I work away from home: love is not for sale.

Exercise 4   **Completing a List Outline of "Home Away from Home"**

Practice

After you've read "Home Away from Home," read the following exercise. Then reread "Home Away from Home," looking for details that will complete the outline.

Beth Nieman wants the parents of the children she cares for to understand her role.

She is a professional who provides specific services and items. (List some

of these services and items.) _____

_____

_____

_____

Yet some parents act as if she doesn't need to make money. (Give one

example.) _____

_____

_____

Others don't understand why she can't care for a sick child. (Explain why

she can't.) _____

_____

_____

She works under tough conditions. (Explain some of the conditions.)

_____

_____

_____

She is not a nanny. (Explain the difference.) _____

_____

_____

In spite of the drawbacks of her job, Nieman likes working at home, near her own children.

WRITING FROM READING "Home Away from Home"

When you write on any of the following topics, be sure to work through the stages of the writing process in preparing your paragraph.

1. Using the ideas and examples you gathered in Exercise 4, write a summary of "Home Away from Home."

2. Beth Nieman says her job has taught her a lesson: Love is not for sale. Write about a lesson you learned at a job. You can begin by freewriting about the job. Try recalling any problems or achievements on the job, and think about what the difficulties or successes taught you.

3. Write an agree or disagree paragraph about one of the following statements:

   Day-care workers have it made.

   Working mothers do not have it all.

   Day-care workers should not be expected to care for sick children.

   Parents should pay a fixed amount at the beginning of each week, whether they bring their child to day care or not.

4. Write a paragraph about what you love—or hate—about your job. Begin with an interview. Have a writing partner interview you. Your classmate should prepare at least six questions before the interview. They may be questions like "What's the best part of your job?" and "What's the worst part?" and "How do you cope with the bad parts?" At the interview, let your partner jot down your answers and ask follow-up questions.

   After you have been interviewed, switch roles. Interview your partner, with your own prepared list of questions.

   At the end of both interviews, give your partner his or her jotted-down responses and take your own. Use them to develop a focus and details for your paragraph.

5. Write a letter to your boss or to the customers, clients, patients, or children you serve at your job. Explain how they misunderstand your job and your role. You may include what they could do to make your life easier.

Grammar for ESL Students

NOUNS AND ARTICLES

A **noun** names a person, place, or thing. There are *count nouns* and *noncount nouns*.

> **Count nouns** refer to persons, places, or things that can be counted:
>
> three *cookies*, two *dogs*, five *suitcases*
>
> **Noncount nouns** refer to things that can't be counted:
>
> *luggage, employment, attention*

Here are some more examples of count and noncount nouns:

count	noncount
joke	humor
movie	entertainment
dream	inspiration
automobile	transportation

One way to remember the difference between count and noncount nouns is to put the word *much* in front of the noun. For example, if you can say *much entertainment*, then *entertainment* is a noncount noun.

Exercise 1 **Identifying Count and Noncount Nouns**

Practice Put **count** or **noncount** next to each word below.

1. _____ housewife

2. _____ fuel

3. _____ equipment

4. _____ carrot

5. _____ interest

6. _____ dignity

7. _____ rain

8. _____ school

9. _____ jewelry

10. _____ goal

401

Using Articles with Nouns

Articles point out nouns. Articles are either **indefinite** *(a, an)* or **definite** *(the)*. There are several rules for using these articles:

Use *a* in front of consonant sounds; use *an* before vowel sounds.

a filter	an orphan
a room	an apple
a bench	an event
a thought	an issue
a necklace	an umbrella

Use *a* or *an* in front of singular count nouns. *A* or *an* means *any one*.

I saw *an* owl.
She rode *a* horse.

Do not use *a* or *an* with noncount nouns.

not this: I need a~~ money.
but this: I need money.

not this: Selena is passing a~~n arithmetic.
but this: Selena is passing arithmetic.

Use *the* before both singular and plural count nouns whose specific identity is known to the reader:

The dress with the sequins on it is my party dress.
Most of *the* movies I rent are science fiction films.

Use *the* before noncount nouns only when they are specifically identified.

not this: He wants ~~the~~ sympathy. (Whose sympathy? What sympathy? The noncount noun *sympathy* is not specifically identified.)
but this: I need *the sympathy* of a good friend. (Now *sympathy* is specifically identified.)

not this: ~~Generosity~~ of the family that paid for my education was remarkable. (The nouncount noun *generosity* is specifically identified, so you need *the*.)
but this: *The generosity* of the family that paid for my education was remarkable.

Exercise 2 Using *a* or *an*

Practice

Put *a* or *an* in the spaces where it is needed. Some sentences are correct as they are.

1. Robert filled the tank with _____ gasoline.

2. The fortuneteller gave me _____ warning.

3. Sometimes _____ rumor can spread lies.

4. Christina went to the market to buy _____ milk.

5. The thief stole _____ sandwich and _____ orange.

6. Last week, Sammy fell in _____ love.

7. Our house is ＿＿＿ example of ＿＿＿ home without ＿＿＿ beauty.

8. ＿＿＿ parrot and ＿＿＿ toddler may not get along well.

9. ＿＿＿ food costs more than it used to.

10. If you want to lose ＿＿＿ weight, you should go on ＿＿＿ diet.

Exercise 3 Using *the*

Practice   Put *the* in the spaces where it is needed. Some sentences are correct as they are.

1. My husband gave me ＿＿＿ support I needed.

2. Isaac has ＿＿＿ faith in ＿＿＿ honesty of ordinary people.

3. Teresa is filled with ＿＿＿ kindness.

4. With ＿＿＿ help of my best friend, I managed to repair the roof.

5. I was ＿＿＿ last one in ＿＿＿ class to finish ＿＿＿ test.

6. ＿＿＿ magazines I like best write about ＿＿＿ sports.

7. ＿＿＿ conference in ＿＿＿ Washington educated me about ＿＿＿ difficulties

   facing single parents.

8. My dog has ＿＿＿ courage of a much larger dog.

9. Giselle likes to walk near ＿＿＿ ocean.

10. One of these days, he will take ＿＿＿ advice I gave him.

Exercise 4 Correcting a Paragraph with Errors in Articles

Connect   Correct the eleven errors with *a, an,* or *the* in the following paragraph. You may need to add, change, or eliminate articles. Write the corrections in the space above the errors.

> The traveling can be a frustrating experience. Last week, I spent four
>
> hours at airport, waiting for plane that would take me to Atlanta. The per-
>
> son at the check-in counter did not announce an delay until one hour after
>
> the plane was supposed to take off. One hour later, we finally boarded the
>
> plane, only to sit for another two hours. During those two hours, the air
>
> conditioning was turned off, and no one offered me the drink or the
>
> snack. Pilot kept coming on the loudspeaker to say he had a news of bad
>
> weather ahead and had to wait. Sitting in the tiny seat, sweltering in the
>
> heat, I felt the anger and an impatience. I experienced bad side of travel.

NOUNS OR PRONOUNS USED AS SUBJECTS

A noun or a **pronoun** (a word that takes the place of a noun) is the subject of each sentence or dependent clause. Be sure that all sentences or dependent clauses have a subject.

> **not this:** Cooks breakfast on weekends.
> **but this:** *He* cooks breakfast on weekends.

> **not this:** My cousin was hurt when fell down the stairs.
> **but this:** My cousin was hurt when *he* fell down the stairs.

Be careful not to *repeat* the subject.

> **not this:** The lieutenant ~~she~~ said I was brave.
> **but this:** The lieutenant said I was brave.

> **not this:** The cat that bit me ~~it~~ was a Siamese.
> **but this:** The cat that bit me was a Siamese.

Exercise 5 **Correcting Errors with Subjects**

Practice

Correct any errors with subjects in the sentences below. Write your corrections in the space above the errors.

1. Your sister Leah she never stops arguing.

2. When the rain began, my roof it started to leak.

3. French fries with their skins on they taste the best.

4. Occasionally on a cold night feels good to sit by a fire.

5. Books make a great gift; can be enjoyed by more than one person.

6. My rabbit Geraldo he likes to be petted.

7. Last week the battery in my cell phone it was dead.

8. Wants to rent an apartment near the college.

9. After leaves his girlfriend, he calls her and talks all night.

10. The most dangerous intersection in town it was near my house.

VERBS

Necessary Verbs

Be sure that a main verb isn't missing from your sentences or dependent clauses.

> **not this:** Carlos extremely talented.
> **but this:** Carlos *is* extremely talented.

> **not this:** Bill called the police when saw the robbery.
> **but this:** Bill called the police when *he* saw the robbery.

-s Endings

Be sure to put the *-s* on present tense verbs in the third person singular.

not this: She ~~take~~ a break in the afternoon.
but this: She *takes* a break in the afternoon.

not this: The plane ~~arrive~~ at 7:00 p.m.
but this: The plane *arrives* at 7:00 p.m.

-ed Endings

Be sure to put *-ed* endings on the past participle form of a verb. There are three main forms of a verb:

present: Today I walk.
past: Yesterday I walked.
past participle: I *have* walked. He *has* talked.

The past participle form is also used after *were, was, had,* and *has.*

not this: We have ~~talk~~ about this plan for several weeks.
but this: We have *talked* about this plan for several weeks.

not this: The baby was ~~amuse~~ by the new toy.
but this: The baby was *amused* by the new toy.

Do not add *-ed* endings to infinitives. An infinitive is the verb form that uses *to* plus the present form of the verb:

to suggest, to revise

not this: My husband wanted me to ~~suggested~~ a family party.
but this: My husband wanted me to *suggest* a family party.

not this: I finally learned how to ~~revised~~ a draft.
but this: I finally learned how to *revise* a draft.

Exercise 6
Practice

Correcting Errors in Verbs: Necessary Verbs, Third Person Present Tense, Past Participles, and Infinitives

Correct any errors in verbs in the sentences below. Write your corrections in the space above the lines. Some sentences do not need any correcting.

1. My car was repaired at the same place where Andy always take his car.

2. In calculus class, I wanted to completed the homework, but I did not have enough time.

3. My parents were pleased with the gift Danielle gave them.

4. Once a week, Nathaniel cleans the bathroom and dusts the living room.

5. That rose bush look healthy, but it needs some plant food.

6. By the time I got to the airport, the passengers had board the plane.

7. One of the most beautiful streets in the city Lincoln Avenue.

8. Today my son is a good swimmer because he has conquer his fear of water.

9. Without a doubt, communication essential in a good marriage.

10. If my father manages to arrive home before dinnertime, he collapse into

    his armchair and take a nap.

Correcting a Paragraph with Errors in Necessary Verbs, Third Person Present Tense, Past Participles, and Infinitives

Correct the nine verb errors in the following paragraph. Write your corrections in the spaces above the errors.

Eileen is the most popular person in her department because she give so much to her fellow employees. Whenever she greets her office mates with a smile or a silly joke, Eileen has the power to turned a dull day into a happier one. Even when Eileen herself is feeling low, manages to make others laugh. She is also a good listener. She offer her total attention and does not judge those who confide in her. She been known to spend hours on the phone with someone in trouble. Everyone feel comfortable talking to Eileen, for she genuinely care about others. She is well-liked because she knows how to responded to others and to brightened their lives.

Two-Word Verbs

Many verbs called **two-word verbs** contain a verb plus another word, a preposition or adverb. The meaning of each word by itself is different from the meaning the two words have when they are together. Look at this example:

I *ran across* an old friend at the ballgame.

You might check *run* in the dictionary and find that it means "to move quickly." *Across* means "from one side to the other." But *run across* means something different:

not this: I ~~moved quickly from one side to the other of~~ an old friend at the ballgame.
but this: I *encountered* an old friend at the ballgame.

Sometimes a word or words come between the words of a two-word verb:

Yesterday I *took* my brother *out* to dinner.

Here are some common two-word verbs:

ask out:	I hope Steve will *ask* me *out* tomorrow.
break down:	If you drive too far, the car will *break down*.
call off:	I will *call* the game *off*.
call on:	He may *call on* you for advice
call up:	Neil *calls* Marsha *up* on weekends.
come across:	Sometimes Joe *comes across* Nick at work.
drop in:	We can *drop in* on the neighbors.
drop off:	I can *drop* you *off* on my way to school.
fill in:	For this test, just *fill in* the blanks.
fill out:	You must *fill out* an application.
hand in:	Harry has to *hand in* his lab report.
hand out:	Marcy will *hand out* the tickets.
keep on:	We can *keep on* rehearsing our music.

look into:	The police want to *look into* the matter.
look over:	Tom intends to *look* the place *over*.
look up:	I can *look* the number *up* in the phone book.
pick up:	Tom went to *pick up* his dry cleaning.
quiet down:	The neighbors asked us to *quiet down*.
run into:	Maybe I will *run into* you at the park.
run out:	We have *run out* of coffee.
think over:	Thank you for the offer; I will *think* it *over*.
try on:	I like that dress; I will *try* it *on*.
try out:	Jack needs to *try* the drill *out*.
turn down:	Lucy wants to *turn* the proposal *down*.
turn on:	*Turn* the radio *on*.
turn up:	The lost keys will *turn up* somewhere.

Exercise 8 **Writing Sentences with Two-Word Verbs**

Practice Write a sentence for each of the following two-word verbs. Use the examples above as a guide, but consult a dictionary if you are not sure what the verbs mean.

1. break down   _____

2. look into   _____

3. fill out   _____

4. run out   _____

5. come across   _____

6. turn down   _____

7. drop off   _____

8. think over   _____

9. call off   _____

10. try on   _____

Contractions and Verbs

Contractions often contain verbs you may not recognize in their shortened forms.

contraction: *I'm* making cookies.
long form: *I am* making cookies.

contraction: *He's* been out of town for two weeks.
long form: *He has* been out of town for two weeks.

contraction: *He's* studying German
long form: *He is* studying German.

contraction: *They'll* meet us at the beach.
long form: *They will* meet us at the beach.

contraction: The *cat's* in the basement.
long form: The *cat is* in the basement.

Exercise 9 **Contractions and Verbs**

Practice In the space above each contraction, write its long form. The first one is done for you.

    She would
1. She'd make a fine manager of a large department store.

2. Sarah's calling a throat specialist.

3. Sarah's called a throat specialist.

4. We'll follow your car.

5. This song's better than the first one.

6. At night, I'm too tired to go out.

7. You're never home when I call.

8. I knew you'd like this restaurant.

9. Tomorrow they'll plan a birthday celebration.

10. The child won't listen to the teacher.

Text Credits

Page 7: Edgar Allan Poe, "The Tell-Tale Heart," from *Great Tales and Poems of Edgar Allan Poe*. Reprinted with the permission of Pocket Books, a division of Simon & Schuster. © 1960 W.S. Press; © renewed 1988 by Simon & Schuster. Reprinted with permission.

Page 74: From John F. Kennedy's Inaugural Address from *The Oxford History of the American People* by Samuel Eliot Morison. New York: Oxford University Press. © 1965.

Page 74: Martin Luther King, Jr., "I Have a Dream" speech. Reprinted by arrangement with The Heirs to the Estate of Martin Luther King, Jr., c/o Writers House, Inc. as agent for the proprietor, © 1963 by Martin Luther King, Jr.; © renewed 1991 by Coretta Scott King.

Page 89: James R. Miller, "The Estimable Mr. Campbell," from *Tropic Magazine* 11/18/90, p. 8. Republished with permission of the *Miami Herald*; permissions conveyed through Copyright Clearance Center, Inc.

Page 147: Edna Buchanan, "The World's Most Dangerous Profession," from *The Corpse Had a Familiar Face* (New York: Random House, © 1987), pp. 11-12. Reprinted with the permission of Random House, Inc.

Page 207: "Isodor and Ida Strauss: Inseparable in Life, Then in Death," from *People* 3/16/98, © 1998 Time Inc. Reprinted with permission.

Page 245: Winston Churchill, "Dunkirk" speech, from *World's Greatest Speeches* by Lewis Copeland and Lawrence Lamm, Editors (Mineola: Dover Publications, © 1973), p. 439. Reprinted with permission.

Page 323: Michael Winerip, "Binge Nights: The Emergency on Campus." © 1998 by The New York Times Company. Reprinted with permission.

Page 326: Ved Mehta, "The Baby Myna," from *Vedi* by Ved Mehta. Reprinted with permission of Georges Borchardt, Inc., for the author.

Page 333: Judith Ortiz Cofer, "I Fell in Love, Or My Hormones Awakened," from *The Looking Glass Shame* by Judith Ortiz Cofer. Reprinted by permission of the publisher of *Silent Dancing: A Partial Remembrance of a Puerto Rican Childhood* (Houston: Arte Publico Press-University of Houston, © 1990).

Page 362: Lillian Gwin, "I Wish." © T.D. Allen. Used with permission of the author.

Page 364: John Grisham, "Death Row," from *The Chamber* by John Grisham. © 1994 by John Grisham, Used with permission of Doubleday, a Division of Random House, Inc.

Page 368: Ronald Takaki, "A Different Mirror," from *A Different Mirror* (New York: Little, Brown, and Co., © 1993) Found in *Border Texts*, Randall Bass (Boston: Houghton Mifflin, ©1999), pp. 593-594. Reprinted with permission.

Pages 373, 376: Gary Klott, "Part-Time Job May Do Teenagers More Harm Than Good." Reprinted with the permission of Knight Ridder/Tribune Information Services.

Page 393: Maya Angelou, "New Directions," from *Wouldn't Take Nothing for My Journey Now* by Maya Angelou. © 1993 by Maya Angelou. Reprinted with permission of Random House, Inc.

Page 397: Beth Neiman, "Home Away from Home," My Turn column, from *Newsweek*, 11/11/96, © 1996 Newsweek, Inc. All rights reserved. Reprinted with permission.

Photograph Credits

Page 293 A, Julie O'Neil/Stock Boston; **page 293 B**, Amy Sancetta/AP/Wide World Photos; **page 321 A**, Scott Cunningham/Merrill Education; **page 321 B**, Evans/Hulton Getty/Archive Photos; **page 360 A**, Hulton Getty/Archive Photos; **page 360 B**, Hulton Getty/Archive Photos

Index